American Settler C

American Settler Colonialism

A History

Walter L. Hixson

palgrave
macmillan

AMERICAN SETTLER COLONIALISM

First published in 2013 by
PALGRAVE MACMILLAN®
in the United States—a division of St. Martin's Press LLC,
175 Fifth Avenue, New York, NY 10010.

Where this book is distributed in the UK, Europe and the rest of the World, this is by Palgrave Macmillan, a division of Macmillan Publishers Limited, registered in England, company number 785998, of Houndmills, Basingstoke, Hampshire RG21 6XS.

Palgrave Macmillan is the global academic imprint of the above companies and has companies and representatives throughout the world.

ISBN: 978–1–137–37424–0 (hbk)
ISBN: 978–1–137–37425–7 (pbk)

Library of Congress Cataloging-in-Publication Data is available from the Library of Congress.

A catalogue record of the book is available from the British Library.

Design by Integra Software Services

First edition: December 2013

Contents

The memorial at Gnadenhutten. Photograph by Wade Wilcox

Preface

Driving on Interstate 77 near Coshocton, Ohio, you are in what used to be the land of the Lenni Lenape, better known as the Delaware Indians.[1] Exiting the Interstate and driving east on US 36, it is only a few miles to the small town of Gnadenhutten ("tents of grace"). There, near the banks of the Muskingum River, you will find the simple, peacefully shaded memorial marking the historic site where for many years in the eighteenth century, Delaware Indians, who had converted to Christianity, lived and farmed with Moravian missionaries of mostly German ancestry.

Gnadenhutten embodied *colonial ambivalence*, as it underscored the wide range of possible relationships between peace and war on the North American borderlands. It represented adaptation, accommodation, and tolerance as opposed to violent conflict between Indians and Euro-Americans. The missionaries showed their willingness to coexist with Indians by establishing the United Brethren mission and striving to save the Indians' souls. The Delaware who lived there embodied ambivalent relations through their willingness to convert to Protestantism, and to embrace pacifism.

Colonial ambivalence (discussed more fully in Chapter 1) existed throughout the North American borderlands over some four centuries of European colonization. The borderlands provided a vast tableau of intercultural exchange, competing desires, diplomacy, accommodation, and resistance. Indians had lived in communities united by regional networks of trade and exchange for centuries before Europeans arrived on the continent. The colonial encounter brought sweeping changes that affected Indians everywhere. Having no choice but to adapt and adjust to the newcomers, they did so in a variety of ways. The indigenes variously exchanged culture and conducted an extensive trade with the interlopers, negotiated with them, allied with them in warfare against other whites as well as other Indians, joined their families and communities, adopted their ways, and converted to the European religions. Some tried their best, as a Shawnee man once put it, to "walk the white man's road."[2]

For their part the Euro-American settlers displayed fear and admiration, revulsion and desire, for indigenous people. They ate with them, traded with them, sometimes lived, raised children, and worshipped with them; exchanged the pipe, negotiated and allied with them; adopted indigenous methods of hunting and of warfare; wore their moccasins and leggings, and learned their techniques of "wilderness" survival; walked on their paths, canoed their streams, and adopted their place names. Newly arrived colonists often expressed shock at the extent to which their "civilized" European brethren had come to resemble the indigenes.

Despite these examples of accommodation and hybridity, Euro-Americans were not culturally equipped to accept Indians as their equals with legitimate claims to the land. They viewed "heathen," transient, hunting-based societies as inferior to Christian settler societies. Palpable cultural differences based on economy, land use, gender roles, spirituality, and much else underscored the distinctions drawn between the self and the other. Euro-American settlers imagined that it was their destiny to take control of colonial space and nothing would deter them from carrying out that project. Many came to view *the very existence* of Indians as an impediment to individual and national aspirations.[3]

Settler colonization thus ultimately overwhelmed ambivalence and ambiguity. Indians, who had used and changed the land for centuries, proved willing to share land with the newcomers but not simply to give it up to the settlers. The Euro-Americans, however, were on a mission to take command over colonial space, a process that entailed demarcation and control, boundaries, maps, surveys, treaties, seizures, and the commodification of the land.

* * *

In the late winter of 1782, a group of militiamen from Virginia and Pennsylvania entered Gnadenhutten, where they found a large group of Indians collecting the corn harvest that had been left behind in the fall. Although the American settlers knew that the Indians at Gnadenhutten were peaceful and mostly Christians, they decided to kill all of them anyway. In a chilling display of the coexistence of democracy and genocide on the American borderlands, the settlers first held a vote on what to do with the indigenous Moravian converts. Indiscriminate slaughter won out.

On March 8 and 9, the Americans executed and scalped 96 Indians at Gnadenhutten. After a night filled with terror, song, and prayer, one Indian after another—including 39 children—was forced to kneel, then bludgeoned to death with a heavy cooper's mallet until the executioner's arm tired and he gave way to a second. Two teenagers—one scalped and secreting himself beneath the carnage of the dead—survived to recount the horror.

The massacre at Gnadenhutten stemmed from the desire of the perpetrators to bring an end to the very colonial ambivalence that the United Brethren mission represented. Enraged by Indian assaults on borderland communities, which had killed friends and family members, the militiamen pursued their quest for blood revenge at the expense of non-combatant Indians who only sought to provide food for their people. The borderland settlers had long resented efforts, first on the part of the British and then on the part of the Continental army, to conduct trade and strategic alliances with Indians. Not all of the militiamen favored the executions, yet most voted for it nonetheless because they did not want to be viewed by their fellow settlers as coddling savages. Many Americans subsequently condemned the atrocity and an investigation ensued, but, as throughout US history, no one would be convicted and punished for killing Indians.[4]

The settlers had no monopoly on blood revenge and indiscriminate violence, which were deeply rooted in indigenous traditions. In the wake of the

Gnadenhutten massacre, after an Indian coalition defeated a settler invasion force in north-central Ohio, the Delaware and their allies slaughtered their captives and subjected the commander, William Crawford, to a hideous array of sadistic torture prolonging the agony of his death. The indigenes stripped Crawford naked; painted his face black for death; cut off his scalp, nose, and ears; and then slow-roasted him at the stake. Crawford's demise permeated narratives of borderland warfare, underscoring the inherent savagery of the Indians and justifying the cycle of borderland violence.[5]

* * *

The killings at Gnadenhutten, like other massacres throughout American and other nation's histories, were not isolated events; rather they reflected a broader history of settler colonization within an even broader history of global colonialism. Whether they wanted to slaughter the Delaware and other Indians or not, the vast majority of settlers wanted them *removed* from the land so that it might be cultivated by a more modern and even providentially destined people. Gnadenhutten signaled that by 1782 the time for ambivalence and seeking out a middle ground was over: the settlers wanted total security, assurance of their exclusive claim to colonial space. The militiamen informed one of the Moravian missionaries in the wake of the massacre, "When they killed the Indians the country would be theirs, and the sooner this was done the better!"[6]

The history of Gnadenhutten—ambivalent relationships giving way to indiscriminate violence and Indian removal—in many respects is the history of the "settlement" of the United States. At the beginning of his book on another massacre, this one of Apaches in Arizona in 1871, Karl Jacoby observes that violence against Indians is "at once the most familiar and most overlooked subject in American history." He argues, "The true magnitude of the violent encounter with the indigenous inhabitants of North America remains unacknowledged even today. So too are its consequences and contingencies unexplored."[7]

Jacoby has identified a paradox that a postcolonial history of American settler colonialism can help us to understand and explain. The history of Indian removal *is* familiar; in a sense virtually every American and many others throughout the world know about it. Popular histories, from *Century of Dishonor* in 1881 to *Bury My Heart at Wounded Knee* in 1970, have long since chronicled and eulogized the dispossession and displacement of the American Indian.[8]

This study goes beyond a simple narrative of massacres and conquest by framing Indian removal within a context of settler colonialism. I narrate a comprehensive history of American Indian removal in order to convey the magnitude as well as the violence of the settler colonial project. I also argue that the long and bloody history of settler colonialism laid a foundation for the history of American foreign policy—and especially its penchant for righteous violence. This study thus connects the history of Indian removal with other nineteenth-century American wars to illuminate patterns of counterinsurgency and indiscriminate warfare deeply rooted in colonial history, carrying through the nineteenth century, and indeed to the present day.

While my own background is in diplomatic history, I have sought to forge connections with other subfields of American history, to reach across disciplines. Such crossings are infrequent because of the surprisingly rigid boundaries erected by academic specialization. Within American history alone, subfields on the pre-Revolutionary era, the early Republic, Western history, Indian history, diplomatic history, military history, and American studies have their own members, annual meetings, specialized journals, and book and article prizes. Balkanization promotes a certain degree of gatekeeping while status and promotion typically derive from archival research in one's own subfield. Synthetic and theoretical work is discouraged as arcane and outmoded; identification of continuities dismissed as simplistic. The "c" and "g" words—colonialism and genocide—are rarely invoked.

Discussion of violent Indian removal thus has become strangely passé. Owing in no small part to the sensational success of *Bury My Heart at Wounded Knee*, many Indians and the overwhelmingly non-indigenous scholars of Indian history have for years steered clear of accounts centered on the victimization of Indians by Euro-Americans. They grasp that a maudlin sentimentalism, ironically, tends to dehumanize Indians by denying them historical agency and leaving the impression that all of the Indians were "killed off" (in fact more than five million people identify themselves as indigenous North Americans today). With justification, scholars thus avoid writing narratives in which Indians function purely as victims of the man's white aggression, with virtually no attention paid to indigenous culture and colonial ambivalence. Scholars in the dynamic fields of Indian history and borderland studies emphasize indigenous cultures and agency, the complexities and ambivalence of specific borderland situations, cultural brokers and go-betweens. In the field of American history, studies focused on Euro-American drives, removal policies, and killing of Indians have been branded Eurocentric or teleological and relegated to the margins.

Indigenous-centered and borderland studies were and are much needed, typically insightful, and make possible a new synthesis incorporating Indian agency and colonial ambivalences into a broader narrative. In this book, that narrative centers on the continent-wide and centuries-long settler colonial project of dispossessing indigenous people. As Indians mounted an anticolonial resistance, American settler colonialism entailed the application of sustained and often indiscriminate violence. Borderland warfare gave rise to an "American way of war," which manifested in the Mexican War, the Civil War, and the "Philippine Insurrection," and indeed has carried over into the twentieth and twenty-first centuries. Counterinsurgency and indiscriminate warfare did not originate in the search-and-destroy operations in the jungles of Vietnam, but rather sunk their roots over centuries of North American settler colonization.

Only by synthesizing and conceptualizing over a broad sweep of American postcolonial history can we address the "true magnitude" and consequences of the "violent encounter with the indigenous inhabitants of North America" to which Jacoby referred. I discuss these issues more fully in Chapter 1, which locates this study within historiography and within postcolonial studies. Chapters 2, 3, 4, and

6 analyze American Indian removal and borderland warfare. Chapter 5 frames the Mexican and Civil Wars as part of a broader history of settler colonialism and borderland violence. The colonialisms of Alaska and Hawai'i (Chapter 7) offer different frames of comparison from the continental experience. Chapter 8 addresses the issue of continuity and discontinuity in the history of American colonialism through an analysis of the history of intervention, indiscriminate warfare, colonialism, and postcolonialism in the Philippines.

Chapter 9 discusses the ways in which indigenous people not only survived but also struggled for change in the wake of the centuries of violent dispossession. The legacies of settler colonialism, integral to postcolonial studies, remain formidable, as they continue to affect the lives of indigenes and indeed of all those who live in colonized societies.

The Conclusion focuses on the internalization of righteous violence within American history and the nation's foreign policy. The violence of empire did not victimize the indigenous people alone. Colonialism "dehumanizes even the most civilized man," Amié Césaire pointed out in *Discourse on Colonialism*. The colonizer "gets into the habit of seeing the other man as *an animal*, accustoms himself to treating him like an animal, and tends objectively to transform *himself* into an animal. It is this result, this boomerang effect of colonization that I wanted to point out."[9] In the Conclusion, I explore the ways in which this "boomerang of savagery" came hurtling back on the United States itself.

* * *

Other scholars have helped me along the way with efforts both great and small, from reading multiple drafts, to offering encouragement, to suggesting literature. In actuality I have hundreds of scholars in multiple subfields to thank for the books and articles that they have written over the years and which inform this study. None of these scholars, mentioned here or cited in the work, should be held accountable for the final product, though many of them made it much better than it otherwise would have been. Shelley Baranowski, Kevin Kern, Margaret Jacobs, Sherry Smith, and one of the preeminent theorists of settler colonialism, Lorenzo Veracini, all read full or partial drafts at various stages and helped me a great deal. Others who read, criticized, and suggested literature include Christine Lober, Maurice and Kathryn Labelle, David Zietsma, Ted Easterling, Kelsey Walker, Andrew Sternisha, Michael Sheng, Elizabeth Mancke, Martin Wainwright, Stephen Harp, Janet Klein, Michael Graham, Constance Bouchard, Lesley Gordon, Benjamin Harrison, Gary Hess, Brian Halley, Philip Howard, Kelly Hopkins, Anne Foster, Eric Hinderaker, David Ryan, Karine Walther, Kristin Hoganson, Daniel Margolies, Wade Wilcox, and Kym Rohrbach. The Hixsons—especially Kandy but also Bud, Emma, and Maiza—always encourage my work. Zoe was always there for a pat on the head or a yawn and a stretch while I was actually doing it.

I thank the University of Akron and the US Army Heritage and Education Center for generous research grants in support of this study. I thank the History Departments at the University of Louisville and Bowling Green State University for inviting me to give, respectively, the prestigious Louis R. Gottschalk and Gary R. Hess annual lectures at their institutions wherein I worked through some of these ideas with the help of some excellent questions from the audiences. Finally, I especially thank Chris Chappell, a senior editor at Palgrave-Macmillan, for taking an immediate interest in the study, and shepherding it through the publication process.

1

Introduction: Settler Colonialism, History, and Theory

This book analyzes settler colonialism over the sweep of Euro-American history. It is neither a simple narrative of conquest nor a study devoted solely to ferreting out indigenous agency within the colonial encounter. The narrative instead identifies ambivalences—the myriad ways in which both the "colonizer" and the "colonized" reconfigured their identities as they traded, allied, assimilated, negotiated, resisted, and otherwise carved out "third spaces" within the colonial encounter. Despite these ambivalences, American settler colonialism ultimately drove an ethnic cleansing of the continent.[1]

I employ the trope of ambivalence as a framework both to incorporate Indian agency and to address the complexity of the colonial encounter. Borderlands history emphasizes local and regional studies and the distinctiveness of each colonial situation. There was no single "frontier," of course, but rather many borderlands with fluid geographic boundaries. Mixed ethnicities and convoluted identities, contestation over sovereignty, and varieties of cultural, economic, and social change characterized the borderlands. Yet underlying the history of all regions was dispossession of the indigenous residents backed by violence.

In the end, settler colonialism was a zero-sum game. Settlers—operating from the bottom up but backed by all levels of government—would accept nothing less than removal of Indians and complete control of the land. As they carried out Indian removal across the breadth of the continent, Americans internalized a propensity for waging indiscriminate violence against their savage foes. Born of settler colonialism, this boomerang of violence would play out over the sweep of US history and help define an "American way of war" in the process.[2]

This study flows from the premise that the United States should be perceived and analyzed *fundamentally* as a settler colonial society. The American "imperial settler state" originated in the context of Indian removal and forged powerful continuities over space and time. American history is the most sweeping, most violent, and most significant example of settler colonialism in world history. American settler colonialism evolved over the course of three centuries, resulting in millions of deaths and displacements, while at the same time creating the richest, most powerful, and ultimately the most militarized nation in world history.[3]

Postcolonial Studies

This book situates itself within postcolonial studies, a term that requires contextualization. The absence of the hyphen distinguishes "postcolonial" from "post-colonial," a term that might suggest, say, the study of India in the aftermath of British colonialism, or Indonesia following the departure of the Dutch. Hence "postcolonial" does not impart a temporal meaning in the way that the hyphenated "post-colonial" might bring to mind post–World War II decolonization. "Postcolonial" relates to colonialism, to be sure, but in much more expansive ways than the hyphenated form.[4]

Postcolonial studies link the colonized past with the present and the future, thereby facilitating analysis over a *longue dureé*[5] of history. The "postcolonial era" is in a sense timeless, thus challenging the historian's penchant for tidy periodizations, insofar as while there are beginnings, there is no end; the legacies of colonialism persist. The field facilitates comparative studies, as colonialism was an international phenomenon that profoundly influenced (and continues to influence) the entire world. Postcolonial studies blend history, culture, and geopolitics within a "context of colonialism and its consequences." They encourage efforts "to look critically at the world and the knowledge and representations that have been made about it."[6] Because postcolonial studies have been defined and used in different ways, one must be wary of those who either condemn or heap praise upon it.[7]

Postcolonial critique draws upon classic theorists including Frantz Fanon, who is sometimes credited with "inventing" postcolonial studies. In *Black Skin, White Masks* (1952), Fanon identified a "massive psycho-existential complex" under colonialism, within which "The black man is not a man . . . for the black man there is only one destiny. And it is white."[8] Fanon's exploration of "the various attitudes that the Negro adopts in contact with white civilization"—the white mask over the black skin—stimulated postcolonial analysis, inspiring a virtual subfield dubbed "critical Fanonism." In *The Wretched of the Earth* (1961), a more revolutionary Fanon inspired anticolonialism as well as the black power movement with his advocacy of violent resistance to colonial oppression. According to Fanon, the West—including the United States, a former colony that "became a monster"—had nothing to offer to true liberation struggles, and he advised, "Leave this Europe where they are never done talking of Man, yet murder men everywhere they find them."[9]

In *Discourse on Colonialism* (1950) Amie Césaire preceded Fanon in emphasizing the ways in which the colonizer destroyed the identity of the colonized through "thingification." The colonized person could not be an individual but rather was a "thing"—a savage, a barbarian, a nigger, and so on. Colonization thus worked to "*decivilize* the colonizer, to brutalize him in the true sense of the word." Similarly, Albert Memmi argued that colonized people were perpetually degraded as the colonizer "emphasizes those things which keep him separate," precluding the evolution of "a joint community."[10]

Building on the work of these classic theorists, as well as on the philosophy of Michel Foucault, Edward Said extended the analytic framework by introducing the concept of "Orientalism." Said showed how literary discourse established a powerful binary between Western modernity—viewed as rational, progressive, manly, and morally and racially superior—and the non-Western other, typically represented as heathen, primitive, treacherous, and de-masculinized. Orientalism shifted attention to the ways in which "colonial knowledge" shaped the "encounter" between the metropole and the periphery in a variety of global settings.[11]

Colonial Ambivalence

Going beyond black skin and white masks, the colonizer and the colonized, Homi Bhaba identified ambivalence within the colonial encounter. Drawing insight from the French psychoanalyst Jacques Lacan's seminars on the formation of individual identity, Bhaba destabilized the sharply drawn binary between the colonizer and the colonized. Bhaba explained that the supposedly all-powerful colonist actually depended on the supposedly totally subservient colonized subject in order to formulate his own identity (e.g., "I am white and civilized, he is brown and savage"). Rather than being fixed or monolithic, colonial identities therefore were constructed, unstable, and required constant repetition and affirmation in order to assert them as being real. Bhaba's insight illuminated a "third space" between the colonizer and the colonized, opening the way for considerations of *hybridity* within the colonial encounter.[12]

Critical to Bhaba's analysis was the ambivalence inherent in the colonizer's desires as well as the indigene's capacity for resistance. The colonizer desired the colonized other, for example for his attunement with nature or sexual liberation, and yet was repulsed by his primitiveness and the dangers that he posed. The slippages and uncertainty within the colonizer's identity, including taking on some of the characteristics of the "savage," produced anxiety and instability. At the same time, ambivalence enabled the colonized other the capacity for agency and resistance because the relations were not as fixed as they appeared to be, but rather were inherently unstable and malleable. Bhaba argued that through, for example, mimicry or mockery the indigene could appear to embrace the colonizer's authority or display his contempt for it. The colonized subject could also appropriate or adapt to the colonizer's resources and knowledge for his or her own uses and benefit. The supposedly helpless colonized subject thus had the capacity to cultivate, as Bhaba put it, "strategies of subversion that turn the gaze of the discriminated back upon the eye of power."[13]

On the North American borderlands, colonial ambivalence complicated relations between settlers and indigenes. Masses of Americans empathized with Indians, condemned treaty violations and aggression against them, and strove to shepherd them to civilization and salvation. Almost none of these people, however, perceived Indians as having legitimate claims to occupy colonial space. They often expressed sympathy for Indians even as they advocated removing them from their homelands in order to "save" them. Countless numbers of Indians went a long way toward accommodating Euro-Americans by trading and interacting with them, negotiating and allying with them in warfare, converting to their religions, and showing a willingness to share space.

The persistence of destabilizing ambivalences and uncertainties ultimately could only be addressed through the virtual *elimination* of the indigene. Arriving in massive numbers, Euro-Americans assumed entitlement to the land and demanded total security from the threat of indigenous resistance. By occupying "middle ground" with Euro-Americans, Indians destabilized the colonizer's identity and his presumed providential destiny to inherit the land. This persistent rupturing of the colonialist fantasy combined with "savage" anticolonial resistance had a traumatic impact on the colonizer. Euro-Americans thus engaged in often-indiscriminate violence aimed at fulfilling the self-serving vision of Indians as a "dying race."

Borderland studies and postcolonial studies have focused mostly on the indigenes and the complexities of local situations. But a history focused overwhelmingly on indigenous peoples and their experiences is one-dimensional. A history of settler colonialism must by definition also "focus on the settlers, on what they do, and how they think about what they do."[14] In this study I attempt to probe into the psyche, the ambivalences, and the resort to violence of the colonizer as well as the colonized. The analysis encompasses the complexity of the colonial encounter but suggests that ambivalence and hybridity created unwanted contingencies and psychic anxieties that tended ultimately to be reconciled through violence.

Settler Colonial Studies

The central arguments of this book are framed by settler colonial studies, a relatively recent and cutting-edge field of inquiry. "Settler colonialism as a specific formation has not yet been the subject of dedicated systematic analysis," Lorenzo Veracini notes.[15] Academic conferences in 2007 and 2008, followed by the launching of a journal dedicated to settler colonial studies, have propelled the new field forward.

Settler colonialism refers to a history in which settlers drove indigenous populations from the land in order to construct their own ethnic and religious national communities. Settler colonial societies include Argentina, Brazil, Australia, Canada, Israel, New Zealand, South Africa, and the United States. What primarily distinguishes settler colonialism from colonialism proper is that the settlers came not to exploit the indigenous population for economic gain, but rather to remove them from colonial space. Settlers sought "to construct communities bounded by ties of ethnicity and faith in what they persistently defined as virgin or empty land," Caroline Elkins and Susan Pedersen point out. A "logic of elimination and not exploitation" fueled settler colonialism. The settlers "wished less to govern indigenous peoples or to enlist them in their economic ventures than to seize their land and push them beyond an ever-expanding frontier of settlement." As Veracini succinctly puts it, "Settler colonial projects are specifically interested in turning indigenous peoples into refugees."[16]

Under "conventional" colonialism the colonizer eventually departs, but under settler colonialism the colonizer means to occupy the land permanently. "Settler colonies were (are) premised on the elimination of the native societies," Patrick Wolfe explains. "The colonizers come to stay—invasion is a structure not an event." Because it was *structural* rather than contingent, settler colonialism extended widely and outlasted colonialism and European imperialism. By a process of conquest and "the reproduction of one's own society through long-range migration," James Belich explains, "It was settlement, not empire that had the spread and staying power in the history of European expansion."[17]

Settlers dispossessed indigenous people by establishing "facts on the ground" through mass migrations backed by violence. Hungry for land unavailable to them in Europe, settlers poured into new worlds, leaving metropolitan authorities struggling to keep pace. "Mobility and a lack of supervision enabled free subjects and citizens to scout for prospects and to squat," John Weaver points out. "All frontiers attracted squatters whose possessory occupation was difficult to supplant."[18]

The triangular relationship between settlers, the metropole, and the indigenous population distinguishes and defines settler colonialism. Settlers sought to remove and replace the indigenous population and in the process to cast aside the authority of the "mother" country. Settler colonies created their very identities through resolution of this dialectical relationship, in which indigenes disappeared and metropolitan authority was cast aside—the American Revolution being a prominent example. Thus, the ability to make both the indigenous and the exogenous metropolitan other "progressively disappear" established "the constitutive hegemony of the settler component."[19]

The speed and intensity of explosive colonization overwhelmed indigenous peoples. As Belich notes, indigenes "could cope with normal European colonization [but] it was *explosive* colonization that proved too much for them." Masses of settlers brought modernity with them, as they hewed out farms, domesticated animals, and built roads, bridges, canals, railroads, factories, towns, and cities, mowing down indigenous cultures in the process. The migrants "destroyed, crippled, swamped or marginalized most of the numerous societies they encountered," constructing new societies at an astonishing pace.[20]

If "sheer demographic swamping" failed to overwhelm the indigenous people, the modern societies linked advanced technology with lethal tropes of racial inferiority and indigenous savagery to effect ethnic cleansing campaigns.[21] "The term 'settler' has about it a deceptively benign and domesticated ring which masks the violence of colonial encounters that produced and perpetrated consistently discriminatory and genocidal regimes against the indigenous peoples," Annie Coombes notes. Settlers could be "dangerous people," Belich adds, "especially when in full-frothing boom frenzy."[22]

This study embraces settler colonialism as a critically important interpretive framework, but one that requires theoretical and historical contextualization.

I accept Wolfe's argument that settler colonialism establishes a *structure*; however, the tendency of structuralism to forge rigid binaries can gloss over historical complexity and contingency. Bhaba's ambivalence thus provides an important contextualizing framework, one that I use to incorporate exceptions, qualifications, gray areas, and middle grounds between the colonizer and the colonized.

Space, Place, and Law

Culturally imagined and legally enshrined conceptions of space and place fueled settler colonialism. Outside of geography "the importance, complexity, and dynamism of space is frequently rendered invisible," yet space, as Doreen Massey observes, "is by its very nature full of power and symbolism, a complex web of relations of domination and subordination, of solidarity and cooperation." Spatiality thus plays a central role in the production of knowledge and power. The way space is conceived, imagined, and framed has political consequences, for example as in the relationship between conceptions of globalization and neoliberal economic policies in the more recent past. As David Delaney points out, "Much of what is experientially significant about how the world is as it is and what it is like to be in the world directly implicates the dynamic interplay of space, law, meaning, and power."[23]

Rather than being an empty void, space in this context is heavily laden with meaning. A culturally imagined and legally sanctioned relationship with the land creates the conditions and contingencies of social relations—the facts on the ground. In settler colonial societies, terms such as "frontier," "Manifest Destiny," and "homeland" assumed powerful symbolic meaning, creating emotional attachments. Legal claims such as the "Doctrine of Discovery" and "domestic dependent nations" bolstered these cultural ties to colonial space, while sanctioning dispossession and removal policies.

Profoundly divergent conceptions of place and space thus played a critical role in the colonial encounter. Over centuries, indigenous people had cultivated deeply rooted spiritual connections with the land from which the colonizer sought to remove them. The spiritual universe of indigenous societies revolved around nurturing and preserving reciprocal relations with the natural environment. This powerful sense of reciprocity carried over into relations with other peoples. When the universe of reciprocal relations was disrupted, indigenous warrior cultures typically lashed out in a quest for blood revenge.[24]

For the settlers, violent indigenous resistance in contestation for colonial space functioned to reaffirm their own powerful constructions of imagined relationships with the land. Eurocentric notions of racial superiority, progress, and providential destiny thus propelled settler colonialism. Europeans denied or derided "primitive" concepts of land use, creating a colonial binary between land wasted by indigenes and land mobilized for progress by settlers. Framing indigenous people as indolent and wasteful justified removal and relocating them onto less desirable spaces. "Europeans' convictions about improvement and waste, their assumptions about supposedly advanced and less advanced peoples, helped make the land rush unstoppable," Weaver points out.[25]

As they linked private property and individual landholding with freedom, progress, and national destiny, under God, settlers assumed control over colonial space. Colonial ambivalence, the relative balance of forces, and alliances determined the pace and timing of the settler advance. In the end, however, settler states would not stop short of establishing their authority over colonial space through mass migration, sanctioned under their laws, backed by violence.

Equipped with a higher manhood and a higher calling, settler colonials boldly conquered the wilderness, the outback; inherited the True North; and reclaimed the land of Zion. Having imagined powerful connections to their chosen lands, settlers defended them violently and at all cost.

Comparative Analysis

Settler colonial studies facilitate comparative analysis that reveals surprisingly similar histories evolving at different places and at different times. "The fact that settler societies resemble one another in several respects is not a consequence of conscious imitation," Donald Denoon explains, "but of separate efforts to resolve very similar problems."[26] As settler colonial studies are relatively new, Lynette Russell notes, "One of the future directions for research include detailed comparative studies."[27]

While this book homes in on American settlement, the United States emerged out of a broader history of global colonialism and especially of British settler colonialism.[28] "The course of American history," Weaver points out, "connects deeply, extensively, and reciprocally with land-taking and land-allocation episodes in the histories of British settlement colonies."[29] The American, Canadian, Australian, New Zealand, and South African settler colonies shared common cultural traits and similar outlooks toward indigenous people—ambivalent attitudes as well as lethal ones—yet important distinctions remained.

Although Canada like the United States was a product of British settler colonialism, geographic and demographic distinctions constructed a different history with indigenous people. In essence Canada had far fewer settlers, far fewer indigenes, and plenty of space to avoid one another for a longer time. Contrary to popular mythology, British Canadians were neither wiser nor morally superior in their handling of Indian affairs; rather they felt less pressured to address the issue. Canadians were also preoccupied with internal divisions between French and English settlers and between maritime and interior provinces.[30] Not until the 1860s did the Canadian policies begin to resemble the American removal policies, but the scale and scope of conflict with the First Peoples was small compared with the United States. "Aside from the 1869 Matisse resistance in the Red River country and the 1885 Matisse and Indian uprising," Roger Nichols points out, "the Canadian record featured little violence particularly when contrasted to what was happening at the same time in the United States."[31]

In southern Africa both the much-mythologized Dutch "trekboers" and British settlers and investors colonized through violent dispossession of indigenous people. As in other settler societies, "the quest for more land continued relentlessly," especially with the discovery of gold and diamonds. The colonizers cheated, killed, and removed the indigenes while the Dutch also enslaved them and, as in the United States and Australia, removed children from their families.[32] In South Africa, as in the United States, Australia, and other settler colonial settings, "warrior resistance played into allegations of savagery, thus confirming unfitness for tribal or individual land title" and justifying violent retribution. Again, however, the scope and scale of the colonial violence, while hardly negligible, did not match the American experience.[33]

The same was true of New Zealand (Aotearoa in the Maori language). New Zealand settlers purported to take a humanitarian approach to the Maori, who were dispossessed nonetheless by legal means in the wake of the disputed Treaty of Waitangi (1840).[34] As in the United States and other settler societies, disease took a severe toll on the Maori. The *Pakeha* (whites) "took it for granted that the Maori population would continue to decrease" as their own proliferated.[35] Thereafter, the settlers moved onto Maori land, as "frontier avarice throttled principal." Beginning in 1860 the New Zealand Wars raged for a decade.[36] "Maori resistance was effective rather than futile until numbers overwhelmed them." The Maori population steadily declined, as in other colonized societies, as they were "dominated demographically" in the wake of massive waves of immigration in the 1860s and 1870s.[37]

The settler state that most closely mirrors the American experience is Australia. As in the United States, the ethnic cleansing of Australia extended across an entire continent, proved genocidal in its effects, and until very recently has been subjected to persistent historical denial. Ambivalence on the part of both colonizers and indigenes materialized in both societies, as did drives for religious salvation and assimilation. Both Australia and the United States adopted "reforms" that entailed cultural genocide, including national campaigns removing children from their families.[38]

At the arrival of European settler colonialism in the late eighteenth century, from 750,000 to 1.5 million "Aborigines" lived on the continent. Ravaged by disease, dispossession, and indiscriminate slaughter, the number had plummeted to 31,000 by 1911.[39] In the early 1640s the Dutchman Abel Tasman was the first European to explore New Zealand, sight the Fiji Islands, and set down on the island south of the Australian mainland that is named after him today. More than a century later the three voyages of the legendary British seafarer James Cook from 1768 to 1779 spurred Anglophone settlement in the Pacific. Cook traversed the eastern coast of the continent and named it New South Wales. On April 29, 1770, he planted the British flag in Botany Bay, about 30 kilometers from modern-day Sydney. Cook made only limited contact with the natives whereupon tensions surfaced immediately. "All they seemed to want is for us to be gone," he noted.[40]

Despite this chilly reception, as in North America ambivalent relations including trade and cooperation characterized the early interaction between the British settlers and indigenous peoples. "Contact between explorers and Aborigines was often friendly and mutually satisfactory," Henry Reynolds points out.[41]

The Europeans often depended on the aboriginal people for food, access to water, and generalized local know-how. Some Aborigines already had exposure to European commodities including pottery, cloth, and metal tools that had arrived through trade routes from Southeast Asia. The new settlers brought iron, guns, and other desirable trade goods.

As in the future United States, ambivalent relations gave way to violence as settlements expanded and the Europeans strove to drive out the indigenes, considered primitive and inferior. Both Americans and Australians displayed "relatively little use for indigenous people and a penchant for considering Aborigines and American Indians as impediments to progress," Benjamin Madley notes. The colonizers perpetrated "a particularly high number of massacres" and displayed "surprisingly congruent tactics despite the fact that they occurred decades apart on separate continents and under different regimes, while targeting dozens of different indigenous peoples."[42] Settler colonization of Queensland, for example, resembled California, as settlers and squatters unrestrained by central government authority orchestrated massive cleansing campaigns replete with indiscriminate violence.[43]

The most significant difference between US and Australian settler colonialism was that the Americans formally recognized Indian possession of the land and thus dispossessed them by means of ostensibly legal treaties, whenever possible. On the other hand, through their embrace of *terra nullius*—"land belonging to no one"—the Australian settler colonials adopted a more extreme version of the Doctrine of Discovery than in the United States. Under *terra nullius* the Australians considered the natives to be British subjects rather than independent peoples hence they would be dispossessed without legal wrangling.[44]

Terra nullius, like American Manifest Destiny, constituted an "imperial fantasy" that enabled Australian settler colonialism and the ethnic cleansing of the continent. A romanticized national history in which people thrust rudely onto the barren shores "down under" became "a good and neighborly" community elided the history of settler invasion and destruction of Aboriginal culture. Colonial discourse depicted Australia as "a wild, untamed space that existed beyond the boundaries of colonial civilization." As Rod Macneil points out, "The creation of a prehistoric landscape enabled colonization to be couched not in terms of appropriation and exploitation, but as progress and redemption."[45]

The similarities between the United States and Australia as well as other British settler societies suggest that American history is not exceptional. On the other hand, the *breadth* and *scope*—and thus the violence—of Euro-American settler colonialism have no parallel, not even in Australia.

Race, Gender, Religion, Nation

Settler colonialism typically unfolds in association with nation building. Constructions, hierarchies, and inclusions and exclusions pertaining to race, class, gender, religion, and nation enable settler communities to cohere. Often these constructions are comingled and mutually reinforcing. The settler community and nation define themselves, expand and police their borders, and project their power into colonial space on the basis of these constructed hierarchies and exclusions. In constructing identity, exclusion of "the other" closes off their narratives and discourses while privileging one's own.[46]

It is in this sense that Fanon pointed out, "Europe is literally the creation of the Third World." Without the colonized other, the European could not define his own identity through manliness, whiteness, godliness, progress, and the civilizing mission vis-à-vis the colonial world. Similarly, as Kevin Bruyneel has argued, "The very identity and meaning implied in the name *America* as the national identity of the United States was in no small part constituted through this nation's real and imagined relationship with indigenous people."[47] Likewise, Australia defined itself in opposition to the aboriginal other.

Neither "the people" nor "the races" actually exist rather they are based on a fictive ethnicity that becomes naturalized within the imagined nation. "For the nation to be itself, it has to be racially or culturally pure," hence it becomes an "obsessional imperative" to drive out exogenous others. Constructions of race, gender, religion, and often a common language construct "a single national project that effectively neutralizes people's differences" and thus enables the imagined community of the nation to cohere. Without these discourses, constructions, and demarcations of space "patriotism's appeal would be addressed to no one."[48]

Colonial varieties of racial formation were often especially virulent as these discourses performed the representational work of sanctioning the extreme violence of slavery and genocide. Racism is an enduring human social formation that preceded modern colonialism and nationalism. Prior to the advent of Darwinian thought there existed an "archaic racism with genocidal potential, constituted by the visual othering of indigenous populations." The discourse of scientific racism piled onto existing racisms and helped justify "the other's expulsion from native lands, economic exploitation, destruction of the indigenous ecosphere and even eventual genocide." Class tensions, closely intertwined with race, played out in colonial encounters. The removal of indigenes from the land created more wealth while promoting the perception among poor whites that they would have greater opportunity for advancement. In any case they could count themselves members of a "master" race.[49]

Gendered constructions complemented racial exclusions as the two became mutually reinforcing under colonialism. "Persistent gendering" marginalized the feminine and thus exalted male power. Competition, aggression, control, power, and other traits of colonialism were distinctly male. Settler colonies exalted manliness, and regeneration of manhood, as they subdued savage foes and "tamed the frontier." Colonialism simultaneously reinforced gendered practices within metropolitan societies, as the emphasis on woman's proper place in the domestic sphere and white men as the protectors of vulnerable women affirmed male authority. On the other hand, women could gain agency by taking part in the colonial encounter, for example as missionaries or in promoting policies of child removal.[50]

Gendered tropes feminized the "virgin" land and its conquest. Gendered colonial discourse often represented indigenous women as queens or alternatively as enticing maidens. Their nakedness and lack of sexual inhibitions aroused desires otherwise repressed in the Christian West. Representations of the dark-skinned indigenous male threat to white women powerfully reinforced repression of the bestial male native yet the rape and enslavement of indigenous women by white men was a common and rarely punished occurrence. Captivity narratives, the specter of miscegenation, and of the proverbial "fate worse than death" pervaded colonial discourse.[51]

Western practices transformed gendered social and economic roles of indigenous people in settler societies. When engaged in civilizing missions, colonial authorities typically tried to convert male warriors into sedentary farmers and relegate women (who performed the agricultural work in most indigenous societies) to a domestic sphere. Colonialism altered family structures and "eroded many matrilineal or women-friendly cultures and practices, or intensified women's subordination in colonized lands."[52] Colonialism enabled paternalist discourse viewing colonized peoples and their children as having undeveloped minds that needed to be molded, scolded, properly socialized, and ultimately the children removed to a civilized environment.

Christian missionaries promulgated many of the gendered Western practices, underscoring the centrality of religion in the colonial encounter. Settler colonials typically viewed their own projects as divinely inspired and providentially destined. Missionaries displayed colonial ambivalence, as they sought to "uplift" indigenes and save their souls, but this sort of paternalism produced cultural imperialism and encompassed genocidal practices such as child removal. Westerners thus showed little recognition or respect for indigenous spirituality. They often linked the "atheistical" and "diabolical" savages with biblical forces of evil. Manifestations of indigenous spirituality threatened these colonial discourses and thus inspired a violent response, for example in 1890 when the Sioux Ghost Dance preceded the Wounded Knee massacre (see Chapter 6). Tightly infused with concepts of space, race, and nation, religious discourse justified and propelled the settler colonial project.

Historical Denial

Historical distortion and denial are endemic to settler colonies. In order for the settler colony to establish a collective usable past, legitimating stories must be created and persistently affirmed as a means of naturalizing a new historical narrative. A national mythology displaces the indigenous past. "The settler seeks to establish a nation, and therefore needs to become native and to write the epic of the nation's origin," Anna Johnston and Alan Lawson point out. "The 'origin' is that which has no antecedent, so the presence of Ab-origines is an impediment." *Becoming the indigene* required not only cleansing of the land, either through killing or removing, but sanitizing the historical record as well.

The critical sleight of hand in propagating a new national narrative was the settler's displacement of the indigene. Increasingly, the settlers depicted themselves and their cultures as indigenous. As the inheritors of a "New World" and cultivators of a "virgin land," the settlers elided their actual historical role as invaders and conquerors of colonial space. "Empty land can be settled, but occupied land can only be invaded," Johnston and Lawson point out. "The word 'settler' was itself part of the process of invasion; it was literally a textual imposition on history."[53]

Even with the removal and marginalization of indigenes onto reservations or Bantustans their existence could not be forgotten entirely, yet that which remained could be subtly absorbed within the dominant culture. In the quest for authenticity the settler colonial societies appropriated the indigenous style of clothing—the buckskinned frontiersman for example—and adopted the "attributes and skills (the Mounties, cowboys, range-riders, gauchos, backwoodsmen), and in this way cemented their legitimacy." They simultaneously romanticized the "noble savage" or relegated the indigenous past to the realm of place names and sports teams, subsuming the violence of conquest within the "liberating frivolity of play." They also cultivated an "imperialist nostalgia," as they produced stories, literature, and images focusing on the inevitable "passing" of the indigenous race, as in the "last of the Mohicans."[54]

These historical representations and cultural constructions notwithstanding, history remains a neuralgic subject in settler colonial societies. Denial and disavowal of the history of violent dispossession of the indigenes characterize settler societies. "Revisionist" challenges invariably meet with denunciation or marginalization rooted in the naïve assumption of the existence of a true and immutable sacred past. Hence in the 1990s "history wars" raged in both the United States and Australia, South Africa conducted "truth and reconciliation" hearings, while the debate over "post-Zionism" roiled Israeli society.[55]

Historical denial helps explain why study of the United States within the context of both settler colonialism and postcolonialism has been relatively scarce and "especially controversial." Even as postcolonial studies "has expanded its scope to include the United States," Jenny Sharpe points out, "it has not addressed its status as an imperial power, past or present."[56] Analysis of American imperialism has always been problematic. For generations, as the legendary diplomatic historian William Appleman Williams pointed out in 1955, "One of the central themes of American historiography is that there is no American Empire." As they narrated the Cold War as a rigid binary pitting the "free world" against "godless communism," consensus historians dismissed the very concept of American imperialism as "a stock expression in the Marxist vocabulary, connoting, to the leftist mind, both the wickedness and decay of capitalism." To the extent the United States engaged in imperial policies, Julius Pratt explained in 1950, "peoples of primitive or retarded cultures" needed "guardians to guide and direct their development" hence the US Empire was "benevolent" and "accepted by those living under it."[57]

While Americans trumpeted the nation's commitment to diversity and democracy both at home and abroad, "The irony of this image in the light of its conquistadorial and slave-holding past required great ideological effort." The "fantasy" that enabled US citizens "to achieve their national identity through the disavowal of US imperialism was American exceptionalism," Donald Pease argues.[58] Structures of denial, disavowal, and forgetting comingled with fantasies of chosenness provided Americans with "an imaginary relation to actual state colonialism."[59]

To the extent Americans have acknowledged the existence of a colonial empire, it is typically associated with the Spanish-American War and the annexations and taking of colonies after 1898. However, postcolonial analysis illuminates a much longer process of colonialism and empire building, long preceding the American Revolution and rooted in settler colonization.[60]

Indigenous Agency and Borderland Studies

For more than a generation now, ethno-historians and specialists in indigenous American history have brilliantly illuminated the agency and ambivalences of Native American history and culture.[61] This scholarship responded in part to a largely one-sided (though nonetheless useful at the time) historiography that emerged from the minority-conscious 1960s, emphasizing the imperial conquest of Indians by white Americans. Under this framing, indigenes functioned purely as victims of aggression, burying their hearts at Wounded Knee following their conquest by whites whose genocidal drives were motivated by "the metaphysics of Indian hating."[62] These works tended to overlook indigenous agency as well as ambivalences and historical complexity, and to accept uncritically the identities of the colonizer and the colonized.

By contrast, studies, focused on the agency of indigenous Americans and ambivalent cross-cultural relations, represent arguably the most productive field in American history over the past generation. By "facing East" instead of West, historians have unearthed a wealth of knowledge on the indigenous tribes, thus transcending the depiction of Indians as mere victims in the inevitable if lamentable passing of the noble race. Influenced in part by postcolonial frameworks, including Bhaba's ambivalence, these scholars have appropriately complicated and nuanced white–Indian relations. They have explored Indian agency in terms of spirituality, culture, gender and social relations, trade and economics, intertribal cooperation and conflict with Europeans as well as other Indians, environmental impact, and much else. Perhaps most important, by illuminating times and places in which indigenes and Euro-Americans and mixed bloods interacted and coexisted with some degree of understanding and mutual benefit, these studies suggest that violent removal was not the only option within the colonial encounter.[63]

Indigenous people thus not only confronted the European expansion, but also *participated* in a complex and contested colonial encounter. For many indigenes the colonizer–colonized dyad was not their primary concern, at least not initially, as their attention remained focused on longstanding relationships with other indigenous groups. Rather than simply bloody rivals from the outset, Indians and Euro-Americans frequently were trade and alliance partners, neighbors, wives, employers, and co-religionists. Powerful "tribes" such as the Iroquois, the Comanche, and the Sioux exerted their influence—often through violence—over other indigenous groupings. Indians (the Iroquois are a good early example) often exploited trade and alliance opportunities with Europeans to advance their economic and security interests at the expense of other indigenes. Because they were different peoples, indigenes only belatedly developed pan-Indian consciousness and alliances and these typically succeeded only in achieving short-term gains rather than an effective long-term resistance against settler colonialism.

Over the past generation scholars tilling the fertile ground of borderlands studies have demolished the concept of static "frontier" in favor of fluid geographical boundaries. Regional and localized conflict and cooperation, drives and aspirations, multiethnic and gendered inclusions and exclusions forged a complex and diverse borderland history. Contravening a simple binary of expansion–resistance, the more recent studies have revealed places and times in which Euro-Americans and indigenes shared an ambivalent albeit often tenuous "middle ground." Other local and regional studies have emphasized indigenous interaction and conflict, underscoring that whites often were not the central players on the various borderlands.[64]

The rich historiography of borderland studies, with its emphasis on blurred boundaries, crossings, and connectivity, transcends traditional preoccupation with the nation-state and thus furthers the agenda of transnational history. Borderlands were by definition places where sovereignty, control over colonial space, was unstable and contested, hence the "centrality of violence in relations within and between borderland communities." However, borderlands also represented sites for cultural interaction, hybridity, and negotiation as well as conflict. The regional and localized histories characteristic of borderlands studies stand on their own but can also, taken collectively, provide the evidentiary framework for contextualizing the history of North American settler colonialism. They also open up possibilities for linking Indian history with the wider global history of indigenous peoples in postcolonial context.[65]

With much of the best work focused on the American southwest, borderlands' scholarship has incorporated not only indigenes but also Hispanics more fully into histories formerly monopolized by Indians and whites. Borderland studies emphasize Hispanic and indigenous agency, sometimes in cooperation other times in conflict, and reveal myriad examples of ambivalence and ambiguity. As with Indians and Europeans, Mexicans and Mexican-Americans were not merely subjects but instead had cultures and agency of their own. Violence between and among indigenes and Hispanics is one of the most significant products of the new borderland scholarship. Until recent years the traditional Turnerian frontier historiography focused overwhelmingly on violence between whites and Indians or whites and Hispanics. But as Nicole M. Guidotti-Hernandez points out, "Mexicans and Indians were not always resisting whites; they often allied with whites against other Indians and Mexicans."[66]

Indians and Hispanics waged brutally violent assaults and military campaigns. They also participated in captive taking, slave trading, and other odious practices traditionally ascribed to the colonizer alone. "Rituals of violence, exchange, and redemption" permeated borderland societies, James Brooks points out in his influential study of the colonial southwest. In these conflicts women and children became "crucial products of violent economic exchange" yet they also enriched the cultures with which they were forcibly conjoined. Violence, paradoxically, over time eroded ethnic distinctions by creating polyglot communities and providing a basis for reconciliation among turbulent, multiethnic borderland societies.[67]

Captive taking, slave trading, and endemic violence were not confined to the southwest or the trans-Mississippi West. Indeed, the mythic allure of "the West" in American cultural memory has established an almost monolithic imagery, obscuring the violent ethnic cleansing, resistance, and ambivalence that unfolded over *centuries* across the entire eastern half of the future United States. In recent years original borderland scholarship focused on Indian enslavement and indigenous complicity in the slave trade transcends the history not only of "the West" but also of "the South."[68]

Historical, anthropological, and archeological studies show unequivocally that the Euro-American settlers had no monopoly on violence, which had long inhered in indigenous societies. However, colonialism with its vast disruptive power intensified borderland violence and spurred cycles of conflict. Euro-American intrusions into indigenous modes of conflict tended to have an accelerant effect on the preexisting indigenous violence. As other scholars have noted, "The frequent effect of such an intrusion is an overall militarization; that is, an increase in armed collective violence whose conduct, purposes and technologies rapidly adapt to the threats generated by state expansion."[69]

Disease and new technologies—especially firearms and the introduction of the horse—dramatically affected the scope and intensity of borderland conflicts. Colonialism thus introduced new pathogens and technologies, forged new economic relationships, and created new rivalries, alignments, alliances, all of which brought incentives and intensification of violence. Indians could exploit trade opportunities or enhance their own security by allying with Europeans against their indigenous rivals. Indigenes could engage in market driven captive taking in return for trade items and in an effort to preserve their own security.

Borderland violence also changed the practices and identities of the Euro-American invaders. They quickly learned from and adopted the indigenous guerrilla style of warfare—skulking in the woods, hit and run and surprise assaults—and incorporated these techniques into their own way of war. Over time they learned that the way to defeat the indigenes, who often proved difficult to track down, was a scorched-earth policy of destroying their crops, killing their animals, burning their villages, engaging in collective punishment, keeping them on the run. Indiscriminate borderland violence, as I argue in the chapters that follow, carried over into the Mexican War, the Civil War, and the Philippine intervention and came to inhere in what has been called an American way of war.

Connecting Disparate Historiographies

Despite the profusion of a rich and original scholarship on indigenous and borderland history over the past generation, Indian history remains less than fully integrated into the overall narrative of American and global history. Historians of Native American history, like those of many other subfields, frequently lament the disconnectedness and marginalization of their subject area. "American

Indian history continues to be characterized more by its intellectual promise than its impact on historical scholarship," Frederick E. Hoxie observed in 2008. That same year Colin Calloway averred that Indian and ethnohistorians had not yet been unable to "push beyond understanding Indian motivations, perspectives, and agency" to re-center the narrative of American history. Joseph Genetin-Pilaw points out that an overemphasis on indigenous agency "limits ability to synthesize" and thus tends to make Indian history "a marginalized, insular, or even ignorable field."[70]

Thus, no matter how rich and productive, an exclusive focus on Indian agency and localized history tends to marginalize the field while also obscuring the broader framework of settler colonialism. Analysis of the great diversity of Indian experiences should not overshadow the "remarkable continuity of basic objectives and results" in the Euro-American removal policy. Taken too far or to the occlusion of the indiscriminate violence inherent in settler colonialism, a focus limited to indigenous communities and agency can function to perpetuate historical denial by elision. As Peka Håmålåinen points out (albeit buried in an end note), "The recent historiographical focus on cross-cultural crossings and collaborations threatens to obscure a fundamental fact about the history of colonial America—that it is in its essentials a story of conflict, hatred, violence, and virtually insurmountable racial, ethnic, and cultural barriers."[71]

The boundaries that relegate indigenous history to the margins or contain it within regional frameworks such as "The West," reflect the remarkable staying power of Frederick Jackson Turner's iconic 1893 essay, "The Significance of the Frontier in American History." Turner subsumed the "fierce race of savages" within the frame of the "frontier" that he rightly claimed was intrinsic to any meaningful understanding of American history. Turner perceived the importance of violence against Indians in forging unity among the disparate American migrants. As he put it, "The Indian was a common danger, demanding united action." Facing the West, Turner showed no interest in what it was like to have been an indigene facing the East. By 1952 Bernard DeVoto could point to the consequences of this neglect, noting, "American historians have made shockingly little effort to understand the life, the societies, the cultures, the thinking, and the feelings of Indians, and disastrously little effort to understand how all these affected the white men and their societies."[72]

By the 1960s, anthropologists and historians had begun developing the history of indigenous Americans but by that time "racial divisions of the past had been canonized in print and academic ritual," and the "pedagogic ruts" had been carved deep. "By the time ethno-history had become a recognized specialty it was too late for it to be anything else," Kerwin Klein explains. "Ethno-history did not transform 'mainstream' American history but became another note, paragraph, page, or lecture shoehorned into an already overloaded semester. The relentless *westward* march of Anglo-Saxons remained the grand narrative framework [without] any hint that things might have worked out differently."[73]

In recent years several scholars have pinpointed postcolonial and settler colonial studies as possible pathways of escape from this long-term pigeonholing of indigenous history. "The postcolonial critique . . . suggests a new way to imagine the relationship between American Indian history and other areas of scholarship," Hoxie suggests. "The most promising aspect of this critique," he adds, "is the formulation of 'settler colonialism.'" Other scholars concur that postcolonial analysis, and specifically the settler colonial framework, offer ways to integrate the indigenous past with not only the broader narrative of American history but world history as well.[74]

Both Indian history and diplomatic history—another notoriously marginalized subfield—could benefit from developing the seemingly obvious yet remarkably undeveloped colonial–imperial nexus. Postcolonial analysis of settler colonialism and indiscriminate warfare establishes convergences that have yet to be fully explored. As Ned Blackhawk points out, "Despite an outpouring of work over the past decades, those investigating American Indian history and U.S. history more generally have failed to reckon with the violence on which the continent was built." Similarly, Richard White notes that scholars of US Indian policy have done "relatively little on what the relentless erosion of Indian land teaches us about the United States in a larger international context."[75]

Through a combination of theory and contextualized narrative, this book directly addresses these perceived conceptual gaps in knowledge.

Historians of American foreign relations have over the past generation taken the "cultural turn" and are now poised to take an "indigenous turn." In June 2012, the Society for Historians of American Foreign Relations, to its credit, invited specialists in indigenous American history to a roundtable discussion entitled, "Is Indian History Part of the History of American Foreign Relations?" The answer I believe is a resounding "Yes," but it is revealing of the insularity of historical subfields (and a dearth of synthetic work) that this question still had to be posed in 2012. As distinct and largely disconnected subfields, American Indian history and US diplomatic history thus are just now beginning to address systematically the connections between continental Indian removal and twentieth-century overseas empire.

An "indigenous turn" within diplomatic history is much needed to remedy a colonialist historiography. The primary focus within diplomatic history on modern nation-states obscures indigenous polities and the considerable agency they manifested over three centuries of "American" imperial history. Leaving Indians out of diplomatic history thus reaffirms colonialism—the "savages" are denied legitimacy; they were not civilized enough to be encompassed within the study of "foreign policy;" they were part of the conquered wilderness of a still Eurocentric world. Moreover, leaving Indians out limits the understanding of US identity and foreign policy and, especially as I emphasize here, of the penchant for indiscriminate violence embedded within it.

Colonial Violence and Genocide Studies

Postcolonial analysis connects American Indian removal not only with diplomatic and military history but also with the global history of colonial genocide. Although American settler colonialism constituted genocide under broadly accepted international definitions (discussed below), scholars of Indian and borderland history have been reluctant to apply the term. As Carroll Kakel points out, "an almost universal reluctance on the part of mainstream American historians to consider 'genocide' in the case of the American Indians" prevailed until "very recently." Historian Gray H. Whaley, who explicitly makes the connection in his 2010 study of Indian removal in Oregon, avers, "The fact that Euro-Americans attempted genocide as a central component of settler colonialism makes it a crucial topic for historical analysis, one that should not be denied."[76]

In recent years the "new genocide studies" have expanded both the conceptual and geographic boundaries in assessing removal policies and indiscriminate killing in a global context.[77] To some extent these studies begin with the knowledge that, as John Docker puts it, "The history of humanity is the history of violence."[78] With the beginning of recorded history in the Western world, discourses of genocidal violence took a prominent place, as revealed by Thucydides in his classis account of the Peloponnesian War. Genocidal tendencies are apparent in both Greco-Roman polytheistic and Jewish-Christian monotheistic traditions. Genocidal violence, gloriously justified as retribution, permeates the Pentateuch. Similarly, Virgil's "Aeneid" (29–19 BCE) forged a Western mythology promoting "honorable justification" for violence against indigenous societies. "In their operation, reception and eventual imbrication in Western history, these texts represent an ethical disaster, with highly destructive consequences for humanity as a whole, especially for indigenous peoples and peoples already in a land coveted by others as chosen and promised," Docker explains. "The practices recommended in these narratives, of ethnic cleansing and extermination of peoples cast as enemies, would now be considered war crimes and crimes against humanity."[79]

Modern definitions of genocide emanate from World War II and the Nazi Holocaust. In 1944 Raphael Lemkin published *Axis Rule in Occupied Europe*, which defined genocide in essence as a conscious plan to destroy a defined group by killing them or undermining their ability to sustain life, through military, cultural, economic, biological, or psychological means. The UN drew on Lemkin's work in its 1948 Convention on the Prevention and Punishment of the Crime of Genocide, defined as "any of a number of acts committed with the intent to destroy, in whole or part, a national, ethnic, racial or religious group." These acts included "killing members of the group; causing serious bodily or mental harm to members of the group;" and other deliberate actions to destroy a group, notably attempting to prevent births or "forcibly transferring children."[80] Under this framework there seems little doubt that Euro-Americans—as well as Australians, South Africans, Argentinians, and other settler colonials—carried out genocidal campaigns against indigenous peoples.[81]

Part of the reason the G-word has been avoided is the all-consuming shadow cast by the Nazi Holocaust. The Eurocentric genocide convention established a framework singling out the Holocaust while obscuring the histories of colonial genocide. Modernist and Orientalist colonial discourses thus remained unpacked in the early postwar era. Killing of Asians, Africans, Native Americans, and Australian Aborigines was seen as an "inevitable" chapter in the evolution of human "progress" whereas the slaughter of Europeans by the Nazis was truly shocking. Perceiving the Holocaust as utterly without precedent elided the history of European colonialism, including the enrichment of Europeans through colonial violence and exploitation. This ongoing occlusion of other holocausts enabled the continuing exploitation of the "developing" world in the postwar era. Moreover, the Holocaust frame became "sacred" to Jews, unifying their religious community in pursuit of the Zionist settler colonial project in occupied Arab territories in the wake of the Nazi genocide.[82]

While the Nazi Holocaust, like all genocides, entailed unique features, scholars now interpret it within a broader frame of colonial genocide. The Holocaust was "an extreme, radical form of behavior that was not unfamiliar in the history of colonialism," Jürgen Zimmerer explains. The scope, intensity, and industrial style distinguished the Nazi genocide, making it "an extremely radicalized variant" yet still part of a broader history of colonial genocide.[83]

Similarities between the American West and the "German East" were not lost on Adolf Hitler and are belatedly being acknowledged by scholars today. "The Early American and Nazi-German national projects of territorial expansion, racial cleansing, and settler colonization—despite obvious differences in time and place—were strikingly similar projects of 'space' and 'race,' with lethal consequences for 'alien' 'out-groups,' " Kakel points out. American settler colonialism and removal policies against the "Red Indians" served as "the primary model" for Hitler and Heinrich Himmler, the two chief architects of Nazi aggression to the east. "The overwhelming success of the American expansionist project invited repetition in a Nazi-German project which, in their fantasies, would one day dwarf its American predecessor," Kakel notes.[84]

The absence of studies of "third space hybridity" reflecting ambivalence between Jews and the Nazi regime is also notable. While the pathological Nazi worldview left little room for ambivalence, scholars do not hesitate to explore ambivalence and ambiguities pertaining to non-Western "natives" who lived under genocidal colonial regimes. While Indians and Aborigines are said to have had agency under colonial rule—and indeed they often did have—Jews function purely as victims within the frame of the Holocaust, which thus continues to be viewed as unique and unparalleled. The chillingly rational Nazi style of slaughter after 1941 was indeed *sui generis* yet it often obscures that in the end more people were summarily executed or starved to death than funneled through the gas chambers.[85]

Often wrongly perceived as incidental or merely punitive, massacres furthered the eliminationist project not only of the Nazis but also in all genocidal regimes. Scholars make a distinction between massacres and genocide, pointing out for example that the former can exist without the latter but not vice versa. Massacres that occur in a genocidal context are not merely retributive or aberrational but rather advance the ultimate goal of annihilating the targeted population. While often justified as retribution or preemption, massacres are typically "more eliminationist than simply punitive in intent."[86] As in other genocidal campaigns, and illustrated in the chapters that follow, American settler colonials carried out indiscriminate assaults and massacres, perpetrated rape, conducted summary executions, confiscated and destroyed property, engaged in collective punishment, removed children, and almost never punished the perpetrators of these war crimes.

Massacres in the United States and other settler societies often targeted women, children, and animals. The killing of women and children was not merely incidental or spur of the moment but rather intrinsic to the ethnic cleansing project. Settlers and military officials understood that Indian cultures depended on the work performed by women such as tanning skins to make lodges, bedding, and clothing as well as gathering, processing, and preserving food. Women of course had the capacity to bear and raise children, which only complicated the ultimate goal of removing indigenous people from the land, thus affirming the logic of killing both women and children. Settler colonials, volunteers, and military officers often openly advocated just that. Similarly, slaughtering buffaloes and horses and the destruction of housing, crops, and food supplies were incorporated into US counterinsurgency warfare. All of these actions served to facilitate the ultimate goal of driving indigenous people out of colonial spaces desired by Americans.

Indians as well as Hispanics on the American borderlands also conducted brutal attacks to further their self-interest. They targeted rival tribes as well as settlers, and these assaults were often both indiscriminate and atrocious. Indigenous violence "played into allegations of savagery" and thereby served to justify retribution and removal policies. Violence on the borderlands thus precipitated a boomerang of savagery, traumatizing settler society, and forging an American way of war.[87]

Psychoanalytic Dimensions

Many scholars and perhaps especially historians have been reluctant to explore psychoanalytic frames, which are often summarily dismissed through application of the derisive trope "psychohistory." As with any serious psychological issue, however, ignoring the problem will not make it go away. Anne McClintock among others has criticized the "disciplinary quarantine of psychoanalysis from history." As Geoff Eley points out, historians "have begun only slowly to explore" the "key role" that "the critical and eclectic appropriation of psychoanalytic theory of various kinds has played" in advancing historical understanding.[88]

Psychological drives and conditions such as trauma, denial, repression, projection, fantasy, guilt, rationalization, narcissism, victimization, and others permeate the history of colonialism and therefore must be considered, however imperfectly, in any effort to gain a comprehensive understanding. "Colonialism colonizes minds in addition to bodies," Ashis Nandy points out, hence it "cannot be identified with only economic gain and political power." Settler collectives are "traumatized societies *par excellence*, where indigenous genocide and/or displacement interact with other traumatic experiences," Veracini points out. The contradictions inherent within settler colonial societies combine "perpetrator trauma" with "stubborn and lingering anxieties over settler legitimacy." These anxieties produce "long-lasting psychic conflicts and a number of associated psychopathologies."[89]

The colonizer, no more than the colonized, could escape the legacies of settler colonial violence. This was the genius of Joseph Conrad's (and Francis Ford

Coppola's) Kurtz. Carried to its logical extreme, as Kurtz reveals, colonial violence overwhelms the psyche of the perpetrator. Colonizers "are at least as much affected by the ideology of colonialism" as the colonized, Nandy points out. "Their degradation, too, can sometimes be terrifying."[90] While much has been learned about colonialism and its impact on the colonized peoples, the cultural and psychological pathologies produced within the colonizing societies are equally important. Accordingly, I probe here into the relationship between psychoanalytic theory and colonial violence.

Fantasy played an important role in the evolution of settler societies and the genocidal violence that accompanied them. For the Americans, the fantasies of "American exceptionalism" and "Manifest Destiny" were driving forces replete with psychic contradictions and traumatic repercussions. In Australia the "national fantasy" of "mateship" obscured the destruction of Aboriginal societies, with attendant psychic consequences. The same phenomenon played out in South Africa, where the trekboers viewed themselves as destined, and in modern Israel under the settlement compulsions of Zionism.[91]

In attempting to carry out their fantasies, to realize their dreams, settler colonials perceived their actions as the performance of good works. Settlement required the courage to cross the sea, enter into the unknown, build cabins, hew out farms, overcome obstacles, raise families, forge communities, worship God, and build the imagined community of the nation. Settlers could take pride in their good works and identify with those perceived as being of the same race and religion who shared their pride and experiences. Those of different (inferior) races and cultures who posed an obstacle to the settlement project manifestly were engaged in wrongdoing. By intruding into settler fantasies and disrupting their good works, the indigenous people were responsible for the consequences that followed—removal, destruction of their societies, death. In these ways fantasy, rationalization, narcissism, projection, and guilt permeated the conscious and unconscious mind of the colonizer, enabling genocidal violence as well as historical denial.

The psychoanalytic theories of Jacques Lacan illuminate these points. "The domain of the good is the birth of power," Lacan explained. "To exercise control over one's goods is to have the right to deprive others of them." Jennifer Rutherford elaborates, "This paradox, identified by Freud and articulated by Lacan, is the manifestation of aggression at the very moment we set out to do good." As the Americans set out to build their farms and communities or the Australians to tame the outback, "an aggressive *jouissance*—a will to destruction"—set in at the expense of those who impeded these projects, namely the indigenous and borderland peoples.[92]

The persistent violence of the colonial encounter, as narrated throughout this volume, stemmed from the repeated disruption of the settler colonial fantasies and projects on the part of the indigenous populations. Not merely the ambivalence and resistance of the indigenous people but ultimately their *very presence* ruptured the settler colonial fantasy. As indigenous peoples appeared to impede the path of the new chosen peoples they menaced the good that inhered in the rational, civilized, progressive, and providentially destined settler project. "Within the frameworks of psychoanalytic discourse, anti-colonial resistance is coded as madness, dependency or infantile regression," Ania Loomba points out. "The inferior being always serves as a scapegoat," the French psychoanalytic theorist Octave Mannoni pointed out, "our own evil intentions can be projected onto him."[93]

As the indigene becomes the force of evil pitted against the good of the colonizing project, the psychic drives within the colonizer rationalize violent repression. Despite all ambivalent efforts to work with him, to share culture, religion, and the benefits of civilization, by putting up resistance the indigene shows that in the end he is a savage who understands only the exercise of power. Righteous violence, however lamentable, is therefore justified. "A true Stalinist politician loves mankind, yet carries out horrible purges and executions—his heart is breaking while he does it, but he cannot help it, it is his Duty towards the Progress of Humanity," the Lacanian philosopher Slavoj Zizek explains. "It is not my responsibility, it is not me who is really doing it. I am merely an instrument of the higher Historical Necessity. The obscene enjoyment of this situation is generated by the fact that I conceive of myself as *exculpated for what I am doing:* I am able to inflict pain on others with the full awareness that I am not responsible for it."[94]

Settler communities are both "civilized" and "savage" and therefore must walk a fine psychic line in forging a collective identity and institutions. In the case of the United States, "There was, quite simply, no way to make a complete identity without Indians," Phlip Deloria explains. "At the same time, there was no way to make a complete identity while they remained."[95] Considerable psychic gymnastics arise from the contradictions involved in cleansing the land of the indigenes while appropriating their desirable characteristics within the maw of the dominant culture, all the while eliding the genocidal past. The colonizer's claims of indigeneity and authenticity require long-term effort but also entail "a cognitive dissonance, a gap between knowledge and belief," a repression of knowledge. Thus the unresolved "historical legacy of violence and appropriation is carried into the present as traumatic memory, inherited institutional structures, and often unexamined assumptions."[96]

In the narrative history that follows, I have made limited yet persistent efforts to incorporate the psychoanalytic drives that permeated the settler colonial project. However challenging for the historian, some effort at incorporating psychological approaches to the postcolonial past "may enable the understanding of the traumatic present."[97]

The history of American settler colonialism sheds light on the past, yet the essence of postcolonial studies is the connection between past and present. As the philosopher Tzvetan Todorov once noted, even as one writes history the present is ultimately more important than the past.[98] The hope is that by interrogating the past we can wedge a small brick into the mortar of a postcolonial future.

2

"People from the Unknown World": The Colonial Encounter and the Acceleration of Violence

Millions of Indians—probably as many, if not more, as lived in Europe—had been living throughout North America for thousands of years when the colonial encounter began.[1] Their cultures and economies differed between places and times but indigenous culture was thriving. The continent was a "stunningly diverse place, a tumult of languages, trade, and culture, a region where millions of people loved and hated and worshipped as people do everywhere."[2]

Characteristics of Mississippian culture (roughly 900–1700 CE) included large communities, towns, and maize culture (agriculture-based spirituality revolving mainly around cultivation of the annual corn crop). Men hunted bear, deer, waterfowl, and turkey, and fished in lakes and streams; women raised corn, beans, and squash, and gathered nuts and berries. In Mississippian culture women gained respect as life-givers and many bands operated on the basis of matrilineal descent.

Some tribes migrated while others settled in cities and towns; others did both by migrating during hunting season and returning to their towns for the winter. Most indigenes were highly spiritual, worshipped their ancestors, and took a keen interest in observable astronomy. They cultivated creation myths and oral traditions, created art and architecture, and played sports. They also engaged in warfare.[3]

In the modern era Americans destroyed indigenous pyramid mounds and other structures while nurturing a Euro-centric history that generally obscured *centuries* of indigenous civilization in North America. Fortunately Cahokia, Chaco Canyon, and hundreds of other less celebrated sites provide evidence for archeologists, anthropologists, and historians. Cahokia, a planned city near the confluence of the Missouri and Mississippi rivers, "had a major impact on the Mississippian world." The city featured a huge public square and was home to thousands of people and more than 200 packed earth pyramid mounds as well as thousands of huts and temples. Cahokia was a "political, economic, and social behemoth," a center from which peoples "scattered across the midcontinent and the Southeast." Chaco

Canyon in northeastern New Mexico was "a political-ritual amphitheater, with audiences of believers and pilgrims standing on the canyon's rim looking down on great houses and up to the sun, the moon, and the stars."[4]

Mississippian era politics and diplomacy centered on chieftains who typically lived in impressive homes built atop leveled-off pyramid mounds. Their power depended on their success at cultivating kinship ties linking surrounding villages and communities as well as their ability to establish exchange relationships with other chieftainships. Archeological evidence shows that Indians did not live in isolated villages but rather established long-distance trade and exchange relationships with other indigenes. Conflicts led to warfare with attendant dislocations and power shifts. "Warfare played a major role in the cycling of Mississippian chiefdoms over the region," John Scarry explains, "and the rise and decline of individual societies."[5]

A "culture of violence" prevailed within Mississippian societies. Europeans thus cannot be blamed for introducing war and violence to North America, as they were already well ensconced within indigenous communities. The chieftains went to war to assert power, gain control of agricultural fields and hunting grounds, enforce tribute systems, and to secure advantages in trade and exchange. "Warfare was an integral part of Mississippian worldviews, and sacred art objects often depicted stylized weapons of war, including axes, swords, maces, and arrowheads," Matthew Jennings observes. The chieftains often consulted priests, as war and spirituality were intimately linked.[6]

A "cult of war" evolved in Mississippian societies as zealous warriors took part in rituals and ceremonies in which the entire community mobilized in preparation for conflict. The chieftains sometimes fielded large armies, which could be divided into squadrons and accompanied by the pounding of drums. At other times indigenous groups engaged in "skirmish warfare, centered on the ambushing of hunting parties." Indigenous people engaged in targeted violence and, less frequently, "indiscriminate slaughter" and ritual sacrifice. Evidence includes mass graves, skulls, headless burials, dismemberment, and distinctive wounds.[7]

Warfare in indigenous cultural traditions characteristically was short and seasonal but cruel and vicious. Indians attacked by surprise, carried out excruciating tortures, took scalps and otherwise mutilated the corpses of the dead. Profoundly gendered, Indian violence was a young warrior's masculine path to glory. Contact with the enemy and taking scalps provided evidence of courage and accomplishment in battle, thereby enhancing the warrior's status in society. Success on the battlefield was a prerequisite for would-be chieftains. With virtually every male needing to prove his worth on the battlefield, indigenous cultures were violent, warlike, and underscored "the brutal side of Indian life."[8]

The killing of some captives and the taking of others characterized the Indian way of war. Indians took into their societies captives—both Indian and European—to replace those who had been lost to war or disease (thus to "cover the dead"). Especially as their populations became ravaged by diseases to which they lacked immunities, many North American Indian tribes employed war and captive-taking to rebuild their numbers. At other times, however, Indians took captives, mainly women and children, to exploit them for sex, labor, trade, and as tools of diplomacy. Captives could be traded for goods or other captives and thus often played an important role in diplomacy and peacekeeping.

Indians routinely carried out torture as a means of displaying power while testing the victim's courage. Some indigenes used mutilation to underscore their dominance or to achieve a more practical purpose, for example cutting off thumbs to prevent a captive from untying his or her bonds. The captive's ability to endure torture with equanimity, even if mockingly so, showed that while you might maim or kill the victim, his or her spirit would not be taken in the process.[9]

Without ennobling indigenous violence and militarism, it is important to point out the cultural context in which these elements functioned. Indigenous people operated on the basis of reciprocal relationships with the natural, human, and spiritual worlds. Just as they would kill animals or exploit nature to eat and to live, indigenous culture allowed for violence against other people. Indigenes viewed war as a natural activity to promote manhood and keep the community strong and secure. Indian culture demanded "blood revenge" for attacks against family or community. Once revenge had been taken, the conflict could end. Violence in such cases was reciprocal and proportionate rather than indiscriminate and total. Pre-contact Indians typically did not engage in genocidal campaigns against their rivals. Indigenous people placed limitations on warfare, which paradoxically could also establish a foundation for peaceful relations once both sides' cultural drives have been satisfied. As gift giving was a critical aspect of indigenous diplomacy, the exchange of captives could serve to mitigate conflict.

While Europeans did not introduce violence and militarism, already well ensconced within Indian cultures, colonialism did profoundly *intensify* indigenous violence. Colonial violence functioned in the context of the demands of a globalizing market economy. While Indians took captives, the arrival of European colonialism precipitated a "frenzy of slaving," the marketing of captives for weapons, ammunition, and other goods.[10] Competition among Indians for access to weapons, to gain a foothold in the global marketplace, or merely to avoid becoming slaves themselves, dramatically accelerated the pace and scale of colonial violence.

The forces unleashed by colonialism undermined the Mississippian chieftain system and sharply increased the levels of violence. Political uncertainty, disease, slavery, and the introduction of market forces shattered equilibrium and introduced powerful and destructive new forces. As David Dye points out, "It was Western contact that was responsible as an agent of change in native warfare patterns."[11]

New Spain, New France, New Worlds

The arrival of the Europeans brought revolutionary changes that ultimately overwhelmed indigenous ways of life. Sailing for Spain in 1492 and believing he had discovered a maritime route to India, Christopher Columbus dubbed the people he encountered in the Caribbean *los Indios*. The name stuck, and remains preferred by many Indian peoples to this day. Many of the names that

Europeans subsequently applied to North American Indian tribes—Creeks, Sioux, and Navaho for example—were also contrived yet they too endure. Most North American indigenous groups identified themselves simply as "the people" or "the true people."

"Indians" have never existed as a single coherent entity rather Europeans invented the homogenizing trope. This invention of "Indians" created the colonial binary of savagery and civilization from the moment of contact. Once the category of "Indians" was created, distinguishing features had to be elaborated. The process of articulating difference creates "the other" through narratives and discourses that persistently reaffirm the fundamental colonial binary.[12]

Despite the polarizing discourse, ambivalence manifested from the beginning, as Indians and Europeans cooperated, accommodated, and adapted within the colonial encounter. Indigenous groups and Europeans engaged in trade and diplomacy and marriage and friendship and all manners of cultural exchange, as well as violent conflict. Whether or not they respected or empathized with indigenous people, the vast majority of Europeans viewed their way of life as superior to that of "savages" and this conceit ultimately drove the colonial encounter. The devastating impact of European-borne diseases, which killed as much as 90 percent of the indigenous population, reinforced the European fantasy that they were a superior people with divine sanction to assume possession of colonial space. The precise impact of the European-borne pathogens remains uncertain, but it is clear that disease combined with warfare, Indian slavery, and sweeping economic and cultural changes transformed indigenous life in North America in previously unimaginable ways.

With Columbus at the helm "New Spain" took the lead in European colonization of the "New World." The Treaty of Tordesillas finalized in 1494 gave Spain the bulk of colonization rights in the Americas; with God and the Pope behind the effort the Spanish believed that no one had the right to oppose them. Following the conquest of the Aztecs and the Incas, Spain established outposts in the Caribbean and worked its way up to "La Florida." In 1513 Juan Ponce de Leon had named the colony noting the beauty of the flora as he traversed the coastline. The Spanish explorer made landfall and conducted trade with the Calusa tribe, but eight years later he would die in conflict with Indians. After a series of colonization efforts failed because of lack of food and persistent conflict with the indigenes, Spain in 1565 established a single enduring colonial outpost in La Florida at St. Augustine.[13]

Spain imported intolerance and militancy, conditioned by centuries of conflict with "infidels" on the Iberian Peninsula. As they had already demonstrated in South and Central America and the Caribbean, the Spanish sanctioned "savage violence against people who were considered 'heathens.' " No one better displayed this uncompromising Christian militancy than Hernando de Soto, a seasoned *conquistador*, who embarked from Tampa on a four-year long scorched earth campaign across the southeast. Accompanied by a 600-men army, 200 horses, pigs, and war dogs, Soto employed the Spanish technological advantages of guns and armor to terrorize, rape, plunder, and kill thousands of indigenous people in a futile search for gold.

"The kind of all-consuming violence that Soto imported was unknown to the chieftains that inhabited the region," Jennings notes. In 1540 at the Battle of Mabila in central Alabama, Soto's army suffered 22 casualties and some 150 were injured, but killed hundreds and perhaps thousands in the army of the chieftain Tuscalusa. Soto died in 1542 and his *entrada* ended the next year but by that time European diseases were spreading rapidly across the continent. Soto's invasion destroyed several chieftainships—on occasion with the help of ambivalent rival Indian allies—as the Spanish invasion undermined indigenous politics and diplomacy.[14]

In contrast to settler colonialism, which would drive the eventual success of English colonization, Spain pursued more of an enclave strategy founded upon the two main institutions of colonization: the mission and the presidio. While the English would remove Indians to establish colonies along the Atlantic seaboard, Spanish colonialism sprawled much more widely and emphasized cultivation of a docile labor force. "Spanish settlement of America was based on the domination of peoples" more than the displacement of them, J. H. Elliott observes.[15] Moreover, beginning with Bartolomé de Las Casas, Catholic reformers condemned the Spanish brutalities against indigenous people of the Americas and sought to shift the emphasis toward saving souls through the establishment of missions.[16]

The Spanish never succeeded in resolving the contradiction between benevolent salvation on the one hand and forced labor as well violence and sexual assaults on indigenous people on the other. Missions spread from the Florida coast in the late sixteenth century across to New Mexico, Arizona, Texas, and California, where the last mission was built in the Sonoma Valley, north of San Francisco, in 1823. Some were more successful than others in securing conversions and cultivation of agriculture and cattle herds but in general the Spanish never succeeded in maintaining their authority very far beyond the walls of the mission and the presidio.

Spain's broad geographic stretch, the absence of a large and secure population of settlers, combined with corruption, inefficiency, and a mounting indigenous resistance, continued to undermine the colonial project over a *longue dureé*. To be sure, thousands of indigenes labored for the Spanish, converted to Catholicism, and became wives and mistresses, but far more stayed away, resisted, or turned to the missions only when they were cold or hungry. The Spanish baptized those Indians who came in or were rounded up but most of the indigenes merely went through the motions of conversion in order to access the mission benefits. The Spanish whipped, mutilated, and sometimes killed the "deviating neophytes" and "apostates and fugitives" who fled the missions. The Spanish violence only produced a broader resistance, spurring raids on the Spanish outposts. At the same time, however, many Indians stayed long enough to learn Spanish and to reconfigure their identities by joining with Hispanics and other indigenes in and around the missions. "This process of reinvention ended any hope that Spain possessed of controlling the borderlands," Gary C. Anderson argues.[17]

The Franciscans kept coming despite their lack of success, expanding the mission system backed to varying degrees by the army even though the two were not always in accord. The friars condemned the soldiers for their sexual relations with indigenous women, set up sometimes by consent and sometimes by force. For their part the priests exploited indigenous laborers, who were required to work from sunrise to sunset, sometimes on a starvation diet, and often punished them severely for noncompliance. As resistance to colonial oppression is inevitable, the indigenes revolted, most famously in the Pueblo uprising of 1680. This violent uprising against Spanish colonialism took the lives of some 400 Spaniards including 21 priests and drove them out of Santa Fe. Other revolts occurred early in the next century along the Rio Grande and at San Diego in 1775.[18]

More debilitating than the revolts, however, were the persistent indigenous raids. Increasingly, skilled equestrian tribes descended on Spanish rancheros in hit-and-run raids targeting horses, cattle, and human captives. Spanish missions converted and made farmers of many sedentary Indians but failed utterly to subdue the raiding cultures known as the Apache and Comanche. These indigenes "raided Spanish farms and ranches, destroyed Spanish property, took Spanish lives, and blocked the arteries of commerce that kept the empire alive," David J. Weber points out. Beginning in 1700 Bourbon reformers sought to pursue a more humane and paternal approach to the indigenes than their Hapsburg predecessors had applied but the effort waned as Indian violence boomeranged on the Spanish. While some continued to emphasize reform and salvation, other traumatized Spaniards called for extermination of the *Indios barbaros.* Conflict alternated with accommodation, peace could turn quickly to war, and both sometimes appeared to exist simultaneously.[19]

Despite the obstacles Spain persisted with its overstretched colonial empire, especially as other European powers posed a threat to it. Following the landing on the Texas coast in 1684 of the French under Robert Cavelier de La Salle, the Spanish established missions and presidios in Texas along the Rio Grande and further north at San Antonio. In sharp contrast to Soto, La Salle's interactions with indigenous groups as he explored the southeast were "exceptionally fruitful and non-exploitative by colonial standards." "New France" had originated to the north in 1534 with Jacques Cartier's advance up the St. Lawrence River and accelerated 70 years later with Samuel de Champlain's founding of Quebec City and reconnoitering of the lake that bears his name.[20]

The French practiced cultural accommodation with the indigenes rather than forcing conversions or attempting to drive them from the land, hence the relationship was less violent than Spain's and far less violent than English settler colonialism. "The French tended to learn [indigenous] languages, to adopt to some degree their ways of living, traveling, hunting, and fighting, and to rely heavily on them for their economic and military success," Cornelius Jaenen points out.[21] "The willingness of the French to adopt and adapt to indigenous culture conveyed respect and thus served to reassure the indigenes and to limit violent conflict." As the French established Catholic missions, forts, and the profitable fur trade, they strove to carve out a "middle ground" of convergence and reciprocal relations in keeping with indigenous cultural traditions.

French Jesuit missionaries and traders ventured into Indian villages, establishing reciprocal relations and tapping into the lucrative fur trade. An exchange economy emerged as the French supplied indigenous people with European trade goods in return for beaver pelts with which Europeans made and sold felt hats. The fur trade was partly responsible for the outbreak of the "Beaver Wars" in which the group of tribes led by the Mohawk and known collectively as the Iroquois (Haudenosaunee) launched merciless assaults on the Huron and other rival bands. Armed and equipped by Dutch and English traders to the east, the Iroquois drove out the Huron and virtually wiped out the Mahicans. The Iroquois, however, could not subdue the French, who reciprocated violent assaults and "burned Iroquois villages in the late seventeenth century."[22]

The Iroquois went to war for cultural reasons as well as to protect their stake in the fur trade. The confederation conducted "mourning wars" with the primary purpose of seizing captives to replenish the confederation for the devastating losses of more than 90 percent of its population to diseases such as measles and smallpox. "A major goal of Iroquois warfare and diplomacy through both the seventeenth and eighteenth centuries was to replenish the populations of Iroquois communities with war captives and refugees," Thomas S. Abler notes.[23] Moreover, in keeping with indigenous traditions, "Young men went to war as a rite of passage to prove themselves as warriors and to gain a reputation among their peers," Timothy Shannon points out. In order to take captives while keeping their own losses to a minimum, the Iroquois engaged in surprise attack. Europeans derisively labeled these hit-and-run assaults the "skulking way of war," but they soon adopted the same tactic, which would become integral to the American way of war.[24]

The Iroquois facilitated English settler colonialism through a mutually beneficial alliance that endured until the American Revolution. In addition to having a powerful indigenous ally, the English also had the advantage of having the Atlantic Ocean at their back. Like the Spanish and the French, the English embraced patriarchy, private property, and Christianity, but the emphasis on the settlement of families and communities distinguished them. The Spanish were spread thin across vast reaches of the continent. Surrounded by indigenous people on the interior, the French traders and missionaries had to find ways to coexist. Overwhelmingly male, the French often took Indian wives and mistresses thus establishing enduring kinship ties with the indigenes. By contrast European women migrated along with men and children to settle in the English colonies. In sum, unlike its two major European rivals, family-based British colonialism proved mobile and resilient over a *longue dureé*, enabling "a steady westward migration towards the agricultural frontier as the threat of Indian attack diminished."[25]

Settler colonialism thus was primarily a British project, with practices distinct from those of France and Spain. British mobility and institutions—the family, private property, Protestantism, and legal structures—anchored settlement in North America as well as Canada, Australia, and New Zealand. English settlers displayed ambivalence and accommodation within the colonial encounter, but "as the balance of numbers tilted in favor of the colonists, the tendency simply to encroach on Indian land became harder to resist." Ultimately, "The removal of indigenous people allowed for the wholesale introduction of British institutions."[26]

The Emergence of the English Settler Colonies

Settler colonialism was not the initial intent of English colonization, which instead was driven by the profit motive. Europeans had long been traversing the Atlantic coast and fishing off the Newfoundland banks by the time of the establishment of Jamestown in 1607. Thus English colonists up and down the coast encountered a few Indians who knew a bit of their language. The Spanish had briefly established a Jesuit mission in Virginia but the friars were driven out.[27] The English had already suffered the "lost colony" at Roanoke Island in 1584 and very nearly met the same end in Virginia. Permanent settlement seemed a virtually hopeless idea in the early years of the seventeenth century, as death and psychic anxiety stalked efforts to establish a viable colony. Under pressure from their sponsors to find gold and other riches, the desperate colonials could not even find food. For years they died by the scores from disease, starvation, and Indian conflict.[28]

Ambivalent relations—a tense mixture of trade and coexistence amid endemic guerrilla warfare and bursts of genocidal violence—characterized the early history of Virginia. The primary Indian chieftain of the region, Powhatan, presided over some 30 indigenous bands, about 7,500 Indians in total across some 80 miles between the James and Potomac rivers. The indigenes engaged in horticulture, foraging, and fishing. They lived in towns but retained the mobility to move around during the temperate months. Women were the primary growers and gatherers while men hunted, fished, and went to war.

Powhatan initially pursued a diplomatic understanding with the European interlopers. In the famous incident of December 1607 Powhatan apparently sought to display his prowess to let live or destroy the English colonists when one of his daughters, Matoaka (Pocahontas), "saved" the English mercenary John Smith from execution. Pocahontas provided an early example of the role women often played as go-betweens in indigenous diplomacy. She also underscores colonial ambivalence, the willingness of some indigenes to adapt and to join European society, as she would marry the tobacco planter John Rolfe in 1614 and convert to Christianity.[29]

The first colonials in Virginia viewed the Indians as "heathen" and "salvages," yet became dependent upon these supposedly inferior people for the basic human necessity of life: food. This unsettling dichotomy weighed on the psyches of the settlers. "English behavior became increasingly aggressive and erratic in a situation in which the Indians, as virtually the sole source of food, held the power," Karen Kupperman explains. The tense colonial encounter played out in violent clashes, guerrilla warfare, massacres, and mutilations, with Indians often getting the best of it. "The Indian killed as fast without, if our men stirred beyond the bounds of the blockhouse, as famine and pestilence did within," one colonist lamented.[30]

With their "Jamestown project" on the brink of collapse, the Virginia Company shifted its strategy from erecting a fortified trading post to establishing a sprawling settler colony with a viable economic foundation. Continually revivified by new shiploads of colonists, the Virginians established a profitable "tobacco monoculture" worked by indentured servants and in subsequent years by African slaves. The investors showed their determination to establish a permanent settlement by sending over "maides young and uncorrupt to make wifes" for the male-dominated inhabitants. By 1620 the colony had grown to nearly 1,000 people who were learning to stay alive while establishing a profitable cash crop. The next year the company dispatched 1,500 more settlers in 21 ships.[31]

The rapidly expanding settler colony posed a mortal threat to the Indians, who not only saw more and more land seized for the cultivation of tobacco but also faced a European assault on their spirituality. The settlers and their sponsors in London were determined to establish a profitable colony but, rather than simply kill and remove the Indians, the ambivalent invaders sought to Christianize the heathen tribes. Moreover, their approach focused on Indian children, reasoning that they were uncorrupted and thus more receptive to conversion. In 1617 King James I directed the Anglican clergy to build "churches and schools" for the education of the "children of these barbarians in Virginia." The Powhatans defied the English king, however, as they summarily rejected efforts to convert them.[32]

Not everyone displayed ambivalence or an interest in saving indigenous souls. Just as the Spanish had fought their infidels on the Iberian Peninsula, the English arrived not far removed from the sixteenth-century dispossession and subjugation of the Irish "heathens" in the largest military conflict of the Elizabethan era. Smith was a veteran of English warfare in the Balkans against the Islamic Eurasian enemy other. He judged the American indigenes "crafty, timorous, quick of apprehension, very ingenious. Some are of disposition fearful, some bold . . . all Savage." Smith likened the "treacherous" natives to "infernal hell hounds" in their style of warfare yet he and his followers would soon emulate the Indian way of war as they sought to drive the indigenes from the land desired by the settlers. In 1609 when conflict erupted in the first Anglo-Powhatan War, Smith pioneered the tradition of irregular warfare in the "New World" by burning and razing Indian homes and agricultural fields. "Inspired by Smith's success," John Ferling points out, "the Virginia Company institutionalized the measures he had pursued."[33]

As tensions escalated over encroachments on land and cultural and spiritual conflict, Powhatan's brother and successor Opechancanough grasped the existential, winner-take-all nature of the settler colonial encounter. In 1622 he launched a surprise exterminatory assault, killing 347 settlers, about a fourth of the colonial population. As the enraged and traumatized colonists recovered, many vowed to rid themselves of the savages once and for all. It would be "infinitely better to *have no heathen among us*" [emphasis added], declared Governor Francis Wyatt, "than to be at peace and league with them." Smith concurred, "We have just cause to destroy them by all means possible."[34]

Ambivalence gave way to genocide as the Virginians now "killed every Indian they could regardless of age or sex." Following months of warfare, the settlers summoned the indigenes for peace talks only to serve them poisoned wine and methodically butcher some 250 of them. Genocidal violence continued to boomerang upon the colonists as well as the indigenes. In 1644 Opechancanough launched a last-gasp exterminatory assault, slaughtering some 500 Euro-Americans in another surprise offensive. Now equipped with an organized militia in each county and forts all along the James River, the Virginians responded with a campaign of annihilation culminating in the execution of the nearly centenarian Opechancanough and the selling of indigenous captives into slavery.[35]

The Tidewater wars ended with the total defeat and ethnic cleansing of Indians thus establishing an enduring framework for the British-American settler colonial project. Demography had overwhelmed the indigenes. The Jamestown settler colonials benefited from a ceaseless influx of new migrants and supplies. Tobacco had given the colony viability within the burgeoning Atlantic world economy. While the Indians fought to defend their homelands, the Europeans displayed boundless energy and determination in their economic drives and convictions of providential destiny to take command of colonial space.

In what became something of an iron law of American history, virtually any effort to impede settler colonial expansion could incite civil tumult *within* the Euro-American communities. As the colonial administrators sought respite from Indian conflict by recognizing indigenous land holdings on the borderlands, the Henrico planter Nathaniel Bacon condemned limitations on squatting and settler expansion in deference to mere Indians. In launching his famous rebellion in 1676, Bacon declared that Virginia and British authorities had "defended and protected" the "darling Indians," who were really "barbarous outlaws" and "delinquents," at the expense of "his Majesty's loyal subjects."[36] Defying Crown authority, Bacon launched search and destroy operations into Pamunkey villages and Occaneechi territory, wiping out even Indians who had refrained from resistance. As the indigenes fled into the forest, Bacon set upon Jamestown and set it aflame before dying suddenly, probably from dysentery.

Bacon's demise ended the rebellion, which nonetheless had underscored the determination of settlers to seize the land on their self-avowed frontiers regardless of what colonial authorities might decree. The rebellion showed that the triangulated settler colonial relationship encompassing Indians, settlers, and metropolitan authority was highly combustible.[37]

Although in other respects "New England" societies bore little resemblance to those in the Chesapeake, settler colonialism and exterminatory warfare against the indigenous inhabitants animated both. Hostile perceptions of the other on both sides limited the prospects of third space accommodation. Prior to the landing of the Pilgrims at Plymouth on Cape Cod in 1620 sporadic exchange relations already had been established between Europeans and indigenes in what became New England. The settlers found that Indians had metal kettles, glass, and cloth items from Europe, and one of them, a Patuxet name Squanto (Tisquantum), spoke a smattering of English as a result of his kidnapping by Europeans in previous years.

Despite his appreciation of Squanto—perceived to be an "an instrument sent of God" to help the settlers fish and plant corn—William Bradford anticipated difficult relations in a land inhabited by "savage people, who are cruel, barbarous, and most treacherous." Unlike the Virginians who came initially with the intent to accrue wealth, Bradford, who became the longtime governor of Plymouth Plantation, landed with the intent to settle permanently.[38] Like Bradford, New England's first Puritan emigrants meant to settle and "did not anticipate permanent peaceful coexistence with the indigenous inhabitants." The Amerindians of the region harbored their own suspicions and thus greeted the Pilgrim and Puritan settlers with distrust. Nevertheless, Massasoit, the Wampanoag chieftain, chose coexistence with the first wave of colonists rather than to wipe them out, as he surely could have done at the outset. As settler colonialism accelerated over the next generation, the New England tribes would be devoid of such options.[39]

Ambivalence as embodied in trade and intercultural exchange prevailed for several relatively peaceful years until the anxiety-ridden Puritans embarked on an unprovoked war of annihilation against the Pequot Indians. The once powerful tribe had been devastated by a smallpox epidemic and was vulnerable. Never doubting their providential destiny to inherit the land, the Puritans launched a preemptive "holy war" to counter "a satanic plot to destroy Christ's church in the wilderness." Content with trading with the settlers, the Pequot "neither desired nor anticipated war with the Puritans," Alfred Cave points out.[40] Once the war began, however, the Mohegan and Narragansett underscored the rivalries among indigenous bands by allying with the Puritans in order to strike back at their longstanding enemies, the Pequot.

Atrocity-filled genocidal warfare characterized New England's first full-scale Anglo-Indian conflict. In May 1637 Massachusetts Bay and its Indian allies launched an exterminatory assault against a Pequot village on the Mystic River. Under the leadership of Captain John Mason the English fired the village and then relished "the extreme amazement of the enemy" as men, women, and children burned to death in the flames. Bradford explained that God had condemned the Indians to the "fiery oven" and their "frying in the fryer, and the streams of blood quenching the same" had exacted a "sweet victory" that brought a "great rejoicing" to the settlers. Troops using dogs hunted down survivors to carry out tortures and executions.[41]

In a struggle pitting the forces of good against evil in the form of the devil's indigenous minions, no amount of indiscriminate killing would be considered too great. "Sometimes," Captain John Underhill rationalized, perhaps to assuage feelings of traumatic guilt within the settler community, "the scripture declareth that women and children must perish with their parents . . . We had sufficient light from the Word of God for our proceedings." The Pequot War "cast a long shadow" as the narrative of martial triumph of providentially destined settlers over devilish and savage foes "became a vital part of the mythology of the American frontier."[42]

Ambivalent relations encompassing trade and acculturation resumed in New England after the Pequot War. More intensely than the Virginians some of the deeply devout Puritans strove to lead indigenous people to Christian salvation. From 1651 to 1674, the Rev. John Eliot established 14 "praying towns" with over 1,000 Indians in residence. He proved to be one of the rare Europeans willing to try to learn Indian languages, though at the same time he insisted that the indigenes conform to the European mode of dress, appearance, and gender roles. The missions of the early New England colleges such as Harvard and Dartmouth also encompassed an effort to Christianize Indians.[43]

The Wampanoag sachem Metacomet, son of Massasoit, embodied the Indian side of colonial ambivalence and appropriation strategies. Metacomet lived among the Puritans and traded with them for years. He regularly communicated with the English (through an interpreter) and went by the European name "Philip" in a display of accommodation toward the colonizer. By this time hundreds of Wampanoag had converted to Christianity.[44]

Tensions escalated over settler encroachments, mounting Indian insecurities as their spiritual and political leadership eroded, and unequal treatment (including capital punishment) accorded the indigenes in the English justice system. Ambivalence waned as the settler colonials broke off relations with Indian groups, including King Philip, and represented all the indigenes as their savage enemies. This Puritan discourse of enmity ultimately drove "thousands of once-friendly Indians into Philip's camp." The "English insistence on subordination and interference in Indian governance," Jenny Hale Pulsipher explains, combined with relentless English expansion, "had convinced Philip that war was his only remaining alternative to preserve Wampanoag sovereignty." Joined by the powerful Narragansett and other tribes, Metacomet led the resistance in what the New Englanders at the time called the Narragansett War.[45]

On the eve of war in 1675 Metacomet explained that the Europeans—"these people from the unknown world"—had grown "insolent and bold," overrunning fields and hunting grounds, breaking agreements, killing Indians, and seeking to "drive us and our children from the graves of our fathers... and enslave our women and children." Now the spirits of those ancestors "cry out to us for revenge." Metacomet and his followers launched an indiscriminate campaign that left a series of New England towns in smoking ruins, littered with dead and mutilated bodies. They mocked and terrorized the English, pinning them down and shouting, "Where is your O God?"[46]

The ferocity of the Indian attacks traumatized the settler colonials and precipitated a boomerang of indiscriminate violence. In order to survive and ultimately to achieve victory, the English adapted to the situation by embracing the Indian style of irregular warfare, which they had previously viewed as savage and dishonorable. Under the leadership of Benjamin Church they now skulked in the woods and launched surprise hit-and-run attacks. The settler colonials bulked up enlistments through the incentive of scalp bounties, which returned five shillings for the scalp of a common Indian (often regardless of age or sex) to 100 shillings, or five pounds, offered for King Philip's hair. From that point forward indiscriminate warfare, ranging, and scalp hunting became powerful weapons in advancing the settler colonial project.[47] Whereas Indians took scalps and trophies to affirm courage and masculinity in warfare, Europeans provided marketplace incentives for the killing and mutilation of indigenous people.

Warfare reinforced masculinity while at the same time altering women's roles as the New England settlers fought for their lives. Both Indians and settler males referred to warfare as a quest to determine which one would "master" the other hence "what was at stake was their very manhood." In the struggle for survival, New England women assumed unprecedented "central and supporting roles" in the traditionally male realm of warfare.[48]

The English possessed superior numbers, material resources, and social cohesion that allowed them to prevail in the Narragansett War. The New England confederation eventually dispatched a 1,000-men army on a campaign to search out and annihilate the indigenous enemy. In April 1676 the English located a

Narragansett fortress at the Great Swamp east of the Chippuxet River and in a reprise of the Mystic River assault put it to the torch as the Indians sat down for dinner. Some 600 Narragansett—roughly half of them non-combatants—died in the inferno. "They and their food fried together," one Englishman exulted.[49]

Several towns had been destroyed and more than 500 soldiers and some 1,000 New England civilians had been killed in King Philip's War. Indian losses were much greater, however, following a genocidal campaign of lynching, murder, and enslavement. Metacomet, a "great, naked, dirty beast" and thus the personification of the savage Indian other, was executed, his body drawn and quartered, and his severed head hung from a pole for decades. The conclusion of the war brought "a shattering defeat for the Indians, who were scattered, sold into slavery, or decisively marginalized."[50]

The extreme violence of King Philip's War made an indelible impression on the minds of the settlers, as "the fear and suspicion of Indians remaining in the colony would persist long after the fighting ended." Indian raids and irregular warfare had so terrorized encroaching English settlements that the hatred and determination to destroy the indigenous enemy became embedded in colonial culture. With bounties being paid for Indian scalps, the fighting men made no unprofitable distinction between combatants and noncombatants. Indeed, as the incentives ran in the other direction, extirpation became "a legitimate act of war." With the "brutish enemy" having caused so much "English bloodshed" in the war, "the rage of the people" turned even on the Christian Indians in the praying towns. As the Rev. Daniel Gookin explained, "All Indians are reckoned to be false and perfidious."[51]

King Philip's War thus illustrated the rewards as well as the traumas of total war against the indigenous savages. In the wake of the conflict, the English increasingly viewed "all Indians who resisted English definitions of authority as enemies." Ultimately the Narragansett War reflected "the unwillingness of the colonists to accommodate native cultures, economies, and land use" and as such presaged "most if not all of the subsequent major wars between natives and settlers during the next two centuries of American expansion."[52]

The violence threw Puritan society into a state of "hysteria" and left its leaders badly shaken. In 1679 the Puritan leader Increase Mather blamed the war on the sinfulness of the settlers and expressed the fear that Englishmen were "degenerating into beasts," as they had "run wild into the woods" and fought the savages in "Heathenish" fashion. "We have [become] shamefully Indianized in all those abominable things," lamented his son and fellow Puritan minister Cotton Mather. "Our Indian wars are not yet over."[53]

In the years following King Philip's War, the remaining Massachusetts Indians were forced to live in small clusters within dramatically reduced homelands. The indigenous people never "vanished" from Massachusetts, they merely disappeared from the English "field of vision." Descendants of the tribes remain ensconced in New England communities to this day.[54]

Disrespect for Indians combined with settler colonial expansion gave rise to indiscriminate violence in New York as well as New England. Dutch traders had settled New York and established Albany and New Amsterdam, both on the Hudson River, as pivotal posts in the fur trade and in securing the alliance with the Iroquois. The Dutch famously purchased Manhattan island for a pittance in 1626 but otherwise made little effort to interact with or Christianize the "entirely savage and wild" Indians that one clergyman found "uncivil and stupid" and beset with "wickedness and godlessness."[55] In 1643 Gov. William Kieft orchestrated a nighttime surprise attack that turned into a massacre of a mixed group of about 80 Indians, mostly women and children. The indigenes struck back, killing among others Anne Hutchinson, the religious dissenter from Massachusetts Bay. The Dutch summoned the famous mercenary John Underhill, "hero" of the slaughter of the Pequot, to oversee the burning of villages and the killing of more than 500 Indians in 1644.[56]

The English seized the colony from the Dutch in 1664 and by the 1670s had solidified their control of the Atlantic seaboard, overwhelming European competitors while killing and driving indigenous people into the woods. The English takeover of New Sweden, founded in 1638 on the Delaware River, did not bode well for the Delaware and Susquehannock Indians, who had not been threatened by the relatively small number of Swedish and Finnish traders in the region. As "great numbers of settlers arrived" in the Delaware valley, Indians who "sought to maintain a traditional lifestyle were displaced westward, while those who remained were forced to adapt as best they could to a new world."[57]

Violence and Indian Slavery in the "Shatter Zone"

The powerful and extremely violent forces unleashed by the colonial encounter shattered indigenous cultures, causing the death and displacement of thousands of Indians, and forcing them to reconfigure their identities. Beginning with the arrival of the Europeans in the sixteenth century, a combination of disease, the introduction of a new market economy, and the explosive growth of Indian slavery dramatically altered the colonial landscape. The modernist Europeans, connected with the international market economy, backed by organized trading companies, and fueled by emerging nation-state ideologies, overwhelmed the preexisting economic and political structures.

Going far beyond indigenous captive taking, the Europeans forged an "international trade in American Indian slaves that led to decimation of entire groups and depopulation of large areas." The brutal history of African slavery, from the Middle Passage to the Civil War, has long overshadowed awareness of the scope and devastating impact of the Indian slave trade. To a far greater extent than popularly recognized, North American slavery was red and white as well as black and white. Indian slavery, not just African slavery, gave rise to the "Old South." The "discovery" of Indian slavery has been one of the most significant developments within history and anthropology over the past generation.[58]

The period from roughly 1540 to 1730 brought the destruction of the Mississippian chieftain system that had anchored indigenous culture and diplomacy since the "Middle Ages." The old system of broad-ranging trade and exchange relations, peppered with episodic warfare and diplomacy, disappeared. Archeological and documentary evidence reveals that the new European slave trade caused widespread death and destruction within indigenous polities. It forced migrations and mass relocations into fortified villages and the coalescence of new groups. Anthropologist Robbie Etheridge described the violent instability of the eastern half of the continent during this era as the "Mississippian shatter zone."[59]

The shattering of indigenous culture was a product of colonialism but Indians were more than passive victims of the violent dislocations. As with African slavery, Indians took a direct role in the slave trade as captors and middlemen. The system could not have worked without them. The tumult and dislocations on the international slave trade forced Indians to reconfigure their identities, which spurred ethno-genesis and the creation of new and powerful indigenous groupings. These included the "civilized tribes" that remained ensconced in the American South until the removal program of the 1830s.

European colonialism did not introduce violence and captive taking, as masculinized warfare had long been integral to Indian culture, but the dislocations it brought intensified the violence that cascaded across the land. Scholars have identified different places and times in which the introduction of colonialism into the "tribal zone" has accelerated and intensified the already existing structures of violence. These changes underscore the significance of "colonial violence and other changes in indigenous life with the rise of the nation state and the incorporation of indigenous peoples into the world economy." The introduction of new and more sophisticated weaponry contributes to the spike in violence but does not fully explain it. Still, "The introduction of firearms led to a revolutionary change in aboriginal warfare."[60]

Though warfare and captive taking existed before the arrival of the Europeans, the various chiefdoms that battled one another had "abided by certain cultural rules. The arrival of the Europeans disrupted these rules."[61] Colonialism introduced violent competition among indigenous groups to gain a foothold in the new globalized market economy. Colonialism sparked an arms race to secure weapons and ammunition as well as horses and other European-introduced technologies that might provide an advantage or enhance the prospects of survival. The slave trade gave rise to a terror-filled environment of long-distance raiding that confronted masses of indigenous people with a stark choice of either taking slaves or becoming one.

Disease and the fur trade, which linked the Midwest and ultimately the Far West with Europe in the globalizing market economy, combined to spark violent competition, destruction, and reconfiguration of indigenous identities. The market extended horizontally to Europe but the shatter zone also extended vertically from the Great Lakes to Florida, radiating death, terror, and arms and slave trafficking across the continent. The colonial encounter thus initiated a "frenzy of slaving that extended from the Atlantic coast to Texas, and from the Ohio River south to the Gulf of Mexico."[62]

In the late seventeenth century, the Iroquois, driven by the loss of the overwhelming majority of their population to disease, launched their "mourning wars" against other tribes in order to rebuild their numbers and secure their position as the pivot in the beaver trade. From their base in the Finger Lakes region of New York, the confederated Five Nations of the Iroquois (Mohawk, Oneida, Onondaga, Cayuga, Seneca) took their aggression further south into the Ohio Valley, seizing captives and forcing other indigenes to flee, remobilize, and reconfigure their identities as new bands. Many of the remaining Hurons relocated on the southern side of the Great Lakes and joined with other Indians to become the Wyandot. The Shawnee formed in the Ohio Valley in response to the threat posed by the powerful Iroquois. Driven all the way south to Carolina, the Erie reconfigured themselves as the Westos and for a time became one of the most lethal tribes in the region.[63]

As the driving force in the Indian slave trade, the English instituted slavery virtually from the outset of colonization. An already existent slave trade accelerated after the Pequot War in which Indian men were killed but women and children sold as slaves. In addition, New England men spoke of their "desire" for Indian women and took them as domestic servants and sex slaves. The settlers of Massachusetts and Connecticut auctioned hundreds of slaves in the aftermath of King Philip's War, including Metacomet's wife and son. Even "savages" who fought *with* the English were enslaved. Despite the outlawing of slavery in New England in the early eighteenth century, the practice continued in the form of "judicial enslavement" for alleged crimes committed by indigenes.[64]

Enslavement facilitated settler colonialism by removing Indians from the land. Thus the English took and sold slaves after the Powhatan Wars. The selling of Indians to international markets in the Caribbean or South America, where the sugar industry depended on slavery, also helped defray the costs of the wars. Later in the seventeenth century, Virginia Governor William Berkeley, citing the need for "revenge" for alleged murders and "mischiefs" carried out by Indians, authorized enslavement of Rappahannock River area tribes.

In launching his Virginia rebellion in 1676, Nathaniel Bacon spurred the Occaneechee to attack the Susquehannock, and then Bacon turned on his allies. After a 12-hour gun battle, the Virginians killed the indigenous men and took mostly women prisoners. During his brief takeover of Virginia, Bacon's Laws included the right to plunder and enslave Indians in order to secure land and labor. This popular law became the only one not overturned after Bacon died and Berkeley restored Crown authority. Thus Bacon's Rebellion was not only a struggle for landed expansion at the expense of Indians but also for control of a profitable Indian slave trade.[65]

The Crown colony of Carolina, founded in 1670, became the epicenter of the eastern woodland shatter zone. Enslavement was not the goal of the Proprietors who received the royal patent for Carolina and sought to Christianize the tribes. However—and typical of triangulated settler colonial settings regardless of place and time—the local government and settler-driven "facts on the ground" outweighed desires expressed in faraway metropolitan capitals. Carolina elites and settlers ignored the wishes of the Proprietors because Indian slavery was lucrative. They pursued a divide-and-conquer strategy of killing, enslaving, and removing Indians from the land to make way for new plantations and settlers. As Jennings notes, "By the time Carolina was founded, the English were savvy enough to recognize the benefits of exploiting existing Indian rivalries."[66]

As they launched the largest slaving enterprise in North America, the Carolinians underscored the connection between war and slavery: "Only through warfare could Carolinians obtain the slaves they desired to exchange for supplies to build their plantations."[67] Carolinians used pressure and incentives, especially guns and ammunition, to spur Indians to attack and enslave other indigenes. Slave-based warfare meant that untold thousands of Indians would die so that others could be captured. Moreover, these assaults triggered the Indian cultural imperative of blood revenge for the killing of family and tribe members, precipitating a boomerang of violent indigenous conflict throughout the Southeast. "As Indian commercial interests intensified," Ethridge explains, "so did warfare and the militarization of those Native groups who sought to control the trade."[68]

By the first decade of the eighteenth century, "all southeastern Indians were either slave traders or their targets." The indigenous Southeast was "a powder keg of anxiety" in which "no one knew who'd be enslaved next."[69] The newly formed Westos transitioned from victim to victimizer as they joined with the Carolina elite and entered into the predatory slave trade. However, settler colonial expansion into the interior soon spurred conflict with the Westos. In 1682 the Carolina settlers allied with migratory Shawnee, whom they called Savannahs, to attack and destroy the Westos as a distinct entity. Like William Bradford in Plymouth, South Carolina Governor John Archdale perceived "the hand of God" in service of "the thinning of the Indians, to make room for the English."[70]

In the 1690s the Carolina slavers provided weapons and trade goods to the Yamasee and other tribes who proceeded to enslave "tens of thousands" of Indians throughout the Southeast and west to Texas and Arkansas. As slaves often had to be moved a long distance, the very young, old, and weak either died or were killed during the initial raids. Slaves were transported in pens to ports for shipment out to the West Indies, South America, or on occasions to northern ports.[71]

The indigenous residents of La Florida suffered the most devastating consequences of the slaving frenzy. Tribes such as the Timucua and Apalachee lived in the northern third of today's Florida. They for the most part successfully resisted French and Spanish efforts at colonization, as relatively few Indians converted or worked willingly for the Europeans. Nearly all of those pulled into the missions resented the friars' demands that they give up dances, celebrations, games, and indigenous spirituality and rituals. In 1597 the attempt to sustain missions on the Georgia coast (Guale) provoked an Indian raid on St. Augustine in response to which Spanish soldiers "burned aboriginal villages and stored crops."[72]

By the early eighteenth century slaving raids from Carolina had carried out a "reign of terror" upon the Timucua, Apalachee, and other tribes of northern Florida. Incentives and the threat of their own enslavement prompted the Yamasee and other mercenary Indians to carry out relentless slave raids against Florida tribes already weakened by smallpox and other diseases. The invaders sacked Spanish missions on the Georgia coast and in Florida, as only St. Augustine survived, and took thousands of Indian slaves back to their benefactors in Charlestown. The remaining Timucua and Apalachee fled either west to join coalescent tribes or south to the swamps. "By the early 1760s," Jerald T. Milanich points out, "the indigenous population of Florida, once numbering hundreds of thousands, was reduced to almost nothing."[73]

Until their destruction in 1704, the Apalachee chiefdom had reproduced itself for 600 years through the traditional system of social, economic, and political legitimation. Colonialism and predatory slave trading "initiated the processes that ultimately led to the end of the Apalachee polity." If not for this, the Apalachees, a strong and distinctive people for centuries, might well have emerged "as a sixth Civilized Tribe" of the Southeast.[74]

Colonial violence and slavery could regenerate as well as destroy indigenous societies. The new societies that formed out of the slaving frenzy included the Creeks, Chickasaw, Choctaw, Cherokee, and Seminole, who would remain on their land for more than 130 years after the dissolution of the Apalachee. Through marriage, fictive kinship ties, adoption, shared language, alliances, and other means, dislocated indigenes coalesced into the new bands. Slavery, colonialism, and ethno-genesis thus reconfigured indigenous identities throughout the shatter zone.

The southeastern tribes who survived the slaving frenzy became slavers rather than enslaved and coalesced into the new tribes. The Choctaw acquired weapons sooner than most other groups and their base in modern-day Mississippi was far enough removed from the slaving epicenter in Carolina to enable them to survive and flourish. Even further west, the Chickasaw amalgamated and became known for mounting large virtual armies of ruthless slavers. The Creeks (named by Europeans because they observed them encamped along streambeds) were born of violence and slaving, as they played a major role as mercenaries in the virtual depopulation of Florida. The Cherokee coalesced in closest proximity to the Europeans, prompting frequent alliances with the English in warfare. The Seminole, from the Spanish *cimarrone*, meaning Indians living away from missions, coalesced in Florida as refugees resisting colonialism and enslavement. Some Africans and small numbers of Europeans also joined these newly coalescent tribes.[75]

Despite the creation of these new and powerful Indian confederacies, the frenzy of slaving delivered so much death and destruction that the indigenes as a whole turned against it and ceased working with the European slave traders. Indians had joined the British in the Tuscarora War (1711–1715) in which South Carolinians helped North Carolinians defeat the Tuscarora. They enslaved some 1,000–2,000 Tuscarora, who had been slavers themselves, and what remained of the tribe removed to the north and in 1722 became the sixth nation of the Iroquois Confederation.[76]

Under the threat of becoming slaves, the Yamasee helped the Carolinians subdue the Tuscarora yet as settlers continued to take Yamasee land the indigenes responded with a major anticolonial war of resistance in 1715. "Suffocated by the British who increasingly encroached on their lands, livelihood and families," the Yamasees struck back ferociously and killed more than 400 colonists and slave traders. The Carolinians responded with a boomerang of indiscriminate violence replete with massacres fueled by scalp bounties. The Carolinians killed masses of Indians, hunted down the remnants of the tribe in Florida, and ultimately "destroyed the Yamasees as a political entity."

The Yamasee War marked the end of the slaving frenzy across the southeastern shatter zone, as "the partnership between British traders and Indian slave raiders was irrevocably broken." The Cherokee and the Creeks had aided the British at the outset but then turned against each other. The Yamasee War thus "catalyzed a Cherokee-Creek cycle of war unprecedented in intensity and scope." Indians continued to take captives and engage in blood vengeance and masculinity affirming warfare, but the frenzy of slave armies and mass raids for sale to Europeans came to an end.[77]

The end of the Indian slave trade after the Yamasee War produced a singular focus on African slavery. Thus, Alan Gallay argues that the Yamasee War marked "the birth of the Old South." Traumatized by the scope of the Yamasee attack, the South Carolinians ever after remained fearful of the potential violence of racially defined others. Over time, phobias of a "black majority" replaced the perception of Indian threat, as South Carolina was to remain the epicenter of American slavery.[78]

Although the "Old South" shifted to African slavery after 1720, Indian slavery, violence, and warfare pervaded the continent, implicating countless Indian groups and all of the colonizing states. Despite the French reputation for cultivating a reciprocal "middle ground" with Indians, New France developed an "extensive system of Indian slavery that transformed thousands of Indian men, women, and children into commodities of colonial commerce." With the burgeoning fur trade centered at the French outpost at Michilimackinac, located at the confluence of Lakes Michigan and Huron, "slavery was embedded in the domestic and economic relationships of the eighteenth century Great Lakes." Indigenous groups, eager to access weapons, tools, and other European goods, brought slaves to the French whether they asked for them or not. As reciprocal relations required accepting as well as giving gifts, even when reluctant the French went along with the human trafficking.[79]

With men often killed during or immediately after slave raids, the Ottawa and Illinois brought captive women to the Frenchmen, who took them as wives and mistresses. French Catholic Church and colonial officials were aghast to learn that the French traders were entering into such relationships in large numbers. Moreover, based on their appearance and practices, the Frenchmen were becoming Indianized—"rendering themselves almost savage"—rather than the Indians becoming Gallicized. Desperate French colonial authorities dispatched "a supply of nubile French girls" to Louisiana but as one official lamented the Frenchmen seemed to prefer Indian women. Indian slavery thus produced a blurring of ethnicity, especially in trade centers such as Kaskaskia, the largest community in upper Louisiana wherein "sexual relations between Frenchmen and Indian women were utterly routine."[80]

Gifting, ethnic mixing, and reciprocal relations did not inoculate French colonialism from war and genocide. The southeastern frenzy of slaving extended to French colonial enclaves, especially Mobile where captive slaves were brought for sale and shipment. As a result of slavery and other tensions, in 1729 the Natchez, the largest indigenous group in the Mississippi Valley, assaulted the French at Fort Rosalie on the eastern bank of the Mississippi. The Indians killed indiscriminately, as more than 200 French died, and put their homes to the torch.[81]

The Natchez assault produced an indiscriminate response from the French, who carried out "a series of vicious reprisals that within two years had decimated the tribe and shattered its integrity forever." Frustrated by the Indian style of guerrilla warfare—they "approach like foxes, fight like lions and disappear like birds," as one French officer put it, the French launched "campaigns of genocidal intent." These early eighteenth-century campaigns targeted not only the Natchez but the Fox and Chickasaw as well.[82]

Slave raids embroiling the Spanish and indigenous people entered Texas from the north. In the early eighteenth century, indigenes descended from the Plains to raid for horses and captives to exchange with Europeans for guns and other goods. "Such raids sent ripples and then waves through native alliances and enmities across Texas, drawing Spaniards into conflict with powerful groups of Comanche, Wichita, Caddo and Apaches through the end of the century," Juliana Barr notes. A coalescence known as Apaches attacked Spanish horse herds, missions, and presidios, provoking an indiscriminate response against the "barbarous enemies of humankind." Whereas Indians took relatively small numbers of captives, the Spanish took far more slaves in their reprisal raids. With slavery formally illegal in New Spain, officials authorized the raids under the Catholic doctrine of just war. Spanish officials dispatched the Indian slaves to Mexico City, Havana, and Veracruz. They took many times more women than men and kept some of these for their own desires. As the frenzied cycle of slavery unfolded in Texas, "The loss of their wives and children drove furious Apache warriors to expand their onslaughts against Spanish horse herds." After decades of raiding, the Spanish and the Apache made peace, leaving the field open in the latter half of the century for the Comanche and Wichita to plague the Spanish rancheros, missions, and outposts.[83]

Centuries of endemic warfare prevailed in New Mexico, where, as Ned Blackhawk points out, Spanish authorities "clearly understood the importance of violence in solidifying colonial rule." The slave trade anchored the Spanish–Ute alliance as the Utes conducted pitiless raids against defenseless non-equestrian tribes further north in the Great Basin. The Ute engaged in "violent subjugation of vassal Indian communities and their women." After torturing and killing most of their male victims, the Ute paraded women and children before potential buyers in annual trade fairs. "The serial rape of captive Indian women became ritualized public spectacles at northern trade fairs." The flesh trade in the southwest was obviously "heavily gendered, with adolescent girls among the prime targets" owing to a high demand for them in New Mexico.[84]

Slavery infused by colonialism came last to the Northwest, the area about which the Europeans knew the least and explored last. Spain, Russia, and Britain descended on the northwest in the mid-eighteenth century, with trade focused mainly on furs, including sea otter pelts sent across the Pacific to China. As elsewhere Indians had long taken and exchanged captives but as in the other regions the European-infused market system introduced new technologies and accelerated the violence. The arrival of colonialism in the Northwest brought a new and more intensive slave trade that unleashed a "cruel system of predatory warfare," as a contemporary European described it.[85]

On the Cusp of the Imperial Wars

The colonial encounter had created an entirely new world for indigenous peoples as well as for Europeans. For the indigenes the colonial encounter brought disease, disruption, enslavement, diaspora, indiscriminate killing, destruction of communities, and loss of ancestral homelands. Violence was nothing new to Indians but the scope and intensity of the colonial violence was unprecedented. The indigenous way of life rooted in reciprocal relations with the natural, spiritual, and human world had been irrevocably changed by the encounter. While Indians sought balance through gift giving, alliance building, social interactions, and performance of rituals, the epidemics and the intensity of colonial violence shattered this way of life. Whereas indigenes viewed nature as there to be exploited in balance, establishing community or moving from place to place as needed for fishing, hunting, planting, and gathering, Europeans sought to establish bounded places, to *possess* colonial spaces.

Individual property rights, commodification of the land, patriarchy, Christianity, and nation-state identity represented radically different and ultimately triumphant conceptions of land use and relations between and among people and the natural world. As Ethridge observes, "The contestants in this imperial struggle who were organized into nation-states held the advantage—Europeans prevailed decisively in this struggle."[86]

The changes brought by the Europeans were not, however, simply imposed on Indians, rather the indigenes often recognized what was happening, adapted, and seized the opportunities available to them. Whereas Indians had trapped animals for food, clothing, and shelter, maintaining the imperative of balance, the Europeans brought a burgeoning global marketplace with them, giving rise to the fur trade, which spurred near-extermination of the beaver for the making of felt hats. Indians sought to access the new technologies and trade goods introduced by Europeans, especially guns and ammunition, but also tools, metals, cloth, and alcohol. They thus accommodated and played a vital role in affirming the European approach to the natural world—that it could be exploited in extremes and imbalance if the market so demanded—in order to get the things they needed or desired.

It has become fashionable to aver that Indians adapted and displayed their own agency within the colonial encounter and that is true. It is also true that the overwhelming majority of them died, their cultures and way of life were shattered beyond recognition, and they now confronted a people in the Europeans whose technologies, economic and spiritual drives, racial formations, and ethnocentricity offered little hope of compromise. They were not doomed to extinction but they did confront a people determined to remove them from the land by whatever means necessary.

Although whole peoples such as the Apalachee, after having thrived for centuries, were virtually destroyed, other Indians adapted and through a process of ethno-genesis created new and powerful confederacies such as the Cherokee, Choctaw, Creek, Chickasaw, and Seminole. They had armed themselves and learned hard lessons through horrific violence, reconfigured their identities, and successfully adapted to the colonial environment. They had finally put a stop to the Indian slave trade, which had entailed perpetual warfare, and now traded relatively more peacefully and profitably within the colonial market system in deerskins rather than in slaves. Having rebuilt their cultures and strengthened their new confederacies, the indigenes recognized that they could exploit the Europeans, who entered into violent competition for control of the continent. During the imperial wars of the eighteenth century, Indians could and did play these Europeans off against one another through often-deft manipulation of trade and alliances. As long as more than one European power remained in contention for the new empire, indigenous people had a fighting chance to keep some of their land and maintain their identities.

3

"No Savage Shall Inherit the Land": Settler Colonialism through the American Revolution

During the eighteenth century, explosive settler colonization established a structural framework that would drive Indians from the land. Trade and diplomacy enabled relatively peaceful relations between Europeans and indigenes in the first half of the eighteenth century. Thereafter, the influx of settlers and the outbreak of the French and Indian War heightened the conflicts involving Indians, imperial authorities, speculators, and settlers. The American Revolution spurred indiscriminate killing on the western borderlands and a determination on the part of the Americans to cleanse Indians from the land.

Under the Doctrine of Discovery, deeply rooted in European tradition, the English colonies laid claim to colonial space, arrogating the right to dispossess the indigenes, deemed heathen and uncivilized.[1] Euro-Americans employed the law as a means of disavowing the colonizing act. In some cases Indians legitimately sold land. Other times speculators and officials cheated them out of land, sometimes in collusion with their own "chiefs" or other tribes. Inaccurate translation and misunderstanding led to nasty surprises and simmering resentments. Even though settlers, speculators, and government officials knew that most land sales and treaties were fraudulent and one-sided, their implications not clear to the indigenous partners, they nonetheless provided the desired veneer of legality. In the final analysis, as Stuart Banner points out, "In the colonial period the Indians sold an enormous amount of land to the English, but in the end they were poorer than when they began."[2]

Both the Europeans and the indigenes had well-ensconced traditions for the conduct of diplomacy, yet a cultural chasm often divided them. For Euro-Americans the primary goals of summitry with Indians were two-fold: to gain control of land for speculators and settlers; and to secure alliances in time of war. As settler colonization grew, Euro-Americans sought written treaties that would sanction land seizures under the authority of the law. Meanwhile, both the English and French courted Indian allies during the course of their long struggle for supremacy in North America. Indigenous groups could and did exploit the imperial rivalry for gifts, guns, ammunition, trade goods, manufactured items, cloth, blankets, and for support against their own indigenous rivals.[3]

Indigenes viewed diplomacy more broadly, as a means to establish mutual respect and kinship ties that would enable relations to go forward. Indians thus focused on the *process* and the *rituals* associated with diplomacy whereas Euro-Americans homed in on the *outcome* of negotiations. Indians, with their cultures rooted in oral traditions rather than writing, often were not fully aware of the terms and significance of the written accords. Symbols and gestures often meant more to them than words. From the indigenous standpoint, if mutual respect and kinship ties had been effectively established, negotiations had succeeded in laying a foundation for future cooperation. Euro-Americans considered the negotiations to be over once a treaty had been signed whereas to Indians the signatures might appear as merely a ritual valued by the other side, but not something to bring an end to the negotiations as a whole.

After often having walked for days if not weeks to arrive at the council fires, Indians might reasonably expect to be greeted with gifts and fanfare appropriate to the occasion of their arrival. Euro-Americans instead often did not hide their contempt for the bedraggled savages coming into their midst. In 1785, for example, when Choctaw diplomats arrived after a two-month trek for a summit in Hopewell, South Carolina, they were tired and hungry and expected to be showered with food and gifts. The Americans instead viewed them as "beggars" and "the most indolent creatures we ever saw."[4]

Once they had arrived at the council fires, Indians, with their emphasis on the process of diplomacy, typically were in no hurry to conclude an accord. If they were tired and hungry, they needed time to rest; if there was alcohol available, they might wish to drink it and enjoy themselves for a few days. Euro-Americans learned to use Indian fatigue, hunger, and desire for alcohol, as well as the allure of guns, ammunition, and trade goods, to secure the kind of agreement they wanted.

The rituals of the council fire took time to unfold and symbolism meant everything. White, for example, was the color of peace, hence if indigenes unfolded a white deerskin upon which the Euro-American negotiator might be invited to sit, such a gesture was highly significant to the tribes, but this symbolism might be completely lost on the colonizer. To Indians a cloudy day might be a bad day to go forward with negotiations and a sunny day a good one. Mutual smoking of the calumet, which took the newly formed kinship ties and understandings to the spirits in the sky by means of the smoke, was highly significant to Indians.

While Euro-American diplomacy was heavily freighted with racial categorization, Indian diplomacy often put more emphasis on gender. With warfare often perceived as a masculine struggle to determine which set of males would rule, an indigenous woman might serve as an envoy to break a masculine impasse and jump-start peace talks. If near the end of negotiations Indian women came into the council fires to embrace the men on the other side, this might represent a meaningful display of recognition of kinship ties, showing the Euro-Americans that they had been "adopted" by the tribe.

Although cultural barriers, double-dealing, and misunderstanding plagued European-Indian accords, diplomacy could keep the lines of trade and communication open and keep the peace or forge alliances in wartime. Indians as well as Euro-Americans sought and often achieved through alliances material gain, political leverage, revenge against their enemies, and an outlet for masculine drives. On several occasions Indian chieftains traveled to Europe, where they were well received by royal courts, reflecting a high degree of colonial ambivalence. Through the painstaking efforts of Indians, Europeans, and go-betweens or middlemen, some of whom had mixed parentage that provided them with essential language skills, many understandings were reached, especially in the first half of the eighteenth century.

The explosive growth of settlement, the structure of settler colonialism, ultimately overwhelmed diplomacy. As the balance of power shifted to the colonizer, land speculators, settlers, and colonial authorities acted unilaterally. Even when colonial officials strove to rein in settlement, squatters and speculators showed contempt for their directives and disregard for Indian claims to colonial space.

Indigenous people were willing to try diplomacy but when it failed they were also willing to take up the hatchet to preserve their homelands. Violent Indian resistance—"savage" attacks on "white" people—traumatized the settlers, inflamed colonial discourse, and led to campaigns of dispossession backed by indiscriminate violence.

Even as they rationalized exterminatory campaigns as a defensive response to Indian savagery, the settlers mastered the Indian way of war. They learned to skulk in the woods, conduct search-and-destroy operations, attack villages at dawn, destroy Indian food stores in winter, take Indian scalps, enslave them, deport their children, and above all relentlessly to take Indian land. Ultimately many Euro-American settler colonials avowed that the "Indian problem" demanded resolution, indeed a final solution.[5]

Amid the campaigns of dispossession and imperial warfare, epidemic disease continued to ravage indigenous people. While millions of Indians became sick and died, millions of settlers arrived and thrived. This dichotomy powerfully fueled the settlers' fantasies of their providential destiny to lay claim to colonial space, to displace a "dying race." As this dialectic played out, ambivalences became unsettling and accommodation with indigenous people less and less necessary.

Indians and the Imperial Wars

Conflict in North America was hardly limited to the "colonizer and the colonized," as indigenes fought indigenes and Europeans battled other Europeans for trade, prestige, and control of the land. Eager to access European goods, and to profit from trade and alliances, indigenous people willingly and often enthusiastically took part in a series of European-inspired imperial wars. Warfare between and among Europeans provided Indian warriors an opportunity to manifest their manhood, to strike back against their indigenous rivals, to access European goods and trade, and to attempt to preserve their lands.

The imperial wars pitted the English, allied with the Iroquois Confederation based in the Finger Lakes region of New York, against the French and their Indian allies on the Midwest borderlands.[6] The major European conflicts were King William's War (1689–1697); Queen Anne's War (1702–1713); King George's War (1744–1748); and the decisive French and Indian War (1754–1763).[7]

Ambivalence and a "long peace" prevailed throughout much of the first half of the eighteenth century between Indians and Euro-Americans. Even as settler colonialism brought increased pressure on Indian land, the Europeans also brought opportunities for commerce and alliances. Indians acted as a buffer between rival Europeans and played a major role in a thriving exchange economy on the borderlands. The indigenes anchored a robust trade in furs, deerskins, foodstuffs, and other items.[8]

Until conflict erupted in the mid-century, Indians and Europeans acknowledged each other's land, and provincial go-betweens helped keep the peace by promoting diplomacy and cultural exchange. The Euro-American intermediaries often learned Indian languages, mastered cultural practices, and established kinship ties. In the end, however, they typically remained implicated in the settler colonial project of dispossessing the indigenes. "No provincial go-between was immune to the land fever that afflicted British America," James Merrell points out. The European go-betweens never lost sight of a "brighter future" in which "Indians would follow the forest into oblivion." Despite the often tireless efforts of both Indian and white negotiators, the "harsh lesson" of the woods was "the ultimate incompatibility of colonial and native dreams about the continent they shared."[9]

By the mid-eighteenth century the explosive growth of settler colonialism undermined the long peace, and ambivalent relations gradually gave way to indiscriminate violence and ethnic cleansing. In 1750 the non-Indian population of about 1.2 million was more than quadruple the number on the continent in 1700. The encroachment of this rapidly growing settler population into colonial space sundered older ties of exchange and alliance linking natives and colonizers. Settlement drove many Indians west, "reducing those who remained to a scattering of politically powerless enclaves," Daniel H. Usner explains. "An old world, rooted in indigenous exchange, was giving way to a new one in which native Americans had no certain place."[10]

In Pennsylvania beginning in the 1680s, William Penn, the Quaker proprietor, had personified colonial ambivalence. Penn and other Quakers believed that Indians like all people possessed the "inner light" from God hence he sought peace with the tribes. At the same time, however, Penn pursued the incompatible goal of selling off lands to generate revenue. "From the beginning, this practical need abraded uncomfortably with his benign intentions toward the Indians," Eric Hinderaker explains. As Euro-Americans pursued profitable land sales and expansion into new settlements, the Delaware and other Indians "were increasingly forced to adapt rapidly or pick up and move."[11]

By the time of the French and Indian War, the British Army exacerbated an already deteriorating situation in Penn's Woods by displaying contempt for the indigenes and their claims to the land. Wedded to the European way of war, the

British dramatically underestimated Indians and in consequence suffered a series of shattering defeats in the war. No one better symbolized the British Army's ignorance of irregular warfare combined with contempt for the "savages" than General Edward Braddock. Before launching his famously ill-fated march to besiege the French at Fort Duquesne, Braddock contemptuously dismissed an offer of alliance from the Delaware leader Shingas. After arriving with his delegation to meet with Braddock in Cumberland, Maryland, Shingas linked Delaware support against the French with securing the lands for the Indians once the French had been driven from the Forks of the Ohio.

Contemptuous of conducting diplomacy with Indians, Braddock declared gratuitously, "No savage shall inherit the land." Shingas replied, "If they might not have liberty to live on the land, they would not fight for it"—at least not on the side of Great Britain. The most prominent settler of Pennsylvania, Benjamin Franklin, warned that the Indians were a force to be reckoned with, but Braddock rejected the advice. The "savages" might be "a formidable enemy to your raw American militia," he told Franklin, "but upon the King's regular and disciplined troops, sir, it is impossible they should make an impression." But make an impression they did on July 9, 1755, as the Indians along with their French allies routed Braddock's army, killing him and more than 450 troops and support personnel in the Battle of the Monongahela. French and Indian losses were minimal by comparison.[12]

Spurned by the British and besieged by the settler colonial advance, the Delaware, Shawnee, Mingo, Ottawa, Potawatomi, and other tribes launched a campaign of terror targeting squatters and backcountry settlements. The peace and ambivalence that had characterized the prior history of Pennsylvania evaporated, as the borderlands became the "scene of chaos and rout, with colonial forces hardly managing even to hinder the raids." As the indigenes lashed out against settler encroachment, their violent homeland defense dealt a deathblow to already waning Quaker calls for toleration. Indian warriors took prisoners and plundered, killing "nearly every male colonist they encountered, often going out of their way to escalate the body count." As they conducted a "psychological terror campaign designed to intimidate and dishearten their opponents," the Indians affirmed the colonial discourse of savagery by mutilating and posing the bodies of many of their victims. Few considered that the indigenes—increasingly outnumbered by the flood of borderland settlers—employed terror as a deliberate tactic of intimidation, one that often worked by prompting reverse migrations.[13]

The indiscriminate borderland warfare fueled a boomerang of retributive violence, a pattern that would play out in American history across the breadth of the continent. By killing and taking the scalps of hundreds of settler victims, the Indians traumatized the Euro-Americans, who increasingly yearned to cleanse them from the land. Settlers acting within a discourse emphasizing Indian terror targeting innocents launched campaigns of extirpation. The colonial press routinely referenced Indian resistance as "murder" and "massacre" perpetrated by "barbarians" and "savages" against innocent men, women, and children. Graphic narratives relayed "careful descriptions of bashed-in skulls and cut-out tongues. Of sharp objects stuck into eyes and genitals." Children learned "to hate an Indian, because he always hears him spoken of as an enemy," explained the settler James Hall. "From the cradle, he listens continually to horrid tales of savage violence, and becomes familiar with narratives of aboriginal cunning and ferocity." Another settler avowed, "The tortures which they exercise on the bodies of their prisoners justify extermination." As Armstrong Starkey notes, "The image of the Indian as a murderous savage was a powerful weapon."[14]

Settler incursions, land and trade disputes, spiritual divergence, alcohol consumption, and war had eroded colonial ambivalence. An "enraptured discourse of fear" and a "horror-filled rhetoric of victimization" had become "all but unanswerable as political discourse" in western Pennsylvania and the Ohio River country. As in future American conflicts, opponents of violent retribution against evil and savage foes quickly became marginalized. "Anyone who professed not to see the dangers," Peter Silver explains, "or who seemed not to care enough about the suffering it relentlessly described, was open to the charge of acting against the best interests of 'the white people.' "[15]

Colonial discourse also emphasized the anxiety-producing threat of Indian captivity of "helpless wives and poor defenseless babes." Since the harrowing saga of Mary Rowlandson in 1682, the captivity narrative had been a staple of colonial discourse, reinforcing gendered frames of helpless women and maidens confronting the proverbial "fate worse than death" at the hands of the savages. To Indians, "captivity was a normal accompaniment to warfare." The captives might be adopted to "cover the dead" or eventually exchanged through diplomacy to facilitate bringing an end to conflict. However, to the Euro-Americans, captivity of "white" people, and their living and residing among the indigenes, ruptured the colonial binary of civilization reigning over savagery.[16]

In 1757 an Indian massacre and seizure of captives outside Fort William Henry on Lake George, New York, broadly affirmed the trope of Indian savagery in colonial discourse. The French under Marquis de Montcalm bombarded and forced the surrender of the English fort, but what followed underscored the Indo-European cultural divide and became a turning point in the war. After accepting Montcalm's terms, the British began their march out of Fort William Henry whereupon Montcalm proved unable to constrain his Indian allies, who descended upon defenseless men and women with knives and tomahawks to kill and also take their customary captives and trophies. The Abenaki, Ottawa, and Potawatomi, among others, killed 185 and took some 300–500 captives.

The Indians had joined the French in anticipation of proving themselves in battle and taking trophies back to their villages, hence Montcalm's reversion to a European-style honorable surrender was a betrayal of them. Moreover, with the English colonies often killing Indians indiscriminately and offering bounties for the scalps of indigenous men, women, and children, the Indians outside Fort William Henry viewed their actions as consistent with the prevailing way of war. Nonetheless, the "massacre of Fort William Henry" cemented the trope of Indian savagery while making a Pearl Harbor or 9/11 type of traumatic impact on the British North American mind. The slaughter outside the fort, vividly recounted in newspapers across the colonies, led to an upsurge in recruitment of thousands of new militiamen.[17]

Although they would long remember the Fort William Henry massacre, the British, desperate to change the course of a war they were losing, now sought alliance with the tribes. Many British colonials had learned a valuable lesson from Braddock's dismissal of Indians and the subsequent debacle at the Monongahela. George Washington, a narrow survivor of Braddock's folly, grasped that Indians were the masters of irregular warfare in the woods. He and others realized that the indigenes alone could provide crucial intelligence on the strength and positioning of the French and their allies.[18]

In 1758, after tense negotiations, the British, the settlers, and representative of 13 tribes came to terms in the Treaty of Easton. The Indians won concessions on hunting grounds and supposedly permanent occupation rights in the Ohio country. British military officials secured an alliance with the tribes against the French in return for pledging to stop settlement west of the Appalachians and to guarantee that Indian lands "shall remain your absolute property."[19] The settlers got an end to the indigenous campaign of terror but the brutal ethnic violence was not forgotten and would return with a vengeance at the end of the French and Indian War.

With British America now fully mobilized, new officers such as James Wolfe and Jeffrey Amherst conducted "wildly violent campaigns" against New France and the remaining Indian "miscreants" allied with the French. Few events better illustrated the embrace of indiscriminate warfare at the moment of British-American triumph than the murderous assault by Rogers' Rangers on the Abenaki village of St. Francis on October 4, 1759. During decades of warfare with the New England settlers the Abenaki had often descended from St. Francis, located north of Montreal, to conduct murderous raids. Major Robert Rogers of Massachusetts, who today "is regarded as the founding father of the American Army's Special Forces units," recruited a force of mostly Scotch-Irish irregulars from New Hampshire, together with some Indian and even a few African-American fighters, to make the audacious trek deep into enemy territory. "Take your revenge," General Amherst charged Rogers, adding the contradictory directive to show "no mercy" and yet to spare women and children.[20]

In an operation much like those that would occur later in places like Sand Creek and My Lai, angry attackers primed for slaughter would make no distinction on the basis of age or gender. Indeed, as so often happened in such attacks, warriors were not even present at the village, leaving mostly old men, women, and children to die by the scores if not hundreds as "the well-disciplined assault swiftly degenerated into an uncontrolled massacre." The villagers, who had celebrated a wedding the night before, burned alive in their wooden houses in the sunrise assault or were bludgeoned or shot dead on the spot. Noting that hundreds of scalps wafted in the breeze around the village, Rogers' Rangers took their own trophies from the dead and plundered the village of valuable metals and icons. "The American frontier could find and un-tether the savage that lay within even the most civilized of men," Stephen Brumwell observes.[21]

The British, aided by their Indian allies, defeated France decisively in the French and Indian War, paving the way for another wave of European settlement. Under the terms of the Treaty of Paris (1763), the British arrogated to themselves all French territory in North America, including indigenous lands, while Spain received the trans-Mississippi Louisiana territory from France. The Indians had cooperated in the war in the expectation that in return the British would reward them with trade and gifts and respect their right to their lands and access to hunting grounds. Yet even though Braddock had been killed in the first major battle of the war, his declaration that "no savage shall inherit the land" still prevailed in the minds of Englishmen. The British had erected a chain of forts in the Upper Great Lakes region from 1758 to 1762 and soon cut off trade with the Indians in weapons and powder, thus precipitating another wave of violent conflict.

The *pays d'en haut* (French term for the "upper country" of the Great Lakes region) had long been a multicultural "middle ground" reflecting the ambivalence of the colonial encounter. Indians outnumbered the French in the region yet became increasingly dependent on the fur trade as well as access to firearms and European trade goods. Indian women married French men, thereby forging kinship ties, blurring identities, and opening up third spaces in the colonial encounter. Trade, ceremonial gift giving, and interethnic mixing thus stabilized French-Indian relations in the region. Many British officials and settlers expressed contempt for the race mixing "interior French" and failed to recognize the critical role they played as "cultural negotiators with Native people."[22]

Emboldened by their victory over the French, British elites expressed contempt for trade and diplomacy with Indians. Amherst, like Braddock before him, had no respect for council fires, gift giving, wampum and calumet exchange, and other tiresome rituals associated with conducting diplomacy with the savages. In contrast to the French, who had long worked within the context of Indians' ways in establishing the middle ground, the preferred British model was one of removal and dispossession. "Never during the colonial period did British or British-colonial officials establish an alliance in North America closely resembling the French alliance with the Indians of the Great Lakes," Gregory Dowd points out.[23]

Following patterns rooted in the centuries-old system of chieftainship, indigenous groups had long pursued exchange relationships in order to access items as a means of ensuring loyalty to the regime. Chiefs whose tribes had become increasingly dependent on European trade goods to maintain popular support often sought war with other tribes, otherwise their young warriors would attack the Euro-American settlements, putting a stop to trade and gifting. War between tribes provided a way to "channel animosities and provide opportunities for young men to acquire status." The British often seized opportunities to provide weapons to the warring tribes as a means of weakening the indigenes as a whole in furtherance of the settler colonial project.[24]

With the French defeated and the British claiming sole possession of the continent, the indigenes now confronted a single European power that, even when willing to engage in diplomacy, lacked the experience and understanding of the French in how to deal with the tribes. While some leaders and mediators grasped the nature of indigenous diplomacy, British Indian policy "was fragmented between the various colonies" and thus depended on local attitudes and conditions. Moreover, the decentralized nature of settler society enabled traders and individuals rather than the state to handle Indian affairs, which broadened the opportunities for fraudulent deals, alcohol peddling, violence, and sexual abuse. Organized trade fairs and diplomacy enabled chiefs to control relations and deliver to their constituents, but with their victory over the French, the British increasingly viewed the Indians as having been enabled by such ceremonies, spoiled by gift giving, and in need of being "convinced of our superiority."[25]

Increasingly tenuous Anglo-Indian alliances fell apart on the southern borderlands. At the beginning of the eighteenth century, the Cherokee, who had coalesced in the southeastern mountains and valleys, backed the Carolinians in the Yamasee War. The English, however, pursued a divide-and-conquer strategy and thus refused to back the Cherokee in a vicious conflict with their rival, the Creeks. The Cherokee nevertheless continued to pursue good relations with the British in order to access European trade goods. Led by Little Carpenter, the Cherokee marched with General John Forbes to drive the French from Fort Duquesne (renamed Fort Pitt) in 1758. However, along the way the Cherokee chieftain grew resentful over the contempt shown to him by the British, who attempted to force European-style military discipline onto the indigenes. Virginia settlers then besieged the Cherokee on their way back home, including "random killings" based solely on their identities as Indians.[26]

As in Pennsylvania, settler encroachment was the ultimate cause of the "Cherokee War" of 1758–1761. Despite the British being "allies," settlers built new homes and towns on Cherokee lands and hunting grounds. As the British became assured of victory over the French, the fragile alliance collapsed and an indiscriminate war soon followed. The Cherokee viewed the alliance as a partnership and perceived the British as penurious in gift giving after the Cherokee cut short the hunting season and risked their lives to go to war against the French. The British resented having to give gifts to the tribes and viewed the Indians as insatiable mercenaries. As British "concepts of status bore an increasingly racial tinge," they expected the Cherokee to show "grateful subordination to British power and wealth" but instead encountered a "haughty" resistance. In the absence of trade and gift giving, the chiefs proved unable to rein in young warriors, who attacked settlements to take away what they wanted. A boomerang of retributive violence ensued.[27]

With the outbreak of war the British-Americans laid waste to Cherokee villages and killed indiscriminately. They summarily executed 22 chiefs who had come to negotiate an understanding. Catawba and Chickasaw warrior allies joined the British and South Carolina rangers in the Cherokee War. In borderland fighting in 1761, Lieutenant Colonel James Grant, sent from New York by Amherst, burned to the ground Cherokee villages and summarily executed noncombatant captives regardless of age and gender. "I had orders to put every soul to death," Grant acknowledged. Already devastated by smallpox epidemic, the Cherokee were left starving and homeless by the "scorched earth campaigns waged by the colonial whites." With many settlers and British officials calling for extermination, it was "the Cherokees' readiness to reach out from their side that made peace possible."[28]

The Catawba, denizens of the Carolina upcountry, allied with the British in the French and Indian War as well as the Cherokee War, but the alliance did not prevent their eventual dispossession. The Catawba received clothing, weapons, ammunition, food, and other supplies but after the wars the British concluded that "the more gifts they get the more proud and devilish they are." The British cut off trade as settlers with their cattle, hogs, sheep, and horses swallowed up Catawba land, hunting grounds, orchards, and burial mounds. They cleared forests, built farms, cabins, fences, wagon roads, towns, and taverns from which drunken men emerged to molest Indian women without fear of legal repercussions. Once the sole proprietors of the piedmont, the Catawba received a small reserve and "existed only on the sufferance of people inclined to cheat them as often as protect them, mock them as readily as befriend them."[29]

With settler colonialism revivified by the victory over the French, the British resumed land sales and squatting in the Ohio River Valley. As settlers streamed down new roads into the Ohio country, ambivalent relations, trade, gift giving, and diplomacy gave way to indiscriminate warfare. Britain had proven ungrateful to its indigenous allies and unworthy successors to the French by cutting off trade in high-demand items, notably guns and alcohol. Moreover, the British Army did not withdraw from the Forks of the Ohio as promised in the Treaty of Easton and also failed to stem the tide of the settler advance.

Dramatically underestimating Indian anger, and unwittingly promoting unity among the diverse bands, the British under Amherst soon reeled from the impact of a pan-Indian uprising. Amherst had shrugged off suggestions of violent indigenous resistance by citing their "incapacity of attempting anything serious." In any case, he would relish the opportunity to "punish the delinquents with entire destruction, which I am firmly resolved on whenever any of them give me cause." Belying such assurances, in the spring of 1763 the Seneca and Delaware joined by the Chippewa, Shawnee, Huron, and Ottawa under Pontiac (Obwandiyag) assaulted forts and settlements throughout the borderlands, killing indiscriminately and sending the Redcoats and the settlers into a panicked retreat.[30]

Indian homeland defense set off a new wave of borderland warfare replete with genocidal intent. Declaring, "No punishment we can inflict is adequate to the crimes of those inhumane villains," an apoplectic Amherst urged policy that would "extirpate this execrable race . . . I wish to hear of no prisoners." In a dispatch on May 4, 1763, Amherst asked, "Could it not be contrived to send the small pox among those disaffected tribes?" Two months later Colonel Henry Bouquet responded, "I will try to inoculate the bastards with some blankets that may fall in their hands." British officials knew of the effects of smallpox before Amherst gave his order and infected blankets and handkerchiefs in fact already had been distributed. But no one could have foreseen the massive smallpox epidemic that would ravage the entire continent, with little regard for ethnic distinctions, from 1775 to 1782.[31]

Stunned and traumatized by the scope of the Indian resistance, Britain attempted to rein in the settlers by issuing the Royal Proclamation of 1763. The Proclamation drew a line proscribing new trans-Appalachian land grants or purchases and requiring a permit for trade on the western side of the mountains. Moreover, the Proclamation outlawed private sales by Indians to settlers or speculators, decreeing that only the Crown could purchase land from the indigenes.

The British had not suddenly decided to respect indigenous homelands or to "protect Indians" from settler colonialism. Rather the Crown, already indebted by the French and Indian War, sought a respite in the violence in order to regroup and get its imperial house in order, in part by raising revenue with new duties on the colonists. In the long run, "removal rather than sustained coexistence" remained the structural imperative behind British Indian policy. In any case, various loopholes in the Royal Proclamation allowed land hunters to continue to survey the Ohio Valley while the "bans on squatting invited scorn."[32]

The Royal Proclamation combined with the new tax levies ignited the colonial rebellion. Shutting off access to new land for settlers was no more acceptable in 1763 than it had been at the time of Bacon's Rebellion. The "Americans" had no intention of respecting Indian ownership of the land or of complying with restrictions on settler mobility. Nor would they go along with the new duties and many other royal initiatives for that matter.

In the triangulated relationship typical of settler colonial situations, the settlers claimed colonial space already inhabited by indigenous people as well as the freedom of restraint from exogenous metropolitan authorities. In the wake of the Royal Proclamation, Americans associated the British with the Indians as impediments in the path of their providential destiny. They continued to pour into the borderlands with disregard for both British and indigenous sovereignty.

Racial formation coalesced in the context of rising American nationalism and indiscriminate borderland warfare with Indians. Increasingly identifying themselves as a superior race of white people, the settlers at the same time were traumatized by Indian violence. The French and Indian War simultaneously prompted Indians to take on a collective racial and cultural identity as well. Spiritual revival, especially the teaching of the Delaware mystic Neolin, accentuated the cultural divide between all "red" Indians and the "white" man. As Neolin's preaching spread across the borderlands, Indians rejected British paternal authority and began to ally more with one another. The settler colonial drive to take Indian land thus fueled a "rising conviction" on the part of the indigenes as well as the Euro-Americans that they were "opposite peoples" who literally lacked common ground.[33]

Indians and the American Revolution

Of utmost significance Indian removal and indiscriminate warfare evolved in tandem with the formation and achievement of American racial and nationalist aspirations. American national identity thus evolved not just in opposition to "taxation without representation," as American schoolbooks long emphasized, but also within the context of a murderous race war driven by settler colonial expansion. Unremitting borderland violence affirmed the increasingly homogenized colonial discourse that framed Indians as a unitary and savage foe in the path of civilization, progress, and national independence. In the face of this unifying discourse, colonial ambivalences degenerated into campaigns of ethnic cleansing.

Materialist motives also drove the American settlers and land speculators. Most colonial elites engaged in land speculation. The Proclamation Line thus infuriated

Washington, a land surveyor and speculator, as well as Thomas Jefferson, Arthur Lee, Patrick Henry, and other American patriots. The colonial elite and land speculators, as Colin Calloway puts it, "saw tyranny in Britain's interference with their ability to make a [financial] killing in the West."[34]

But the elite men of the cities and plantations were generally not those who actually performed the bloody work of cleansing the land of the indigenous other. "The pressures that inspired Indian hating did not descend from the top down, but arose from the bottom up," Patrick Griffin explains.[35] Thousands of men, women, and children of divergent European ethnicity knew little about land speculation; only that they intended to carve out a stake of their own where they could build farms, homesteads, and outposts for trade. On the eve of the American Revolution, more than 50,000 "whites" lived on the trans-Appalachian borderlands beyond British ability to control them. British officials invariably described these squatters as "low" and "the very dregs of the people." But they also realized the squatters and settlers were "too numerous, too lawless and licentious ever to be restrained."[36]

The Indians on the borderlands "now confronted a people who were, in a sense, stateless," Starkey explains. "The frontier thus became a very unstable place and the potential for violence almost unlimited."[37] Traumatized by Indian violent resistance and determined to occupy colonial space, the settlers stepped up the indiscriminate killing of Indians. As the English trader, go between, and land speculator George Croghan noted, settlers "thought it a meritorious act to kill Heathens whenever they were found."[38]

In late 1763 and early 1764, a Pennsylvania mob known as the Paxton Boys, determined to exterminate a "nest of perfidious enemies," seized 14 Indians from protective custody in Lancaster for summary execution and mutilation. As one settler explained, "the storm that has been so gathering has at length exploded." The "piecemeal ethnic cleansing" of the Paxton Boys "crystallized long-simmering hatreds into explicit new doctrines of racial unity and racial antagonism." Declaring that all Indians were "enemies, rebels, and traitors," the Pennsylvania governor made the colony a free fire zone, thereby authorizing settler colonials "to embrace all opportunities of pursuing, taking, killing, or destroying" Indians. The by now time-honored practice of offering bounties to scalp hunters flourished, including special rewards for the scalps of women and children.[39]

Settlers drove Indians off western Pennsylvania and eastern Ohio lands, forcibly repatriating any "white" children as well as adults that they found. These settlers wanted no vestiges to remain of ambivalent ethnic mixing and intercultural relations. Scores of men but especially women and children did not want to leave the tribes for "civilization." As an observer at the time put it, they "parted from the savages with tears." Many later escaped and tried to return to their Indian way of life. These "white savages" seem to have responded positively to a "strong sense of community" and a freer, less anxiety ridden indigenous lifestyle.[40]

In an effort to provide a legal veneer for opening up new lands for the inexorable encroachment of settlers, the British turned to their longstanding allies, the Six Nations of the Iroquois Confederation. The ambivalent Iroquois—whose pan-Indian consciousness, as it turned out, would arrive too late for their own self-interest—proved perfectly willing to sell out the Ohio Indian tribes when it served their purposes. Having already savaged the Ohio Indians during in the "beaver wars" over control of the fur trade in the mid-seventeenth century, the Iroquois now undermined them through diplomacy. In 1768 the Six Nations signed the Treaty of Fort Stanwix (near present-day Rome, New York) with the British.

The "Stanwix line" supposedly resolved the Euro-Indian boundary question by confining settlement to the east and south of the Ohio River. The deal rewarded the Iroquois with silver and trade goods and also opened lands from New York to Kentucky to speculators. The Stanwix Treaty was an especially egregious accord in a long and notoriously dishonest history of Anglo-American diplomacy with indigenous people. Under this "cynical compact," Timothy Shannon points out, the Iroquois "sold thousands of acres of land hundreds of miles away from them to agents whose official credentials barely disguised their private interests." Among those cashing in was the influential go-between William Johnson, who had established kinship ties with the Six Nations through his marriage to Molly Brant (Konwatsi'tsiaienni), from an influential Mohawk family.[41]

Insidious diplomacy only deepened the conflict, as the Ohio Valley Indians, settlers, and speculators were primed for war. On the eve of the American Revolution the innocuously entitled Lord Dunmore's War broke out when the eponymous Virginia governor overturned royal decrees against speculation in Indian lands. Virginia surveyors, settlers, and speculators promptly claimed the colonial space of "Kentucky" as their own. Their encroachment precipitated violent resistance by many of the Shawnee, who would lose their Kentucky hunting grounds thrown open for settlement by the Stanwix line.

Dunmore's War stemmed from a spate of indiscriminate killings of Indians in 1774, some perpetrated by drunken settlers who murdered the indigenes for sport. The killings included the pregnant sister of the Mingo chief Logan, who had embodied colonial ambivalence by living alongside settlers and counseling peace with them. Logan did not hesitate to seek blood revenge, however, as he took 13 settler scalps. Logan declared that through this *proportionate* violence he had satisfied the need for retaliation over the like number of murders of his people, in keeping with indigenous cultural tradition. The conflict could have ended there but Dunmore, declaring that the Indians should be "severely chastised," precipitated a wider war of *indeterminate* violence by ordering the destruction of entire Indian towns and villages and moreover, in deference to the ultimate goal, the seizure and sale of their lands. Dunmore, as Richard White put it, thus "demonstrated how murders occasioned by rum and backcountry settlers could serve the desires of more discreet men to become wealthy."[42]

The difference between Logan and the settler invaders underscored larger cultural distinctions. "Indian culture continued to have some means of limiting the horrors of war," Starkey explains. "The settlers seem to have inhabited a harder world and to have been equipped with very insecure moral anchors. The step to total war was easier for them than it was for their Indian opponents."[43]

At the very time that Dunmore drove Indians from their villages, the First Continental Congress simultaneously began the process of driving the British from the future United States. The American Revolution, framed in historical discourse as a struggle for freedom and self-determination, was simultaneously a campaign to drive Indians out of colonial space. Whereas the Crown had sought however haltingly to regulate westward expansion, land-grabbing settlers received the backing of local and national revolutionary governments in a "dramatic inversion of the earlier model of imperial development." For squatters who had already begun to settle on the borderlands without authorization, Hinderaker points out, "the language, the ideas, and the urgency of the American Revolution all helped to validate their scramble for western lands."[44]

Revolutionary War discourse inculcated the binary of savage Indians impeding enlightened patriots in pursuit of liberty, thus rationalizing driving Indians from the land. The Declaration of Independence excoriated King George for unleashing "on the inhabitants of our frontiers, the merciless Indian savages, whose known rule of warfare is undistinguished destruction of all ages, sexes, and conditions." By blaming the British for inciting Indians, the Americans dismissed the indigenous people as mercenaries, eliding the legitimacy of Indian homeland defense. Subsequent campaigns of Indian removal could be obscured beneath the larger frame of the Revolutionary struggle for the triumph of republicanism over monarchy. The British "were a useful enemy," Andrew Cayton explains, "in that they made it easier to reconcile conquest and liberty."[45]

As the British once again turned to alliance with "the savages" to chastise the rebellious colonials, the Mohawk leader Joseph Brant (Thayendanegea) spearheaded Indian resistance. A prominent example of colonial ambivalence, Brant could hardly be called a savage, as he had graduated from the future Dartmouth College and embraced the Anglican Church. Brant, whose sister had married the go-between William Johnson, "presented a hybrid persona—both genteel and native." Brant gleaned that a British victory in the Revolutionary War offered the only hope of containing the relentless American drive against *all* Indian homelands. The British and their Indian allies thus sought to destroy and terrorize vulnerable pockets of rebellion in the backcountry in order to undermine morale and divert American military resources from other battlefields.[46]

In July 1778 in the Wyoming Valley of Pennsylvania, the Iroquois Confederation joined British forces under Colonel John Butler in a massacre of settlers. The attack centered on the township of Wilkes-Barre, which had been named for rebellious Whigs in the British parliament and had become an American rebel stronghold. In the wave of murder, torture, scalping, and mutilation that followed, the Indians, Butler's rangers, and Tory allies killed 227 while taking only five prisoners. "The massacre of the Wyoming Valley militia illustrated the savagery of frontier fighting and civil war at their bloody worst," Glenn Williams observes.[47]

The Iroquois Confederation would pay a devastating price for allying with the British in the massacre. The Iroquois had long enjoyed relatively peaceful relations with settlers in the Mohawk valley. It was "not until the American Revolution that the Iroquois and New York colonists experienced the same destructive and racially charged warfare that Pennsylvania, Virginia, and other British colonies had experienced much earlier," David Preston notes.[48]

In 1779 the Wyoming valley assault led to a boomerang of exterminatory violence against Loyalists and especially the Iroquois. Under orders from Washington, General John Sullivan's forces routed Loyalists and razed some 40 Iroquois villages in the Finger Lakes region of New York. "The immediate objects of this expedition are accomplished," Sullivan reported to Washington, "total ruin of the Indian settlement, and the destruction of their crops, which were designed for the support of those inhuman barbarians, while they were desolating the American frontiers." Washington pronounced the success of a campaign that had been designed to "relieve our frontiers from the depredations to which they would otherwise be exposed." The Iroquois, who froze to death or died of starvation in droves, ever after dubbed Washington "the Town Destroyer." Washington's search-and-destroy campaign bore "striking similarities with other operations conducted by the US Army later in its history," Williams notes.[49]

American settler colonialism continued to center on the Ohio Valley, a colonial space that Americans now claimed as their own western "frontier." Patriotic discourses exalted yeoman farmers and the spread of republicanism, thus downplaying the self-interested motivations of squatters and land speculators. The settlers constructed forts or "stations" as a means of survival as they "carried the military organization of the frontier settlements to a higher plane." As Indian attacks intensified in the summer of 1777, the Kentucky militia girded for indiscriminate warfare.[50]

Confronted with an existential threat, the indigenes of the Ohio Valley diverged as to how best to respond to the mounting American assault. Zealous young warriors, angered over the loss of their homelands, hunting grounds, and way of life, prepared to fight to the death while ambivalent community elders searched for a diplomatic solution. In 1777, the Shawnee leader Cornstalk blamed some of the borderland violence on the warrior zeal of his own "foolish young men" and embarked on a peace mission. A settler mob in Point Pleasant responded to his call for nonviolence by imprisoning and then executing and mutilating Cornstalk and his son. "Everyone among the Shawnees knew that Cornstalk had been the tireless advocate of accommodation and peace," John Mack Faragher points out, "and their outrage was immeasurable." Meanwhile, other groups of settler colonialists in and around Fort Pitt killed innocent Delaware and Seneca Indians. As a result of this wave of indiscriminate violence, ambivalence lost ground and advocates of extermination ruled the day. The Ohio Indians sought unsuccessfully to recruit Cherokees and Creeks against the Long Knives (settlers), explaining it was "better to die like men than to dwindle away by inches."[51]

Some Revolutionary Americans, George Rogers Clark among them, advocated genocide. "To excel them in barbarity is the only way to make war upon Indians and gain a name among them," avowed Colonel Clark as he launched a raid into southern Ohio and Indiana replete with indiscriminate killing of Indian women and children. In February 1779, Clark sought to make an impression on British territorial Governor Henry Hamilton, notorious among the Americans as the "hair-buyer" for his incitement of the borderland tribes. While Hamilton and his British charges looked on from inside the gates, Clark demanded the surrender of the British fort at Vincennes and drove home his point by bludgeoning an Ottawa Indian named Macutté Mong. After being struck in the head with a tomahawk outside the gates of the decrepit British fort, Macutté Mong withdrew the weapon from his own skull and handed it back to his executioner, mocking his inefficiency. Clark ordered the indigene, still alive, thrown into the Wabash River whereupon he and other captives drowned. When Clark, in the words of Hamilton, with "his hands and face still reeking from the human sacrifice," subsequently took the surrender of the fort, he declared that as to the Indians "for his part he would never spare man, woman or child of them."[52]

The same genocidal drives underlay the Gnadenhutten massacre (discussed in the Preface) in March 1782. A growing number of American settlers could perceive Indians only as savage foes, regardless of their religious conversion and lack of aggression. As one man observed after Gnadenhutten, "On this side of the mountain . . . the country talks of nothing but killing Indians and taking possession of their lands."[53]

Indiscriminate ethnic violence raged across the border lands throughout the Revolutionary War. As Indian prisoners brought no reward, Americans killed them for their scalps, which could be redeemed for cash. When, as often happened, no men of fighting age could be found in a village, the invaders burned the homes and crops, leaving the survivors to forage or starve. "American troops and militia tracked through the Susquehanna, the Allegheny, the Scioto, Miami, and Tennessee valley, leaving smoking ruins and burned cornfields behind them."[54]

The American War of Independence accelerated violent dispossession of Indians in the southern states as well. The Creeks had granted the British a huge land cession in 1763 in return for the promise that their remaining lands would be free of Euro-Americans. But no paper agreement could put a stop to the settlers who flooded into Georgia regardless of Creek claims or British paper restrictions. Ensconced in Florida since the establishment of St. Augustine in 1565, Spain could hold back the tide of American settler colonialism for another generation or two but no longer, as it turned out.[55]

In Carolina American patriots issued "a call for Cherokee genocide" to put an end to ambivalent relations on the borderlands. Race mixing and middle-ground relationships in the backcountry had been a target of the Carolina Regulators, backed by the elite in Charlestown, in the late 1760s. They promoted, as Tom Hatley explains, a "message of support for white on red violence among out of power social groups," which extended to Georgia as well. Many of the settlers had been traumatized by years of conflict with Creeks, Cherokees, and other Indians and longed to cleanse them from the land.[56]

In 1776, raids against borderland settlements carried out by young Cherokee warriors provided the "moment" that many Carolinians had been awaiting to unleash an indiscriminate campaign. Eager rebels called for "the first warfare of our young republic" to be a campaign in which the "awe and dread of the power of the white people" would be driven into "the breast of the Indians." Even previous proponents of ambivalence, such as William Henry Drayton, called for destruction of "every Indian cornfield, and burn every Indian town" and either to enslave or to "extirpate" indigenes. The man who immortalized the phrase "merciless Indian savages," the Virginian Thomas Jefferson, called for the Cherokees to "be driven beyond the Mississippi."

Facing a genocidal assault, the Cherokee abandoned their villages. "We are now like wolves," one of them lamented, "ranging about the woods to get something to eat."[57] The Carolinians admired the Cherokee towns even as they destroyed them, commenting on the fine agricultural fields and "white man-like improvements" in the settlements. Dragging Canoe, leader of the Cherokee warrior faction, advocated fighting back against the scorched earth campaign, declaring that it "seemed to be the intention of the white people to destroy us from being a people." Backed by the British the Cherokees waged an indiscriminate conflict with the settlers throughout the Revolutionary War. In 1782, the settlers ordered their blacksmiths to make special new cutlasses for "intensely violent attacks on the tribe." In 1785, two years after the British recognized American independence, the Cherokee signed a treaty at Hopewell, S.C. establishing a western boundary. The Cherokee had few illusions that the treaties with the whites would hold water; such accords, or "talking leaves," could be expected like leaves to blow away in the wind whenever it suited the Americans to violate them.

Most Cherokee moved deeper into the Appalachian hills and valleys where they "built farmsteads much like those of their American neighbors" and where they remain to this day. Determined Protestant missionaries rode into the backcountry but found the Cherokee little interested. The tribe was, as one member explained, "Too well acquainted with white people to be converted easily." Though decimated by the Revolutionary War era conflict, as they had been a generation earlier, the resilient Cherokee would soon thrive once again until the next major American cleansing campaign targeted them in the 1830s.[58]

During the Revolutionary War, Indian combatants reciprocated the exterminatory violence replete with torture whenever they had the opportunity. In the Battle of Blue Licks in northern Kentucky in August 1782, the Shawnee and Delaware, joined by some 50 Loyalists, soundly defeated the Americans after luring them into a foolhardy frontal assault. Despite such ephemeral victories, the Ohio Valley Indians had already suffered a shattering blow the previous year albeit indirectly when the Americans and their French allies defeated the British Army under General Charles Cornwallis in a culminating battle of the Revolutionary War. Under the Treaty of Paris (1783), the British sold out their Indian allies by recognizing US independence and handing over to the Americans the vast colonial space ranging from the Allegheny Mountains to the Mississippi River and south to the Gulf Coast. As the Creek leader Alexander McGillvray put it, the British had "most shamefully deserted" their Indian allies.[59]

In 1786 the Americans launched a bloody raid through southern Ohio fueling another eight years of exterminatory warfare. The irregular forces burned eight Shawnee villages, disregarding whether these were hostile Indians or not. In a reflection of the simmering hatreds and erosion of ambivalence on the borderlands, Hugh McGary, a Kentuckian who had led the foolish charge at Blue Licks, slaughtered an elderly chief named Moluntha with a tomahawk blow to the head. Moluntha advocated indigenous accommodation to American settler colonialism, represented the Shawnee peace faction, had no connection with the Blue Licks battle, and flew the American flag over his village in Ohio, but he was slaughtered nonetheless.[60]

Among the combatants at Blue Licks as well as the destruction of the Shawnee villages in 1786 was the legendary frontiersman Daniel Boone, who well embodied the transition from ambivalence to ethnic cleansing that characterized the American borderlands. Boone had led the first wave of settlers who "had come west precisely to escape hierarchy and control, and in their radical notions of independent action they resembled no group more than the Indians." In 1777, Boone had been captured by the Shawnee and forced to run the gauntlet. He survived the beating as if he wore a shell on his back; hence the Shawnee dubbed him "big turtle," or Sheltowee, and decided that he could live. Boone was then taken in by Blackfish, the Shawnee chief whom in the Indian tradition "covered the death" of his own son in warfare through adoption. Blackfish came to love Daniel Boone like a son. Boone evolved his hybrid personae in captivity, including intimacy with Indian women. He eventually escaped, went back to Kentucky, and survived a trial for treason for having trucked with the Indians and the British. Eager to reestablish his patriotic bona fides, Boone joined Clark in the scorched earth campaign across Ohio and into Indiana—a state whose name would not convey ultimate ownership. Boone, who had lost two sons and a brother at the hands of Indian violence, helped burn down the stores and villages of the very people who had adopted him, including Old Chillicothe, the center of Shawnee civilization.[61]

During the American Revolution the borderlands became a colonial space of existential violence. Indiscriminate warfare against Indians, which peaked at the very "moment" when Americans achieved their revolutionary ambitions, left a powerful imprint on the emergent national identity. Under the drives of settler colonization, the Americans would not share space or conduct diplomacy on equal terms with the indigenous people. Settler colonialism was a zero-sum game in which only the "unconditional surrender" of the enemy could stem the violence.

Historical denial, projection, and rationalization accompanied the American settler colonial project. Though the British and the Americans were the invaders of space already occupied by other societies, they blamed the "merciless Indian savages" for the violent conflict. They viewed ethnic cleansing as fantasy fulfillment, a reflection of the preordained march of civilization and progress. Colonial and revolutionary discourse depicted Indians as primordial savages and indiscriminate killers thus eliding indigenous ambivalence as well as the genocidal tendencies of the settlers. If anything, as Starkey, White, and other scholars have suggested, the Euro-Americans freed themselves of the restraints of the scope of violence more easily than did the Indians.

Wars had been waged from the arrival of the first Europeans to the end of the American Revolution, yet history has obscured these conflicts. Many of these wars—William's, Pontiac's, Dunmore's—took on innocuous personal names or no name at all. This absence of meaningful names reflected "the unspoken recognition that there was little that was noble about them," Cayton observes.[62]

Shrouded behind a Revolutionary discourse emphasizing the triumph of republicanism were the drives to dispossess and destroy the putatively savage indigenous other. The Americans streaming into the borderlands joined by land speculators and the "founding fathers" back east were determined to take the land and to kill or remove those who stood in their way. The time for trade and diplomacy, compromise and coexistence, had now passed. The Americans sought a final solution to the problem that had long plagued settler expansion onto a "frontier" they called their own.

4

"The Savage and Common Enemy of the Country": US Settler Colonialism to the Mississippi River

Long before Buffalo Bill and later Hollywood romanticized the "Wild West," Indians were driven out of the vast colonial spaces of the eastern half of the North American continent. In the early decades of the nineteenth century, as they faced relentless and unprecedented pressures, indigenous people became divided on how best to respond to the American settler-colonial juggernaut. Through trade, conversion to Christianity, intermarriage, and establishing kinship ties, many Indians had begun to acculturate to Euro-American society. In view of the demographic swamping, these indigenes viewed violent resistance as futile and, while still maintaining their identity as Indians, wanted to get on with their lives.

Other indigenes rejected acculturation and accommodation. They believed that Indians could survive only by retaining indigenous ways, including warfare, and resisting American cultural imperialism as well as the expansion of settlements. During this period, bands such as the Shawnee and the Creeks became bitterly divided over the best means to cope with the settler onslaught. The Americans exploited these divisions to further a national campaign of Indian removal.

As in other settler colonial settings in global history, the Americans confronted the indigenes with "facts on the ground." As immigrants poured into the country, migrating west and south, settlers overwhelmed the indigenous cultures and forced them out of colonial spaces regardless of the degree of their ambivalence or willingness to acculturate. Crucially, the War of 1812 and the US takeover of Florida left Indians bereft of European allies and more vulnerable than ever to American aggression.

The United States preferred to disavow colonialism by dispossessing Indians through legal means, an effort that culminated in the Indian Removal Act (1830). In this landmark act, Americans openly debated and then legislated a national campaign of ethnic cleansing. The stormy debate that ensued over the

Indian Removal Act underscores that Americans, too, were often divided over Indian policy during the early national and antebellum years. Many Americans opposed Indian removal, many others lamented but acquiesced to it, yet still other Americans—especially those living on the borderlands—relished the dispossession and destruction of the savage foes.

Racial formations and national self-righteousness anchored denial and rationalization of Indian removal, as well as the expansion of slavery. Americans viewed themselves as a chosen nation, expanding republicanism and leading the world toward liberation from monarchy and aristocracy. The United States was a sovereign nation-state and as such had a right to settle in defined spaces, whereas Indians were nomadified as primitive hunter-gatherers, children of the forest, warlike people who could not adapt to a rational existence such as tilling the soil while their wives anchored the domestic sphere.[1] Americans proved adept at overlooking the considerable number of indigenes who defied these stereotypes and showed themselves willing and able to acculturate.

As a progressive nation, nothing less than an "empire of liberty," Americans were by their very identity performing good works. Accordingly, inferior races in the path of progress had to give way, or in the case of blacks, they had to perform the labor required for the greater good of mankind. National narcissism thus fueled denial and rationalization of the settler colonial project.

During the early national, Jacksonian, and antebellum eras, Americans cultivated a discourse of nostalgia for the inevitable "passing" of the noble savage. The incorporation of Indians into the symbolic past thus coincided with the actual removal of the tribes to lands west of the Mississippi River. At least since William Bradford at Plymouth, North American settlers had attributed the devastating impact of their diseases to a higher plan from God to displace the savages. No guilt or responsibility had to be assumed in the ebullient young republic for a "dying race" whose fate was the inevitable consequence of providential design.

Framing removal as the best possible solution for Indians assuaged guilt and rationalized ethnic cleansing. Even many Americans who expressed paternal concern for Indians advised that the most prudent course was for them to withdraw to the west, otherwise the least civilized among the white men living within the putatively civilized society might kill them. Ironically, then, it made little difference whether American colonial discourse was benevolent or hate-filled, as they produced the same policy: removal of Indians from colonial spaces desired by whites.

With hundreds of thousands of settlers flowing into the country, indigenous people east of the Mississippi had no choice but to adapt. They did so through a variety of strategies, distinct to time and place including acculturation, trade, alliances, diplomacy, use of the American legal system, spiritual revival, and warfare. Indian violence, however, continued to boomerang against the tribes in a vicious cycle of aggression and retribution. Indian violence traumatized settlers, affirming the colonial discourse of savagery, defying the narrative of a vanishing race, and igniting never deeply subsumed genocidal tendencies. Americans thus engaged in warfare and perpetrated massacres, work that attempted to turn the narrative of the dying race into reality.

Indigenous strategies, whether of accommodation or resistance, ultimately failed because Indian removal inhered in the structure of settler colonialism. Americans left no cultural space for Indians under the fantasy frame wherein it was the white man's providential destiny to take sole command of the continent. Thus, Americans would accept nothing less than removal of Indians from all but a few pockets of the land east of the Mississippi River.

Legacies of the Revolutionary War

Despite their exaltation of freedom and liberty, the American Revolutionaries "shared none of these gains with the Amerindians." Liberated from the restraints formerly imposed by the British, American settlers and speculators descended on their new "frontier" with determination to drive Indians off the land. "The Indian will ever retreat as our settlements advance upon them," George Washington declared in 1783. "The gradual extension of our settlements will certainly cause the savage as the wolf to retire; both being beasts of prey though they differ in shape."[2]

The new nation sought "to place a legal cover" on Indian removal by asserting that the indigenous people had lost all rights to lands east of the Mississippi because some had sided with the British during the Revolutionary War. While the United States depicted the Indians as defeated people, the indigenes, having won most of the Revolutionary War battles and with plenty of fight left in them, did not see it the same way. Americans thus "constructed a national mythology that simplified what had been a complex contest in Indian country, blamed Indians for the bloodletting, and justified subsequent assaults on Indian lands and cultures."[3]

The British Empire had been cast aside but a new form of triangulation emerged, as settlers continued to drive indigenous removal while the federal government sought to gain control of the colonial project. In the Commerce Clause of the US Constitution (1787), the Congress assumed the power to "regulate Commerce with foreign nations, and among the several States, and with the Indian tribes." As uncivilized natives, Indians could not be perceived as "foreign nations" yet the foundational legal document did require the United State to conduct diplomacy with them albeit a diplomacy of annexation. In 1790 the Federal Intercourse Act provided the national government the exclusive right to extinguish Indian title, regulate trade, and negotiate treaties.[4]

Pressing economic motives conjoined with the drives of settler colonization to fuel dispossession of the tribes. Even though it had survived the struggle against the British, the United States remained surrounded by enemies and plagued by a sizable war debt accrued in the Revolutionary War. Only by occupying and converting colonial space into private property could the Americans generate the revenues needed to retire the war debt, address the claims of war veterans, and appease land speculators. Moreover, by seizing Indian land, the United States could better secure its borders against the lurking world powers of Spain, ensconced in the south and eager to foment settler rebellion there, and the British who continued to occupy forts in the northwest until the mid-1790s. The United States sought to gain control of the fluid and expanding borderlands, to build trading posts and military outposts to secure settlement and preclude alliances between Indians and foreign governments.

Viewing aggressive settler colonial expansion as vital for the survival of their young republic, Americans took land from Indians in huge chunks, by treaty cessions if possible, by violent aggression if necessary. "In a series of 'treaties' dictated to the Indians in the mid-1780s," Stuart Banner notes, "the Confederation government confiscated Indian land without paying any compensation." By the mid-1790s, Dorothy Jones concludes, the "great disparity of power" between the United States and indigenous people had forged a treaty system "so unequal that it can only be called colonial."[5]

While both state and federal governments took action from the top down, they were responding to pressures that emanated from the bottom up. The loyalty of settler colonialists to the new republic depended on the backing they received in the taking of Indian land. At least since Bacon's Rebellion (1676) in colonial Virginia, whites had shown that they would rebel against any government that attempted to prevent them from carving out new lands on the self-avowed "frontier." Ever aware of factionalism, the American founders feared the prospect of class warfare or civil tumult unless the country continued to expand and open new lands to squatters, settlers, and speculators.

Both the State of New York and the federal government moved systematically to dispossess the Iroquois, now considered a "subdued people." As General Philip Schuyler told the Six Nations in 1783, "We are now masters and can dispose of the lands as we think proper or more convenient to ourselves." As Alan Taylor points out, the "dual process of dispossessing Indians and creating private property constructed the state of New York, the United States and the British Empire in Canada."[6] New York forced upon the Iroquois vast land cessions for a fraction of their value. The Iroquois resisted vigorously, as they sought to preserve a tenuous hold on their land through negotiations, by proposing leases instead of land sales, and offering direct payments to Americans to stay out of Indian land. They also sought to preserve the Haudenosaunee legal system and cultural practices rather than be subjected to those of New York.

The Mohawk Indian "half-breed" Joseph Brant used his English fluency to appropriate the American discourse of liberty as a strategy of resistance. He and other Iroquois leaders pointed out that Americans were denying them the "natural rights" so eloquently exalted in the Declaration. But the Iroquois, the Cherokee, and other once formidable tribes had suffered a series of crippling blows. The indigenes "reeled from the triple disaster of smallpox, war, and abandonment by their British allies." Nonetheless, scholars note, "The concessions wrung from British and American governments over the colonial and early national eras are testimony to Amerindian political acumen in the face of daunting pressures."[7]

To the west, the Northwest Ordinance (1787) provided a modernist framework for incorporating colonial space into the new nation. The Ordinance, typically framed in American History as the seminal accomplishment under the Articles of Confederation, as it provided for "orderly settlement," laid the groundwork for dispossession of the actual residents of the "northwest." The Ordinance facilitated the incorporation of vast tracts of land comprising the future states of Ohio, Indiana, Illinois, Michigan, and Wisconsin.

The language of the Northwest Ordinance formally disavowed aggression against Indians and the expansion of slavery. The Ordinance proscribed slavery in the territories and then states (some Americans took their slaves into them anyway) and declared, "The utmost good faith shall always be observed towards the Indians." The Ordinance claimed that Indian "lands and property shall never be taken from them without their consent; and, in their property, rights, and liberty, they shall never be invaded or disturbed, unless in just and lawful wars authorized by Congress." The Americans pledged to prevent "wrongs being done to them, and preserving peace and friendship with them."[8]

This discourse of disavowal suggested a degree of American respect for Indian peoples and their property rights incompatible with the settler colonial project. Settlers backed by all levels of government refused to consider compromises that might infringe upon what a subsequent generation would call "manifest destiny." In order for the new republic "to reach its mythological destiny," Frazer McGlinchey observes, "there was to be no 'middle ground' culturally or literally on the future landscape to develop in the Northwest Territory."[9]

As was so often the case, Thomas Jefferson, the architect of the "empire of liberty," personified American ambivalence as well as aggression toward the native peoples. The author of the original Northwest Ordinance (1784), Jefferson voiced profound respect for the indigenes, yet he also "had a working knowledge of the Doctrine of Discovery and used it against the Indians nations."[10] Jefferson displayed empathy for the indigenes in his *Notes on the State of Virginia* (1785), which included the famous though perhaps apocryphal "Logan's Lament." These were statements the Mingo chief supposedly made about having tried his best to get along with the whites only to have his family victimized by atrocity at the outbreak of Dunmore's War (see previous chapter).

The apparent empathy within Jefferson's colonial discourse belied his own knowledge of and personal investment in dispossessing native peoples on the Virginia borderlands. Jefferson perceived Indians as having natural rights, as long as their life, liberty, and pursuit of happiness did not extend to ownership of the land. Jefferson's empire of liberty thus "was keen on land but not on people."[11] Moreover, settler colonialism—landed expansion for the yeoman farmer and slaveholder—anchored Jefferson's Democratic-Republican Party, the most powerful political force in early American history. "For a Jeffersonian Republican administration, the idea of siding with Indians against Americans who sought land would be laughable," Robert M. Owens points out.[12]

Jefferson's ambivalence was invariably paternal and quickly turned bellicose when the native "children" stood in the path of settlement. Jefferson thus "played a major role in one of the great tragedies of recent world history, a tragedy which he so eloquently mourned: the dispossession and decimation of the First Americans," Anthony F. C. Wallace observes. "It was a process now known as 'ethnic cleansing.'"[13]

This ambivalence—a professed empathy for the plight of the indigenes comingled with willingness to remove or exterminate them—epitomized American settler colonial discourse. Jefferson and others offered the same rationalization that Andrew Jackson would employ in 1830, that segregation and removal policies served to protect Indians from the potential genocidal violence of the settlers. Americans thus cleansed Indians from their lands while explaining that removal was the best thing for them, otherwise the settlers might kill them. This was no mere ruse: the US leaders understood that given a chance, settlers *would* kill Indians who got in the way of their expansionist drives. "It is in the highest degree mortifying to find that the bulk of the frontier inhabitants consider the killing of Indians in time of peace to be no crime," Timothy Pickering, Indian commissioner for the United States, observed. The "frontier miscreants," he added, were "far more savage and revengeful than the Indians."[14]

Other officials alluded to the boomerang effect and the pathological nature of colonial violence. "The Whites and Savages will ever prevent their [sic] being good neighbors," Secretary of War Henry Knox explained in 1787. "With minds previously inflamed the slightest offense occasions death—revenge follows which knows no bounds. The flames of a merciless war are thus lighted up which involve the innocent and helpless with the guilty." Despite his seeming ambivalence, Knox like Jefferson and other US leaders could quickly turn lethal when faced with indigenous recalcitrance. When Indians resisted settlers in western Ohio, Knox authorized General Josiah Harmar at Fort Washington (Cincinnati) to "extirpate, utterly, if possible" the indigenous "Banditti."[15]

Ethnic Cleansing of the Ohio Valley

General Arthur St. Clair, the governor of the Northwest Territory, displayed the same willingness to exterminate behind an ambivalent discourse of empathy. He acknowledged that blaming violence on the "savages" obscured the aggression that inhered in settler colonialism. "Though we hear much of the injuries and depredations that are committed by the Indians upon the whites," he observed, "there is too much reason to believe that at least equal if not greater injuries are done to the Indians by the frontier settlers of which we hear very little." Yet the same man ruled out a negotiated settlement with the "indolent, dirty, inanimate creatures" and soon led a disastrous assault against the Ohio Indians.[16]

Ethnic violence raged south of the Ohio River as settlers and Indians engaged in brutal campaigns of irregular warfare. Indians killed some 300 "Kentuckians" from 1783 to 1787 but the latter would not be outdone. "Kentucky pioneers continued to kill their Indian friends as readily as they did their enemies," Stephen Aron ironically observes. Irregular and scorched-earth warfare proved decisive in cleansing the future Bluegrass state. "Once Kentuckians discovered the vulnerability of Indian villages and cornfields, they burned and plundered with devastating effect."[17]

Indians responded to settler colonial expansion with more concerted efforts to craft pan-Indian alliances. Charismatic leaders who had proven themselves during the Revolutionary War—Brant, Alexander McGillvray of the Creeks, the Miami chief Little Turtle, and Blue Jacket of the Shawnee—attempted to forge alliances of homeland defense. Other Indian tribes joined the resistance, including the Mingo, Wea, Potawatomi, Piankashaw, Kickapoo, Mascouten, Munsee, Sauk, Ottawa, and Ojibwa (Chippewa).

North of the Ohio River, a broad coalition of tribes united under Brant's diplomacy as embodied in the United Indian Nations document of 1786, which called for the natives to speak with "one mind and one voice." The vast majority of indigenous people refused to recognize the huge cessions of Indian land, which had been extorted from the tribes for a fraction of their value in the treaties of Fort Stanwix (1784), Fort McIntosh (1785), and at the mouth of the Great Miami River (1786). Brant now proposed the Muskingum Compromise, which offered a boundary line drawn along the Muskingum River in southeastern Ohio between the Stanwix line and the line drawn at the coerced Fort McIntosh treaty, which had ceded virtually all of the Ohio Valley. Invoking the Indian imperative of blood revenge, Brant warned that if the United States rejected diplomacy, the Indians would "most assuredly, with our united force, be obliged to defend those rights and privileges which have been transported to us by our ancestors."[18]

American settler colonialism thus confronted a determined, last-gasp Indian resistance in Ohio. In 1790, the Shawnee under Blue Jacket, joined by the Miami under Little Turtle, decisively repulsed a foolhardy traditional, European-style US military assault led by General Harmar near the (modern day) Indiana–Ohio border. With the Kentucky militia forced into a desperate retreat, St. Clair mobilized an armed force for "vengeance" and "utter destruction" of the Shawnee and Miami, but the Americans instead suffered yet another humiliating and total defeat.

On November 4, 1791, the Americans—disorganized, poorly equipped, absent effective scouts, and blundering headlong into battle much as British General Edward Braddock had done in 1755—suffered a total rout in which some 650 were killed, including 69 of 124 commissioned officers, and 270 wounded, the casualties including scores of women and children. Many of the dead had their mouths stuffed with dirt to mock their lust for Indian land. The indigenes suffered only 21 warriors killed and 40 wounded in the slaughter on the Wabash River. With two and a half times the number dead as Custer's command would suffer at Little Big Horn, it was the worst defeat the army would ever suffer in battle with Indians, yet few Americans know of it today.[19]

The Indian confederates celebrated their decisive victory, but were under no illusions about their future prospects in view of the relentless settler colonial advance. "The pale faces come from where the sun rises, and they are many," Little Turtle lamented. "They are like the leaves of the trees. When the frost comes they fall and are blown away. But when the sunshine comes again they come back more plentiful than ever before."[20]

Some ambivalent Americans in the east blamed the shocking defeat on the headlong rush of the settlers into Indian Territory. Secretary of War Knox responded, however, that even if "it should be admitted that our frontier people have been the aggressors," the federal government had tried to come to terms with the tribes, thus "justice is on the side of the United States."[21] Knox's comment epitomizes the American approach to Indian removal: it would seek to accomplish the project humanely and through diplomacy but when Indians resisted giving up colonial space, "justice" was on the side of military aggression and ethnic cleansing.

Americans mobilized for violent retribution under the command of General "Mad" Anthony Wayne, who declared his eagerness to lay siege to the "haughty and insidious enemy." Provided with an (at the time) massive $1 million federal appropriation, Wayne mobilized an infantry of 2,200 men backed by 1,500 Kentucky volunteers eager for revenge. Underscoring the limitations of the pan-Indian movement, ambivalent Choctaw and Chickasaw mercenary "scouts" came up from the South to assist the US assault on the northern tribes. In the by now deeply rooted tradition, irregular forces were offered bounties for as many scalps as they could deliver. Wayne methodically constructed forts at Greenville, Fort Recovery (the site of St. Clair's defeat), and further north at Fort Defiance. The Indians held out the hope of assistance from the British, still ensconced in the northwest forts, but their former allies instead in 1794 agreed to withdraw under the Jay Treaty from the territory they had formally already ceded to the Americans in the 1783 Treaty of Paris.[22]

Wayne's careful planning and mobilization led to a decisive victory flowing from a by now well-ensconced American style of counterinsurgency warfare. Wayne unleashed his rangers on Indian villages and cornfields throughout the Miami and Maumee River Valleys. American History texts focus on the anticlimactic Battle of Fallen Timbers (1794) but it was the scorched-earth campaign against Indian homes and agricultural stocks that shattered the resistance. Wayne "laid waste the Indian country along the Maumee, destroyed even the British agents' houses and fields." The Americans "left evident marks of their boasted humanity behind them," the Shawnee-raised "white" Alexander McKee sardonically observed, noting that the invaders scalped and mutilated their victims and unearthed graves.[23]

Adorned in a scarlet jacket and gold epaulets, Blue Jacket met Wayne in the field to surrender the upper Ohio country to the American general. The ambivalent Shawnee chief had associated closely with the British and French, lived in a nice home with his French-Shawnee wife, owned livestock and black slaves, traded in alcohol, and sent his son to Detroit for education. Wayne and others grasped the importance of co-opting indigenous leaders such as Blue Jacket, who was soon provided with bribes and given a commission in the US Army. Blue Jacket thereafter cultivated the Western lifestyle and indulged his taste for liquor.[24]

On August 3, 1795, with the Americans having proven "relentless in their determination to terrorize the Indians of the Wabash and the Maumee into accepting their wishes," representatives of the Delaware, Shawnee, Miami, Wea, and Piankashaw signed off on the loss of their homelands following elaborate ceremonies. Little Turtle held out as long as he could before acquiescing to the Treaty of Greenville, which the president signed and the US Senate ratified.[25] The indigenes gave up claims to south-central Ohio and a portion of Indiana in return for trade-goods, annuities, and promises that would not be fulfilled of preservation of their remaining pockets of land from additional settlement. With the Indians defeated, the white population of Ohio rocketed from 5,000 in 1796 to 230,000 by 1810.[26]

The decade following the Greenville Treaty proved "simply disastrous for the Indians on the Wabash and its tributaries." The settler influx brought influenza and smallpox epidemics while depleting the forests and animal populations. The Miami, Shawnee, and Delaware villages suffered "the full effects of spatial, ecological, and cultural dislocation." Even William Henry Harrison, governor of the Indiana territory, condemned his countrymen for their "monstrous abuse" of the land, pointing out that the average hunter killed more game "than five of the common Indians."[27]

Harrison, a Virginian who imported African-Americans as "de-facto slaves" into the future Hoosier state, had complete authority over Indian policy and set about to clear the indigenes from the land. Harrison was "especially relentless, resourceful, and ruthless" in dispossessing Indians. He rationalized that US expansion advanced civilization and generated revenue and taxes. Moreover, white American settlement enjoyed divine sanction. There was "nothing so pleasing to God as to see his children employed in the cultivation of the earth," Harrison explained to the indigenes while appropriating three million acres of their land at the Treaty of Fort Wayne (1809).[28]

Indian Homeland Defense in the "War of 1812"

Though driven out of the Ohio Valley, indigenes mobilized resistance in the Indiana territory behind two charismatic leaders, the Shawnee brothers Tecumseh and Tenskwatawa. The latter, like many Indians had fallen into drunkenness and despair but pulled out of it and underwent a powerful personal spiritual revival. Soon known as The Prophet, Tenskwatawa preached that the whites and their ways were evil and the path to salvation lay in a return to Indian ways of living, dressing, speaking, worshipping, and consuming. If Indians could unite against settler colonialism and shed themselves of the contamination of pale face culture, they might yet survive, the brothers and their followers believed.

The spiritual resistance movement was intertribal, "integrated the religious and the political," and spanned generations. Tenskwatawa's message echoed the Delaware prophet Neolin, who had called for rejection of "white people's ways and nature" on the eve of the Indian resistance at the end of the French and Indian War. Tenskwatawa gave Indians hope, spurred cultural renewal, and cleared the way for his brother to mobilize violent resistance. Many indigenes responded to the appeal to return to Indian ways out of a growing conviction that commercial engagement with whites had weakened them, both spiritually and materially. The whites had introduced disease, alcoholism, and prostitution while the fur trade and other extractive industries had depleted resources and fostered economic dependence. Market forces had eroded the indigenous way of life while Christianity threatened spiritual and cultural traditions. By casting off the white ways, Indians rejected dependency and sought to regain control of their lives and, they hoped, to preserve their lands as well.[29]

As would occur at Wounded Knee, South Dakota, in 1890, Indian spiritual revival aroused powerful American anxieties followed by indiscriminate violence.

By clinging to colonial space desired by Americans and attempting to revivify their spirituality, Indians were refusing to play their designated role as a "dying race." By uniting Indian bands, they were defying the American divide and conquer strategy. Thus the movement would have to be stopped and resistant Indians dispossessed or killed.

Despite his contempt for the Americans, who had killed his father and two brothers and driven him from his burning village as a boy, Tecumseh proved willing to try diplomacy. However, his meeting with Harrison in 1810 at Vincennes went badly. The governor had no intention of compromising with a savage. From his sitting position on the ground—having deliberately turned down the white man's offer of a chair in which to sit like a "civilized" man—Tecumseh explained to Harrison, "You have taken our lands from us and I do not see how we can remain at peace with you if you continue to do so." Tecumseh urged Harrison to convince James Madison to return lands confiscated in the Treaty of Fort Wayne or else the president could "sit still in his town, and drink his wine, while you and I will have to fight it out." When Harrison responded lamely that Americans had forever shown a "uniform regard to justice," Tecumseh, according to Harrison, leaped to his feet and "with the most violent gesticulations and indications of anger" stalked out of the meeting.[30]

While Tecumseh traveled south to organize pan-Indian resistance, Harrison set out with 1,200 soldiers to destroy Prophetstown, the center of the Indian spiritual renewal. On November 7, 1811, the Indians attacked Harrison's approaching forces along Tippecanoe Creek. The unprepared Americans suffered much heavier casualties than the outnumbered indigenes, who were eventually forced to abandon the attack and melt into the countryside. They burned Prophetstown behind them. Harrison represented the battle as a glorious triumph over British-incited savages and infused his report with melodrama—"To their savage fury our troops opposed that cool and deliberate valor which is characteristic of the Christian soldier." Harrison emerged from the modest battle as "the hero of Tippecanoe," a legacy that helped him claim a short-lived presidency 30 years later.[31]

The battle of Tippecanoe actually settled nothing, but the subsequent War of 1812 would prove as devastating for Midwestern Indians as the Revolutionary War had been for those living in the eastern states and the Ohio Valley. Known primarily as the second American war to secure independence against the British, the history of the conflict, as with conventional histories of the Revolutionary War, obscures the US campaigns of Indian dispossession. The War Hawks, a congressional faction representing the new "western" states, had agitated for war out their desire to drive Indians from the land in order to free up colonial space for their constituents.[32]

Irregular warfare between Americans and Indians replete with atrocities on both sides raged across the borderlands during the innocuously entitled War of 1812. As was usually the case, open warfare undermined ambivalence and ignited the American impulse to exterminate the "merciless Indian savages." Jefferson declared that the Indian resistance would "oblige us now to pursue them to extermination, or drive them to new seats beyond our reach." The sage of Monticello projected US settler colonial aggression onto the British and the Indians, rendering them the aggressors thereby rationalizing American settler colonialism as a purely defensive reaction.[33]

While glossing over their own indiscriminate killing, Americans publicized Indian massacres as confirmation of the primordial savagery of the indigenes. In January 1813, a group of Indians, having swilled a case of American whiskey, slaughtered 30 to 40 wounded Americans in eastern Michigan following the Battle of River Raisin, the largest battle of the War of 1812 and a defeat for the United States. The American press was aflame with stories of the killings, but as Armstrong Starkey points out, "the 'massacre' occurred against the background of indiscriminate American scorched earth tactics in the Indian villages."[34]

In September 1813, following a series of setbacks, including a reprise of their Revolutionary War invasion of Canada, the United States took control of the Great Lakes in the Battle of Lake Erie and the British began to retrench. Disgusted once again with the unreliable European ally, Tecumseh declared the British were "like a fat animal that carries its tail upon its back" but, when frightened, "drops its tail between its legs and runs off."[35] The indigenous war effort deflated with the news that on October 5 Tecumseh had been found dead and mutilated after the battle on the Thames River. Exhausted by the Napoleonic wars, the British settled for burning Washington, DC, and withdrawing. In December 1814, the Treaty of Ghent brought a return to the status quo ante.[36]

The death of Tecumseh and their abandonment by the British left Indians demoralized whereas American patriotic fervor soared in the wake of the War of 1812. Like the Revolution of 1776 and the Louisiana Purchase (1803), the War of 1812 powerfully affirmed the national fantasy of providential destiny to inherit the continent. In the postwar "era of good feelings," a sense of "revitalized national strength, liberal individualism, and godly affirmation of the republic surfaced everywhere in peace commemorations."[37]

The War of 1812 created "a powerful anti-Indian faction in the national government" including the War Hawk congressmen and two future presidents, Harrison and Jackson. Support for settler colonialism by means of ethnic cleansing thus provided the foundation for a successful political career in the United States. The Battle of the Thames alone "produced a president, a vice president, three governors, three lieutenant governors, four senators, twenty congressmen, and a host of lesser officials."[38]

As in the Revolutionary War, the Treaty of Ghent excluded the Indian savages from any involvement in the white man's diplomacy. The French dictator Napoleon Bonaparte had sold off a monumental portion of Indian land in the Louisiana Purchase and the British had now done the same thing to their Indian allies. The Americans laughed off a half-hearted British proposal of an independent Indian nation in the Old Northwest. Having won most of the battles on the upper Great Lakes and upper Mississippi Valley during the War of 1812, the indigenes could scarcely believe that they once again would be denied the fruits of their victories at the negotiating table. The tribes faced an ominous future with the ouster of the British. Determined "to expel the British entirely from the Indian country," the Americans proceeded to construct new forts on the upper Mississippi River and along the western shore of Lake Michigan.[39]

To gain the British signature on the Ghent Treaty, the United States disingenuously pledged in Article IX to make peace with the Indians and "forthwith to restore to such tribes or nations, respectively, all the possessions, rights, and privileges which they may have enjoyed or been entitled to" before the war broke out.[40] This insincere pledge was as empty as its counterpart in the Northwest Ordinance hence the indigenous people again faced a reinvigorated tide of righteous American settler colonial expansion.

Many Americans living along the borderlands had been traumatized by their defeats at the hands of the Indian savages. The humiliating US surrender of Fort Detroit, for example, came in the wake of a British general's threats to unleash on the Americans "the numerous body of Indians who have attached themselves to my troops." Having now survived the second war with Britain, many Americans longed to destroy the "merciless" savages to ensure that they never again posed such a threat. Like the Pennsylvania settlers who besieged Gnadenhutten, these western settlers sought total security—a final solution to the Indian problem.[41]

With the exterminatory impulse at the forefront, the Americans proved equally hostile to the considerable numbers of Indians who had fought *with* them in the War of 1812. In western Ohio, the remaining Shawnee, Wyandot, Seneca, Miami, Potawatomi, Ottawa, and Kickapoo had joined in the battle, often under coercion. As one Ohioan explained to the Indian residents of the Buckeye state, "War is our trade and you cannot live quiet and take no part in it." The War of 1812 "especially divided the Shawnee," as more members of the tribe had fought against Tecumseh than with him at the Battle of the Thames. The indigenes had shown their ambivalence by fighting other Indians, thereby "rejecting the binary racial and ethnic division" that prevailed strongly among Americans.[42]

The Shawnee who had sided with the Americans nonetheless endured persistent harassment from borderland settlers because they were racialized as Indians rather than respected as allies. During the War of 1812 the Kentucky, militia betrayed an inclination to attack any and all Indians on general principles. With news of the River Raisin massacre, "settlers burned many Shawnee cabins, stole their livestock, and physically abused several Shawnee tribesmen." Settlers tried to assassinate the "progressive" Shawnee chieftain Black Hoof, who had joined Harrison in the invasion of Canada, shooting him in the face as he conferred with a US general.[43]

Many Indians had been moved onto newly created reservations and received federal annuities but others had settled successfully and begun to acculturate within Ohio communities. These ambivalent indigenes had learned to provide for themselves and wanted to live with their white neighbors. "We have good homes here" and had invested the "labor and pains to make them," a Shawnee explained. These Indians had successfully adapted, fought on the American side in the war, and were "willing to walk the white man's road." Yet when they tried to claim "all the privileges of the white male inhabitants" their actions aroused opposition from "the honorable part of this community," a resident of Bellafontaine declared. In 1824, citing drunkenness and occasional violent clashes between whites and "roving Indians," the Ohio governor pronounced the remaining Shawnee "morally depraved" and thus subject to removal.[44]

Forced by the Treaty of Miami Rapids (1817) into a small reserve near Black Hoof's village at Wapakoneta, Ohio, the Shawnee built cabins, raised crops, and sent their children to schools. The American settlers, viewing the Indians as "out of time and place in the linear conception of 'progress,'" drove them out of Wapakoneta and appropriated their lands and cabins. In the two decades following the War of 1812, "the Americans forced most Shawnee to yield their lands and to seek refuge across the Mississippi." Told in 1831 that they would get no legal protection and thus "might be beaten or killed by white men," the remaining Shawnee contingent at Wapakoneta had no choice but to sign a removal treaty.[45]

Just as the Prophet, Tecumseh, and other spiritual leaders had predicted, efforts to accommodate the Americans came to grief. While Indians manifested colonial ambivalence through their willingness to live and fight with Americans against other Indians, the United States exalted the superiority of white people. Indigenous people had shown that they would transcend a common identity as Indians in order to keep their homes and try to carve out some cultural space within US society, but Americans in this period were intent on affirming the racial identity of the country as a white man's republic. While slavery expanded dramatically in the South, Americans north of the Mason–Dixon Line exalted whiteness with no less enthusiasm than their southern brethren.[46]

The war and continuing settler colonial expansion finished off the ambivalence embodied in the "middle ground" in which Indians and Euro-Americans, mainly French, had lived, traded, and intermarried in mixed communities since well before the advent of the United States.[47] As settlers flooded into the territories after the War of 1812, ethnic cleansing soon followed. As they entered the federal union, Kentucky (1792), Tennessee (1796), Ohio (1803), Indiana (1816), Illinois (1818), Michigan (1837), Iowa (1846), and Wisconsin (1848) simultaneously drove out not only Indians but also "half-breeds." As with African-Americans, in a republic that celebrated the purity of the "white race," mixed bloods were considered members of an inferior order of humanity.

Many Trails of Tears

While historical discourse has focused overwhelmingly on Indian removal in the Southeast—and especially on the infamous Cherokee "Trail of Tears"—the "equally egregious behavior of people in the Old Northwest has generally escaped historical notice." Death, disease, corruption, and perfidy characterized Midwestern Indian removal in the aftermath of the War of 1812. "Rations supplied to emigrating Indians were so spoiled that militia accompanying the removal refused to eat them," Susan Sleeper-Smith explains, "and Native women were forced to prostitute themselves to obtain food for their families." Michigan Indians escaped the worst of it, as many Ottawa and Ojibwa migrated to relatively undesirable lands in the northern portion of the territory and the upper peninsula near the Canadian border. Americans removed only some 650 out of about 8,000 Michigan Indians, hence by 1853 about a third of the indigenous people still living east of the Mississippi River resided in Michigan.[48]

As settler colonialism, patriotic nationalism, the market economy, and military fortifications converted colonial space into American space, Indians were driven across the Mississippi River. The staggering influx of settler colonials destroyed indigenous hunting grounds and cultural autonomy. Wisconsin, for example, grew from 11,000 people in 1836 to more than 300,000 by 1850. In Illinois land sales catapulted from less than 100,000 acres a year in 1829 to two million acres in 1836.[49]

As the Sac chief Black Hawk discovered, Americans meant to cleanse the eastern side of the Mississippi of Indians. The roots of the so-called Black Hawk War dated to 1804 when Harrison "negotiated" a huge land cession from an unrepresentative group of Sac and Fox Indians that he had plied with liquor. Later, the Sacs, Foxes, Winnebago, and other tribes had been inspired by Tecumseh and the Prophet to resist American settler colonialism in modern-day Illinois and Wisconsin. Many young warriors destroyed the property of whites and attacked and murdered them with a vengeance. After a campaign of irregular warfare, US volunteers put down a Winnebago "rebellion" in 1827 and used the occasion to seize additional Indian land. "The Winnebago war of 1827 convinced most Indians in the region that the Americans were too numerous and powerful to contest by force of arms," John Hall notes, "but some retained the hope that a pantribal alliance could punish white transgressions and establish a more favorable balance of power."[50]

Black Hawk and the Sac had not wanted war—they crossed the Mississippi on a hunt for increasingly scarce game—and neither were they aware of the vast cessions of Indian land. Once fighting erupted in 1832, Black Hawk waged a powerful resistance as he held off a much larger force in the Battle of Wisconsin Heights. However, at the subsequent "Battle" of Bad Axe—actually a massacre—a large federal force and hundreds of volunteers killed some 500 Indians. Many of the indigenes were "needlessly and ruthlessly slaughtered." Some Americans tried with limited success to stop others from killing innocent women and children. One volunteer boasted that the irregular forces "killed everything that didn't surrender" including "three squaws [who] . . . were naked" after having been sexually assaulted.

Consistent with other settler colonial settings, the Bad Axe massacre was neither isolated nor incidental but rather capped off the cleansing campaign. It was a "great misfortune" that women and children had been killed, a volunteer mused, but the "Ruler of the Universe" had seen fit for the battle to transpire in that way. Moreover, the Indians were "the savage enemy and the common enemy of the country" and thus deserving of their fate. Despite such demonizing discourse, many Indians, ambivalent about conflict with the Americans, rallied behind the accommodationist Sauk chief Keokuk, who opposed the war and eventually displaced Black Hawk as the leader of the tribe. Keokuk "attempted to walk a tightrope" as he strove "to placate American officials while at the same time protecting his people from both the [marauding] Sioux and unruly white settlers."[51]

The federal government exploited the "savage" resistance in the Black Hawk War to rationalize extension of settler colonialism across the borderlands. As the Americans removed Indians from land in present-day Iowa, the Sac and Fox coalesced into a single tribe, migrated to Kansas, and were later forced into the Indian territory of Oklahoma. Americans continued to exploit their ambivalent Indian allies for military assistance only to abandon them once the conflict came to an end. Potawatomi and Winnebago bands had allied with the United States in the Black Hawk War but their "fidelity would be forgotten in the rising demand that all Indians be removed beyond the Mississippi." As one Winnebago belatedly concluded, "We think the Big Father does not care for us any longer, now that he has all our best land." Within two decades "virtually the entire region passed into the hands of the federal government," Patrick Jung points out.[52]

Settler colonialists in the southeastern United States orchestrated the most well known Indian Removal program in American History. The Cherokee had long occupied mountainous regions of Kentucky, Tennessee, North Carolina, and Georgia; the Creeks (Muskogee) had vast holdings in what became the states of Mississippi, Georgia, Alabama, and Florida; the Seminole split off from the Creeks in Florida while the Choctaw and Chickasaw lived further west in the Mississippi territory. All would be subjected to a relentless campaign of state and federal ethnic cleansing and each would have its own "trail of tears."

Though culminating in the 1830s, southeastern Indian Removal had been a gradual process driven by the settler colonial project. The Cherokee, their population already halved from 1700 to 1775 by smallpox and other diseases, suffered further devastating losses in the American Revolution. When they had joined the Shawnee and British in resistance, American settlers vowed to "carry fire and sword into the very bowels of *their country.*" (emphasis added). Americans conducted scorched earth campaigns against Cherokee villages, crops, and stores. By the end of the American Revolution the Cherokee population had dropped to some 10,000 and they had lost three-fourths of their homelands and hunting grounds and more than half their villages. Squatter and missionary invasions followed, backed by the Jefferson administration, which took additional land cessions in treaties of 1804 and 1806.[53]

All the tribes felt the effects of the Revolutionary War, disease, squatter infiltration, erosion of hunting grounds, and cultural dissolution. The Creek resisted American settler colonialism in the Revolutionary War era. Although the governor of Georgia vowed, "Your conduct towards us long since has authorized our putting flames to your towns, and indiscriminately killing your people," the settlers could not yet carry out their palpable desire to extirpate the Creeks.[54] To the west the Choctaw and Chickasaw, "nations" remained intact as well.

The American victory in the War of 1812 eroded the ambivalence toward the indigenous people and paved the way for the Indian removal campaign. Most Americans agreed with John C. Calhoun, whose grandfather Patrick Calhoun had been killed in a Cherokee raid at Long Cane in the Carolina backcountry. Calhoun declared that victory over Britain and its Indian allies in the War of 1812 had brought an "important change." With the British ally driven out of the west, Indians had now "ceased to be an object of terror," hence there was no longer any need to negotiate with them. Instead, "Our views of their interest, and not their own, ought to govern them." In 1824 Calhoun placed the new Office of Indian Affairs under his supervision within the Department of War.[55]

Divisions within the tribes facilitated the emerging American cleansing campaign. By the 1790s the Creeks had split into rival Upper and Lower bands, the former more acculturated, *mestizo*, economically well heeled, and by now "deeply alienated from most Creek traditions and the vast majority of the Creek people." The most prominent representative of this group was McGillvray, the son of a Scotsman and a Creek woman, who upon his death in 1792 left a landed estate with some 300 heads of cattle and worked by 60 slaves. In an effort to preserve their own privileged position, the Upper Creeks embraced "civilization" over Indian ways and "ceded to the United States the very hunting grounds that most people depended on for survival." During the "hungry period" of the 1790s, "wealthy Creeks continued to fare well, while hunters and hoers suffered without relief." Accommodation to Euro-American culture thus brought class conflict and "an astounding degree of inequality" to Indian country. The arrival of Tecumseh into Creek country on the eve of the War of 1812 sowed further divisions, as the Upper Creeks disdained the Shawnee leader's efforts to mobilize pan-Indian resistance to the Americans while the Lower Creeks embraced it.[56]

A "devastating civil war" within the Creeks unfolded in concert with the War of 1812, a reminder that savage conflict was not limited to clashes between whites and indigenes. The Lower Creeks—now called Red Sticks for the red clubs they carried in solidarity with Tecumseh's pan-Indian cultural revival—attacked settlers and mixed bloods viciously and indiscriminately. On August 29, 1813, the Fort Mims Massacre north of Mobile marked the apogee of this violence, as the Red Sticks slaughtered some 500 mixed-blood Creeks and white settlers. On March 27, 1814, in the culmination to a scorched-earth campaign through Creek country, General Jackson led a 2,500-man force of Tennessee militia, Upper Creek, and Choctaw allies against the Red Sticks. After hemming them in at Tohopeka or the "Horseshoe Bend" of the Tallapoosa River, Jackson's forces slaughtered more than 800 Red Sticks—557 in the battle and some 300 more who plunged into the river and tried unsuccessfully to swim to safety. "To make the body count accurate," Andrew Burstein notes, "the Tennesseans sliced off the tips of the dead Creeks' noses one by one."[57]

In the Treaty of Fort Jackson, signed on August 9, 1814, the US war with the Creeks formally ended with a massive annexation of more than half of all Creek land, a huge swath of colonial space across the American southeast. Thus, as with its Indian allies in previous wars, the United States had no intention of rewarding the ambivalent Indians for their wartime alliance by allowing them to keep their land but instead would take it for the benefit of land speculators and settlers. Although the Upper Creeks eventually received compensation for destroyed property, the war within had fatally compromised the Creeks as a whole.

Like Jefferson, Jackson embodied ambivalence toward the natives, an ambivalence that easily gave way to indiscriminate killing and removal. Jackson allied and fought side by side with Indians, sometimes spoke admiringly of them, yet he had long viewed the indigenes as a menace "constantly infesting our frontier." Writing to Harrison after the Battle of Tippecanoe, Jackson declared, "The blood of our murdered countrymen must be avenged... That banditti must be swept from the face of the earth."[58] An unapologetic slaveholder, whose first purchase as a single man was a 19-year-old slave girl, Jackson had become a self-made borderland elite in Tennessee but needed military heroism on his resume in order to realize his national political ambitions. Following Horseshoe Bend, Jackson became Major General in the US Army, the highest rank in the nation. His victory over the British in the Battle of New Orleans in January 1815 made Jackson the country's most popular military hero since the venerable Washington. Well representing American ambitions, Jackson set his sight on Florida and characteristically would brook no opposition in his determination to "liberate" the peninsula from the Spanish and the Indian "banditti."

Spain had occupied Florida for three centuries but American settlers, filibusterers, and the federal government strove to bring an end to Spanish colonialism in the southeast. Spain had lost Florida once, after the French and Indian War in 1763; got it back in the Treaty of Paris in 1783; and then allied with Britain and the Florida Indians against the Americans in the War of 1812. In response to American filibustering expeditions into Spanish East Florida on the eve of the War of 1812, Spain encouraged Indian assaults and guerrilla attacks on American settler enclaves.

The Spanish and the southeastern tribes fully grasped the US intent and attempted to band together to ward off an American takeover. The indigenous tribes proved willing to recognize Spanish possessions in exchange for recognition of their own. In contrast to the aggressive Americans, Spain recognized lands that "legitimately and indisputably" belonged to the tribes. Spain pursued indigenous-style kinship ties, offered the Indians "lavish tribute," and no longer sought to convert them to Catholicism. In a culminating treaty at the Fort of Nogales in 1793, the Alabama, Creek, Choctaw, Chickasaw, Cherokee, and Tallapoosa accepted Spain's "protection" and in return the tribes recognized Spanish Louisiana and Florida.[59]

Americans damned the Spanish "Dons" as dishonorable for taking on "savages," but even more disturbing than colluding with the Indians was Spain's deployment of runaway slaves, so-called "maroons" that Americans considered "the vilest species" of opponent. Ambivalence and mixed loyalties still prevailed in Florida, where the settlers had long traded and interacted with Indians. But as the indigenes began "setting fire to their plantations, and ravaging their farms," Americans set out to drive the Indians and the Spaniards from the land in the wake of the War of 1812.[60]

Under Jackson's hyper-aggressive masculine drive, Americans launched their assault on Spanish Florida in the so-called First Seminole War. The reference to the Seminole was generic, encompassing Creeks who had migrated south to Florida but also Alachua, Miccosukee, Tallahassee, and Apalachicola Indians. After Horseshoe Bend, Jackson sent the Seminole and Red Sticks in flight to the Apalachicola swamps of West Florida. The United States built Fort Gadsden and other military posts and laid siege to the so-called "Negro Fort" where blacks and Indians were holding out along the Apalachicola River. On July 27, 1816, a red-hot cannonball fired from a US gunboat hit the magazine at the fort, blowing to pieces at least 40 defenders and forcing the remaining resistance to disperse.[61]

The explosion and burning of the "Negro Fort" carried important symbolic value to the Americans, who may have inflated the body count in using the figure of 300.[62] As to the fatal bomb, "The great Ruler of the Universe must have used us as instruments in chastising the blood-thirsty and murderous wretches that defended the fort," a brigadier general explained. Jackson took as a green light (not that he would have heeded a red one) James Monroe's non-response when he informed the president that he could take all of Florida from the Spanish within 60 days. After razing several Seminole villages, Jackson, on April 6, 1818, seized Fort Marks from the Spanish, hanging two British subjects in the process. Secretary of State John Quincy Adams provided Spain a face-saving diplomatic gloss through the subsequent Adams-Onîs or Transcontinental Treaty (1819), which formally turned over Florida and, significantly, also recognized US boundaries to the Pacific Ocean. Once again Europeans had signed over to the Americans land inhabited by tens of thousands of indigenous people. Americans would learn, however, that the indigenes would not go from Florida (or the West) without a long and bitter fight.[63]

Jackson's regenerative violence opened new lands for settler colonialism and slavery and propelled him to the White House, where he made Indian Removal his top priority. Characteristically, nothing would deter him: Indian resistance, political rivals, weak-willed eastern reformers, even the Supreme Court, all would be swept aside. Yet Jackson was the agent not the progenitor of the removal program. Indian removal inhered in the structure of settler colonialism, which began evolving long before Jackson or the United States itself had come to exist. The style may have been Jackson's but the substance represented continuity with previous American and Euro-American history of advancing "civilization" by driving indigenous people from the land.[64]

Proponents of the Indian Removal Act (IRA) of 1830 overcame opposition to secure passage of a full-blown, nationally legislated program of ethnic cleansing. The legislation invoked the familiar discourse of disavowal, as it provided funding for "such tribes or nations of Indians *as may choose* [emphasis added] to exchange the lands where they now reside" for "districts" west of the Mississippi River that were not currently part of any state or territory. Indians of course did not "choose" removal nor did the United States keep its pledge to "forever secure and guarantee to them, and their heirs or successors, the country so exchanged with them." Secretary of War John Eaton openly declared that treaties with Indians were never meant to be permanent. A member of the House committee on Indian affairs acknowledged that treaty making was an "empty gesture" meant to appease the "vanity of tribal leaders."[65]

Indian removal dramatically underscores the zero-sum nature of settler colonial expansion, as the Americans strove to remove all Indians regardless of their level of acculturation. Indian removal targeted the "five civilized tribes" of the southeast who had done the most to appropriate the culture of "civilization." Thousands of indigenes spoke English, lived and dressed like Americans, had adopted white gender roles, and even owned slaves. Many Americans who "thought it had been right to supplant the savage hunter with the civilized farmer" now questioned whether it was right to "remove the Indian farmer so the white farmer could enjoy his country."[66]

The IRA aroused intense opposition from masses of Americans. The opponents came overwhelmingly from north of the Mason–Dixon line and many linked the defense of Indians with their growing opposition to slavery as well as to what they perceived as overweening Southern political influence over the nation. Women proved especially active in the opposition and were behind a massive anti-removal petition campaign that went before the Congress. Many of those who defended the indigenes but ultimately lost the battle went on to found organizations such as the American Antislavery Society.[67]

Many of the opponents of Indian Removal and of slavery were Protestant reformers who pointed out that many Indians had acculturated and converted to Christianity. Protestant missionaries, aided by the federal Civilization Act of 1819, had long been streaming into Indian country to save souls, a project that gained momentum with the spread of the Second Great Awakening. Indians were among the tens of thousands of converts in the midst of fiery Methodist revivals. Many Indians, especially mixed bloods, responded to the emotional call, which to some complemented Indian religious traditions. Other Indians merely feigned conversion as a means of getting their children an opportunity for education in the mission schools. In 1822, for example, a Choctaw leader wrote, "We wish to follow the ways of the white people. We hope they will assist us in getting our children educated."[68]

Turning a deaf ear to antiremoval as well as antislavery forces, Jackson and his southern stalwarts meant to appropriate colonial space from any and all Indians. The settlers and speculators of Georgia, Alabama, and Mississippi wanted Indian land for themselves and together with the hero president they prevailed over the ambivalent opponents of Indian removal. The invention of the cotton gin and the profitability of cotton in the burgeoning market economy made the drive for dispossession all the more urgent. Moreover, gold had been discovered on Cherokee land in 1829. With wealth, progress, and white supremacy on the line, Georgia politicians branded Indians "useless and burdensome" and a "race not admitted to be equal."[69]

Despite the blatancy of Jackson and his constituents, Americans drenched the removal program within a rationalizing discourse of benevolent paternalism. As Indians were "a vanishing race," removal was the only means to protect these "children" from harm. Even opponents of Indian Removal such as Jackson's rival Henry Clay dubbed Indians "essentially inferior" as well as "rapidly disappearing" and "destined to extinction." Lewis Cass averred in a familiar refrain that removal was the "only means of preserving the Indians from utter destruction." As a result of "popular acceptance of the theory of the Vanishing American," Brian Dippie points out, "the humanitarian argument for removal was not easily refuted." As the Frenchman Alexis Tocqueville sardonically observed, "It is impossible to destroy men with more respect for the laws of humanity."[70]

The ambivalent among the Choctaw, who had fought with Jackson against the Red Sticks and again at New Orleans, found that their indigeneity far outweighed their acculturation and loyalty to the United States. "Jackson played into the naiveté of the Choctaws, who up to this point actually thought they were a valued ally and friend to the United States," Donna Akers explains. The Choctaw reasoned that they had become integrated into the nation's market economy, as they had shifted from selling deerskins in an exchange economy to successful cattle farming.[71]

Despite such expectations Jackson, whom the Indians called "Sharp Knife," made it clear to the Choctaw that "he would stop at nothing to obtain their dispossession and exile." After forcing the Treaty of Dancing Rabbit Creek (1830) down the throats of the Choctaw, Eaton mendaciously reported to Congress that the tribe had consented to voluntary removal. The Treaty of Dancing Rabbit Creek thus "was procured with the rankest sort of dishonesty and foul play on the part of the US government negotiators." From 1831 to 1836, the United States dispossessed the Choctaw of 11 million acres and forcibly removed some 12,500–14,000 of them from Mississippi to the Indian Territory of Oklahoma.[72]

Plagued by the disorganization, unscrupulousness, and insufficient funding that characterized the entire removal program, as many as a third of the Choctaw died along the way or shortly after arrival in the Oklahoma Territory. Cholera and other diseases ravaged their ranks. In 1830 the leadership of the Chickasaw, who lived north of the Choctaw in Mississippi, met directly with Jackson and pleaded that they "cannot consent to exchange the country where we now live for the one we have never seen." Sharp Knife responded that in reality they had no choice and Eaton informed the Chickasaw that if they refused to sign the removal treaty, "the President in twenty days would march an army into their country" to drive them out. After the Chickasaw signed off on removal in 1832, between 500 and 800 of the 4,000 Chickasaw forced out of homes died en route to the west.[73]

The largest genocidal removal campaigns involved the Creeks and the Cherokee. Even before Jackson took office, and with the backing of President Adams, the Creeks had been driven out of Georgia and their homelands reduced to a five million acre tract in Alabama. Neither the United States nor Alabama respected the wishes of the remaining Creeks, as "there was an overwhelming popular demand to be rid of them once and for all." Following the signing of a compulsory treaty in 1832, land agents defrauded the Indians while aggressive settler colonials burned their farms and seized their land. By the mid-1830s, hundreds of Creeks roamed the countryside searching for food and shelters.

The Creeks mounted a violent resistance in the "Creek War" of 1836 but they could not overcome the relentless squatters backed by the state and federal governments. Alabama militia and federal forces captured some 2,500 Creeks, put them in chains and crowded them onto barges for the trip down the Alabama River and over some 800 miles of land for the three-month journey to Oklahoma. A total of nearly 20,000 Creeks were removed, including "the friendly disposed part of them" who had fought with Jackson against their Red Stick rivals. During the removal of 1834–1837, some 3,500 Creeks died en route or shortly after arrival in Oklahoma. More than 300 died in a single steamboat accident on the river. All along the way observers commented on the near nakedness and emaciation of the barefoot Indians, alternately freezing and overheated, and trailed overland by packs of wolves ready to prey on the weak or the dead and discarded.[74]

The Cherokee displayed the highest levels of resistance, hybridity, and acculturation by editorializing, lobbying, petitioning, and mounting a formidable legal challenge to the ethnic cleansing campaign. In the War of 1812, the Cherokee had "demonstrated their desire to remain at peace with the United States"; moreover, hundreds of them had fought with the Americans.[75] A large number of Cherokees were Christians and mixed bloods. The tribe held 15 million acres with abundant farms and livestock and worked by hundreds of slaves. The Cherokee had a written constitution with three branches of government and had established their own police forces.

As they moved toward declaring complete sovereignty as an independent nation within the southern states, the Georgia legislature struck back by declaring only a month after Jackson's election that all Indians living within the state's boundaries would come under its jurisdiction in six months. The Cherokee sued and the issue reached the US Supreme Court. Chief Justice John Marshall's court had previously ruled unanimously in *Johnson v. McIntosh* (1823) that Indians were "fierce savages, whose occupation was war, and whose subsistence was drawn chiefly from the forest" hence the United States under the Doctrine of Discovery could legally "extinguish the Indian title of occupancy." In his March 18, 1831, decision on *Cherokee Nation v. Georgia*, Marshall rejected the Cherokee claim to be a foreign people, declaring instead that they were a "domestic dependent nation." In the subsequent decision in *Worcester v. Georgia* (1832), the last of the "fateful trilogy," the high court declared unconstitutional the State of Georgia's claim that its laws could govern the tribes.[76] The Cherokee took the ruling as "a ringing declaration of Indian sovereignty," but one that neither Jackson nor the Georgians had the slightest intention of accepting.[77]

The Cherokee refused to abandon their homelands to the encroaching settlers even when it became clear that Jackson encouraged the Georgians to ignore the federal judicial mandate. When a tiny minority succumbed to the pressure and signed the Treaty of New Echota in 1835, the vast majority of Cherokee denounced them as traitors and eventually assassinated the collaborationists. Jackson, however, signed the treaty, which the Senate ratified by a single vote over intense opposition. The treaty gave the Cherokee a two-year grace period to vacate the state. When they failed to do so, Jackson's handpicked successor Martin Van Buren dispatched federal troops, who rounded up Indians at bayonet point and put them in stockades. By mid-June 1838, the general in charge of the Georgia militia "proudly reported that not a single Cherokee remained in the state except as prisoners."

In the subsequent "trail of tears," a minimum of 4,000 and possibly as many as 8,000 of some 18,000 Cherokee who were removed died in the stockades or en route. "At every step of their long journey to the Indian territory," Robert Remini notes, "the Cherokees were robbed and cheated by contractors, lawyers, agents, speculators, and anyone wielding local police power."[78] Lacking food, shelter, medicine, and other provisions, the Cherokee perished in droves.

The Forgotten "Florida War"

While the Cherokee put up the best legal fight, the Seminole exploited geography and their alliance with free blacks to mount the strongest and most prolonged military resistance in the entire history of American settler colonialism. The United States took the Florida territory from Spain by treaty but the Seminole and their allies would not go without a determined fight that dragged on for seven years to the consternation of the US government and its military. The so-called Second Seminole War erupted in 1835 in the midst of the IRA, lasted to 1842, and was followed by a third Seminole War in 1856 that lasted another two and a half years.

The inglorious counter-insurgency wars—obscured in American History even though they commanded national attention at the time—further ensconced the American way of war. On December 28, 1835, the Seminole and their black allies defeated a US assault force under Major Francis L. Dade, who died in the battle that Americans immediately labeled a "massacre." Dade thus "became the Custer of his day as leader of a doomed force whose annihilation captured the nation's imagination."[79] The shocking news of the defeat, replete with Indians and more ominously African-Americans taking trophies and committing atrocities, traumatized Americans and spurred hundreds of recruits from the adjacent southern states.

Through their effective resistance the Seminoles were defying the narrative of the inevitable triumph of civilization over savagery and of America's continental destiny. They thus had to be removed no matter what the cost. On the Christmas Eve of 1837, a combined force of 380–480 under Colonel Zachary Taylor lost a battle on the shores of Lake Okeechobee, though Taylor claimed victory anyway and received promotion and national acclaim. By this time, "The Florida War had degenerated to a fierce guerrilla war that the United States appeared to be losing," John and Mary Lou Missall note. Jackson found no peace in retirement at his Hermitage plantation, as he fulminated against the "disgraceful" and "humiliating" war. Alternating tropes of race and gender, the Old Hickory branded the white men in Florida "damned cowards" and vowed that "with fifty women" he could "whip every Indian that had ever crossed the Suwannee."[80]

Nothing better illustrated American intolerance of indigenous ambivalence than the fate of the Seminole resistance leader Coacoochee. In 1841, with his forces exhausted from navigating the swamps of the Everglades, Coacoochee surrendered to the ironically named William Tecumseh Sherman at Fort Pierce. Put on trial, he explained that the Seminole had "asked for but a small piece of these lands, enough to plant and to live upon, far south, a spot where I could lay my wife and child. This was not granted to me." A witness at the trial, John Sprague, observed, "Here was a chief, a man whose only offense was defending his home, his fireside, the graves of his kindred, stipulating on the *Fourth of July*, for his freedom and his life."

The United States put in camps and then removed Coacoochee and some 3,000 other Seminole. About 1,500 Americans and an unknown number of African-Americans and Indians died in the counterinsurgency war. The Second Seminole War "was forgotten almost as soon as it ended ... It had been an unpopular, dirty little war, and no one wanted to talk about it."[81] As with a small Cherokee community that held out in the mountains of North Carolina, a band of Seminoles remained in Florida (to this day) and successfully resisted removal yet again in the Third Seminole War.

The Passing of a Noble Race

By the time of the Seminole wars, a comforting national mythology rationalized removal and assuaged feelings of traumatic guilt over the American cleansing campaign. The inexorable forces of history rather than the Americans themselves were driving Indians from the land. The pervasive "cultural myth" of the "Vanishing American ... accounted for the Indians' future by denying them one, and stained the issue of policy debate with fatalism," Dippie explains. "The fate of the aborigines was predestined. Their demise reflected no discredit on American institutions or morality," as removal had been preordained by "benevolent Providence."[82]

As Americans carried out the cleansing campaign and gained control of the land east of the Mississippi, they internalized discourses centering on the inevitable passing of the "noble savage." The Pocahontas legend, which transformed early Indian relations from conquest into a love story, flourished in narratives and on canvas. James Fennimore Cooper's "Leather-stocking tales" promoted the noble savage stereotype as well as mourning for the inevitable passing of the tribes. Cooper's *The Last of the Mohicans: A Narrative of 1757* (1826) reassuringly dated the Vanishing American to a generation before the United States had even been created. Just as a later generation would feature Sitting Bull in the Wild West shows, Americans compelled the Sac chief Black Hawk to travel through the eastern United States in burlesque appearances as a symbol of the once powerful but now subdued Indian warrior. Black Hawk later renounced his own performance as a sham.[83]

Artistic representations promoted the maudlin mythology of the Vanishing American. A burned-out portrait artist from Philadelphia, George Caitlin, resolved to travel west and convert his art into "a monument to a dying race." During the 1830s Caitlin visited 48 tribes and made some 470 Indian portraits. "Caitlin's lament" raised ambivalent awareness of the decimation of Indian life and culture while reinforcing the notion of the Indians' inevitable demise before the advance of a chosen people.[84]

The cultural narrative of the passing of the noble savage became so pervasive that many Americans in the east appeared to forget or never learn of the violent removal of the indigenous tribes from their midst. In the generation to come, many of them would criticize settlers west of the Mississippi for representing the Indians as savages and treating them accordingly. But such expressions of ambivalence would not obstruct the course of the empire. Fired by a renewed sense of Manifest Destiny, American settler colonialists set out to cleanse the land not only of Indians but also of Hispanics who impeded their path to the Pacific Ocean.

5

"Scenes of Agony and Blood": Settler Colonialism and the Mexican and Civil Wars

The "Mexican War" was an extension of the borderland violence that had been ongoing for centuries and deeply implicated in American national identity. The term "Manifest Destiny" may have been new but removing putatively inferior people from colonial space was not. After centuries of Spanish colonialism, the southwestern borderlands had a polyglot character with considerable ethnic mixing between Indians and Hispanics. "Mongrel" peoples such as these lacked legitimacy in American eyes and could not be allowed to impede civilization, progress, and acquiring of new lands by white settlers.

Within a generation the triumphalism of the Mexican War had been replaced by internecine conflict. In the Civil War the boomerang of savagery came hurtling back onto the United States with a vengeance. The effort to incorporate the vast territories taken from Mexico exacerbated the sectional crisis over slavery—which was challenged primarily where it did not already exist—and propelled the Americans into the depths of civil tumult.

Both the Mexican and Civil Wars became counterinsurgency wars replete with indiscriminate killing and collective punishment. Underscoring the continuities within an American way of war, the Mexican and Civil wars shared much in common not only with each other but also with the centuries of warfare with the Indian tribes. All reflected the powerful sway of nationalist fantasy—the Indian and Mexican wars to dramatically expand the chosen nation, the Civil War to prevent the dissolution of the "last best hope of earth."[1]

The Civil War complemented Indian removal insofar as both the Union and the Confederacy agreed that the "Negro problem," like the Indian problem, needed to be resolved primarily through strategies of elimination. In order to achieve its providential destiny, Americans needed to clear geographic space for white men and their families to the exclusion of Hispanics, Indians, and African-Americans. The vast majority of Northern anti-slavery forces, as is well known, did not advocate inclusion of African-Americans into society, just as most supported removal of the indigenes. The South sought to preserve slavery whereas the preferred solution of the Union at the outset of the war, including President Abraham Lincoln, was colonization. While many ambivalent reformers advocated uplifting and assimilating Indians, Hispanics, and African-Americans, most Americans preferred to rid the nation of these highly problematic alien races.

Indians and the "Mexican War"

The "Mexican War" has been poorly understood because Indians until recent years did not factor into its narration. In fact the indigenes played a profound role in destabilizing the Spanish borderlands; weakening the newly independent nation of Mexico; and making Texas, the southwest, and California ripe for the Yankee picking. Borderland studies have discredited the notion of fixed boundaries, especially in regions of mixed ethnicity such as the North American Southwest. Rather than a war between the United States and Mexico, the conflict was a war for the extension of American settler colonialism into the colonial space of California and the contested borderlands of the Southwest.

Beginning in the late sixteenth century, Spain had tried, but failed to establish colonial authority through the mission and the presidio (see Chapter 2). Most indigenous people successfully resisted Spanish efforts to remold them into "sons of God and vassals of Spain." By the mid-seventeenth century horses became widely available and various Indian groups exploited this new technology to raid and to terrorize the Spanish outposts as well as other indigenous groups. Even the Bourbon reformer King Carlos III, who had implemented a more benevolent approach to the indigenes, became so incensed over Apache raids that in 1772 he called for "vigorous and incessant war" and even "extermination" of the "mob of savages." By their own introduction of horses, sales of weapons, and efforts to establish colonialism, "Spaniards, like other Europeans, pushed indigenous conflict," David Weber notes, and "war became endemic."[2]

Despite the inability of Spain to establish colonial authority outside of its mission and presidio enclaves, intermarriage and sexual liaisons over the generations produced people of mixed blood. By the nineteenth century the North American Southwest constituted a hybrid "third space" of ambiguous ethnicities and ambivalence with no single authority. Exchange economies existed alongside brutal violence rooted in the tradition of raiding and spurred by slave trading and the warfare associated with it.

A series of events in the early nineteenth century increased the scope and stakes of violent contestation in the Southwest. The Mexican independence movement, the influx of American settlers, and the migration of various Indian tribes into and around the region spurred violence and uncertainty. In 1821 the opening of the Santa Fe Trail linked the Southwest with central Mexico and with the eastern US market economy, creating increased trade and political instability. That same year, after a decade of struggle, Mexico gained its independence from Spain, thus inheriting an unstable northern frontier that it would prove utterly unable to control.

The revolt against Spain destabilized an already weak imperial authority from Texas to California. Spain never controlled the northern borderlands but it had established colonial structures of defense, trade, and alliances with indigenous groups, all of which dissolved with Mexican independence. Mexico thus was a newly independent, sprawling, disunited territory with power centered in Mexico City and maintained primarily by the Catholic Church and a privileged aristocracy. The weak central government and regional differences fostered separatist movements, frequent rebellions, and banditry. "It would be decades before the country would unite politically," Douglas Richmond notes.[3]

Rather than Mexico being an integrated nation with control of its borders, the lands were contested among a variety of indigenous groups: *Tejanos*, *Neuvomexicanos*, *Californios*, and increasingly, American settlers. Indian raids, slave warfare and trading, and all manner of violent conflict between and among indigenes, Hispanics, and others raged across "a thousand deserts." From California to Texas, "Mexico's northern border with independent Indians became a far more violent place than it had been in the late Spanish era," Weber notes. Indians, Hispanics, American traders, and people of mixed ethnicity all had been "born into worlds steeped in violence," Ned Blackhawk observes, and "had become accustomed to and fluent in its uses."[4]

By far the most formidable indigenous group in the Southwest was a coalescence known as the Comanche, from a Ute word meaning "enemy." Highly skilled equestrians, confirmed opportunists, merciless raiders, and enthusiastic slave traders—the Comanche "were the dominant people in the Southwest" from the mid-eighteenth to the mid-nineteenth centuries. They "halted the expansionist Texas in its tracks and carved out a vast raiding domain in northern Mexico."[5]

The Comanche were a masculinized raiding culture yet women played crucial roles in the community and often in diplomacy as well. Cultivation of the male warrior culture went through stages, as boys began as sheepherders until they could go out on raids to prove themselves as men and warriors. Political leaders earned and maintained their status through performance in warfare. Like most indigenous groups, the Comanche lived by blood revenge: any attack on the tribe would precipitate a ruthless and relentless counterassault. On the other hand, women sometimes went as envoys to pursue diplomacy.[6]

For decades the tribe ranged across "Comancheria," a broad territory centered on the Texas panhandle but extending outward in every direction into several future American states. In the late eighteenth century, the Comanche traded captive slaves for guns and ammunition. The Comanche brilliantly exploited their access to markets extending in all directions, which enabled them to raid and trade across a broad swath of the Southwest and into the Rockies and the Plains. The massive buffalo herds throughout the grasslands sustained the tribe with plentiful food, clothing, and shelter. The combination of arms, equestrian skills, and a favorable location for trade and security undergirded Comanche supremacy.[7]

Comanche raided, enslaved, and killed but their reputation for ruthless militarism sometimes overshadows their allure to indigenous people. Captives willingly stayed with the tribe and other indigenes joined the Comanche coalescence or sought to ally with them. Until the buffalo herds declined and the American settlers overwhelmed them, no other band in the Southwest enjoyed the power and prestige of the Comanche.[8]

With the majority of the Mexican population living in central Mexico, the northern borderlands were terrifyingly vulnerable to attacks by Comanche and other Indians. By the mid-1820s the Comanche and other tribes "raided ranches and towns at will, killing cattle and carrying off people." Like the Comanche, the Kiowa, a militarized warrior society, engaged in raids. Further West the Navaho, Utes, and indigenes generically lumped as Apaches also plagued the Mexican borderlands with raids and captive taking. The Mexican cattle industry suffered millions of dollars in losses.[9]

Brutal Indian raids wreaked "breathtaking systematic carnage" turning the northern third of Mexico into "a vast theater of hatred, terror, and staggering loss," Brian DeLay points out. As Mexicans defended themselves, killing hundreds of Comanche and other Indians in the process, their efforts ignited an "extraordinarily cruel war for revenge." Motivated to avenge the deaths of their own, the invading tribes strove to capture, kill, rape, scalp, dismember, and mutilate their foes. In the years leading up to the American-Mexican War, death and destruction stalked Mexico's northern borderlands.[10]

The assaults by the Comanche and other tribes so weakened northern Mexico as to pave the way for the US triumph in the ensuing war with Mexico. As Pekka Håmålåinen points out, "The stunning success of American imperialism in the Southwest can be understood only if placed in the context of the indigenous imperialism that preceded it."[11]

The Ethnic Cleansing of Texas

The weakness and vulnerability of Mexico to Indian attack accounts for the desperation move in which Mexico authorized migration of American settlers into Texas shortly after Mexican independence. Although Mexico ostensibly required the migrants to become citizens and embrace the Catholic Church, these requirements could not be enforced. Americans, primarily from the southern states, soon outnumbered the *Tejanos*—the longtime Hispanic residents of Texas—and in time would take control of the territory and establish it as a slaveholding republic.

From the 1820s to the early 1830s ambivalent relations prevailed between the American settlers and the *Tejanos.* Although racism, tensions, and violent clashes occurred in early Texas history, the American settlers and the *Tejanos* found "much common ground." The *gringos* and the *Tejanos* shared similar living patterns including the growing and grinding of corn, raising livestock, and shared entertainments such as fandangos, gambling, horse races, and breaking of wild horses. However, as the Anglos began to outnumber the *Tejanos* on Mexico's northern frontier, they increasingly emphasized the otherness of the Spanish-speaking, Catholic people they called "Mexicans" to emphasize their foreign character. The Texans increased the level of "indiscriminate violence" against *Tejanos.* At the same time, "Manipulation of the legal system led to land loss" for the *Tejanos.*[12]

The Texans declared their independence in 1836, prompting Mexico to send in the army, which proceeded to massacre hundreds of Texas-Americans at the Spanish missions Alamo and Goliad. As nothing else could have, these massacres provoked outrage and a boomerang of violent retribution. On April 21 Sam Houston surprised the army of Antonio Lopez de Santa Anna at San Jacinto and won the decisive "battle" for Texas independence. The Texans killed without quarter at San Jacinto, as attested by the mind-boggling disparity in the death toll: 630 Mexicans to nine Texans. The Texans had their revenge for the Alamo and Goliad, but the indiscriminate killing had only just begun. Found hiding in the bush, Santa Anna preserved his own life by agreeing to Texas independence.[13]

Captors of a sprawling multiethnic territory, the Texans embarked on a campaign of cleansing the state of Indians and removing or relocating *Tejanos* as well. "Texans gradually endorsed (at first locally and eventually statewide) a policy of ethnic cleansing that had as its intention the forced removal of certain culturally identified groups from their lands," Gary C. Anderson explains. The Texas Rangers, immortalized in the state's lore as mythic frontier heroes, functioned as a vigilante assault force targeting Indians and *Tejanos*. "Rangers killed indiscriminately, they robbed, and they raped," Anderson recounts. "Their goal was to spread terror so that neighboring Native groups would leave."[14]

By the 1830s American settler colonials mostly from the slaveholding South had arrived in Texas in sufficient numbers to begin a nearly half-century-long campaign of removal and indiscriminate killing of indigenous people. Not all Texans advocated ethnic cleansing of Indians, yet for the most part ambivalence about killing or removing of the savages was unwelcome in the Lone Star republic. Houston, who had been friendly with many Cherokee back in his native Tennessee, tried to make the case for drawing distinctions between "good Indians" versus "murderous hordes of wild Indians" but most Texans did not care to discriminate and thus shot down Houston's efforts to negotiate land agreements with the Texas tribes. Instead, "racial hatred became compatible with honor" and "Indian hunting" a "sport" as a "culture of violence" prevailed in Texas.[15]

While frontier mythology saturates the entire history of the American West, few histories have been as distorted as that of Texas. Under the dictates of Texas mythology, "Indians, brutal and bloodthirsty, were always at fault, and Texas Rangers were saviors, brave and righteous in their actions," Anderson explains.[16] While popular accounts continue to appear with heavy emphasis on Indian depredations and righteous retaliatory violence,[17] the settlers killed far more Indians than vice versa while driving out the indigenes, including those seeking accommodation.

Captivity narratives and horrid tales of savage violence and depravity triggered by a few incidents in the mid- to late-1830s became hegemonic in the colonial discourse of Texas. These incidents included most famously an Indian assault in June 1836 on the Parker Fort, which the Texas Rangers had used as a base of operations against the tribes. The indigenous raiders killed five settlers and took five prisoners, one of who, Rachel Plummer, wrote a lurid captivity narrative following her release. Texas lore elided the Ranger assaults for an exclusive focus on the murders of innocent settlers as well as the rape of "Granny Parker"—a rape that actually did not happen. One of the captured women, Cynthia Ann Parker, in subsequent years famously chose to remain with her Comanche husband and children, including her son and legendary Comanche leader Quanah Parker.[18]

Texas colonial discourse and its political leaders rationalized "the indiscriminate killing of Indians." Governor Mirabeau Lamar, a Georgian, advocated "absolute expulsion" of the "wild cannibals of the woods." By 1842 Lamar's war had cleansed Indians from the central valleys of Texas, thereby opening up productive farmland for settler colonialism. Vigilantes such as John Baylor, who had his own army, killed indiscriminately with the knowledge that no American would be prosecuted in Texas merely for killing Indians. As the Texas newspaper—aptly named "The Whiteman"—explained, "The killing of Indians of whatever tribe [is] morally right" and "we will resist to the last extremity the infliction of any legal punishment on the perpetrators."[19]

The colonial discourse of Indian savagery obscured ambivalent indigenous efforts to negotiate for agreed-upon borders but the Texans opted for wholesale ethnic cleansing. As Anderson notes, "Warfare was honorable to Indians, but so was negotiation." A good example of the willingness of Indians including the "bloodthirsty" Comanche to negotiate—along with the willingness of Texans to kill them—came with the Council House massacre, typically rendered in Texas mythology as the Council House "fight." The Comanche delegation arrived in San Antonio to negotiate in March 1840 but when they brought with them only one captive to turn over, the Texans responded by attempting to incarcerate the entire delegation. When the Comanche tried to flee, the Texans opened fire, killing 35 Indians compared with seven or eight Texans dead, some of them from friendly fire.[20]

As proud slaveholders who had orchestrated their own Indian removal campaign in the 1830s, Americans in the southern states especially identified with the Texans and viewed their incorporation into the United States as both desirable and inevitable. But once he had safely returned to his estate, Santa Anna reneged on his pledge of Texas independence and the Mexican government indignantly rebuffed President Andrew Jackson's offer to purchase Texas. In 1837 the United States formally recognized Texas independence. Hostilities between the Texans and Mexicans continued episodically for the next few years. In 1842 Mexicans attacked and occupied San Antonio, but the Texans retook the city in a battle marked by "horrendous bloodshed and atrocities."[21]

Fully aware that Mexico was not in control of its northern borderlands, President James K. Polk and his generals "intended to make the most" of Mexico's weakness. "Americans had come to see and to describe the whole Mexican north as a vast theater for an unfolding race war between mongrel Mexicans and the most savage and politically undeveloped of American Indians," DeLay explains. "This observation informed U.S. expectations about Mexico's willingness to sell its northern territory, Mexico's ability to defend the territory, and the way in which northern civilians would receive the U.S. Army."[22]

As a providential nation on a mission to take control of colonial space, Americans could justify aggression to resolve racial ambiguities and extend the "empire of liberty." Indians, *Tejanos*, *Neuvomexicanos*, and *Californios* were beneath Americans in the formation of racial hierarchies and thus could be removed through violence. In 1845, the hour of "Manifest Destiny" arrived, as the United States provoked war with Mexico in order to annex Texas and to take California and the southwest. A "messianic conception of the American people as the chosen agents of God's will," Manifest Destiny blended "revolutionary nationalism, evangelical Christianity, and material self-interest."[23]

While choosing a path to war against Mexico, Polk backed down from a fatuous claim to the 54-degree line of latitude in the northwest, thus averting a potential casus belli with the fellow "Anglo-Saxon" British. In 1846, the Oregon Treaty freed the United States of concern that Britain might intervene on Mexico's behalf or try to take California for itself, neither of which, however, had been on the agenda in London.[24]

Showing that his claim to expansive boundaries without historical justification was not confined to Oregon, Polk asserted a southern American boundary at the Rio Grande rather than the Nueces River. War could be averted only if the Mexicans accepted not only the unprecedented new border with Texas but also the loss of California and New Mexico. The vast terrain of New Mexico encompassed not only the modern-day Southwest (west Texas and the states of Arizona and New Mexico) but also nearly all of contemporary Nevada and Utah and stretched east as far as Nebraska. The Americans thus demanded Mexican capitulation to extraordinary new boundaries that would strip the nation of more than half its territory. The Mexicans had not even accepted the loss of Texas, hence there was no chance they would acquiesce to the American demands. In June 1845, Polk sent General Zachary Taylor to the banks of the Rio Grande, an "extraordinarily provocative move [that] made war all but inevitable."[25]

Feverish with Manifest Destiny, many politicians and much of the press and the public issued "hysterical calls for war in a toxically racist tone." Having recognized Texas and pushed the US Army into disputed territory, Polk had done all he could to bring on a war and merely had to await the almost certain clash. The men in Taylor's army knew why they had been sent south of the Nueces. Col. Ethan Allen Hitchcock declared that the US government sought "to bring on a war, so as to have a pretext for taking California and as much of this country as it chooses." Lieutenant Ulysses S. Grant likewise acknowledged, "We were sent to provoke a fight but it was essential that Mexico should commence it."[26]

On April 25, 1846, Mexican troops obliged by ambushing a squadron of Taylor's patrolling dragoons, killing 11 of them. Polk now had the pretext he sought for the legislation he sent to Congress not asking for a declaration of war but rather declaring that one already existed. Despite "all our acts to avoid it," Polk mendaciously asserted, a state of war existed "by act of Mexico," which had "shed American blood on American soil." In truth, Mexico had refrained from going to war over the loss of Texas and never encroached on US soil. Determined to use violent aggression to carry out Manifest Destiny, the US Congress reflected popular sentiment as it voted 174–14 in the House and 40–2 in the Senate to wage war.[27]

Although they were roughly the same size in 1846, Mexico and the United States evolved on wholly divergent trajectories, which influenced the outcome of the war. The Enlightenment, with its powerful impetus to the accumulation of knowledge and notions of progress, propelled the American colonies and the future United States but it largely bypassed Spain and the Catholic Church hierarchy. Whereas the United States had come into existence in a revolutionary era and received crucial support from France and other European powers, Mexico struggled after independence in 1821 to establish its nationhood at a time when the European powers had restored monarchies and committed themselves at the Congress of Vienna (1815) to fighting off liberalism.

In sharp contrast, the United States, benefiting from 50 years' more experience than Mexico as a republic, had forged a powerful, crusading national identity framed at mid-century as Manifest Destiny. A magnet for immigrants, the United States had grown to some 22 million people, more than triple Mexico's population of about seven million, on the eve of war. The Louisiana Purchase (1803), the Transcontinental Treaty (1819), in which Spain recognized US borders to the Pacific, and the Monroe Doctrine (1823), in which the United States asserted its separation from Europe and intention to dominate the Western Hemisphere, powerfully affirmed the drive for continental hegemony. The United States did not have a large army but one that had grown increasingly professional since the establishment of West Point in 1802. More important, legions of volunteers including many seasoned Indian fighters would turn out for the conflict. By contrast, the Mexican army, like the economy and society of the young republic, was in disarray.

Like the Indians, the Mexicans found themselves squarely in the path of a crusading nation committed to an almost boundless settler colonial expansion. Many Mexicans remain resentful of the "North American invasion," a war with "geographic consequences and repercussions that are still felt today."[28] Some Mexican writers and intellectuals have acknowledged, however, that in view of the inability to control the northern borderlands, the Mexican government should have perceived the realism of selling a portion of the land, including California, to the crusading Americans who in any case meant to take it one way or the other.[29]

Mexicans living on the borderlands at the time displayed a high degree of ambivalence. With the outbreak of war, the Hispanics on the borderlands were "caught between two opposing forces." *Tejanos* and *Neuvomexicanos*, especially, had significant economic ties with the American settlers. In California and the northern borderlands, "Shaky financial conditions and a stream of U.S. immigrants prevented Mexico from maintaining healthy ties to frontier societies."[30] At the same time, however, the Mexican government appealed to their national identity and devotion to Catholicism in a holy war against the invaders. As "American and Mexican national projects collided" in northern Mexico, "cross-cultural and cross-class alliances and counter-alliances . . . played out at the local level."[31]

With the outbreak of the war, many of the ambivalent *Tejanos*, *Neuvomexicanos* and *Californios*, especially elites, were receptive to siding with the Americans. Many *Tejanos* initially supported Texas out of frustration with the inept government in Mexico City. The Mexican government dramatically underestimated the disillusion of people who lived far from the center, which would enable the invaders to exploit separatist tendencies. The Americans were well positioned to exploit these cleavages until the chauvinism, and indiscriminate violence of the US volunteers alienated the borderland residents and propelled a longer and bloodier war.

Unleashing the Volunteers

Like the previous Indian Wars, and the Civil War and the Philippine conflict to come, indiscriminate violence, massacre, and collective punishment characterized the "American way of war" in Mexico. Once hostilities commenced, American volunteers primed to kill became the vanguard of Manifest Destiny. Volunteers outnumbered army regulars by almost two to one, as Americans remained leery of standing armies long associated with Red Coats and British tyranny. Most Americans had little respect for the regular army "hirelings," many of whom were immigrants and Catholics, whereas they perceived the 59,000 volunteers as venerable "citizen soldiers" and bulwarks of republicanism. Americans celebrated the tradition of volunteer militias, which they credited with redeeming the "frontier" from the savage Indians. Polk distrusted the regular army while exalting volunteers as "free citizens, who are ever ready to take up arms in the service of their country when an emergency requires it."[32]

Masses of men, especially in southern and western states, responded with rabid enthusiasm to Polk's request for 50,000 volunteers. They hailed not only from Tennessee, "the volunteer state," and other southern states, but also "from all quarters of our glorious Union . . . in one great common cause." Many times more volunteers turned out than needed. Ohio met its quota within two weeks. Massachusetts rallied to the cause as the largest town hall meeting in the history of Lowell was a pro-war rally. Herman Melville found New Yorkers "all in a state of delirium" in which "military ardor pervades" and "nothing is talked about but the Halls of the Montezumas." "Yankee Doodle" became the theme song of the Mexican War, thus connecting it with the original fight for liberty in 1776. It was the "order of Providence," a Methodist clergyman and Louisiana volunteer declared, to show the Mexicans "the blessings of liberty" through violent aggression and annexation.[33]

Buoyed by "a war mood that approached hysteria," the American public thus embraced the volunteers and proved willing to overlook their indiscriminate violence. Some Americans got a hint of things to come as the volunteers descended on communities nearby their training camps where they could be seen "swaggering about with bowie knives." The volunteers got into fights in which they "bruised, mangled, shot and stabbed each other." They "crowed like bantam cocks, shouted 'show us the Mexican niggers.' " Nonetheless, the volunteers remained popular, as young women decorated their camps and brought them cakes and other treats.[34]

In May 1846, as Taylor's forces defeated the Mexican army in a bloody fight at the northeastern city of Matamoros, packs of volunteers descended on the city. The streets quickly "filled with drunks carrying bowie knives, rifles, and pistols, which they used at the slightest provocation" as Matamoros devolved into "a state of anarchy."[35] Looting was the most consistent crime committed by the volunteers but murder and rape were not uncommon. The leaders of the irregular forces "scarcely attempt to interfere with them to prevent these depredations," an Army officer lamented.[36]

Had the US occupation been disciplined, the United States would have been well positioned to exploit the widespread Mexican ambivalence, thus making for a shorter and cleaner war. But as David Clary points out, "The litany of drunken brawls, fights, gang rapes, stabbings, shootings, arson, robberies, theft, livestock rustling, looting and desecration of churches and other crimes ended any hope for cooperation before the Army of Occupation had been in the area a month."[37]

The invaders transformed Matamoros into "a conquered city much the receptacle of all the dregs of the United States," Colonel Samuel R. Curtis of 3rd Ohio Volunteers recorded in his diary on August 4, 1847. "Murder, rapine and vice of all manner of form prevails and predominates here." Curtis had no love of Mexico, a "barbarous Catholic country" and a "den of thieves, robbers, and assassins." It was his fellow volunteers, however, who shocked him most. "It is a disgrace to our country for our own citizens are much worse than the Mexicans who are mixed up with them," he declared. Even though many of the daily acts of murder, robbery, theft, and rape were enthusiastically documented in the bi-weekly Matamoros newspaper *American Flag*, the "brutal crimes committed by the regular and volunteer soldiers in Mexico went unpunished."[38]

As the Catholic Church represented an alien and undemocratic power to the Protestant US volunteers, they engaged in "robbing and killing priests, raping nuns, looting altars, and desecrating holy buildings. Taylor issued orders against this behavior but did little to stop it." Texas Rangers near Saltillo tore down a crucifix, dragged it through the street, and trampled the parish priest. When the people resisted, the Rangers turned their violence upon them, "sparing neither age or sex in their terrible fury."[39]

Taylor deplored the violent disorder and clearly perceived that it would undermine the war effort by eroding Mexican ambivalence and strengthening guerrilla opposition. "Were it possible to rouse the Mexican people to resistance, no more effectual plan could be devised than the very one pursued by some of our volunteer regiments," Old Rough and Ready lamented. "There is scarcely a form of crime that has not been reported to me as committed by them."[40]

Just as Taylor feared, within months a guerrilla war of resistance prevailed in Mexico. Indiscriminate killing, robbery, and sexual assault by the US volunteers inspired a vengeful hatred that prompted the Mexican people to engage in sniping, sabotage, hit-and-run attacks, and other tactics of irregular warfare. "We meet the inhabitants sullen, sulky, and with the best disposition in the world to cut the throats of each and every one of us," an Army officer wrote.[41] Livid over hit-and-run attacks and other "dishonorable" behavior, the Americans responded by branding any armed Mexican a bandit subject to summary execution.

The scarcely trained volunteers—abetted and encouraged by camp followers comprised of liquor salesmen, gamblers, and prostitutes—proved reminiscent of Indians and borderland settlers back home. Regular army officers frequently referred to the volunteers as "Mohawks," likening them to Indian savages.[42] Many of the volunteers were indeed borderland settlers well-schooled in Indian warfare and contemptuous of external authority. Lacking discipline and routine, their camps were often filthy breeding grounds for diseases that ravaged the ranks. They had no use for drills, discipline, rank, and supervision of any kind, though they remained close-knit within their own units. Most of them craved action and showed no reluctance to kill noncombatants.

US volunteers demonstrated violent and undisciplined behavior that many observers associated with "the wild Indians." Like indigenous warriors, the volunteers desired to take the spoils of victory and to return to their communities as heroes. "The propaganda surrounding the war was nakedly opportunistic and expressly promised plunder as the right of the volunteer," Paul Foos explains. Volunteers signed on with promises of "roast beef, two dollars a day, plenty of whiskey, golden Jesuses, and pretty Mexican girls."[43]

Undisciplined and poorly led, the volunteers "act[ed] more like a body of hostile Indians than of civilized whites," declared army regular George Meade, the future hero of Gettysburg. "They rob and steal cattle and corn of the poor farmers" and committed violent crimes "for no other object than their own amusement." In a typical incident recounted by an army surgeon, some Texas volunteers in the midst of raiding a farm for horses and pigs shot to death the owner, his little son, and two servants when they came out of their home in protest. The slaughter went unpunished.[44]

The US public had no interest in trying Americans for crimes against Mexicans any more than it had for crimes against Indians. Volunteers committed violent crimes, including murder and rape, with impunity because of a weak US code of military justice. While the army could and often did severely punish men within its own ranks, Taylor and others did not have the same legal authority over the volunteers. The law required that citizen violators of orders and the rules of war be tried in civilian courts. Almost invariably, however, volunteer offenders sent off to New Orleans for trial found little difficulty in gaining release by obtaining a writ of habeas corpus. In May 1846, General Winfield Scott proposed changes in the law to address the problem but Congress failed to act.[45]

As Taylor's army moved from Matamoros into the interior, the Mexican army put up strong resistance before surrendering Monterey amid "tremendous slaughter and destruction."[46] Beginning in September 1846, the occupation of Monterey would last two years, the longest of any Mexican city, and was atrocious from beginning to end. Taylor again established no security patrols hence the populace was subjected to the "beastly depravity and gross outrages of the volunteers," a disgusted Lieutenant Daniel H. Hill observed.[47]

Indiscriminate violence worsened after the Battle of Angostura (also known as the Battle of Buena Vista), one of the bloodiest fights in US history up to the time. Santa Anna was back (minus one of his legs) and at the forefront of an army with superior numbers. The Mexicans fought tenaciously, killing 270 and wounding some 400 others in Taylor's army, while 591 of its own men were killed and more than 1,000 wounded. Superior US artillery turned the battle of Angostura, the last regular armed confrontation in northern Mexico. The region thereafter became a theater of vicious guerrilla attacks followed by a US scorched-earth response.

Virtually all signs of ambivalence had disappeared as a result of the violent pathologies of the American volunteers. "The smiling villages that welcomed our troops on their upward march are now black and smoldering ruins," a regular confided. "The march of Attila was not more withering and destructive."[48]

One of the most infamous atrocities of the war occurred in response to the ambush of a weakly escorted US wagon and mule train north of Monterrey. The Mexican attackers killed and mutilated several teamsters, took others prisoner, and destroyed property. To avenge the assault, Taylor sent his most brutal force, a unit of Texas Rangers under Captain Mabry "Mustang" Gray. The Texans descended on the nearest pueblo and dragged 24 men, who had nothing to do with the wagon train assault, out of their beds, tied them to posts, and shot them in the head. The news of this atrocity traveled fast and incited guerrilla resistance throughout northern Mexico.[49]

No one disputes that the worst offenders in the course of an almost uniformly atrocious US campaign in Mexico were the Rangers and other Texas volunteers. Hardened by years of conflict with Indians as well as *Tejanos*, the Texans well remembered the Alamo and Goliad. They regularly took their revenge against innocent people. "The mounted men from Texas have scarcely made one expedition without unwarrantably killing a Mexican," Taylor grumbled.[50]

The Ranger volunteers carried themselves with a certain gangland panache, as they wore colors, cultivated bushy beards, and packed multiple weapons, both guns and audacious bowie knives, which they employed with unbridled enthusiasm. At the outset of the occupation of Monterey, Texas volunteers summarily slaughtered at least 100 non-resisting citizens and torched the city. They committed "murder, rape, and robbery . . . in the broad light of day," complained Hill, the future Confederate general. "The Mexicans dread the Texans more than they do the devil, and they had good reason for it," a soldier wrote in his diary.[51]

While it was typical of Army regulars to criticize the conduct of their rival volunteers, even the other volunteers condemned the Texas Ranger companies for their gratuitous violence. However, the Texans were familiar with the southwestern terrain and valued for their work as both scouts and light cavalry. Despite their "reign of terror upon the countryside," the utility of the Texans to the army "meant that no questions were asked when they went on rampages against civilians."[52]

In the last week of 1846, a band of Arkansas Volunteers known as the Rackensackers matched the depravity of the Rangers as they "celebrated Christmas with an orgy of rape, murder and destruction." In response to the killing of one man from their company, the Arkansas volunteers trapped and slaughtered 25 to 30 men, women, and children who had fled into a cave. Army Private Samuel Chamberlain provided a graphic account of the incident. When his group of regulars arrived at the scene, they aimed their weapons at the volunteers who were in the midst of killing and mutilating the unarmed Mexicans. "Women and children were clinging to the knees of the murderers and shrieking for mercy." Chamberlain had no love for the Mexican "greasers" but the indiscriminate slaughter, capped off when a "savage cutthroat marched out with a swagger and gave a fancy Indian dance," sickened him. Taylor declared that the incident put an "indelible disgrace upon our arms and the reputation of our country" but, as was routine, it went unpunished.[53]

Despite such protestations, Taylor had unleashed US forces in response to banditry and irregular warfare targeting his troops and supply lines. Taylor inflicted collective punishment for guerrilla attacks by ordering the burning of villages located in the vicinity. Meanwhile, the volunteers "committed rape and pillage . . . while the democratically elected officers looked the other way." A pro-war correspondent form New Orleans doubted "that *negroes* in a state of insurrection would hardly be guilty" of such crimes. A sergeant in a volunteer regiment acknowledged privately that Americans were beginning to "act as *Guerrillas*, and have been killing, I fear, *innocent* Mexicans as they meet them . . . This has led to reprisal and recrimination until it is dangerous to be out alone."[54]

The scorched-earth tactics carried out by Taylor's army of occupation "transformed much of northeast Mexico into a moonscape," as Clary puts it. Opportunistic Mexican bandits and desperados preyed on their fellow citizens as well. The people of northern Mexico were thus "plundered by both sides, their lives often taken and their wives and daughters outraged and carried off."[55]

The War on the Western Borderlands

Neuvomexicanos displayed ambivalence at the outset of the war as a result of their disaffection of Mexico City combined with extensive trade ties with the Americans on the Santa Fe Trail. While Taylor's army incited a guerrilla war by laying waste to northern Mexico, General Stephen Watts Kearney marched the Army of the West from Fort Leavenworth to Santa Fe to lay claim to colonial space for the United States. In the summer of 1846, Kearney sent advance notice that his approaching army represented no threat to the citizenry as his purpose was "seeking union with and ameliorating the conditions of the inhabitants." Many New Mexicans hoped that the US Army could rein in the marauding Indian tribes that plagued the Santa Fe trade.[56]

Despite Kearney's noble intentions, ambivalence quickly gave way to simmering resentment as the Americans once again alienated the resident Hispanic population. Kearney angered *Neuvomexicanos* by putting in charge a group of US merchants who reaped the profits from sales of stock and supplies to the newly arrived army while the Hispanics got the crumbs. At the same time, a wide array of Indian tribes—Apaches, Comanche, Kiowa, Ute, and Navaho among them—seized upon the disarray brought on by the war to step up their own depredations against the Mexicans, the Americans, and each other.[57]

In January 1847, the impoverished pueblo Indians and Hispanics lashed out against the US occupiers and Mexican collaborationists. In Taos, long the center of American trade and settlement, an angry mob broke into the home of Governor Charles Bent to murder and decapitate him as his wife and children fled through a hole in the wall of their adobe abode. The ethnic violence lasted a few weeks until volunteers and vigilantes variously butchered, arrested, and scattered the "rebels" who were said to be committing treason in their native land. The Americans killed some 150 insurgents, while only seven of its men died.[58]

In California as in New Mexico the US invaders alienated an ambivalent Hispanic population otherwise predisposed to favor them over the distant and incompetent Mexican government. The collapse of the Spanish mission system in the 1830s had weakened Hispanic unity in California and made many like the ranchero Mariano Vallejo receptive to breaking away from Mexican authority. Descending from Sutter's Fort, the "Pathfinder" John C. Frémont, accompanied by Kit Carson (the actual finder of mostly long extant Indian paths) and a motley crew of mountain men and adventurers, proclaimed the "Bear Flag revolt" in June 1846. The US Navy, which had landed at Monterey, sanctioned Frémont's proclamation of Californian independence. Commodore Robert F. Stockton gratuitously named himself the ruler of the territory. Frémont and Stockton quickly alienated the *Californios* through their racist arrogance, which included the arbitrary arrest and imprisonment of Vallejo and others. By the time Kearney arrived from New Mexico, California like northern Mexico had become inflamed with guerrilla resistance.[59]

Having seized California, New Mexico, and Texas, the United States had seemingly realized its expansive settler colonial ambitions but the violence would not end until Mexico formally acknowledged American sovereignty over the new lands. As with Indian removal, Americans sought a veneer of legality as a means of disavowing the colonizing act. Polk demanded a formal peace treaty that would end the guerrilla resistance and rationalize the US aggression by providing it with a diplomatic gloss. As Mexico refused to accommodate the Americans, Polk decided to initiate a wider war by invading Central Mexico and marching on the capital to compel recognition of the US conquests.

The US commander, Winfield Scott, had been appalled by the atrocities committed by the volunteers in northern Mexico. "Our militia and volunteers," he lamented, "if a tenth of what is said to be true, have committed atrocities—horrors—in Mexico, sufficient to make Heaven weep." Scott declared it had been "unchristian and cruel to let loose upon any people—even savages—such unbridled persons." Scott cracked down on the liquor trade and issued an order creating military commissions to try both regulars and volunteers for war crimes. Scott would jail offenders, subject them to public whippings, and even hang a handful of murderers and rapists during his campaign but ultimately the atrocities could not be curbed.[60]

Despite his professed sensitivity to the "minds and feelings" of the Mexican people, Scott ordered a campaign of indiscriminate bombardment of Vera Cruz, a port city of 6,000 people. Rules of war forbade assaults on noncombatants yet Scott pummeled the city with "awful destructiveness."[61] About 350 soldiers and some 400 civilians died from the US artillery barrage in March 1847 compared to 13 US deaths. An army private recalled "the report of the bomb and then a heart-rending wail of the inhabitants that was awful, the women and children screaming with terror." The bombardment destroyed cathedrals and hospitals as "scenes of agony and blood follow one after the other." "My heart bled for the inhabitants," Robert E. Lee told his wife.

The Mexicans finally surrendered the city but irregular warfare roiled the surrounding countryside. Scott responded by branding all Mexican resistance as criminal behavior rather than wartime belligerence and thus authorized summary executions and collective punishment. As in the Vietnam War more than a century later, any dead Mexican was deemed a rebel just as any dead Vietnamese would be counted a "Viet Cong." As Taylor had done, Scott levied "taxes" on Mexican towns as punishment for attacks by unidentified guerrillas. If they did not pay, the towns were summarily destroyed.

The merciless US response to irregular attacks only encouraged more Mexicans to take up guerrilla resistance. As Scott mobilized for an assault on the capital, a Mexico City newspaper warned that the Americans were coming to "burn our cities, loot our temples, rape our wives and daughters, and kill our sons." Given the character of the US occupations, the Mexicans assumed that they had nothing to lose by fighting to the death.[62]

In September 1847, as Scott's forces took Mexico City in a blood-drenched fight, the elite citizens of the capital city opted for an ambivalent collaboration with the US occupiers. They soon regretted the decision. The Americans strolled around Mexico City with their guns out "in order to strike fear into us," one citizen recalled. "They entered homes and searched and looted at their pleasure, taking whatever they wished."[63]

While elites tried to placate the invaders, the common people of the city fought back, as they cursed, stoned, shot, and stabbed the occupiers whenever they got the chance. Livid over sniping, assassination, and hit-and-run attacks, the Americans lashed back with extreme violence, sexual assault, and theft. The occupation "corrupted our men most fearfully," Hill wrote in his diary. "Many of them were perfectly frantic with the lust of blood and plunder." For months an "undisciplined and officially discountenanced war between soldier and civilian continued," Clary points out, as "Scott's army turned one of the great cities of the Western Hemisphere into a hellhole."[64]

Guerrilla attacks prompted a boomerang of genocidal violence. The Texans again took the lead as on one occasion they slaughtered some 80 people in a two-hour shooting spree in response to the death of a single Texan, a revered figure known as "Cutthroat." Similarly, Army General Joseph Lane ordered his men to burn the entire town of Huamantla after Major Samuel Walker, had been killed in battle (as opposed to an irregular assault). Unleashed on the town, the troops, "maddened with liquor," proceeded to carry out "every species of outrage" including gang rapes, breaking into homes, and wanton slaughtering of people and animals.[65]

As both the press and the public had celebrated the volunteers as the heroic vanguard of Manifest Destiny, there was little cultural space for discourse on atrocities. As with Indian conflict, Americans rationalized the indiscriminate violence of the Mexican War, if acknowledging it at all, as the unfortunate consequence of the march of civilization and progress over racially inferior peoples. The antiwar press sometimes publicized accounts of the indiscriminate violence in Mexico but heroic narratives overwhelmed the few critical accounts. Americans ignored the indiscriminate killing and framed the aggression as a providentially sanctioned war of liberation. Polk and other proponents of the war exercised a chilling effect over war critics by questioning their patriotism and, as in future US wars, equating criticism of the war with undermining the troops in the field. Ambivalent anti-war sentiment existed and persisted throughout the war yet "Polk received almost everything he requested from Congress."[66]

For a time it appeared that the drives of settler colonialism literally knew no bounds as most US citizens appeared to favor punishing Mexico's insolent resistance to Manifest Destiny by seizing control of the entire country. As the Americans approached the fabled halls of Montezuma, the "All-Mexico" movement gained momentum with the press and public. "Your ancestors, when they landed at Plymouth" dealt with the Indians by "cheating them out of their land," Sam Houston declaimed at an All-Mexico rally. "Now the Mexicans are no better than the Indians, and I see no reason why we should not go in the same course now and take their land." The sentiment extended beyond the slave-holding South. Absorbing and democratizing Mexico was work "worthy of a great people," the *New York Herald* averred.[67]

Relentless guerrilla resistance precluded the United States from securing battlefield gains much less extending its authority to "All Mexico." The prolonged conflict had "sapped the morale and resilience of the invaders." After torturous efforts owing to deep divisions between Polk, diplomat Nicholas Trist, and Scott as well as disputes on the Mexican side, the Treaty of Guadalupe-Hidalgo brought a merciful end to the Mexican War in 1848. As with the movement for Indian assimilation (see next chapter), Article IX of the treaty invited Hispanic residents of the newly annexed US territories to become US citizens as long as they pledged not to "preserve the character of citizens of the Mexican Republic." Mexican vulnerability to Indian depredations was not forgotten, as Article XI of the treaty required the United States to "forcibly restrain" incursions by the "savage tribes" into Mexican territory.[68]

Texans celebrated the victory over Mexico, which allowed them to resume the ethnic cleansing of Indians from the lone star state. In 1845, Texas claimed complete control over "all the vacant and un-appropriated lands" within the state as a condition of entrance into the Union. By dispossessing Indians, the Texans could retire debt through the sale of the newly seized land while carving out ranches and communities for slaveholding settlers. The Indians in Texas included not only the mobile and aggressive raiding cultures notably the Kiowa and Comanche, who continued to unleash brutal raids against white and *Tejano* settlements, but also more sedentary bands, including the Cherokee, Shawnee, Chickasaw, Choctaw, and Kickapoo, who had migrated after being removed from the east.

As the allure of cheap land catapulted the settler population from 140,000 in 1845 to 600,000 in 1860, Texans became increasingly intolerant of Indians. In the summer of 1847, "the state granted white speculators vast tracts of public land even though Indians resided there." Texans seized the lands and hunting grounds of Indians, variously known as savages, barbarians, or more imaginatively as "Red Niggers" or "Red Vermin."[70] The Indians soon "recognized that Texans intended not only to take all their land, but to conduct a war to exterminate them," Philip Weeks notes.[71] The indigenes would not go quietly, however, as "Indian hostilities constituted the single most important factor in the development of Texas until the 1870s," Jesus de la Taya points out.[72]

The Texans targeted ambivalent and non-hostile tribes as well as the Lipan Apache even though they had helped hunt down and kill their blood rivals the Comanche. During the 1850s the Rangers, settlers, and the US Army "struck randomly" against indigenes and killed indiscriminately, Peka Håmålåinen notes. "Ranger companies and spontaneously organized Texas militias killed all Indians they could find" in order to drive them from the path of settlement. By the late 1850s, Indians other than in the Texas panhandle had been driven onto reservations or otherwise were considered "hostile" and subjected to summary execution.[73]

Displays of colonial ambivalence by whites were not popular and on occasion proved lethal in Texas. In September 1859, Bureau of Indian Affairs agent Robert Neighbors, one of the few Texans who opposed the indiscriminate killing of Indians by "malicious white men," was murdered by means of a shotgun blast in the back. By that time Texas had been cleansed of thousands of Indians from dozens of indigenous and immigrant tribes. While many Texas Indians would have accepted enclaves within the state, the Texans opted for ethnic cleansing over ethnic diversity. Though they "had many opportunities to end the violence," the Texans instead pursued their campaign of murder and expulsion to its logical end.[74]

Freebooting Colonialism

The conclusion of the Mexican War dimmed neither the broad appeal of the Manifest Destiny fantasy nor the desire for new frontiers of American settler colonial expansion. As the budding sectional crisis curbed state-sponsored expansionism, filibusterism stepped into the breach. Filibusterism—the word derived from French and Spanish versions of the Dutch term freebooter—had long been closely connected with the drives of settler colonial expansion. Aaron Burr and interested followers, Andrew Jackson among them, had considered the prospects of forging a separate nation of squatters between Spain and the United States early in the century. A few years later George Mathews had launched a covertly US-backed filibustering expedition in Spanish Florida. The seizure of Texas, as Robert May notes, might be considered "the most successful filibuster in American history." Similarly, Fremont's proclamation of the Bear Flag Republic in California was tantamount to a filibustering expedition.[75]

Though often dismissed or overlooked because of the strange character and frequent futility, antebellum filibusterism reflected mainstream Manifest Destiny and settler colonial expansionist drives. Much like squatters, filibusters routinely violated the US Neutrality Law of 1818 as well as international law yet thousands of Americans could not have cared less as they eagerly joined these expeditions. Many more thousands of Americans—and not just Southerners—cheered them on and grieved over their failures.

The discovery of California gold at Sutter's Mill only nine days after the signing of the Treaty of Guadalupe Hidalgo accelerated settler colonialism. Streams of Americans crisscrossed the continent, dreaming of riches but soon wracked with disappointment. As most of these were young men, the gold rush left in its wake "a pool of latent filibusters."[76] Moreover, the rush across the continent had highlighted the need for a trans-isthmian canal in Central America while exciting renewed American covetousness of Baja ("Lower California"), Cuba, and Mexico.

In 1851, Spanish officials in Cuba captured and executed by means of the garotte Narciso Lopez, a Venezuelan who had landed a small army in an effort to claim the Caribbean island for the United States.[77] Manifest Destiny fantasists mourned the demise of Lopez through pronouncements, paintings, songs, and poetry decrying the evil Spanish Dons ("Ten thousand soldiers in a moment rise, To drive the harlot Spain from her Cuban prize"). President Millard Fillmore condemned filibustering but he and other Whigs perceived the popularity of the freebooters and the widespread view that Baja and other areas of Mexico should have been annexed during the late war. Even some of those wary of filibusterism still supported the end if not the means to achieve it. "We can philosophically 'bide our time' and patiently wait the unfolding of the 'Manifest Destiny' whose strides are so gigantic, so certain, so rapid and so wonderful," the editors of the *Alta California* rhapsodized.[78]

William Walker, the most famous or infamous among the *filibustero*, launched separate attempts to seize Baja and Sonora from Mexico. All failed and one of the invaders, a former California state senator named Henry Alexander Crabb, ended up with his head on display in a jar of mescal in the Mexican village of Caborca.[79] Walker, a bright and charismatic but unstable Tennessean, recruited financial backers and followers for an assault on Baja, which his small invasion force proclaimed they had carried out after killing a handful of Mexicans. Apparently attempting to emulate Fremont's Bear Flag revolt, Walker fashioned a crude new flag, hoisted it, and proclaimed the new "Republic of Lower California" in 1853.[80]

Like most Americans Walker exalted the superior Anglo-Saxon race and pledged to liberate the "wild, half savage and uncultivated" colonial space for American settlement. The New Orleans *Daily Creole* declared Walker would bring "Anglo-American institutions" to the "feeble descendants of the once haughty and powerful Spaniard." But the small invasion force lacked basic necessities such as food, water, and medicine, all of which prompted a characteristically irrational move by Walker—an extension of his invasion into Sonora. Although the would-be *conquistador* crossed the Sea of Cortez and proclaimed a new Republic of Sonora in 1854, everywhere they went the Yankee invaders "met with hostility by officials, peasants, and even bandits." The expeditionary force barely limped back across the border to San Diego whereupon federal officials had Walker arrested. However, "Popular sentiment so favored Walker that a jury declared him innocent of filibustering after just eight minutes of deliberation."[81]

Frustrated by Mexican resistance, Walker focused on Nicaragua where colonial ambivalence created the prospect of a successful extension of American settler colonialism into the Central American isthmus. The Liberal political faction in Nicaragua initially encouraged Walker to establish a US colony in their country, not only to help overcome their Conservative rivals amid Nicaragua's civil tumult but also to usher in Yankee commerce and know-how that they hoped would uplift their impoverished nation. These same ambivalent visions of modernity had prompted Nicaraguans to sign a contract with Cornelius Vanderbilt's transit company, which required it too to establish agricultural colonies along the transit route. Above all, the Nicaraguans wanted to see the Americans build a canal through their country, as they expected prosperity to follow. These Nicaraguans badly misjudged Walker, however, and would bitterly regret it.

Though only a few hundred in number, Walker's "American Phalanx" won a quick victory in 1855 over the Conservative forces in Granada, thus briefly solidifying his reputation as a conquering hero. Americans back home hailed the glorious triumph of Manifest Destiny, prompting some 10,000 additional settlers and adventurers to flock to Nicaragua. While Conservatives took up guerrilla resistance in the countryside, Walker quickly alienated his ambivalent Nicaraguan supporters as well. The Liberals and the Nicaraguan peasantry soon discovered that Walker's plans to siphon off all of the good land to the US migrants mimicked the neo-feudal policies of the Conservatives. Moreover, the "Daring Grey Eyed Man of Destiny" viewed all Nicaraguans as "mongrels." As nations characterized by an "amalgamated race" were bound to fail, Walker decided to legalize slavery as a means of separating and clarifying the racial formation in Nicaragua. Horrified, the Liberals saw their country become the only one in Latin America to reinstitute slavery. After a fraudulent election in 1856, in which Walker proclaimed himself the new president of Nicaragua, other Central Americans and especially Costa Ricans rallied to drive Walker and his "Immortals" into the sea and back to the United States.[82]

This bizarre chapter in the history of American colonialism had in common with the Indian and Mexican wars indiscriminate violence and destruction. "For two long years, Walker and his troops waged a brutal war against Nicaraguans and other Central Americans as they tried to create an American empire in the region," Michael Gobat explains. Walker's followers—an amalgam of true believers, racial purists, and violent adventurers reminiscent of the Mexican War volunteers—"brought great destruction to Nicaragua" as they left "thousands of dead" in their wake. Walker infamously and gratuitously put Grenada to the torch, igniting a fire that lasted for ten days and left one of oldest cities on the continent in smoldering ruins. "Walker's intoxicated men looted and raped as they torched house after house, working from the suburbs toward the city's center."[83]

Enthusiasm for providentially destined expansion was so great that the nation invariably rallied behind the filibustering expeditions no matter how futile or irrational. Walker became a celebrity—feted in New York City, sitting for a Matthew Brady daguerreotype, and the focal point of demonstrations, parades, and torchlight processions for the martyred American heroes of the battle for Nicaragua. The administration of Democrat Franklin Pierce had even briefly recognized his claim to represent the legitimate government of Nicaragua.[84]

Walker had no regret of the violence in Nicaragua, explaining, "Whenever barbarism and civilization ... meet face to face, the result must be war."[85] Walker returned three times until his capture by the British navy, which turned him over to Honduran authorities. Suddenly a keen supporter of international law, Walker claimed protection as a prisoner of war but the Hondurans ignored the pleas and had him summarily executed by firing squad on September 12, 1860.

The Crisis of American Settler Colonialism

The American Civil War was a crisis provoked by settler colonialism. Like many of the prior Indian wars (see Chapter 2), the Civil War was in essence a borderland conflict over slavery albeit on a more massive scale than anyone imagined. The expansion of settler colonialism into the new western territories in the wake of the Mexican War ignited the internecine conflict. The Civil War thus ultimately flowed from the incomplete progress of nation building as exacerbated especially by slavery or more accurately by the politics (as opposed to the morality) of slavery.[86]

Like the Indian savages and the Mexican mongrels, the Confederate rebels defied and disrupted the imagined community of the nation by making an independent claim on sovereignty. By clinging to what many now saw as a reactionary and immoral practice in slavery, the South undermined the national fantasy of America as a land of the free and a model for the world to emulate. By mid-century, with new lands opened up, a religious revival in force, and an antislavery movement gaining momentum, slavery had now become a problem *for white people* in America.

In the Civil War Americans turned their penchant for righteous violence onto themselves rather than projecting it as a unifying force against the indigenous savage or the Hispanic other. The romanticized history of the Civil War—the way that Americans choose to memorialize and remember the epic clash between the Blue and the Gray—occludes a striking level of rage-filled irregular and indiscriminate violence reflecting continuity with the Mexican and Indian wars. The great battles such as Antietam and Gettysburg, which brought on the bloodiest days in national history, figure prominently in American memory of the Civil War. Far less well known, however, Americans in communities throughout the South, the West, and the central borderlands wantonly killed one another in localized indiscriminate blood feuds.[87] In recent years scholars have increased the estimated death toll from 620,000 to 750,000 on the basis of census data and more sophisticated evidence of the massive toll of irregular warfare.[88]

Though not a race war like the Mexican and Indian wars, the localized guerrilla conflicts of the Civil War otherwise reveal a striking continuity with the earlier history of American warfare. These struggles were "extremely brutal, with combatants 'Othering' their enemies in order to validate the most horrific acts of retribution." Both Confederate and Union partisans "dehumanized their opponents as criminals or bushwhackers or Tories."[89] Only a handful of scholars (in the context of a gargantuan Civil War literature) have focused on this "uncivil war," the "punitive war," and the "savage conflict."[90]

Combatants made frequent references to the Indian wars as they applied a ready vocabulary of "savagery" and "barbarity" to their new domestic enemies. Just as "the people of the Southern borders had slaughtered the Indians who stole their cattle," a Richmond, Virginia, editor avowed, they would "shoot the Yankees who steal their Negroes." Let the Yankees invade, declared *DeBow's Review*, and the people of the South "will become as savage as the Seminoles and twice as brave."[91]

By the summer of 1862, the Civil War had already taken on the character of a full-scale, atrocity-filled guerrilla conflict. Following the passage of the Partisan Ranger Act of 1862, the Confederacy unleashed irregular forces such as those led by John Mosby of Virginia—the "Grey Ghost of the Confederacy"; John Hunt Morgan of Kentucky; and Nathan Bedford Forrest of Tennessee.[92] Some of the most atrocious indiscriminate violence occurred in Missouri, which remained in the Union but was a slave state with masses of Confederate sympathizers. The pro-slavery Missourians viewed Northerners and neighboring "Jayhawkers" as degraded by their "sickly sycophantic love of the nigger" and intent on "crushing us of the South as a people." Unionists viewed the pro-South Missourians as "bushwhackers," "dregs," and "pukes" who "should be punished for their secessionist, slaveholding sins." In this climate of extreme hatred, with men on both sides believing they were doing God's will, "rampant and seemingly random violence" prevailed in Missouri before, during, and after the Civil War.[93]

Indiscriminate violence in Missouri metastasized after the stunning attack on Lawrence, Kansas, led by the rebel guerrilla William Quantrill. After plundering and killing some 180 civilians in front of their wives and families, the raiders put the city to the torch and rode back to the Missouri backcountry.[94] Traumatized Unionist forces responded with indiscriminate violence of their own, including summary executions of suspected bushwhackers. "The contest for the supremacy in this state must be made a war of extermination," Union General Ben Loan declared. As in the Indian Wars and the Mexican War, punishment for indiscriminate killings was exceedingly rare. Not surprisingly, in the wake of Quantrill's raid, Kansas Governor John J. Ingalls applauded the "take no prisoners" attitude and dismissal of "red tape sentimentalism" on the part of "Jennison's Jayhawkers," which he lauded as "a band of destroying angels."[95]

Pathological violence reigned in Missouri. In September 1864 "Bloody Bill" Anderson, a participant in Quantrill's Raid, and a group of about 80 men stopped a train and found that it held two dozen unarmed Union soldiers on furlough. They were forced to strip, then summarily executed and mutilated. As a Union officer later reported, "seventeen of them scalped, and one had his privates cut off and placed in his mouth." When a Union patrol responded to the attack, Anderson's heavily armed gang chased them down and ultimately killed and mutilated a total of 146 Union soldiers and three civilians. The Union army eventually hunted down and killed Anderson and posed his body for photographs. Similarly, another bushwhacker, Alfred Bowman, who claimed to have killed 40 pro-Union men, was beaten to death with an iron tool and his mangled corpse displayed for masses of citizen onlookers at a Union outpost.[96]

Arkansas plunged into "unrestrained guerrilla conflict" as the Mississippi River to the east and the ample swamplands and Ozark Mountains to the west made the Razorback state an ideal breeding ground for guerrilla war. From Memphis, William Tecumseh Sherman warned Arkansas officials, "You initiate the game, and my word for it your people will regret it long after you pass from earth."[97]

Bushwhacking guerrillas ignored the Yankee general by picking off Union troops, attacking steamboats, federal riverboats, and carrying out hit-and-run raids, but Sherman proved as good as his word. The Union army hunted down guerrillas with orders to "shoot them whenever found ... not one of them is to be spared." The federals conducted search and destroy operations, "taxed" the people and burned their homes, towns, and businesses, leaving the state in ruins. As guerrilla and outlaw bands ran wild, and Union retribution showed no restraint, the Civil War became "a time of terror" for Arkansas residents.[98]

Early in the war in Tennessee, Southern irregulars rounded up more than 1,000 Unionists, sending many to prison in the Deep South, and summarily executed an unknown number of others. In a notorious incident in 1864 after a battle in Saltville, VA, Tennessee rebels executed 46 African-American soldiers while several whites lay injured on the battlefield. As the federals retook Tennessee later in the war, Unionists got their revenge by carrying out summary executions of their own.[99]

Despite a vigorous suppression policy in Kentucky, including summary executions, rebel guerrillas flourished in the Bluegrass state. One notorious partisan, Henry C. Magruder, who had taken part in Morgan's raids, was charged with 17 murders, mostly of captured Union soldiers. Magruder also plundered Union homes, burned alive an African-American man, and violated southern gender codes by raping the wife of a Union soldier and six other "young ladies" at a school. Kentucky Unionists wounded and captured Magruder but kept him alive so that he could be hanged before a teeming crowd in Louisville in 1865.[100]

Unsurprisingly, some of the most egregious violence of the Civil War unfolded in Texas, where pockets of pro-Union sentiment prevailed in much of north Texas. In 1861, as Texas joined the Confederacy, the Texas Rangers "wrested control of the state from federal authority," forcing out the Unionist Governor Sam Houston. Declaring that there was no place in Texas for federal sympathizers, Houston's successor ordered "every exertion to effect their *extermination* as soon as possible."[101]

Rumors of a supposed Jayhawk invasion spurred indiscriminate slaughter and mob justice before, during, and after the Civil War in Texas. In August 1862, Rangers and vigilantes descended on six counties populated primarily with German immigrants and carried out "a bloodbath in which more than thirty Germans were killed and nearly that many wounded." In another area of the state, James G. Bourland, a slaveholder and politician soon dubbed "the Hangman of Texas," orchestrated the execution of some 40 alleged Unionists in what became known as the "Great Hanging" of 1862. Determined to extirpate Unionists, Texas briefly contracted with the infamous Missourian Quantrill to round up suspected deserters but his indiscriminate killing of them made Governor Henry McCullough squeamish. "I appreciate his services, and am anxious to have them," he explained, "but certainly we cannot, as a Christian people, sanction a savage inhuman warfare, in which men are to be shot down like dogs, after throwing down their arms and holding up their hands supplicating for mercy."[102]

Neighboring Louisiana, with its river traffic and swamp havens as well as "blurred loyalties and simmering animosities" proved to be "a near perfect incubator for guerrilla warfare." The Union seizure of New Orleans profoundly embittered the city's residents and spurred guerrilla opposition throughout the state. As irregulars conducted sniping and sabotage missions, the federals responded with unrestrained violence of their own. In August 1862, Admiral David Farragut indiscriminately shelled Donaldsville while General Benjamin Butler's army sacked Baton Rouge, plundered homes, destroyed the town, and shipped its art and riches off to the north. Displaced people, deserters, and criminals created a climate conducive to depredations, panic, and despair both during and well after the war.[103]

Sherman's "March to the Sea" late in 1864 has long been singled out as uniquely vindictive in its ruthlessness. In actuality the same style of punitive war had long since become the norm for the Union army. Sherman and Grant—"two of punitive war's greatest proponents"—had concluded as early as 1862 that the only way to respond to persistent rebel resistance and guerrilla assaults was through summary execution and collective punishment of southern communities. The Union generals viewed the Partisan Ranger Act as a dishonorable and inexcusable resort to guerrilla warfare for which the South deserved undiscriminating retribution. They seized upon a code of wartime behavior developed in 1863 by the German Francis Lieber, which deemed irregulars as ineligible for protection under the international laws of war.[104]

With Union forces suffering the traumatic effects of sniping, bushwhacking, partisan raids, and other guerrilla assaults, the federals authorized "a destructive, often murderous, orgy of retaliation." The Union taxed and torched southern cities and towns that refused to turn over guerrillas. Like American attacks on Indian communities, "no real effort was made to determine if the targeted towns and villages did, in fact, house or supply guerrillas before they were set aflame," Clay Mountcastle notes. "Entire towns, sometimes cities, were destroyed and the inhabitants forced to flee even though these locations had no real operational or strategic value." Summary executions "became so routine that the killing of captured guerrillas required little or no justification in dispatches."[105]

By the time Sherman's army marched to the sea, his primed and hardened veterans had already internalized indiscriminate warfare as a matter of routine. Sherman's army meted out punishment to the rebels, burning their homes, farms, and stores, but at the same time continued to take losses as they navigated through a "gauntlet of guerrillas" during the five-month drive on Atlanta.[106] Sherman's army ratcheted up the destruction in South Carolina, carrying out a deliberate reign of terror aimed at ripping the heart out of the southern rebellion. South Carolina guerrillas fought to the bitter end, however, as they "hanged, shot, or slashed the throats of over a hundred federals."[107]

The war would end in Virginia, where in 1864 the Union army under General Philip Sheridan conducted a scorched-earth campaign through the Shenandoah Valley. Sheridan deliberately targeted Loudon County, the home of the longtime Union tormentor, the "Grey Ghost" Mosby, leaving it destitute and in smoldering ruins. The federals plundered and burned everywhere they went, slaughtering farm animals and living off the land, but whenever a Blue-clad soldier strayed too far from the ranks, others would find "our dead comrades suspended conspicuously from the limbs of trees along our line of march," a Union soldier recalled. General George Crook ordered his troops to "destroy all substance for man or beast," to leave behind "a belt of devastation . . . where these bushwhackers are harbored." The Union army "continued to exterminate guerrillas" until Lee finally faced up to the inevitable and surrendered at Appomattox Court House.[108]

By the time of Lee's surrender, guerrilla war could no longer be sustained amid waning popular support in the South. Deserters, pro-Union resisters, escaped slaves, and outlaws plagued the war effort. The mountains of north Georgia had long been inflamed with "vicious local struggles between Confederate deserters, Unionist guerrilla bands, outlaws, and scattered militia companies." In North Carolina, "Bands of destitute deserters roamed the Tar Heel State, plundering homes and wreaking havoc, often upon their own neighbors."[109]

Guerrilla resistance had boomeranged back against the Confederacy. The irregular war had intensified and prolonged the conflict, heightened the destruction, and ultimately ensured that Union strategy and occupation policies had become increasingly draconian. Like the volunteers in the Indian and Mexican Wars, thousands of southern men had wanted to maintain their freedom of movement, avoid regimentation and taking orders, to fight on their own terms. In 1864 the Confederate leaders, recognizing that the irregular war had offered a pretext for "depredations" and "grave mischief," repealed the Partisan Ranger Act.[110]

Sectional hatred kept the South in a state of violent upheaval for years after the war's end. "Union men and former Confederates alike appeared willing to continue their blood feuds after Appomattox," George Rable notes. In opposition to Reconstruction policies, southerners, both "organized and unorganized, intimidated, whipped, hanged and shot Union men, blacks, and Republicans of both races." Accustomed to rejecting authority and carrying out violent assaults, many former guerillas became Klansmen or Night Riders. Others like the James and Younger brothers in Missouri became outlaws.[111]

While violence was commonplace during Reconstruction, as usual "nowhere was it more pervasive and deadly than in Texas." Divisions, hatreds, and "the persecution of freed slaves and Union men contributed to leading Texas to the nation's highest homicide rate by 1870," David P. Smith explains. The wartime hatreds between Confederates, Unionists, deserters, and outlaws "spilled over into the postwar years and lingered in smoldering partisanship for decades."[112]

White Americans gradually restored national unification through racial solidarity in which violence could be focused once again on the South's African-American population. Racial formation and phobias of miscegenation and "black rule" provoked staggering levels of violence to be directed at African-Americans with virtual impunity, as it was "no sin to kill a nigger."[113] Moderate southern whites could be subjected to violence or at a minimum branded as traitors for supporting Yankee Reconstruction policies, which gradually gave way to the "redeemers." A different sort of irregular resistance continued as the South mounted "successful guerrilla warfare against Republicanism."[114] By the time of the 1876 election and subsequent compromise, redemption and counterrevolution were already virtually complete.

Caught in the Middle: Indians and the Civil War

Indians, even those who had been forcibly removed to "Indian country," could not escape the torment of the Civil War. The conflict among the whites offered opportunities for some Western tribes such as the Comanche, who exploited the war to increase the tempo of their raiding in Texas and the Southwest, but for most indigenes the Civil War was as destructive to them as it was to Americans of the North and the South.

Those Indians who joined "the war between the two fires" out of a "desperate hope of obtaining a larger and more secure land base" would be disappointed.[115] The outcome of the Civil War ultimately strengthened the Union and the military while spurring industrialization, homesteading, and railroad development, all of which would help Americans destroy indigenous cultures.

Some 20,000 Indians served in the Civil War, mostly but far from exclusively on the Union side. For some Indians the conflict offered an outlet for their masculine warrior drives while others hoped simply to improve their lives through military service. In the northeast, the Pequot and Mohegan joined the Union cause as mercenaries because they were extremely poor and had few other opportunities. In Michigan, the Ottawa and Ojibwa hoped to improve their declining status in the wolverine state through military service. The Delaware and Seneca also aided the North, the latter inspired partly by Grant's selection of the Seneca Ely Parker as his military secretary. In the South the Pamunkey of Virginia and the Lumbee of North Carolina fought against the Confederacy in hopes of liberation from their increasingly precarious enclaves within those states. Conversely, the Catawba had become collaborationists to survive in South Carolina and thus served as volunteer infantrymen in the Army of Northern Virginia.[116]

The Civil War badly divided and severely damaged the southeastern tribes who had been forcibly relocated west into the Indian Country. Their "entire social fabric disintegrated" as farms, homes, schools, and churches were destroyed in the conflict.[117] Thousands of Indians became refugees. The devastation resulted partly from the neutral space and vulnerability of Indian Country, as Unionist forces raided from Kansas to the north and southerners entered from the south and east. More importantly, however, the tribes divided against each other and amongst themselves as they joined in the spirit of internecine strife.

The Civil War badly divided the Cherokee, with most eventually siding with the Union, though it had been slower than the Confederacy in seeking their support. The Choctaw and the Chickasaw sided with the South, while the Seminole and the Creeks like the Cherokee were divided in their loyalties. "Over the course of the war these factions, in concert with Union and Confederate troops, savagely fought each other, devastating the Five Tribes," David La Vere points out.[118]

After the Civil War the United States cited partial indigenous support for the Confederacy as a pretext for taking additional land away from Indians. With the crisis of the Union resolved, American settler colonialism was back on course.

6

"They Promised to Take Our Land and They Took It": Settler Colonialism in the American West

At mid-century the overland trails, the seizure of vast new lands from Mexico, and the gold rush sent settlers streaming across the continent. The population of the American West soared from about 1 million in 1815 to 15 million by 1860. Before federal Indian agents could negotiate treaties, which Congress often declined to ratify in any case, American settlers and territorial governments often took the "Indian problem" into their own hands. In Texas, across the Great Basin, and in Arizona, California, and the Oregon Territory, Americans perpetrated massacres as they drove indigenous people out of colonial space. Many Americans openly advocated genocide.

The US military sometimes condemned unprovoked settler violence yet the Army also perpetrated massacres and its leaders shared the settlers' contempt for Indians as well as the desire to eliminate them. The Army went on the offensive in the post–Civil War era and fought countless battles and skirmishes with indigenous bands. The Civil War militarized the nation and empowered a generation of army officers and enlisted men who would wage an uncompromising style of warfare against the indigenes. Technological innovation and industrialization, especially the trans-continental railroad, made Indians and their cultures appear that much more primitive and destined to "vanish."

Americans sought total security, as they meant to put a stop to Indian raiding, slave trading, and other vestiges of what they perceived as the wild and savage Indian way of life. Following on the heels of Manifest Destiny, visions of a powerful, modernizing continental empire left no cultural space and only the assigned physical spaces of reservations for Indians.[1]

The legendary "Wild West" has cast such a powerful spell over American history and popular culture that scholars have been anxious to debunk it.[2] "The history of 'the West' was in fact the history of the entire nation," they point out. "We can best know the history of the American West if we read it as a chapter in the much larger history of European colonialism."[3] All of this is true, and yet the West *was* wild in that explosive settlement occurred so rapidly that it often preceded the arrival of military or civilian authority, thus leaving outnumbered bands of indigenes vulnerable to often-indiscriminate settler aggression.

As most Americans viewed the indigenes as "an obstruction to national self-interest and commercial expansion," the tribes had either to be removed from the desired land or to be exterminated.[4] The United States thus implemented a policy of "enforced sedentarism." This policy, typical in other settler colonial situations (Bantustans, Occupied Territories, etc.), entailed driving Indians onto reservations.[5] If they resisted, the Army and settlers claimed justification to wage exterminatory warfare.

Indigenous Americans thus faced unprecedented pressures in this final, often manic, phase of continental ethnic cleansing. Ambivalences proliferated, to be sure, as Indians allied with the Americans against other tribes to pursue their self-interests or merely to survive. As Americans violated treaties and pushed Indians out of "Indian country," they forced these refugees to encroach on the land of other Indians thus promoting interethnic conflict. As in the past the extreme pressures of colonialism divided Indians within their own tribes, often generationally as young warriors waged violent resistance against the settlers while older leaders futilely strove for accommodation in the face of the uncompromising settler advance.

Reformers mostly in the East loudly advocated justice for Indians. They expressed the putatively humanitarian desires to civilize and Christianize the indigenes, "reforms" that ultimately led to the movement for Indian assimilation. Yet even these humanitarians pursued a genocidal agenda of destroying Indian communities and cultures, notably by removing indigenous children from their families.[6] In addition to assaulting the Indian way of life, the assimilationist Dawes Act (1887) enabled the seizure of millions more acres of colonial space for settlers. In the continuous pattern of Euro-American history, the drives of settler colonialism ultimately trumped colonial ambivalence.

Indian Removal from "Indian Country"

As with the "Old Northwest," settler colonialism in the midsection of the continent has been marginalized in American History. Both the southeastern Indian Removal, with its infamous "Trail of Tears," and the subsequent "Wild West" phase have overshadowed removal from what became the American heartland. Indians in this region, however, faced not only a flood of settlers but also the arrival of other indigenous tribes as Americans pushed them off lands to the east. The impact of colonialism thus radiated out across the Mississippi, spurring inter-indigenous violence in addition to the violence associated with dispossession carried out by the Americans.

In the confluence area where the Missouri and Mississippi Rivers conjoined marking the "gateway to the West," a tradition of inclusiveness and ambivalence dated back to the French style of colonialism in "upper Louisiana." As Indians and Europeans worked the exchange economy, the different peoples interacted and coexisted in the region, though not always seamlessly. Sexual liaisons and intermarriage were common, forging kinship ties between Indians and Europeans.

As Americans flooded into the lower Missouri, the region transitioned "from ethnic mixing to ethnic cleansing."[7] Following the War of 1812, as growing numbers of Americans migrated in with their captive slaves, Missouri entered the Union as a slave state in 1820. The American immigrants encountered Shawnee and Delaware Indians who had been made refugees from the US takeover of the Ohio Valley. They would now be forced out once again. "Scornful of Indian holdings," American settler colonials "squatted where they pleased, that is, on any lands they deemed vacant." They demanded that indigenous people be removed to "some more remote part . . . better suited to Indian pursuits."[8]

During more than 30 years as governor of the Missouri Territory, William Clark of Corps of Discovery fame secured treaties removing tens of thousands of Indians from the lower Missouri Valley. The initial treaties merely provided for peace and friendship but in years following the War of 1812, as American power grew and the Indians' ability to resist dissipated, Clark "negotiated" removal of the tribes to the west. In actuality, as in the southeast, the terms of removal began to be "dictated, rather than negotiated." The indigenes lacked the numbers and weaponry to put up a fight against the masses of settlers pouring into Missouri.[9]

Clark's willingness even to conduct diplomacy with Indians did not sit well with the settler-driven Missouri territorial assembly, which in 1820 voted him out of office for being "too good to Indians." Thomas Hart Benton, the most powerful Missouri politician and a champion of Western settlement, labeled Indians "a palpable evil." He called for their prompt removal from the land to "make room for the spread of slaves." A huge forced cession of Osage land soon followed. "Reduced to its essence," Stephen Aron explains, "the problem was simple: more white people wanted more land, which required Indians to be displaced." Hence the US government backed the local population in carrying out the "ethnic cleansing of Missouri."[10]

The Indians most affected in both the Missouri and Arkansas River valleys were the Osage, who had been the power brokers of the region. The Osages long conducted trade with the relatively small numbers of Spanish, French, and English who did not appear to pose a threat to their power. The Osages kept the focus of their aggression on the neighboring Quapaw, a traditional rival, as well as incoming Cherokee, Shawnee, Delaware, and other Indians who had been driven off land to the east. The Osages and the Cherokee clashed violently on several occasions. Having viewed other indigenous groups as the more serious threat to their hegemony, the Osages were slow to react to the Americans until it was soon too late to respond effectively.[11]

West of Missouri the US Congress established a vast and putatively permanent "Indian country." Under the Indian Removal Act of 1830, the United States had shrouded the cleansing campaign behind the pledge to "forever secure and guarantee" the new Indian lands. In 1834 congressional legislation formally created the new Indian country, a huge swath of colonial space stretching from Oklahoma across the Great Plains to modern-day Montana. The Indian Trade and Intercourse Act of 1834 also established regulations governing non-Indian entry, trade, land sales, and the sale of weapons and alcohol.

The substantive legislation establishing the new Indian country reflected ambivalence by advancing the settler colonial project while ostensibly providing for humane treatment of the Indian. Many Americans rationalized their support for Indian removal on the humanitarian grounds that the indigenes would be "better off" once they were provided with land and opportunity further west. In urging Indians to exchange their land east of the Mississippi, Lewis Cass, the Michigan Democrat who served as Andrew Jackson's secretary of war, offered the "solemn promise" that the new lands would be "reserved for the red people; it will be yours as long as the sun shines and the rain falls."[12]

Such promises came up empty, as the putative Indian country proved "ineffectual and a failure from the beginning." Americans were already trickling west on the Santa Fe Trail, but the trickle soon became a flood on the Oregon Trail, which cut through the heart of the Indian country. As belief in the existence of a "great American desert" gave way to the more accurate perception of the Plains as a bountiful heartland, Americans would seize the land from the "semi-barbarous nomads," the "solemn promises" such as those made by Cass notwithstanding. The Mexican War followed by the Kansas-Nebraska Act (1854) ended all doubts that Indians would once again be removed. As Senator Stephen A. Douglas, architect of the Kansas-Nebraska Act, explained, the "Indian barrier . . . filled with hostile savages" must give way to farmers, railroads, commerce, and American destiny to conquer all the land from sea to sea.[13]

American Indian Removal thus remained a structurally ensconced, continuous project, as settler colonialism now drove the paradoxical removal of Indians from Indian country. The approach to the indigenes living in the middle of the continent was the same one Americans had pursued on the other side of the Mississippi: they would be resettled further west to make room for American migrants. The policy undertaken in Indian country thus "was a revival of the government's removal program in a manner not widely publicized or understood."[14]

Rather than a vast, unbroken land in which indigenous cultures could thrive or at least survive, Indian country inexorably shrank into isolated and often depressed Indian Bantustans. Indians found themselves increasingly outnumbered by the American influx as they continued to be ravaged by epidemic diseases, notably smallpox. The plight of the Nebraska Indians proved fairly typical. In 1800 some 14,000 Indians—Pawnee, Omaha, Ponca, and Otoe-Missouria—held some 30 million acres in eastern Nebraska. Following a "century of dispossession," only about 10 percent, overwhelmingly the Omaha, remained.[15]

The dispossession began in earnest in the 1840s as officials called for removal of the four Nebraska tribes to facilitate settler colonialism. Indians had to be cleansed from the land "so as to leave an ample outlet for our white population to spread and pass towards and beyond the Rocky Mountains." Indians were not fooled by the pale-face promises that they would be removed to good land. "If it is such a good country that you offer," a member of the Potawatomi delegation inquired in 1842, "why does not our Great Father send his white children there?"[16]

Indigenous logic fell on deaf ears; moreover, few settlers showed concern for the Nebraska Indian and thus opposed the expenditure of government revenues on behalf of indigenous refugees. "When it came to Indians in territorial Nebraska," David Wishart points out, "sympathy and understanding were as scarce as good timber." Even Americans who expressed an ambivalent desire to see Indians "domesticated, improved, and elevated" at the same time had their eyes on the "large surplus" of "fine agricultural lands" that would be freed up for sale. The tribes were forced to sell their land "for much less than its fair market value."[17]

Although weakened by dispossession and disease—as well as regular onslaughts from the predatory Sioux tribes to their north—the Nebraska Indians sometimes fought back against the settler colonial invasion. Inevitably, Indian homeland defense boomeranged back against the bands in the form of a militant settler backlash. "If the Government will not protect the inhabitants of Nebraska against these red rascals," vowed *The Nebraskian* from Omaha City, "then we are in favor of calling out the militia and scalping the tribe." A minority who empathized with the plight of the Indians was invariably marginalized. A prominent land surveyor condemned the "lackadaisical sympathy" expressed on behalf of Indians, declaring that he would prefer "to exterminate the last mother's son of them from the face of the earth." After being forced onto reservations, where they endured "season after season of grinding poverty and steadily declining population," most of the Nebraska Indians were eventually driven out of the territory entirely. While Indians at other times and places were able to rebuild and reconfigure their identities, "Life only got worse" for the Nebraska tribes.[18]

Removed to the Oklahoma Territory the "civilized tribes" of the Southeast rebuilt their lives, but clashed with the indigenes already living in the region. American settler colonialism thus forced Indians to "invade" other Indian lands. Whereas to most Americans "Indians" were (and to a considerable extent still are) perceived as a unified entity, the tribes forced into close contact differed profoundly from one another. In many cases town-dwelling, agriculturally oriented "civilized tribes" came into contact with the more mobile equestrian, bison-hunting tribes of the Plains states. These indigenous groups had different histories and lifestyles and little more in common than many of them had with Americans.

Well before the Indian Removal of the 1830s Cherokee, Creeks, Kickapoo, Sauk and Fox, Potawatomi, Shawnees, and Delaware had migrated toward the Plains. The Pawnees, Osages, Omaha, Caddo, Wichita and to a lesser extent the Comanche and Kiowa—were among the tribes threatened by this influx. Some bands, including the Kiowa, Comanche, and Apaches suffered a significant blow from a smallpox epidemic perhaps ushered in by the newly arrived tribes in the late 1830s. The Plains bands raided the settlements of the incoming Indians, who fought back, but accommodation and cultural borrowing also occurred.[19]

As they settled into their new homes in the Oklahoma Territory, the Five Tribes "created an amazing renaissance. They re-created their national governments, reestablished their newspapers, and rebuilt their schools and churches."[20] Because they were civilized—a term they freely used to describe themselves—the Five Tribes viewed themselves as superior to Plains Indians. Adopting the classic colonialist binary, they viewed the equestrian, bison hunting, and raiding cultures of the southern Plains as "savage" peoples. But the tribes, who had long considered the southern Plains their homelands and hunting grounds, viewed the Ohio Valley and the Southeastern tribes as encroaching upon their territory.

The Cherokee, Choctaw, Creek, Chickasaw, and Seminole embraced the politics of racial separation that had created Indian country. They proclaimed their territories a "red man's country" as they strove to keep whites out and, true to their Deep South roots, they sought to control the lives of black people living in Indian country. "Nation-building in Indian Territory meant racial separation, notions of 'blood purity,' and the power of race in the making of space," as James Ronda puts it.[21] As they had done in the South, the Cherokee and other tribes built prosperous farms and communities, recovered from the wreckage of the Civil War, and then weathered the assimilation movement. In the late nineteenth century Congress opened up the Oklahoma Territory for a land rush of settlers, squeezing the indigenes off their land and into internal Bantustans, yet they persevered and some thrived.

Conflict between the "progressive" civilized tribes and the "traditional" Plains Indians produced diplomacy and ambivalent relations as well as raids and violent clashes. The Shawnees, Delaware, and Kickapoo gradually came to terms with the Wichita and Caddo. The Creeks called councils with the Southern Plains tribes and strove to establish kinship ties, sometimes bringing in the Seminole as well; however, the Choctaw and Chickasaw "saw their western neighbors as savage inferiors, trespassers, and raiders and wanted as little to do with them as possible." The Cherokee tried to keep their distance from the "savage" Plains tribes as well.[22]

The "Great Triumvirate" and Forced Removal to Reservations

The Civil War strengthened the federal government, militarized the nation, propelled unprecedented numbers of settlers and soldiers into the West, and thus dramatically advanced the settler colonial project west of the Mississippi River. In 1862 alone the Union Congress passed the Homestead Act, the Pacific Railroad Act, and the Morrill Land Grant Act—all of which spurred settler migration. "More in fact was done during the Civil War to incorporate the West than in any comparable period," Elliott West notes.[23]

By the end of the Civil War, some 20,000 US troops were serving in the West, thereby enhancing "the state's capacity to police as well as punish Indians." US Army officers reflected the ambivalence of the broader US society, as many sympathized with Indians and believed that settlers and the government had treated the tribes unfairly. At the same time, however, the officers viewed the indigenes as primordial savages and typically proved willing to fight fiercely against them.[24]

The Civil War empowered a handful of generals skilled in the conduct of relentless irregular warfare and backed by thousands of combat veterans. Generals Ulysses S. Grant, William T. Sherman, and Philip H. Sheridan, "the great triumvirate of the Union Civil War effort formulated and enacted military Indian policy." They sought to remove Indians to facilitate the transcontinental railroad as the spearhead of the capitalist development of the West.

As they had done in subduing the Confederacy, Grant, Sherman, and Sheridan would authorize indiscriminate warfare and collective punishment to crush the national enemy. The three generals thus "applied their shared ruthlessness, born of their Civil War experiences, against a people all three despised, in the name of civilization and progress."[25] The subsequent removal campaigns or Indians Wars underscore the continuity of the American way or war.

While violent ethnic cleansing ultimately would comprise the essence of Western Indian removal, ambivalent discourse pertaining to Indian policy grew powerful in the postbellum years. The antebellum antislavery movement followed by abolition left a legacy of humanitarian sentiment that influenced the debate over Indian policy in the post–Civil War era. The violence of the Civil War traumatized many Americans who now condemned the application of mass violence against the tribes. They viewed Indian removal as inevitable and appropriate but insisted the savages should be educated, taught to farm, and graced with Christianity.

For the Western settlers and the vast majority of Army officers, ambivalent attitudes toward Indians posed a threat to the settlers and delayed the inevitable. Like most Army officers, Grant, Sherman, and Sheridan chafed over the relocation of the Bureau of Indian Affairs from the War Department to the Department of Interior upon its creation in 1849.[26] In 1883 Colonel Frank Triplett expressed a common view in colorful language, as he condemned "junketing peace commissions, composed of low-brow, thick-lipped, bottle-nosed humanitarians" who were "the inferiors of the savages in every manly trait."[27]

After ascending to the White House in 1869, Grant announced a new "Peace Policy" toward Indians to appease mostly eastern critics of violent Indian removal. Grant named his wartime aide Ely Parker, a Seneca, as the first indigenous commissioner of Indian affairs. Grant also appointed Quakers to head Indian agencies across the country. In 1873, alluding to ambivalent expressions of guilt within the society, Grant called for "good faith" effort at uplifting Indians in order "to stand better before the civilized nations of the earth and in our own consciences."

Despite such discourse, the "peace policy" demanded unconditional surrender of Indian homelands and hunting grounds and relocation onto reservations. In 1871 Congress terminated treaty making with Indians, who henceforth would be approached exclusively as a subjugated minority population. The "peace policy" and the subsequent movement for Indian assimilation signaled an effort to institute internal colonial rule once Indians had been militarily subdued.

Reminiscent of the Indian Removal Act, indigenes were "voluntarily" to remove to reservations where they became dependent on the unreliable Americans for food and sustenance. The palpable impulse to exterminate lurked just beneath the surface of the "peace policy." As Grant warned, "Those who do not accept this policy will find the new administration ready for a sharp and severe war policy." As thousands of Indians would prove unwilling to acquiesce to cultural genocide, the "peace policy" in actuality assured the continuation of mass violence.[28]

Although he acknowledged, "No doubt our people have committed grievous wrong to the Indians," Sherman longed for a violent resolution of the conflict. He reasoned, much as the Nazis would do with respect to Jews and other *untermenschen*, that the Indian problem "will exist as long as the Indians exist." This was an ominous discourse given that in 1865 the War Department gave Sherman command over a vast area of colonial space from his headquarters in St. Louis to the Continental Divide, an area he meant to clear of "free roaming" Indians. Sherman bitterly resented Indians' ability to conduct raids and return to the sanctity of the reservation, all the while being depicted as victims by the naïve eastern humanitarians. Sherman's preferred approach was "extermination if need be; displacement for certain," biographer Michael Fellman explains. "Without any doubt Sherman's overall policy was never accommodation and compromise, but vigorous war against the Indians."

Sherman could reflect calmly on the Indian problem on occasion but whenever the tribes offered violent resistance, "his never very subdued rage would break out, and his genocidal urges would pour forth." In order to eliminate the problem altogether, Grant, Sherman, and Sheridan pursued an aggressive war against the Plains Indians. The three generals "would work in perfect accord on this issue."[29]

The third member of the Indian war triumvirate, Sheridan, had during his posting in the Northwest lived in an intimate relationship with an Indian woman named Sidnayoh of the Klickitat tribe. He departed the northwest when the Civil War broke out and never acknowledged her publically, though she did visit him in Washington years later. His own intimate relationship notwithstanding, Sheridan called the Northwest Indians "miserable wretches" and eventually called for their extermination. The Irishman dismissed the peace policy, explaining contemptuously that when a white man murders someone, "we hang him or send him to the penitentiary. If an Indian does the same, we have been in the habit of giving him more blankets." During the winter campaign of 1868–1869, Sheridan took the surrender of a Comanche chief, Tosawi, who professed his peaceful intentions. "Why am I and my people being tormented by you?" he asked Sheridan. "I am a good Indian." Sheridan famously replied in front of a witness: "The only good Indians I ever saw were dead." Whether a quip or a Freudian slip, the expression was not far removed from Sheridan's actual sentiments.[30]

The Cheyenne Massacres

One of the more infamous atrocities in American history, at Sand Creek in 1864, illustrates how massacres functioned not as isolated and episodic events but rather as engines of the larger genocidal removal project. Beginning in 1859, as the Colorado gold rush brought Americans pouring into the Rocky Mountain region, the indigenous people of the area faced an increasingly precarious existence. As miners built camps, the army built forts, capitalists built railroads, and hunters slaughtered bison, Indian land and hunting grounds withered away.

The settler colonial influx brought an end to decades of ambivalent relations and multiethnic coexistence as symbolized by Bent's Fort, the trading post established on the Arkansas River in southeastern Colorado. Since the early 1830s, Cheyenne, Arapaho, and other Indians had exchanged goods peacefully with American trappers and traders at the adobe fort. Founder William Bent and his brothers forged kinship ties, as they had married Indian women. Their mixed blood and multilingual children evolved hybrid personae, as they drifted between both the Indian and American worlds. As late as 1858, "many Kiowa, Comanche, and Cheyenne . . . had been uniformly friendly," Elliott West points out, "but the gold rush and its many repercussions were transforming the central plains." Ambivalence gave way as American adventurers and settlers poured into the country, shattering the indigenous cultures in the process. Bent spoke of "the failure of food, the encircling encroachment of the white population, and the exasperating sense of decay and impending extinction with which they are surrounded."[31]

Under immense pressures from unprecedented and unforeseen forces, Indians divided within their own bands over how best to respond. Younger warriors such as the Cheyenne "dog soldiers" were eager to prove their manhood by standing up to the whites. They wanted to continue raiding and fighting while older chiefs such as Black Kettle, concluding that resistance would prove futile against the endless mass of settlers, sought out paths of accommodation instead. Black Kettle would find, however, that accommodation would prove equally futile with the Americans. These debates echoed discussions within tribes and among Indian confederations throughout the course of Euro-American history, as discussed in earlier chapters.

While the Yankees and Confederates killed each other in the east, a race war between Indians and Americans erupted in Colorado. The dog soldiers of the southern Cheyenne went beyond raids and began to conduct "an indiscriminate war on all whites." When a settler family only 25 miles southeast of Denver was found dead on their farmstead in June 1864, residents placed their scalped and mutilated bodies on a wagon in the city, posing an infant son and four-year-old daughter between their dead parents. While Colorado's inflamed population cried out for an exterminatory response, Black Kettle pleaded for accommodation and kinship. The chieftain called for "peace with the whites. We want to hold you by the hand. You are our father."[32]

Despite Black Kettle's ambivalent plea, Coloradans responded with a perfidious massacre at Sand Creek. Insisting that they had no desire to kill peaceful Indians, Colorado officials authorized Black Kettle and some 600 Cheyenne followers to encamp at the isolated spot on the eastern Colorado plains along the creek. Colorado's territorial governor John Evans, a physician from Chicago with no experience in Indian affairs, and Methodist minister John Chivington, who had organized Denver's first Sunday school, shared responsibility for the subsequent massacre.

Like the settlers who slaughtered Indians at Gnadenhutten, the Coloradans wanted to put an end to ambivalence and to demonstrate that their state was no place for Indians. By driving out the indigenes, Evans would prove that Colorado was safe for settlers, thus increasing migration and hastening the path to statehood. Chivington, the head of Colorado's militia who had won a decisive battle for the Union at Glorieta Pass in northern New Mexico, now wanted to carry out Jehovah's fiery wrath on the Indians and "half-breeds," who represented the sin of miscegenation. "The Sand Creek camp, with its ethnic sloppiness and its tangle of links that bound an older social order, was an intolerable affront," West explains.[33]

At sunrise on November 29, 1864, Chivington and a force of 700 volunteers, backed by four howitzers, perpetrated the Sand Creek Massacre. An attack was the last thing anticipated by Black Kettle, who flew an American flag high on a lodge pole in the camp and had been given "no reason to expect anything but a long, dull, hungry winter." "I heard him call to the people," George Bent, who was encamped at Sand Creek, recalled. Black Kettle urged the Cheyenne "not to be afraid, that the soldiers would not hurt them: then the troops opened fire from two sides of the camp." Chivington's forces slaughtered some 150 peaceful Indians and looted and burned their lodges before withdrawing.[34]

Rationalizing the genocide, Evans declared, "The benefit to Colorado of that massacre, as they call it, was very great for it ridded the plains of the Indians." While the *Rocky Mountain News* praised "the brilliant feats of arms in Indian warfare," the army condemned the attack and an extensive federal investigation charged Evans and Chivington with responsibility for the "gross and wanton outrages" perpetrated at Sand Creek. "Fleeing women holding up their hands and praying for mercy were brutally shot down; infants were killed and scalped in derision; men were tortured and mutilated," the federal commission found.[35]

Outrage over the Sand Creek massacre spurred the US Congress to create the Indian Peace Commission in 1867. The federal government also ratified treaties that were signed that same year at Medicine Lodge Creek in Kansas. The signatory bands of Comanche, Kiowa, Cheyenne, Apache, and Arapaho received cash payments and pledges of food, clothing, tools, schools for their children, and other services in return for relocating onto reservations from which they would be allowed to go on buffalo hunts south of the Arkansas River. The United States did not, however, provide the promised provisions nor did it uphold its pledge to keep intruders off the designated Indian land. For their part the indigenous bands did not cease their raiding and resistance, hence the peace effort collapsed almost immediately. "Marred by obscure meanings, mutual misconstructions, and uneasy compromises," Peka Håmålåinen explains, "the final agreement was a typical U.S. Indian treaty."[36]

As the Medicine Lodge treaties broke down, Sherman reveled in the prospect of waging the kind of warfare that had made him famous in the North and infamous in the South. "I cannot represent two opposing views, for a man of action must have positive plans," he explained. "Now this must come to a violent end." The ruthless army campaign combined with the depletion of the bison—which the Plains Indians had been overhunting before the Americans arrived—meant that the "hunting-based economy rapidly spun into a deep depression from which it would never emerge." As Americans and their cattle and sheep poured into Colorado and the Wind River range of Wyoming, "Native inhabitants slipped into long-term poverty" while "white residents profited by their losses."[37]

As diplomacy collapsed, Sheridan, in command of the army of the West, went on the offensive culminating in a massacre of peacefully encamped Cheyenne on the Washita River just east of the 100th meridian. At dawn on November 26, 1868, Lieutenant Colonel George A. Custer of the Seventh Cavalry led the assault on the camp, as his regimental band blared a jolly Irish dance tune. The Americans and their Osage scouts killed indiscriminately, 103 Indians in all, burned the camp, and systematically shot and cut the throats of some 700 horses and ponies. This carnage was designed to cripple the Indians by depriving them of food in the winter and mobility in the spring. Among the Indians killed was Black Kettle, whose luck had run out after surviving the Sand Creek massacre. Custer ordered a timely retreat before a large encampment of Indians downstream could respond to the attack. In so doing, he left behind a column of men who would be killed and mutilated.[38]

The Killing Fields of California

Preceding the dispossession of the Plains tribes was a genocidal campaign against of the California Indians. In a recent study, Benjamin Madley found "evidence of hundreds of massacres and mass killings perpetrated against California Indians" constituting an "American genocide." Colonial ambivalence thus found little traction with the American settlers of California. Free of government oversight, they carried out orchestrated campaigns of mass murder.[39]

As a result of the gold rush, settlers poured into California too fast for the federal government and its treaty-making prerogative to gain traction. Thus Americans dealt with California much like the settlers in Australia, treating the territory as *terra nullius* (empty or uninhabited land) thus obviating the need for treaties. By the time federal agents arrived, surveyed the situation, and drew up treaties to dispossess the bands in a civilized legal fashion, it was already too late. In 1851–1852, Californians rejected the federal treaties, which they claimed would hand over "the finest farming and mineral lands" to tribes "wholly incapable, by habit or taste, of appreciating its value."[40]

Treating California as empty land was brutally ironic insofar as the territory at one time probably had the highest density of indigenous people on the continent. The Indian population, estimated at about 300,000 in 1769 when the Spanish built their first missions on the Pacific coast, had been halved by the time of the 1849 gold rush. Over the next decade, it plummeted another 80 percent, to around 30,000 Indians, as a result of murder, disease, famine, and declining birth rates. By 1900 only about 15,000 Indians remained in California.[41]

Separated by almost a century, both Hispanic colonialism and American settler colonialism had a shattering impact on indigenous Californians. As the Spanish Franciscan missionaries sought to force labor and conversion on them, the coastal Indians suffered the "brutal effects of mission policies." Many adapted but most resisted and stayed away from the missions and presidios. In 1680, the massive Pueblo revolt drove the Spanish out of Santa Fe. In 1775, hundreds of Indians assaulted and burned to the ground the San Diego Mission. Such revolts prompted the Spanish to "put down resistance with shocking brutality, killing, maiming, or enslaving Indians who defied them."[42]

Holding their own in an ambivalent colonial setting for some 80 years, Indians in the California interior interacted with Spanish missionaries, mission refugees, Mexicans, and American settlers. Relegated primarily to the coast, neither the Spanish nor the Mexicans successfully colonized the interior tribes of California—only the American settler colonials ultimately would cleanse them from the land.

Following the revolt from Spain, Mexican rancheros broke up the mission system and took control of coastal California. The dominant rancheros during the period in which Mexico laid claim to California (1821–1846), men such as Mariano Guadalupe Villejo, "emerged both wealthy and popular after he and his followers attacked and murdered over 200 Wappos in 1834." Indigenous people on the coast, both men and women, worked for the rancheros while Indians from the interior plagued the Mexicans with raids in which they stole stock, especially horses.[43]

As in northern Mexico, persistent Indian raids weakened the rancheros and eventually made their land ripe for the American taking in the Mexican War. In 1846, as the United States launched its invasion of the Mexican territory, some Indians joined with the Americans to oust the despised Mexicans. In 1847, the assistance of indigenous allies helped force the Hispanics to surrender Los Angeles. Peace with Americans was not the norm, however, as traders and trappers had gradually infiltrated the interior regions of California, coming into violent conflict with indigenous people.[44]

The California gold rush brought a surge of settler colonialism followed by waves of indiscriminate killing. In 1851 the first civilian governor of California, Peter Burnett, sanctioned "a war of extermination . . . until the Indian race becomes extinct." The "white" population of California catapulted from 92,000 in 1851 to 380,000 by 1860. The gold rush ebbed but California's bountiful agricultural land lay before the hordes of new migrants like ripened fruit. As a result, "the living space for Indians on the margins of white society steadily eroded." Settlers labeled the indigenous people "Diggers," apparently because some of the tribes collected acorns to eat and grind into flour. The pejorative term reflected a perception of the indigenous Californians as animal-like *untermenschen*—"about the lowest specimens of humanity found on earth," as one settler put it—thus rationalizing campaigns of extermination.[45]

From the 1850s to 1871, a "series of massacres" left the Yana, who had long inhabited a Delaware-sized swath of northern California, "virtually exterminated." In a familiar pattern, settlers first undermined traditional land patterns and access to food and water, then responded to episodic Yana stock raids with "retaliatory massacres" that "escalated to state-sanctioned killing and removal." The settlers sought "total extermination," the creation of an "Indian-free environment."[46]

Settlers carried out massacres—a series of Sand Creeks—in US-occupied California, as the Americans "surpassed Spaniards and Mexicans in their brutal treatment of Native Americans." Colonial ambivalence was in short supply in California as land-hungry settlers and their militias "murdered thousands of Native Americans, and enslaved thousands more." The Army occupied California but "did nothing" to stop the slaughter and sometimes joined in. In 1849, the Army slaughtered an estimated 135–250 Pomo Indians in the Clear Lake area of northern California. The soldiers, making no distinctions of age or gender, speared babies with their bayonets and hurled them into a creek.[47]

In the early 1850s, the Tolowa Indians of northwestern California and southwestern Oregon "were nearly obliterated following the arrival of Anglo-Americans." The Tolowa population plummeted from perhaps 5,000 to fewer than 1,000 Indians in just a few years. Diseases took their toll but so did a campaign of slaughter that began with isolated killings, proceeded to organized massacres, and ended with state-supported campaigns of extermination. Federal officials drove the surviving Tolowa onto dismal reservations for "a destructive new cycle of incarceration, escape, recapture, and re-incarceration," Madley notes. The Army acknowledged that reservation Indians "are continually exposed to the brutal assault of drunken and lawless white men; their squaws are forced and, if resisted, the Indians are beaten and shot."[48]

Genocide permeated the golden state. A militia captain reported killing 283 Indians and forcing 292 others onto a reservation at Mendocino. The Yuci Indians suffered the most extensive assault as their population came down from 12,000 to some 600 in a decade beginning in 1854. "There were so many of these expeditions," a settler recalled. "We would kill on average fifty or so Indians on a trip." An Army major acknowledged that the settlers had carried out a "relentless war of extermination... They have ruthlessly massacred men, women, and children." Unapologetic settlers inundated the California legislature with demands for honoring the scalp bounties that had been offered as an incentive for Indian extermination.[49]

Most of the killing was unprovoked and indiscriminate. The California Indians had carried out some raids against the settlers but rarely attacked them violently. Even the extermination-minded San Francisco-based newspaper *Alta California* acknowledged in 1851, "Their depredations, wherever and whenever committed, were not aimed at human life but leveled at the property of their white neighbors... Instances of Indian cruelty were rarely heard." That same year, the San Luis Rey Indian leader Antonio Garra attempted an armed revolt against settlers in southern California but it generated little response before Garra was captured and hanged.[50]

Despite the overall lack of provocation, the settlers showed little ambivalence over the indiscriminate killing. In 1850, *Alta California* rationalized that the destruction of the inferior Indian "race" was "unavoidable." Another San Francisco newspaper chimed in, "Extermination is the cheapest and quickest remedy."[51]

On several occasions treaties had been negotiated with the Indians, but with the California delegation opposed, Congress repeatedly failed to ratify them. A few reservations aside, by 1860 "the government had more or less abandoned the uphill struggle to protect Indian land in California." The remaining indigenous Californians were left devoid of civil rights and subject to the whims of the settlers. Many Indian women suffered sexual assault or went into prostitution. Between 1850 and 1863, some 10,000 Indians were sold into servitude. American slave traders often killed the parents of Indian children so that they might be seized and trafficked.[52]

Displaying an ambivalence that distinguished him from the militant army triumvirate, General George Crook forthrightly declared that the California settler colonials were the sources of the violence and he even lamented having to protect them "when our sympathies were with the Indians." The Shasta Indians of California had been "forced to take the warpath or sink all self respect, out of the outrages of the whites perpetrated upon them," Crook explained. The settlers obeyed "little or no law" with respect to Indians, hence "It was of no infrequent occurrence for an Indian to be shot down, in cold blood or a squaw to be raped by some brute. Such a thing as a white man being punished for outraging an Indian was unheard of."

Yet Crook served as a general in an army whose ultimate mission was to clear the land for settler colonial expansion by white people. Like many ambivalent Americans over the *longue dureé*, Crook expressed empathy for Indians but had no hesitation about the ultimate project of driving them off the land and onto reservations to make way for the more advanced civilization.[53] "To those [Indians] who were willing to learn and do the right, he was an uncompromising friend," an Army contemporary recalled, but to those "who persisted in wrongdoing," Crook was "a scourge and a terror, a veritable gray wolf."[54]

Settler colonials in the Far West conducted ethnic cleansing campaigns against Chinese immigrants as well as the indigenes. The gold rush had lured thousands of Chinese into northern California but most of them would be deprived of their mining or land claims and driven out. Americans carried out some 200 roundups between 1850 and 1906, reflecting a systematic campaign to rid the United States of Chinese. "Surely the term *expulsion* doesn't fully represent the rage and violence of these purges," Jean Pfaelzer argues. "What occurred along the Pacific coast, from the gold rush through the turn of the century, was ethnic cleansing."

The Chinese "fiercely and tenaciously fought" to live and work in the United States and to exercise full rights of citizenship, but the Californians demonized the "rat-eating Chinaman" and responded with violent aggression. "As with Indians, to whom whites often compared the Chinese, the way such killings were carried out revealed a deep, almost feral hatred," David Courtwright notes. "Chinese men were scalped, mutilated, burned, branded, decapitated, dismembered, and hanged from gutter spouts." In 1882, the cleansing campaign became national policy, as the US Congress passed the Chinese Exclusion Act terminating all Chinese immigration.[55]

Ethnic Cleansing from the Great Basin to the Western Slope

When the Spanish arrived in the Great Basin, a vast terrain of colonial space between the Sierra and Rocky Mountains, indigenous tribes of the region competed for the metals and horses they brought with them. The Spanish and the Mexicans clashed with the powerful Ute Indians but as both the Hispanics and the Ute found that they could not conquer one another, they began trading in captives taken from other Indian tribes. "Using Indian women for sexual and domestic labor and trading Indian children for horses and other goods, Ute, New Mexican, and American slavers further displaced Paiute and non-equestrian Shoshone groups from their accustomed lands and waterways," Ned Blackhawk explains. "Slavery, rape, and horse-raiding remained colonialism's most visible legacies."[56]

Often victimized were the Shoshone, the people who in 1805 with Sacagawea acting as an intermediary had provided Lewis and Clark with the directions and fresh horses they had needed to cross the Continental Divide. Though like Pocahontas, Sacagawea became a mythic figure in American history; in fact, she was a slave and did not marry the legendary frontiersman Toussaint Charbonneau, rather he purchased her. Sacagawea was one example of the "multiple coercive traffics in women [that] became essential to European-Indian interaction" on the borderlands.[57]

For a time the Shoshone and other tribes benefited from the fur trade with the British and then the American trappers, who at the same time "exploited their material and later military advantages over Indian groups for sexual service." In the 1820s, conflict erupted between the Bannocks, a Shoshone band, and large communities of American traders and fur trappers. In response, the legendary trapper James Beckwourth—who had fought in the Seminole War and would later serve as a scout at Sand Creek—led a massacre against the Bannocks on the Green River in which hundreds of scalps were taken. Although some question the reliability of Beckwourth's account, enough evidence exists to show that "the rendezvous trapping system accelerated the violent deterioration of many indigenous communities."[58]

As American settler colonialism flowed across the Rockies in the ensuing decades, traffic on the overland trails disrupted indigenous life. The settlers' stock drained and polluted water sources. The establishment of mining districts in Montana and Nevada brought more hordes and herds. Anxious emigrants, in fear of "wild" Indians, attacked any indigene that approached them. Indians raided and fought back as the colonial encounter descended into "degenerative cycles of violence and reprisal between Shoshone and emigrant groups" as well as "renegades, deserters, and thieves." In 1854, in the "Ward massacre," Shoshone killed and mutilated 19 emigrants from Missouri, 25 miles east of Fort Boise.

By 1863, with Americans demanding a final solution to the problem of Indian depredations on the Oregon Trail, the army perpetrated one of the most egregious Indian massacres in US history on the Bear River near the Utah–Idaho border. A "combination of a militarized Indian policy and aggressive volunteer forces" best explains "this moment of overwhelming state violence against unsuspecting Indian families," as Blackhawk describes the massacre. On January 29, 1863, Army Colonel Patrick E. Connor issued orders to "destroy every male Indian whom you encounter" and to "immediately hang them, and leave their bodies thus exposed as an example of what evil-doers may expect." The attackers went out of control, killed hundreds of Shoshone, raped women, and slaughtered babies. Some 160 surviving women and children were left "standing alone on a corpse-littered field" in the winter snow with no food or shelter. Settlers heaped praise on the soldiers and volunteers while Connor received promotion to brevet major general. Like Evans in Colorado, Utah Governor James Doty declared the massacre was salutary because "it struck terror into the heart" of the Shoshone, who "now acknowledge the Americans are the masters of this country." The Bear Creek massacre long went unacknowledged—the battleground in Idaho served for years as a trash dump—but has since been reconstructed as a historic site.[59]

The Cayuse and Nez Perce had joined the army in a federal campaign to hunt down Shoshone. Indigenous "scouts" and laborers, often refugees, comprised a "second-class racialized work force." Marginalized and dispossessed by settler colonialism, Indians across the borderlands collaborated with the Americans.

Often "reservation captivity or war with the U.S. regime" were the only other options available to these men, though others joined to manifest their warrior manhood and to strike back at the traditional enemies of their tribe, as was the case with the Cayuse and Nez Perce against the Shoshone.[60]

The powerful Ute displayed colonial ambivalence by allying with the Americans against other tribes, but much like the Iroquois Confederation in the previous century collaboration could not prevent their own eventual dispossession. The Ute sought to preserve their autonomy by aiding first the Hispanics and then the Americans at the expense of the Shoshone, Paiutes, and other weaker tribes. The US takeover of New Mexico and California undermined the Ute by shutting down markets for their aggressive slave raids and trade. The Ute tried to revive the slave trade with Mormon emigrants, who sometimes purchased slaves under duress when Utes appeared with their captives, usually Paiute women and children, and threatened to kill them on the spot if the Mormons would not buy them.[61]

The Utes clashed with the Mormons whose settler colonialism dramatically impacted lands, streams, and hunting grounds undermining indigenous subsistence patterns. Some Mormons viewed Indians as among the lost tribes of Israel hence their leader Brigham Young—like William Penn back east in a previous era—strove for accommodation. Like Penn, however, Young also wanted to control the land and commerce of the region. Thus once again settler colonialism overshadowed humanitarian impulses.[62]

Violent clashes erupted among the Mormons and various Indian communities throughout the 1850s. In 1853–1854, Ute and Mormon militias clashed and captive Indians were summarily executed during the so-called Walkara War, named for a Ute chieftain known for horse thievery and slave trading. In 1853 Paiute warriors were the apparent perpetrators of the killing of eight Americans on a scientific expedition led by John Gunnison, an advocate of violent Indian removal. Settlers subsequently murdered the lawyer for the alleged perpetrators demonstrating that efforts to mount a legal defense for crimes committed by Indians were tantamount to treason punishable by death. From 1865–1867, scores of Mormons and Ute died in the so-called Black Hawk War, a last gasp Ute guerrilla campaign named for a Ute leader whose actual name was Antogna.[63]

The dividing line between the Utah and Colorado territories cut squarely across Ute lands. In 1855, following Ute depredations against cattlemen in Colorado's San Luis valley, settlers responded by slaughtering 40 Ute near Salida. The clashes with cattlemen "played into the hands of Colorado's promoters and politicians" who, as they would demonstrate again at Sand Creek, "believed the presence of any Indians, good or bad, was an obstacle to progress." In 1855, Indian agents negotiated a treaty and land cession, which the Ute signed but in a familiar pattern Congress declined to ratify.[64]

As Americans continued to flood into Colorado after the gold rush and the Homestead Act, Coloradans strove to clear the western slope of the Rockies. The Ute leader Ouray personified ambivalence and deft diplomacy, as he held off the Americans for as long as possible. Ouray and many of his Ute followers had adapted to the Americans and settled into successful lives as ranchers and sheepherders. Ouray was feted in New York, Boston, and Washington but the treaties he signed ultimately proved ineffectual. "The bulldozer of American removal hit the Rockies hard," Blackhawk explains, "and it kept moving, scaling the nation's tallest peaks and descending into mountain valleys in search of the next Native community to uproot."[65]

Following the Civil War, Sherman urged the Ute to confine themselves to a reservation or risk removal but Ouray refused. "They will have to freeze and starve a little more, I reckon, before they listen to common sense," Sherman responded. The army thus reversed its ambivalence toward the Ute, which it had previously recruited for an ethnic cleansing campaign against the Navaho in the Arizona territory. "Such mercenary activities," Virginia Simmons points out, "endorsed by the federal government, ran counter to its goal of getting the Indians to settle peacefully on reservations and to become farmers." In 1879, following the Battle of Mill Creek in which Ute killed the Indian agent Nathan Meeker and ten others, Coloradoans would settle for nothing less than removal or extermination. Two years later the Ute were rounded up in a camp north of Montrose and moved to an area of Utah beyond the bounds of what had been their homeland for 500 years. Settler colonials rushed in to stake their claims on former Ute land in western Colorado.[66]

Genocidal Violence in the Southwest

The Civil War famously brought an end to slavery in the American South and less famously brought an end to it in the Southwest. Prevalent throughout the borderlands but especially well entrenched in the Southwest, slave trading, mostly in women and children, anchored economic and often diplomatic relations through exchanges of captives. The slave trade encompassed brutally violent seizures, but these captives typically acculturated to their new communities creating the multiethnic society characteristic of the region. As James Brooks found, "Captured women and children served as objects of men's contestations for power while simultaneously they enriched the cultures in which they found themselves lodged through their own social and biological reproductive potential."[67]

The Americans appreciated neither the ethnic mixing nor the enslavement, which the Civil War had permanently discredited. By the 1860s the United States was wiping out the human trafficking and replacing it with a modernist capitalist economy rooted in the cattle industry, mining, and consumption. Regionally integrated indigenous exchange systems were displaced by a modern nation-centered economy fueled by industrialization and linked by the railroad. Indian removal followed logically from the destruction of the Indian economies and exchange systems.

Among the indigenous tribes to have been heavily victimized by slave raids were the Navaho, but the Diné also conducted raids of their own for captives as well as cattle, horses, mules, and sheep. At the same time, like the "five civilized tribes," the Navaho had long done what Americans said they wanted of Indians, as they had become effective agrarians and herders. They would be violently dispossessed nonetheless.

From 1864–1868, the United States, assisted by the Ute, Hopi, and Zuni, launched an "onslaught on the Navahos and their way of life." In 1858, war had broken out with settlers over a Navaho killing of a white man's slave. At least 200 Navaho died in eight battles over a four-month period. Following the Mexican cession, the Americans had constructed Fort Defiance in 1851 in the Arizona Territory, which the Navaho unsuccessfully assaulted in 1860.

The legendary trapper Kit Carson, now serving as Manifest Destiny's premier scout, led the assault on the Navaho redoubt at Canyon de Chelly in northeastern Arizona. The campaign featured indiscriminate killing and a scorched-earth assault on cornfields, water resources, and the flourishing orchards of peach and other fruit trees. "The maelstrom of destruction and death brought by Carson and his men and their Native allies had the desired effect," Peter Iverson notes.

In 1864, in an incident not unlike the Trail of Tears or even the Bataan "death march" of World War II, some 8,000–9,000 poorly provisioned Navaho were sent on their "long walk" to the barren land of the Bosque Redondo in eastern New Mexico. Hundreds escaped to the hills and canyons to avoid the walk, which was not a single procession but several disjointed compulsory treks. Yet all had in common privations of disease, starvation, and arbitrary execution. If children or the elderly could not keep pace, they were summarily executed or left for the trailing wolf packs. The Americans executed several pregnant women or recent mothers who could not keep up. More Indians perished after arrival in New Mexico, where the alkaline river water at the fort was virtually undrinkable, and where they were prone to devastating assaults by the nearby Comanche. Navaho women were forced into prostitution around Fort Sumner.

The Navaho persisted, resisted, conducted a determined diplomacy, and ultimately overcame the attempted genocide by negotiating a return to their homeland in a remarkable triumph of colonial ambivalence. Continuing to insist on the illegitimacy of their removal to the barren sands, the Navaho leaders achieved an audience in Washington and exploited the rising "peace policy" movement in 1868 to successfully negotiate a treaty that allowed them to return to Canyon de Chelly. The treaty was a "great triumph" for the Navaho and is one of the main reasons why the tribe has flourished and is the second most populous in the United States today behind the Cherokee.[68]

Less fortunate were the tribes most known for their militant raiding cultures, the Comanche, the Kiowa and the Apaches. In Texas the tumult of the Civil War offered the Comanche and the Kiowa a window of opportunity for retribution, but the violence boomeranged back against them in the familiar dialectic of American settler colonialism. Ever opportunistic, the Comanche renewed their raids on Texas settlements, took captives, and preyed on the cattle drives emanating from the Longhorn State. With the Confederacy in defeat, Indians drove Americans back about 100 miles in the first ten months of 1866—"the worst ten-month period in the history of the Texas frontier."[69] The Texans rallied, however, as the Rangers continued to assault Comanche villages, "slaughtering men, women, and children by the hundreds."[70]

In the mid-1870s, a series of clashes known as the Red River Wars culminated the ethnic cleansing of Texas. The fighting began at Adobe Walls in June 1874 when well more than 200 Comanche, Cheyenne, and Kiowa warriors attacked a handful of American buffalo hunters who were killing the bison on Indian hunting grounds. The entrenched and well-armed hunters held off the attack, which gave the Army a pretext to encircle and destroy the Panhandle tribes. Sheridan encouraged mass slaughter of the buffalo, noting approvingly in 1875 that by "destroying the Indians' commissary" the hunters "have done more in the last two years to settle the vexed Indian question than the regular army has done in the past thirty years." The Comanche and other tribes also bore responsibility for the decline of the buffalo, however, by "slaughtering vast numbers of bison for subsistence and for trade."[71]

In September 1875, the Red River campaign culminated when the army drove the Comanche, Cheyenne, and Kiowa out of a large encampment at Palo Duro Canyon. US forces burned the village and slaughtered more than 1,000 horses. The destruction left the Indians "facing grim winter circumstances: their horses were killed; lodges, clothing, and robes burned; and winter food stores destroyed. For most," Frederick Rathjen explains, "making their forlorn way to their agencies was the only alternative left, humiliating though it was." The Indian population of Texas thus plummeted from about 35,000 in 1835 to just a few thousand relegated to hardscrabble reservations in 1875.[72]

Although the Apaches would become one of the most reviled tribes in American history, and stock villains of the Hollywood Westerns, Americans had allied with some Apache bands against the common foe during the Mexican War. The Apaches had long plagued first the Spanish then the Mexicans, who searched in vain for an "efficient means to exterminate... the barbarian Apache."[73] The Apache learned, as did all other Indians over the *longue dureé*, that alliance with the Americans invariably proved ephemeral.

In 1861, a dispute over an exchange of captives prompted the Chiricahua Apache Cochise to kill and mutilate four Americans. The army responded by executing Cochise's captive wife, nephew, and several children. From that point Cochise and his band attacked and killed Americans without restraint as indiscriminate warfare prevailed on both sides. The *Arizona Miner* proclaimed a "great battle of civilization to overthrow the barbarians and teach them that white supremacy... is decreed of God." Another writer averred, "Extermination is our only hope, and the sooner the better."[74]

Genocidal violence prevailed, as President Lincoln's envoys informed him that "Indians are shot wherever seen" in the Arizona territory. In 1863, a group of Apaches were being fed after they were invited in for a parley when suddenly some 30 of them were shot to death by prearranged plan. In 1866 a physician relished "a great slaughter of Apaches" and offered a company of Arizona volunteers "a dollar's worth of tobacco for every Apache they kill in the future." A rancher offered a blow-by-blow account of an Apache hunting expedition in which "altogether we killed fifty-six Indians." Aided by rival Apache scouts, the army reported killing 29 Apaches in 1865; 154 in 1866; 172 in 1867; and 129 in 1868. Settlers did not keep such records but killed and captured hundreds more as a "shared code of violence" existed between civilians and the military. Some planted bags of sugar laced with strychnine to kill Indians as they would wolves or other wild animals.[75]

Obscuring their own aggression, Arizona settlers rationalized the genocide as righteous retribution for "inhuman butchery of white men by Indian murderers." Stories, some true and others wildly exaggerated, of Apache raids, murders, and rapes permeated the Arizona settler community and served to justify indiscriminate slaughter. As the settlers allied in genocidal campaigns against the common enemy, the Apaches, Arizona authorities were able "to reconcile the deep sectional animosities still lingering in the territory" in the wake of the Civil War.[76]

Nothing better illustrated the tolerance for genocide in Arizona than the Camp Grant massacre of non-resistant Apache. Much like the slaughter of Indians at Sand Creek and myriad other American sites, these murders facilitated settler colonialism by helping to clear the state for white American supremacy. At dawn on April 30, 1871, more than 100 Mexicans and Papago Indians along with a few whites—but all under the direction of the leaders of the Arizona territory—killed and mutilated at least 108 Apache camped along a stream on a refuge in the Aravaipa Canyon some 60 miles northeast of Tucson. Women were brutally raped and slaughtered, some babies bludgeoned to death, others taken for adoption or sold into slavery. "In less than half an hour not a living Apache was to be seen," recalled a participant, who relished the killing of "the most bloodthirsty devils that ever disgraced mother earth." This participant failed to mention that all but two of the slaughtered Apache were women and children. The suggestion that the "bloodthirsty" Indians posed a threat to the white community elided that these Indians had surrendered and were peacefully encamped under military authority.[77]

As happened so often on the American borderlands, colonial ambivalence materialized through the willing participation in the massacre of other Indians and also in this case of Mexicans. The Papagos (Tohono O'odham) and the Mexicans "purchased political and economic enfranchisement in the Arizona Territory, however temporary, through physical and sexualized violence against the Apache," Nicole M. Guidotti-Hernandez explains. "They sought not only economic gain but racial differentiation from *indios barbaros*."[78]

The US Army condemned the unauthorized settler assault, which the commander of nearby Fort Grant described as "but another massacre, in cold blood, of inoffensive and peaceful Indians who were living on the reservation under the protection of the Government." The overwhelming majority of Arizona settlers, however, applauded the mass killings. The organizers of the slaughter went on to become the most prominent citizens of Tucson. The massacre was so popular that for years, people who were not there claimed to have taken part. Settlers in nearby states heartily approved as well. The *Alta California* praised the massacre as "one of the most important victories ever achieved by the white men over the savages in Arizona" and envisioned "the extermination of the Apaches." A Colorado newspaper cheered the Camp Grant massacre as the latest "of those victories for civilization and progress" much like their own at Sand Creek. "We only regret that the number [of killings] was not double."[79]

In 1871 for the first time in Arizona history the perpetrators were indicted and put on trial for killing the Indians, but a jury took only 19 minutes to exonerate them. Despite the Army criticism, "the massacre appeared far more ordinary than extraordinary at the time," Karl Jacoby points out. Killing Apaches was nothing remarkable and certainly nothing for which settlers or their auxiliaries ought to be incarcerated. In April 1873, the Army itself slaughtered 76 Apache men, women, and children trapped in the "battle" (in which only one Indian auxiliary died on the federal side) of Salt River Cave. All resisting Apaches in Arizona eventually were rounded up and either killed or dispatched to reservations.[80]

The notoriety of the Chiricahua Apache Geronimo (Goyaalé) reflects the American penchant for elevating a single Indian "chief" to exaggerated prominence. Geronimo and a small band of Chiricahua eluded Crook and a large federal force in the mountains and deserts of Arizona and New Mexico for years.[81] Rarely showing mercy to the settler victims of his raids, Geronimo 's violence obscured that most Apache had long since acquiesced to US authority. In September 1886, after a week of negotiations, Geronimo finally surrendered to General Nelson Miles at Skeleton Canyon in the Chiricahua Mountains.

Although he "would much prefer" to hang Geronimo, Secretary of War R. C. Drum instead exiled the Apache chieftain to Florida for safe keeping but later moved him to Fort Sill in Oklahoma, where he died and is buried along with his wife in a remote corner of the base. In 1918 members of Yale's Skull and Bones secret society—among them Prescott Bush, the father and grandfather of two future US presidents—reportedly unearthed and pilfered Geronimo's bones as a prank. Despite being on an Army base the stone burial mound with an eagle for a crown has repeatedly been desecrated over the years.[82]

Indian Removal from the Northwest

The fur trade created cultural space for ambivalent relations between Euro-Americans and Indians in the Pacific Northwest until explosive colonization overwhelmed the tribes. European and American trappers often took Indian wives and mistresses, establishing working relations with the bands. The fur traders, however, referred to the indigenes in Oregon as "Rogues" and thus left a legacy of racial othering. Most of the thousands of settlers who arrived on the Oregon Trail lumped the indigenes together as a unitary "doomed race" with no legitimate claim to colonial space.[83]

By the time of the Oregon Treaty with Great Britain (1846), settler colonials had begun to close in on the Indians of the northwest. That same year, Carson, blaming the Klamath Indians for an attack on his camp, led a slaughter of an Indian fishing village called Dokdokwas on the Upper Klamath Lake. "I wanted to do them as much damage as I could," Carson later explained, so he burned the village to the ground, which he called "a beautiful sight." A disappointed John C. Fremont arrived on the scene "too late for the sport." Carson and Fremont "continued to kill Indians in a desultory fashion" as they circled Klamath Lake but "in all likelihood" the Modoc and not the Klamath had attacked Carson's camp hence the victims were altogether innocent Indian men, women, and children.[84]

Cleansing campaigns erupted in the Northwest in the wake of the Whitman massacre, a case of religiously inspired ambivalence that came to grief. Long-simmering tensions over trade and cultural issues culminated on November 29,

1847, when Cayuse Indians killed 14 Americans, including the ethnocentric Presbyterian missionary couple Marcus and Narcissa Whitman. They had engendered resentment upon arrival in the region by taking over the home of a Cayuse headman at Waiilatpu. Like most missionaries the Whitmans compelled Indians to change their economies, gender relations, and spiritual way of life. The indigenes of the Walla Walla valley soon viewed Marcus Whitman as a shaman and blamed him for a measles epidemic that ravaged the tribe. Narcissa quickly gave up on saving the Indians and began to hate and fear them instead. After the Whitman killings and in an effort to protect the tribe as a whole, the Cayuse turned over five men said to be responsible for the murders. These Indians were quickly convicted and executed—but not before being baptized and "saved." The Cayuse tribe scattered and broke up as the Americans forced many of its members onto Oregon's Umatilla reservation.[85]

The Whitman massacre provided settlers with the opportunity they relished to launch a cleansing campaign against the indigenes "infesting" the land. "We came not to establish trade with the Indians," a settler acknowledged, "but to take and settle the country exclusively for ourselves." As in California, the federal government arrived too late to head off "squatter sovereignty" backed by "violence and outrage." Indian agents belatedly negotiated treaties, which the settlers opposed and the US Senate rejected in 1852. Pressured by the settlers, the federal government provided "monies from the national treasury, reimbursing militia expenses" to cleanse the Oregon Territory.[86]

Settlers followed by the army conducted indiscriminate campaigns not only against the Cayuse but also against the Klamath, Kalapuyas, Molalas, Clackamas, Chinooks, and other Oregon tribes. In the mid-1850s they completed the violent dispossession of the indigenous residents of southwestern Oregon, the Puget Sound area, and the Yakama Country on the Columbia Plateau. Settler discourse rationalized ethnic cleansing citing the threat of a pan-Indian "uprising" but unity among the various bands was "tenuous and never approached the scope of a grand tribal alliance."[87]

Little cultural space for ambivalence remained in the wake of the Whitman killings. Although not everyone favored indiscriminate slaughter, by the mid-1850s "the ranks of the extermination-minded Euro-Americans swelled, counter-discourse waned, and no colonist did much to prevent the massacres of native people." As Whaley notes, "Settler colonialism made the citizenry's extermination attempts seem warranted in the tense atmosphere of southwestern Oregon in the 1850s."[88]

In 1855 Oregon's first territorial governor Isaac Stevens, a zealous proponent of Manifest Destiny and railroad development, forced the indigenes to sign over their land in treaties or face "extermination." Lacking subtlety, Stevens told Yakima chief Kamiakin at Walla Walla in 1855, "If you do not accept the terms offered, you will walk in blood knee deep." Stevens simultaneously served as governor, head of the Pacific Railroad Survey, and though he had utterly no expertise on Indians and would have preferred their "extermination" he also landed the key position of superintendent of Indian affairs for the territory. "Stevens' principal aim . . . centered on extinguishing Indian title to the lands in the Pacific Northwest in order to promote the settlement of the region." Miners and settlers soon clashed with Palouse, Yakama, Walla Walla, and other tribes on the Columbia Plateau in what became known as the Yakima War.[89]

The Nez Perce, whose land had been spared from dispossession under the 1855 treaties, joined with the Americans in the Yakima War. In fact, US–Nez Perce relations had been amicable since Lewis and Clark spent a month resting with the tribe—a visit that gave Clark time to impregnate a Nez Perce woman.[90] In 1858 the discovery of gold brought miners flooding onto Nez Perce land and found the Americans declining to enforce the restrictions against white settlement.

Following the pattern established by Stevens, the Americans tried to force a hasty acquiescence to landed aggression on the Nez Perce leader Chief Joseph (Heinmot Tooyalakekt). They promised schools, teachers, churches, and houses, but Chief Joseph pointedly replied that the Nez Perce had no interest in adopting any of the white man's ways, that they only wanted to be left alone on their land. Vexed by the concept of savages rejecting the benefits of civilization, the Americans moved to dispossess the unreasoning Nez Perce.[91]

Thus the Nez Perce War, one of the most famous and romanticized of Indian resistances in the history of American settler colonialism, broke out in 1877. A bloody outburst in June replete with killings and rapes of white women by the previously peaceful Nez Perce traumatized the settler colonials. The Nez Perce took flight and repeatedly outmaneuvered and defeated their army pursuers. The army caught up with the Indians in western Montana, surprising and damaging them at the Battle of Big Hole. As the army killed off the stragglers, mostly women and children, at the encampment, the Nez Perce regrouped and closed in on the Americans behind a wall of fire they had deliberately set. The retreating army barely avoided a Little Big Horn type rout when the wind changed direction pushing the fire back into the faces of the Indians, who were soon on their way again, though weakened by the battle. The Nez Perce passed through the newly created Yellowstone National Park, killing and capturing a handful of astonished tourists. Aided by Cheyenne and Sioux scouts, Miles finally tracked down the Nez Perce before they could reach the Canadian border.[92]

A romantic mythology centering on Chief Joseph arose in the wake of the long chase. Following his capture in 1877 Chief Joseph told Miles, "From where the sun now stands I will fight no more." The matter-of-fact statement underwent a culturally induced conversion, emerging in the poetic lexicon of the noble savage as, "I shall fight no more forever." Like Pontiac, Tecumseh, Black Hawk, Sitting Bull, Crazy Horse, and Cochise, among others, Joseph—described as a "light colored Indian" and a "red Napoleon"—came to embody the brave and tragic but also inevitable submission of the proud Indian to a more advanced civilization. "The story of native peoples was distilled into an account about one leader selected by Anglo-Americans to serve as the tragic figure of the noble savage attempting to hold onto 'primitive' ways of life and native land," Robert McCoy explains. The tragic epic offered drama, pathos—and the inevitability of the triumph of civilization over the Vanishing American. In 1879 Chief Joseph did say something profound, however, when he observed, "Whenever the white man treats the Indian as they treat each other, then we shall have no more wars."[93]

Reminiscent of the Navaho, Chief Joseph never gave up on returning to his homeland. The famous chief shrewdly played into the ambivalent American sentiment when he declared, likely falsely, that he had converted to Christianity. This declaration, along with his acceptance of the mantle of noble savage chieftain, enabled "Joseph" to negotiate in 1885 his return along with 268 followers from Kansas to a reservation in Idaho.[94]

Like the Nez Perce, the Modoc Indians of extreme southern Oregon violently resisted settler colonialism. Led by Captain Jack (Kintpuash), the Modoc were an offshoot of the Klamath tribe that had been forced to sign over some 21 million acres of prime land in Oregon in an 1864 treaty. The Modoc, too, had consented to give up their land in the Lost River Valley but that treaty lay dormant in Washington D.C. With the issue thus unresolved, high tensions, Indian raids as well as killings of settlers, and the determination of Americans to remove them brought on the war. Some 50 Modoc dug in to a series of naturally fortified lava beds across the border in California and fended off a much larger invasion force of Army regulars and volunteers. The Modoc killed more than 80 Americans while suffering few casualties of their own. "That was the most terrible night ever experienced by me," recalled a US cavalryman.[95]

The Modoc agreed to a peace parley but when the Americans arrived on April 11, 1873, Captain Jack perfidiously executed General Edward Canby on the spot. Following the murder of the unarmed US Army general along with a Methodist minister, both under a flag of truce, the Army drove the Indians out and executed Captain Jack, among others. The Army removed other Modoc to Oklahoma, which by then was the well-established "dumping ground for unwanted Indians."[96]

The US Army removed indigenous survivors of the cleansing campaigns in the Pacific Northwest, but they found little hope for meaningful life on the undesirable reservation land. Moreover, "Soldiers continued the rape and abuse of Native women that had been perpetrated by colonials before removal of the Indians." The Klamath received a reservation within the range of their former homelands in the 1864 treaty, but they and other tribes lost the bulk of their reservations in subsequent land seizures by settlers.[97] In 1878 when hundreds of Bannocks and Paiutes broke out of their treaty lands in Oregon, Idaho, and Nevada, the Army tracked them down and killed scores of Indians. Armed sweeps across the Northwest pursued the "renegade" and "mongrel" Indians, but the so-called Sheepeaters, actually Bannocks, Shoshone, and Weiser, held out in the high mountains that could only be accessed by invaders during a few months of the year. In the summer of 1879, the army tracked down these Indians as well and forced them onto reservations.[98]

To the east in the Montana territory, the Blackfeet Indians gained a reputation for indiscriminate violence, but this was mainly in response to provocations by the American trappers. They exaggerated Blackfeet violence in an effort "to induce the federal government to intervene militarily to make the region safe for American trappers and traders." By mid-century, the Blackfeet suffered from disease, relentless American in-migration, and widespread addiction to "the white man's water."[99]

On January 23, 1870, as President Grant trumpeted his "peace policy" back in Washington, D.C., the US Army carried out the "Massacre on the Marias," attacking a peaceful village and killing 173 Blackfeet, including 90 women and 50 children under the age of 12. The soldiers also slaughtered more than 300 horses. A *New York Times* account condemned the "wholesale slaughter of women and children," as only 15 of the dead were fighting aged men of ages 12–37. But as John Ewers notes, "The white settlers in Montana, who had called repeatedly for military aid to put an end to Blackfoot depredations, vigorously approved the army's action." Sherman and Sheridan authorized and defended the massacre, which they later blamed on the victims even though the Blackfeet had been peacefully encamped and not hostile. "If a village is attacked, and women and children killed, the responsibility is not with the soldier," Sheridan explained, "but with the people whose crimes necessitate the attack."[100]

The Great Sioux Wars

One of the most formidable of the Western Indian tribes, the bands collectively lumped as the Sioux, carried out a series of trauma-inducing attacks on the Americans before they could be subdued. During the antebellum era in Minnesota (where the Sioux had been driven by the Ojibwa), Little Crow (Thaoyate Duta), leader of the Santee Sioux, strove for accommodation with the in-flooding settlers. By the Civil War, however, the Santee bitterly resented their dispossession and depressed living conditions on their Minnesota reservation. With their game depleted, the Indians neared starvation as the Americans devoted their resources to the Civil War rather than meeting their treaty obligations to provide for the reservation Indians.

In August 1862, the Santee launched a Nat Turner-like bloody assault, as the Indians went farm-to-farm slaughtering mostly German immigrant families in what became the largest Indian massacre of settlers in American history. Before the Army could rein in the rampage, 400–600 settlers and some 140 soldiers had been killed. In the wake of the traumatic massacre, even prominent Minnesota women and other former advocates of benevolence toward Indians now insisted on their removal or extermination. With the enraged Minnesotans demanding vengeance, authorities sentenced 303 Indians to death for the uprising. After conducting a review of the proceedings Lincoln reduced the number to 38 executions, including Little Crow despite his initial opposition to the genocidal assaults. On the day after Christmas in 1862, the Army hanged the indigenes in the largest mass execution in US history.[101] US military expeditions "rampaged across the northern plains in the wake of the 1862 Minnesota Sioux uprising" as "soldiers and eager volunteers" carried out "indiscriminate actions" and drove the northern Missouri tribes further west.[102]

The western Sioux flourished on the upper Great Plains, often at the expense of other tribes upon whom they ruthlessly predated, including the Pawnee, Crow, and Kiowa. Tensions between the Sioux and the Americans surfaced from the outset, as in 1804 Meriwether Lewis informed the Sioux—the "vilest miscreants of the savage race"—that their great father in Washington meant to "distroy" them if they resisted eventual US rule. By the 1840s, American settlers flowing across the Oregon Trail complained of aggressive Sioux bands demanding tolls for passing through colonial space. The Sioux proved willing to conduct diplomacy, however, and signed on to the pivotal Fort Laramie Treaty of 1851 in which several tribes promised safety to migrants in return for annuities.[103]

Relentless settler colonial migration, fort, road, and railroad building, gold mining, and squatting doomed diplomacy with the Sioux and led to war on the upper Plains. In August 1854, a Sioux band killed 30 men at a trading post near Fort Laramie after being confronted by John L. Grattan, "a hotheaded young lieutenant" who had vowed to rid the Plains of Indians. This clash kicked off the so-called First Sioux War, which culminated in the slaughter in 1855 of at least 86 Sioux, more than half women and children, at Blue Water Creek near the Platte River in contemporary Nebraska. Some 70 women and children were taken captive after the Army assault led by General William S. Harney, who had been campaigning against Indians since the Black Hawk War in 1832.[104]

The Army began to surround the Sioux with forts, precipitating another clash in December 1866 when Captain William Fetterman led a force of 80 men out of Fort Phil Kearney in the Powder River country. They fell directly into a trap set by the young militant Oglala Sioux Crazy Horse (Tashunka Witko), whose relatives had been killed by Americans. The Indians proceeded to wipe out and mutilate the entire US force in the "Fetterman Massacre." Demonizing ambivalent "Indian lovers" for their peaceful approach to the tribes, a livid Sherman demanded a war waged with "vindictive earnestness against the Sioux, even to their extermination, men, women, and children." Despite this characteristic explosion of rage from Sherman, Indian agent William Armstrong acknowledged, "There is no doubt that the whites have committed greater depredations on those Indians than the Indians have on the whites."[105]

With an extirpative war on the horizon, the Oglala under Red Cloud (Makhpiyaluta) called for a diplomatic solution. In April 1868, with the "peace policy" forces mobilizing in Washington, the United States agreed to a second Fort Laramie Treaty under which it guaranteed the Sioux that they could keep in perpetuity the western half of present-day state of South Dakota, including the sacred Black Hills, as the Great Sioux Reservation. The Indians would also be allowed to roam and hunt in "un-ceded Indian territory" in the Powder River region further to the west, which was to be closed to Americans. The ongoing settler colonialism, the discovery of gold in the Black Hills, and the US desire to construct the Northern Pacific Railroad across the Sioux land soon made a mockery of the second Fort Laramie accord. As the United States reneged on its treaty obligations, Sheridan in 1874 dispatched Custer with a huge expeditionary force to confirm the existence of the gold and consider a site for another fort.[106]

Assisting Custer were the Crow Indians, well known for their "tireless devotion to martial glory" and "warrior societies." This service would help the Crow to hang onto a reservation in the eastern Montana flatlands, though the Army did remove them from their homelands in the mountain valleys of western Montana. For decades, conflict "over access to the buffalo herds, rivalries over trade and simple revenge fueled round after round of attack and counterattack" among the Crow and Sioux as well as the Blackfeet, Shoshone, Assiniboine, and Cree. The Crow had a special loathing for the Sioux, who had over the years attacked and killed masses of Crow and destroyed their lodges. Though willing to serve in a martial capacity, especially against the Sioux, efforts to "civilize" the Crow failed completely. The Crows "hate the white man's language and the white man's mode of life," Armstrong reported.[107]

Some of the Crows tried to warn Custer about the trap awaiting him, but while the dashing Civil War hero would not listen. He viewed the savages as superb horsemen adept at hit-and-run raids, he judged them ultimately lacking in the discipline and cohesion needed to field an effective army in battle. Conventional wisdom held that primitive Indians were incapable of organizing large enough fighting forces to defeat a US Army contingent of any size. Even after the Lakota chief Sitting Bull (Tatanka Iyotake) had shown his "strong medicine" by defeating Crook at the Battle of the Rosebud in mid-June 1876, Americans could not conceive that a disaster like the Greasy Grass (Little Big Horn) was even a remote possibility.[108] The popular and self-promoting Custer, well known for his long blond hair, heroics at Gettysburg, as well as the Washita attack, had a reputation for aggressiveness in battle. Ignoring the warnings of his Crow scouts, Custer divided his forces and plunged into the fatal battle. On June 25 the amassed army of Lakota, Northern Cheyenne, and Arapaho warriors overwhelmed the Seventh Cavalry, killing 268 in all and wounding 55 more. The Indians took scalps and mutilated the bodies before leaving the field in complete triumph.[109]

As with the Indians' decisive victory over General St. Clair in 1791, it was only a matter of time until the Americans—traumatized by the defeat that marred the Centennial celebration—regrouped with a boomerang of violent retribution. Miles adopted a strategy of relentless pursuit and harassment to wear down the Sioux. "Keep them constantly on the move . . . allow them no rest," he advised, hence the Indians would be unable to hunt or provide for themselves. Over time even the most militant Sioux succumbed to "the army's potential to inflict catastrophic damage combined with unreliable food supplies."[110]

Crazy Horse, who had joined Sitting Bull in defeating the Seventh Cavalry, would not turn himself in until he received a promise of being granted his own reservation on the Tongue River. Crook described Crazy Horse as "fascinating . . . the finest looking Indian I ever saw . . . his face and figure were as clear-cut and classical as a bronze statue of a Greek god. When he moved, he was as lithe and graceful as a panther, and on the warpath, he was as bold as a lion, and as cruel and bloodthirsty as a Bengal tiger." Awe-inspiring sentiments notwithstanding, Crook broke his promise of providing reservation land to Crazy Horse, who was then stabbed to death when he attempted to leave confinement.[111]

Red Cloud came to regret his ambivalence and the willingness he had displayed, often in the face of sharp criticism from other Indians, to conduct diplomacy with the Americans. "They made us many promises," Red Cloud acknowledged, "more than I can remember, but they never kept but one. They promised to take our land, and they took it."[112]

Genocidal "Reform" Efforts in the Nineteenth Century

Ambivalent reform efforts throughout the nineteenth century were fundamentally ethnocentric and genocidal, as they functioned to destroy the Indian way of life. Reformers perceiving themselves as humanitarians sought to "civilize" Indians through assimilation, education, and conversion to Christianity. However, there was nothing humanitarian about the means to the end of civilization, as the dispossession, child removal, and assimilation programs used compulsion and the threat of starvation to force compliance.[113]

Often driven by evangelical Protestantism, many Americans lamented the "passing" of the Indian and the cruel treatment to which indigenous people had been subjected. Helen Hunt Jackson emphasized the broken treaties and broken promises toward Indian peoples amounting to a "century of dishonor," as she entitled her 1881 bestseller. Others condemned widespread corruption and inefficiency in the government's administration of Indian affairs. In 1878, an investigation ordered by Secretary of the Interior Karl Schurz concluded that the Indian Bureau functioned as "simply a license to cheat and swindle the Indian in the name of the United States." General Miles, a national hero in "winning the West," agreed that the time had come to "raise them from the darkness of barbarism to the light of civilization."[114]

Such humanitarian sentiments and lamentations failed to redirect the fundamental policies of dispossession and cultural genocide. The Seneca Ely Parker pursued a cautiously limited agenda as Grant's commissioner of Indian affairs, one focused on treaty enforcement and a methodical approach to assimilation. He achieved neither. The genuinely reformist Indian Rights Association also failed to sway Gilded Age policymakers.[115]

The US Congress, responsive to the settlers, often failed to ratify treaties and to authorize funds for payment of promised annuities. The Congress was often at odds with the executive or otherwise divided in the postbellum era but, moreover, "They saw appropriations not as payments for massive land cessions," Jacki Rand points out, "but as handouts to a broken people they no longer needed to fear or respect." Rather than the incremental program suggested by Parker, "a policy agenda founded upon Indian confinement moved forward with brash intensity." The Office of Indian Affairs pursued "a program of coercive assimilation coupled with dispossession" until the Indian New Deal of the 1930s.[116]

Throughout American history myriad treaties with Indians contained provisions for education to instill "civilization," provisions that assuaged guilt and disavowed the colonizing act. Missionaries took the forefront of ethnocentric efforts to Christianize and acculturate Indians. Established in 1810, the American Board of Commissioners for Foreign Missions promoted Christianizing and civilizing efforts. From 1837 to 1893, the Presbyterian Church's Board of Foreign Missions sent more than 450 missionaries to live among 19 tribes. In 1819, Congress passed the Indian Civilization Act to promote Indian education to help prevent their "decline and final extinction" while "introducing among them the habits and arts and civilization."[117]

As in colonial Australia, the United States forcibly removed Indian children from their homes and communities and placed them in reeducation camps. Like massacres and warfare, child removal advanced the settler colonial project. "Indigenous child removal," Margaret Jacobs explains, "constituted another crucial way to eliminate indigenous people, both in a cultural and a biological sense."[118] Missionaries in the trans-Mississippi West advocated removing children who would otherwise be "constantly under the supervision of their Heathen parents," as one put it. Compulsory Indian education became an important tool for Schurz, charged by President Rutherford B. Hayes to reform the Indian Bureau in the wake of the corruption scandals of the Grant Administration. These proselytizing Christians received support from Hayes, who avowed, "The children being removed from the idle and corrupting habits of savage homes are more easily led to adopt the customs of civilized life."

The federal government sometimes withheld rations and annuities to force compliance with the child removal program. When the Hopi resisted sending their children to a boarding school in Arizona, the government enforced a quota system on the tribe. By 1890, some 12,000 children from the trans-Mississippi tribes were undergoing forced reeducation.[119]

In 1879, the prototype "school for savages" opened in an abandoned Army barracks in Carlisle, Pennsylvania. Under the motto, "Tradition is the Enemy of Progress," the Carlisle Indian Industrial School relentlessly pursued the "kill the Indian, save the man" strategy of forced acculturation. Directed by an Army disciplinarian, Richard Henry Pratt, and backed by the national organization "Friends of the Indian," Carlisle provided English-only instruction and forbade any use of indigenous languages. Indian youth, often sick and terrified from their ordeal of capture, transport, and separation from their families, were given new names, had their hair cut, were dressed in military style clothing, and compelled to abandon their own cultural and religious practices and to adopt Christianity. Pratt's version of ambivalence envisioned "a multiracial society where everyone acted like Anglo-Saxons of the Judeo-Christian persuasion."[120]

Carlisle's legacy can be summed up with these statistics: in its first 24 years, only 158 students graduated while 186 died at the school, mostly of disease, by the time it closed in 1918. Their graves are the only remnant of the school one can find on the Carlisle Barracks today. More of a primary school than a high school, Carlisle did allow scores of Indians to obtain jobs, many of them provided by the federal government, yet the majority of students returned to reservations in the West. Separated from their families for years, if not permanently, many students from Carlisle and other Indian schools could not adapt to an indigenous culture from which they had been removed yet neither could they find a place in white society.[121]

For all its humanitarian cant, the motive behind the movement for Indian assimilation was dispossession of more indigenous people. "Instead of breaking with the past use of violence and force," Jacobs explains, the assimilation movement was "part of a continuum of colonizing approaches, all aimed ultimately at extinguishing indigenous people's claims to their remaining land."[122] To the extent that Indians remained on the land coveted by white Americans, the "Indian problem" remained unsolved even after military conquest. The putatively benevolent assimilation program addressed the problem by removing more Indians from their land and Indian children from their homes.

In 1887 Congress passed the centerpiece of the drive for Indian assimilation, the General Allotment Act or Dawes Act, which subdivided reservation land into 160-acre individual plots while freeing up "surplus" land for sale to settlers by the US Government. The "humanitarian" shift from removal to assimilation thus opened additional colonial space for settlers and speculators while at the same time launching a program of cultural genocide. "Politicians and philanthropists heralded land in severalty as the thing that would finally, definitively solve the nation's Indian problems," Andrew Denson notes.[123]

The patently ethnocentric policy undermined Indian culture and community, including a direct assault on the family. Americans sought to transform Indian gender relations by making men into farmers, women into domestics, and removing Indian children from the family altogether. Theodore Roosevelt accurately described allotment as "a mighty pulverizing engine to break up the tribal mass."[124]

Under the Dawes Act, which prevailed from 1887 to 1934, American Indians lost 86 million of the 138 million acres they possessed in 1887. In the wake of the allotment program, Stuart Banner points out, "the pattern of land tenure in the West had been completely transformed—the Indians retained virtually no land that was not part of a reservation."[125]

The ambivalent "reform" movement thus remained a distinctly colonial project, one that echoed the age-old solution of solving the Indian problem by removing Indians from the land desired by settlers. Many tribes, like the Kickapoo, "resisted civilizing attempts and remained unequivocally unchanged at the end of the reservation period." Rather than achieving assimilation, the Dawes Act instead cemented the status of Indians "as a permanent underclass even more dependent on the federal government." As a humanitarian measure, "the allotment system proved an unqualified failure," Philip Weeks sums up.[126]

After centuries of ethnic cleansing and Indian removal, the Dawes Act allowed Indians to have their own land—but only after they severed relationships with their tribes and thus became non-Indians. Thousands of Indians assumed US citizenship under the legislation when they qualified for an individual allotment. In the ceremony granting citizenship, the Secretary of the Interior called indigenes forward, handed them a bow, and had them shoot an arrow. He then declared, "You have shot your last arrow. That means that you are no longer to live the life of an Indian. You are from this day forward to live the life of a white man. But you may keep the arrow."[127]

Unsanctioned Fantasy and the Massacre at Wounded Knee

As dispossession and genocide advanced in tandem, any effort by reservation Indians to revivify their traditional cultures—or even *fantasize* about reviving them—ultimately brought on violent retribution. Having come in or been rounded up in the months and years after their triumph at the Greasy Grass, the Sioux gradually adapted to life on the reservation. "Progressives" among the Sioux urged education and acculturation. Many men had become successful cattle and horse herders. However, with the eruption of the "Great Dakota Boom," American settlers demanded that additional land be carved out of the Sioux reservation. At the same time, the division of the territory into the states of North and South Dakota in 1889 set off political anxieties and infighting in Washington.[128]

Lacking the capacity for violent resistance to the renewed campaign of dispossession, the Sioux responded with the spiritually inspired Ghost Dance. Not unique to the Sioux, the Ghost Dance envisioned the revival of their culture, prosperity, and autonomy. The Ghost Dance, as Jeffrey Ostler suggests, is "best understood as an anti-colonial movement" albeit a nonviolent one.[129]

The Ghost Dance defied both the assimilation and settler colonial projects through its revival of Indian spirituality and cultural autonomy. Indian traditionalists subverted the colonial regime by violating reservation rules, keeping their children out of schools to teach them Indian ways, and practicing their own religion rather than Christianity. Moreover, the Ghost Dance envisioned the disappearance of the white man accompanied by the return of the bison and the revival of the Indian way of life. As with the Shawnee Prophet in the 1810s, Americans could not tolerate even the *vision* of such a turn of events. Only one fantasy was sanctioned on the "American frontier," the fantasy of American providential destiny to monopolize colonial space.

The Lakota ghost dancers "never contemplated using arms" to bring about the new world. The new religion "was not in any way warlike or calculated to provoke war since it taught the doctrine of non-resistance," recalled General G. W. McIver, who served in the Sioux wars with the Seventh Cavalry. "The Ghost Dances were religious in character, bearing a resemblance to Methodist revival meetings," McIver observed, "and were not war dances intended to inspire a warlike spirit."[130]

As the Ghost Dance flourished, Miles informed Red Cloud that he had "no objections as far as I am individually concerned to you enjoying yourselves, as long as it does not go too far." Red Cloud responded that the Ghost Dance was not unique to the Sioux, that other tribes around the country were practicing the same form of spiritual awakening. "If there is nothing in it, it will go away like the snow under the hot sun," the Sioux leader explained, counseling patience. As Miles's patience wore thin "the clamor raised by white settlers" prompted the decision to bring in masses of troops to forcibly disarm Indians who were not in rebellion.[131]

On December 15, 1890, after the largest US military force sent anywhere since the Civil War arrived on the Pine Ridge reservation, tensions escalated with the murder of the revered Sitting Bull, roused out of his sleep in his cabin, and killed along with one of his sons.[132] On December 29, as the disarmament campaign unfolded, an Indian rifle was accidentally fired skyward, setting off the massacre. The panicked cavalry "began shooting in every direction, killing not only Indians but also their own comrades on the other side of the circle," an infantryman recalled. "The Indians were then being hunted down and killed." Five-barrel Hotchkiss guns "sent a storm of shells and bullets among the women and children, who had gathered in front of the tipi to watch the unusual spectacle . . . mowing down everything alive." Some 150 Indians died in the initial outburst and another hundred or so were hunted down and killed in the next few days.

"There can be no question," an investigator determined, "that the pursuit was simply a massacre, where fleeing women, with infants in their arms, were shot down after resistance had ceased." No one knows the precise death toll, as the Indian men, women, and children were buried in a mass grave. Twenty-five troopers died, mostly from friendly fire in the initial outburst.[133]

A century later a congressional resolution acknowledged the massacre and expressed the "deep regret" of the United States, but offered no compensation. At the time of the slaughter, Miles, in an effort to justify the violence as well as the unprecedented 18 Congressional Medals of Honor handed out for bravery in "battle," mendaciously claimed to have uncovered "a more comprehensive plot than anything ever inspired by the prophet Tecumseh." The general claimed that "a hungry, wild, mad horde of savages" had been preparing a pan-Indian uprising.

By then a septuagenarian, Sherman cheered on the massacre from the sidelines, explaining that the more Miles "kills now, the less he will have to do later." The wizened American warrior did not know it, but the Indian wars, fittingly punctuated with a massacre of captive peoples, were coming to an end.[134]

7

"Spaces of Denial": American Settler Colonialism in Hawai'i and Alaska

In the nineteenth century American settlers systematically dispossessed the indigenous Kanaka Maoli—Hawaiian islanders, or the "true people." While dispossession of North American Indian tribes is a familiar subject, Hawai'i has occupied "a space of denial in the consciousness of American history."[1] On these volcanic islands of the northern Pacific, the United States launched a global empire while plantation owners reaped massive profits from the sugar industry. Exploiting the spread of devastating disease, enforced labor, legal structures, and the threat of militarism, Americans undermined indigenous authority, leading to a takeover in 1893, annexation of the Islands in 1898, and statehood in 1959.

Settler colonialism in Alaska, analyzed in the latter part of this chapter, inverted the usual pattern of bottom-up settler, squatter, and commercial expansion. Flowing instead from the top down, Americans first purchased Alaska—virtually sight unseen—and only then embarked on settlement into the vast borderlands of the far Pacific Northwest. When the US Army hoisted the American flag over the Russian-American Company headquarters at Sitka in October 1867, the United States had neither recognized indigenous Alaskans as American citizens nor entered into any treaties with them. The Americans knew virtually nothing about the local tribes nor did they care to learn about them. What they did "know" was that the United States had bought the land, was the bearer of civilization, and thus would continue its tradition of deciding the fates of primitive people.[2]

Although they entered the Union as the 49th and 50th states, Alaska and Hawai'i are typically framed within a context of international diplomacy rather than domestic expansion. Both Pacific states, however, were settler colonies in which the United States took control of noncontiguous colonial space while severely marginalizing the indigenous populations. The absence of mass violence in both Hawai'i and Alaska distinguished the two from the indiscriminate violence of the Indian Wars, the Mexican War, and the Civil War. The impact of colonization on the indigenous peoples of Hawai'i nonetheless constituted a cultural genocide while the impact on the Alaskan natives was deleterious at best.

Colonial discourse justified and rationalized US settler colonialism in Hawai'i and Alaska just as it had on the mainland. Colonial ambivalences, both similar and dissimilar to the cleavages within continental settler colonialism, materialized in both territories. The two states are thus part of the continuous history of American settler colonialism over the *longue dureé*. Indeed, many argue that they remain colonies today.

The American transition from continental juggernaut to international power pivoted on taking command of the colonial spaces categorized as Alaska and Hawai'i. The settlement projects anchored rising US power in the northern Pacific, thus providing a foundation for the subsequent imperial thrust into the Philippines, Guam, and other commercial, strategic, and cultural outposts across "Oceania." Settler colonialism in Hawai'i and Alaska deepened American connections with China, Japan, Korea, Russia, Indochina, and the Philippines, with ultimately profound consequences.[3]

The Creeping Colonization of Hawai'i

Like other indigenous peoples, Hawaiians had long-established linkages between the land, the sea, spirituality, and way of life. In their isolation from other cultures, the islands (collectively about the size of New Jersey) went about their business of farming, fishing, loving, worshipping, and fighting without disruption until the Europeans arrived. Although they would be perceived as primitives in colonial discourse, Hawaiians had developed a diverse agriculture, irrigation systems, and extensive public works, all without any concept of absolute ownership of the land. The Hawaiians did, however, operate a quasi-feudal system in which the monarch possessed ultimate authority over use of the land, which he subdivided between regional chieftains, while commoners labored under often cruel and exploitative conditions.[4]

The Kanaka Maoli, like many Indian societies, adopted ambivalent strategies of accommodation and appropriation in response to the colonial encounter. Hawaiian leaders chose to accommodate the *haole* ("whites") by adopting many of their ways, including Christianity. The Hawaiians employed mimicry and appropriation strategies as a middle way response between capitulation and what would have been a futile violent resistance. Yet appropriation as a strategy of resistance would ultimately prove as futile for the Hawaiians as it had for Indian societies. As on the continent, settler colonialism was a zero-sum game in which the colonizers would settle for nothing less than dispossession of the indigenes and complete authority over the islands.

As in North America many Americans expressed their empathy for the indigenous residents and strove to convert them to Christianity and to lead them to salvation. Inter-ethnic marriages, sexual liaisons, and sexual exploitation were also widespread in Hawai'i even as they became a source of Protestant angst. Missionaries, more influential in Hawai'i than on the mainland, made particular efforts to regulate the Hawaiian body as they campaigned against nakedness and the lack of sexual inhibition in Hawaiian culture.

Although not the first Westerner in Hawai'i, Captain James Cook's arrival in Waimea Harbor, Kauai, in January 1778 was a turning point. As he had done in Australia several years earlier, Cook, on his third Pacific voyage, continued to establish place names, proclaiming new sites on the world map for the modernist West. Cook named the islands after the 4th Earl of Sandwich, a backer of his voyages, and he and his men etched names on rocks and trees in various sites across the Pacific. By providing place names and sites on the map, Cook and other Western explorers established "discursive possession" with the implied right to return and to colonize.[5]

Masses of Kanaka Maoli initially welcomed Cook and his men. The common folk provided fresh food while indigenous women made unmistakable "their intentions of gratifying us in all the pleasures the Sex can give," an officer on board recorded. Hawaiian mythology underwrote perceptions of Cook as Lono, the ancient god of nature, fertility, and music. Cook played along.[6] Despite the tumultuous welcome, one of Cook's lieutenants found cause to kill a Hawaiian man on the Englishmen's first day on shore, a prelude of violent clashes to come.

The Englishmen were again well received on a return voyage in which they made landfall on the largest Hawaiian Island. This time, however, the sailors wore out their welcome after a month of gorging, pilfering souvenirs, and womanizing, of which Cook disapproved but proved powerless to stop. The English departed but returned unexpectedly to Kealakekua Bay after only three days at sea in order to repair a broken foremast on the *Resolution*.

This time the Kanaka Maoli received Cook and his men with hostility. To some it appeared Lono had returned "to deprive them of part if not the whole of their country," as a journalist sailing with Cook recorded. Within days an officer recorded, "We have observed in the natives a stronger propensity to theft than we had reason to complain of during our former stay; every day produced more numerous and more audacious depredations." Livid over the theft of a cutter from his other ship, *Discovery*, Cook rashly decided to punish the Hawaiian king personally, though the sovereign had no involvement in the theft.

On Sunday, February 14, 1779, defenders of the king intercepted Cook and his undersized punitive force. Cook personally shot to death at least one of the 17 Hawaiians who died in the club, dagger, and gun battle that ensued just offshore. As the British began to retreat a Hawaiian clubbed Cook in the back of the head. He was then stabbed, submerged, and killed along with four of his charges. The enraged British sailors retaliated, as "dozens of unarmed women, children, and men were slaughtered and dismembered by the English in the twenty-four hours after Cook died."[7] The Hawaiians gave Cook a ritual funeral reserved for a chief before handing over some of his bones for a sailor's burial at sea a few days later.[8]

The battle at Kealakekua Bay was neither the first nor the last clash between Europeans and Hawaiians. Beginning with Cook and his men, Europeans killed indigenes in episodic clashes, often over charges of theft. The only known massacre reminiscent of the previous American wars occurred in the early 1790s at Olowalu on Maui. In that egregious incident Captain Simon Metcalf, a British-American surveyor and Pacific Northwest fur trader, orchestrated the killing and wounding of perhaps "several hundred" Hawaiians in retaliation for the killing of just one of his own men.[9]

Like Indians, Kanaka Maoli perished overwhelmingly from disease rather than direct clashes with the Europeans. Sailors, traders, and missionaries brought venereal disease, measles, small pox, influenza, and a wide variety of other maladies to the unsuspecting and un-inoculated islanders. Estimates vary, as always, but from an indigenous population at the time of Cook's arrival of at least 400,000, and perhaps more than twice that amount, only about 135,000 Hawaiians remained in 1823. In 1893, the year of the US takeover in Hawai'i, the native population had plummeted to about 40,000. By that time many Hawaiians, who had long circulated throughout Oceania, had left the islands as seamen or to pursue other opportunities.[10]

As Europeans began to arrive in the islands in large numbers—British, Spanish, French, Russian, and American—they exploited Hawai'i as a port of provisioning for whaling and for trade. The Europeans traded guns, ammunition, nails, cloth, trinkets, and grog to the Kanaka Maoli for water, food, vegetables, firewood, and women. More and more of these Europeans chose to stay in the island paradise, already renowned for its beauty and astonishingly agreeable weather.[11]

The United States ultimately proved to be the most tenacious colonizer of the Hawaiian Islands. With experience and colonial discourse honed over decades of Indian dispossession, the Americans were well equipped for the colonizing project across the Pacific. "American settlers largely applied their view of Indians and land ownership to Native Hawaiians," Linda Parker notes.[12]

Beginning in the 1820s, the Americans—mostly from New England—began to insinuate themselves into Hawaiian society and gradually to subvert it. Hawaii was thus "drawn within New England's circuit of Pacific transactions, which included both commerce and missions." Established in 1816 at Williams College, the Foreign Mission School trained missionaries for service in Hawai'i and also brought Hawaiians back to the college in far western Massachusetts for religious study.

Fired by the Second Great Awakening and the antebellum reform movements in the United States, missionaries flocked to Hawai'i. They marked progress in saving souls, as by mid-century more than 20 percent of Hawaiians had converted to Protestantism. The civilizing mission included industrial education. In 1836 the Americans opened the Hilo Boarding School for Boys on the eastern coast of Hawai'i, which became a model for the Hampton (Virginia) Institute for the education of freed slaves. "The negro and the Polynesian have many striking similarities," opined Samuel Chapman Armstrong, the son of missionaries. "Of both it is true that not mere ignorance, but deficiency of character is the chief difficulty, and that to build up character is the true objective point in education."[13]

Weakened by disease, Hawaiians saw little prospect in violent opposition against the technologically superior Europeans hence they sought to use the Westerners for their own ends. Like the American Indians, the Hawaiians had contended amongst themselves for supremacy in the islands before the Europeans arrived. Kamehameha I eagerly traded with the *haole* for guns and other technologies that helped him defeat his domestic opponents in violent conflict and unite the Hawaiian Islands under his monarchy in 1795. The king subsequently employed carpenters and other skilled Europeans to bolster his power, giving many of them land to live upon and to farm in return.[14]

Kamehameha I and other Hawaiians, like the American Indians, had no concept of private property or individual appropriation of land in perpetuity. When Kamehameha gave the Europeans land in trade or in exchange for services, he meant that they could *use* it, not that they could *own* it. The Europeans, of course, saw things differently and from the outset pressed the Hawaiians for conversion to a Western system of legally sanctioned fee simple individual land ownership.

Kanaka Maoli elites soon grasped the threat posed by the Western intruders and sought to preserve Hawaiian sovereignty through ambivalence and adaptation. "The Hawaiian king and chiefs adopted aspects of 'civilized' society in an effort to claim an autonomous space in the world of nations," Sally Engle Merry explains. They recognized the powers that inhered in Western law and culture and sought to appropriate them. Kamehameha III and his chiefs accommodated missionaries, sanctioned conversion to Christianity, and adopted Anglo-American law as the "central act of appropriation." Beginning in the mid-nineteenth century, Hawaiian monarchs prepared meticulously, adorned themselves in European-style clothing, and had their portraits taken and circulated to show they were legitimate and civilized in appearance.[15]

The adoption of Christianity destabilized spiritual life in the islands and further undermined the popular authority of the chiefs. In response the chieftains "chose to ally themselves with the American missionaries and take on the mantle of Christian authority." Hawaiian elites gradually syncretized the Calvinist message with Hawaiian spirituality as a means of "shoring up their hegemony" in the society. The chieftains made a practical decision to accommodate the missionaries rather than traders, who might be inclined to cheat them, or sailors prone to drunkenness and violence. From the missionaries they could learn English and Western ways to better adjust to the colonial condition.[16]

Neither acceptance of legal structures nor conversion to Christianity could preserve Hawaiian sovereignty. Thus no matter how much Western culture they proved willing to appropriate, the Hawaiians, like the Indians, ultimately would be constituted as landless premodern others in the eyes of the *haole*. Hawaiians thus "never escaped their racially inscribed difference."[17]

Before all of this had become clear, the Hawaiian monarchy sought to advance its own position by tapping the Western settlers for their cosmopolitan knowledge, trade goods, and technical expertise. The monarchs and their chiefs adjusted Hawaiian society, law, customs, and culture as part of the broader strategy of resistance through appropriation of Western ways. Hawaiians allowed missionaries and others to live on land only to discover that the *haoles* now claimed the land as their own. As the chiefs and other elites accommodated the Westerners, they gradually lost control of their authority over the land and Hawaiian society.

Indigenous Hawaiian sovereignty thus succumbed to a "slow, insinuating invasion of people, ideas, and institutions."[18] The settler colonials had a program—taking command of Pacific colonial space—and possessed a variety of modernist means to achieve it. Under no circumstances would they allow Hawaiians to impede their path to progress, profits, and the extension of American imperial destiny. "The idea that this floating, restless, moneymaking, go-ahead white population can be governed by natives only, is out of the question," the missionary Richard Armstrong declared in 1847. "The time has gone by for the native rulers to have the management of affairs, though the business may be done in their name."[19]

Kanaka Maoli turned from accommodation to more direct means of resistance when they perceived that the settlers intended to hold the land permanently, but these efforts withered before Western legal precedents, technology, racial formation, and, when necessary, gunboats. The Americans sent warships in 1829 to secure collection of debts owed by chiefs to US merchants. The US warships revisited in the 1830s as the Western interlopers put pressure on Hawaiians to reform their land tenure practices by giving the *haole* more power to exploit the land and to own it. The British and French also menaced the monarchy for land rights and the right to transfer land ownership. Between 1836 and 1839, the appearance of the American, British, and French warships "secured the protection of certain property rights for foreign residents" of the Islands.[20]

The strategy to adjust to colonialism through appropriation and accommodation not only proved futile, but also further divided Hawaiians amongst themselves. As Hawaiian elites sought, for example, to meet the increased demand for sandalwood, they exploited the commoners ruthlessly in the tropical forests. Cut out of land ownership and subjected to hard labor, heavy taxes, and cruel treatment, their lives often rigidly controlled, the common people of Hawai'i did not live in an island paradise, rather many lived in fear and subjection. Rank and file Hawaiians could see that the *haole* were changing the landscape, denuding the sandalwood forests, and spreading disease, yet colonialism offered a ray of hope to commoners for potentially improving their plight.[21]

Whether consciously or unconsciously, the settler colonials exploited divisions among indigenous Hawaiians to their own benefit. American missionaries frequently expressed sympathy for the plight of commoners and sought to uplift and convert them. "Native conversion to Christianity and Western laws enabled *haole* to become powerful authorities in Hawaiian society while managing the systematic destruction of the relationship between chiefs and people," Jonathan Osorio explains. "It was the dismembering of that relationship that crippled the Natives' attempts to maintain their independence and identity."[22]

During the 1840s, while American settler colonials on the mainland seized Texas, New Mexico, and California, their brethren oversaw the enactment of a constitution and new laws securing Western land rights in Hawai'i. Hawaiians resisted the threat to their sovereignty whether posed by the British or the French but now increasingly by the United States. The Kanaka Maoli assembled in mass meetings to protest the accelerating dispossession and attendant loss of sovereignty. In the end, however, "The *haoles*' power and influence proved too strong for the Hawaiian government to withstand."[23]

Legalizing Dispossession

As with treaties made with the Indians, Americans sought to dispossess the Hawaiians under the law, the primary form of disavowal of the colonizing act. The establishment of the new land laws provided a veneer of legality, increased the indigenes' sense of powerlessness, and legitimated dispossession as a marker of inevitable progress, under God. "Most significant transformations in nineteenth century Hawai'i came about as legal changes: in ruler-ship, in land tenure, in immigration, and especially in the meaning of identity and belonging." The law provided "not just the instrument for the dispossession of Natives," Osorio explains, "but continual evidence of superiority of the West, a superiority that made that dispossession, in the minds of the *haole*, inevitable."[24]

In 1848, the year the Americans secured their gains from Mexico by treaty, the Great Mahele or land division proposed to convert the ancient Hawaiian land tenure system to the Western mode of individual ownership in fee simple. The Western businessmen as well as the New England Protestants perceived the primitive Hawaiian monarchy as failing to develop the land in the name of progress. A Western system of individual land holding would attract more investors and settlers, ultimately enhancing land values and advancing their own economic interests on the islands. The Americans assured the Kanaka Maoli elites that "the influence of Anglo-Saxon energy in the councils of the nation would operate more than any other cause to the benefit and preservation of the Hawaiian race."[25]

At first the King and the chiefs "laughed very heartily" at the notion that they could be duped into giving up traditional land tenure system for the Western colonial model. Gradually, however, through their "great cunning and perseverance," as Kamahameha put it, the Americans insisted that the Mahele by increasing land values would bolster the power of the monarchy and the Hawaiian elites. Many chieftains were dubious, warning the king, "You must not sell the land to the white man," but in the end, as Stuart Banner notes, "As in most settler societies throughout the world, it was the settlers' desire that would prevail."

In 1850 the Hawaiian monarchy acquiesced to the Great Mahele. Henceforth land that had for centuries belonged to the Hawaiian monarchy could now be sold to anyone. Aware of developments in the wider colonial world, Kamahameha knew that the British had assumed sovereignty in New Zealand in 1840 while France in 1842 took Tahiti and the Marquesas. The Americans had defeated Mexico and secured control of the North American Pacific Coast. The king's *haole* lawyers and advisers emphasized that in the event of conquest of the Islands as opposed to the Mahele, the monarchy and the elites would forfeit their land rights and lose everything. In the end Kamahameha acquiesced and the Mahele did enable many elite Hawaiians to retain land holdings.[26]

In the ensuing years, as the pressures of colonialism mounted, both the chiefs and commoners sold their lands to foreign buyers. Well-meaning albeit ethnocentric US missionaries had ensured that under the Mahele, commoners could secure ownership of their land by filing claims, but many did not understand the provision and were soon dispossessed of what little land they held. Many Hawaiians "did not realize that they surrendered all rights to use of the land." Still others lost their land to indebtedness, failed mortgages, or unpaid taxes amid the steady erosion of indigenous land rights. As with Indians, some Hawaiians lost their land to unscrupulous methods, as drunk and illiterate people signed away their rights.[27]

Coincident with the Mahele, the California gold rush propelled a wave of American migration across the Pacific, as many of the men and far fewer women made their way from California to Hawai'i. Sailors, whalers, and missionaries, still mostly from New England, flocked to the Islands. "Some of the New Englanders came to do good, others to do well for themselves, and some to do both," Merry observes.[28]

In addition to establishing Western legal and economic structures, the settlers sought to infuse their morality in the islands. Colonialism was heavily gendered and intent on regulating the physical bodies as well as the minds of the Kanaka Maoli. As with the campaign for Indian assimilation, to the extent possible the settlers implanted and policed Western gender roles and the notion of the nuclear family. These policies toward indigenous Hawaiians often "were modeled after Native American prototypes."[29]

While plantation owners focused on exploiting the bodies of the predominately male labor force, the Americans also insisted that Kanaka Maoli women define themselves as wives and mothers who would anchor the domestic sphere. The change may have brought a measure of relief for some Kanaka Maoli women, who also worked in the sugar fields for a wage that was less than half of what men were paid.[30] Yet these women found that the missionaries could be just as harsh and uncompromising in the domestic sphere as the planters were with the men in the fields.

Protestant missionaries compelled Kanaka Maoli women to comply with Western norms pertaining to clothing, cleanliness, eating habits, sexual restraint, and other cultural practices. The New England missionaries insisted that Hawaiian women's bodies should be enveloped in clothing and made available only to their husbands. Under the dictates of civilized society, Hawaiian women could not be allowed to go about in the nude or only semi-clad, especially with so many Western men around the islands. Sexuality, the Westerners stressed, should be confined to marriage and otherwise quarantined in brothels to meet the demands of the hopelessly sinful sailors and other transient males.[31]

Colonial discourse pertaining to Kanaka Maoli men and women did not always reflect a benevolent desire to uplift the indigenes. As in North America, many missionaries deployed the "rhetoric of revulsion" toward the "wretched creatures." They judged Hawaiian women as "filthy . . . ignorant and lazy . . . lack everything like modesty," and generally "in great need of improvement." Many Americans viewed the Hawaiians as fearsome in their "wild expressions of countenance, their black hair streaming in the wind as they hurried over the water." Protestant missionary Hiram Bingham perceived "destitution, degradation, and barbarism, among the chattering and almost naked savages." Given their "deep pagan gloom" one had to wonder, "Can such beings be civilized? Can they be Christianized?"[32]

Ultimately, the Hawaiians could only be seen as primitives. "As to the multitude," the *Missionary Herald* declared in 1833, "they are without feeling, without serious reflections, and without thought. Their minds are dark, their hearts insensible."[33]

Sounding very much like Narcissa Whitman amidst the Cayuse in the Walla Walla valley of Washington, the missionary Clarissa Armstrong could not abide the people whose souls she was ostensibly trying to save. "Week after week passes and we see none but filthy, wicked heathen with souls as dark as the tabernacles which they inhabit," she complained in 1831. The more extreme the hostility they expressed toward the indigenes, "the more the missionaries could present themselves as courageous, righteous, and worthy," Houston Wood notes. "Whether depicted as animals or as children, Kanaka Maoli remained in the missionaries' rhetoric as beings who require the supervision of settler Americans."[34]

With their ethnocentrism trumping their ambivalent desire to uplift, the Americans displayed almost complete contempt and intolerance for Kanaka Maoli culture. They targeted sex, drinking of spirits, gambling, and recreation involving display of the body such as dancing, swimming, and surfing. "Anything that was not customary for Americans was deemed wrong for Hawaiians," Patricia Grimshaw explains. The Western-imposed judicial system made criminals of Kanaka Maoli for practices in which they had engaged for centuries. The settler colonials imposed fines, imprisonment, forced labor and public humiliation for nakedness, multiple sexual partnering, and spiritual observances, all deeply rooted in indigenous culture. As Wood points out, "Missionaries and their friends loudly proclaimed that dancing, flirting (lewdness), making love, sharing possessions (spendthriftness), taking off clothes, drinking *awa* and sour potatoes were crimes" though they "had practiced forms of these customs probably since before Jesus was born." Adds Merry, "The arrogance of the Americans and their certainty of their cultural and, by the end of the nineteenth century, biological superiority became unmistakable."[35]

As so often occurred under settler (and other forms of) colonialism, the colonizer's drives and discourse of good works proved to be forces of destruction for indigenous people. Although many Americans did sincerely strive to save the souls and improve the economic plight of the Hawaiians, settler colonialism took their land and cultural imperialism undermined their way of life. Even as they sought to convert and uplift the islanders, the same predominantly New England families "gradually converted the independent kingdom into a sugar plantation economy in which many of the Hawaiian commoners became landless peasants and destitute urbanites."[36] Immigrants could more easily assimilate into this new society while Hawaiians were marginalized and impoverished.

The Sweet Taste of Annexation

As the Americans took charge of the land, the emergence of a fabulously profitable sugar industry paved the way for the US political takeover of the islands. Jamaica, Cuba, Haiti, and Puerto Rico had preceded Hawai'i as profitable sugar islands. Beginning in 1875 with the elimination of trade barriers through reciprocity agreements, the Hawaiian sugar industry experienced "an explosion of growth," as the planters were able to sell their product duty free to a tariff-protected US market. "Due to the Great Mahele, the Gold Rush, the American Civil War, and the Reciprocity Treaty," Ronald Takaki explains, "the Hawaiian sugar industry experienced meteoric success."[37]

The Hawaiian sugar industry flourished behind "latifundia-like colonization by a small elite holding huge parcels of real estate." Five dominant firms, held or managed by a tight-knit group of elite intermarried families, "controlled the banks, hotels, utilities, and above all the land," Bruce Cumings explains. By 1911, journalist Ray Stannard Baker declared Hawai'i was not merely a tropical paradise but also "a paradise of modern industrial combination. In no part of the United States is a single industry so predominant as the sugar industry in Hawai'i."[38]

Beginning in the mid-nineteenth century, the sugar plantation owners began to import foreign labor to do the backbreaking work in the sugar fields, work that was considered inappropriate for white people to perform themselves. In four years after the reciprocity agreement of 1875, 2,300 immigrants arrived in the islands from Asia, initially mostly from China, to work in the sugar industry. Over the ensuing decades the sugar elites extended their importation of low-cost labor to Japan, Korea, and the Philippine Islands.[39]

While American elites exploited cheap labor for massive profits from Hawaiian sugar cane, expansionists and naval enthusiasts coveted Hawai'i for strategic reasons. Hawai'i had featured prominently in Secretary of State William Seward's targets for US expansion but he had been confined to the purchase of Alaska and the Midway Islands, located some 1,300 miles northwest of Honolulu. By the 1880s another ardent expansionist secretary of state, James G. Blaine, viewed "the Hawaiian islands as the key to the dominion of the American Pacific."[40] By the late nineteenth century the naval theorist Alfred Thayer Mahan, Theodore Roosevelt, and other architects of the "large policy" of US imperial expansion viewed Hawai'i—and especially the coveted port at Pearl Harbor—as essential to the rise of the United States as an Asian power. Hawai'i and other islands provided the coaling stations and trans-Pacific trade centers that were crucial to Pacific expansion and establishment of the "Open Door" to trade with China.[41]

With backing in Washington, the Americans who had taken control of the land and established highly profitable sugar and fruit plantations, set their sights on terminating the monarchy and seizing direct political control of the Islands. As with the "Vanishing American" back on the mainland, expansionists argued that the Hawaiians were dying out and that the United States had already established de facto control. An 1874 tourist guide proclaimed, "If our flag flew over Honolulu we could hardly expect to have a more complete monopoly of Hawaiian commerce than we already enjoy."[42]

Under these circumstances, Americans argued it made no sense for the backward indigenes to retain even titular authority over the Islands. By the late nineteenth century, Social Darwinist sentiment bolstered a wave of overseas colonialism and imperialism. The Western powers engaged in a "scramble" for Pacific outposts that mirrored the scramble for Africa. Europeans as well as Americans undertook the "white man's burden" of spreading civilization by force over "primitive" peoples perceived as unable to keep pace with the modern world.

"Whether the Hawaiians were doomed because of their paganism, their devotion to their chiefs, their want of private property, their laziness, their lack of sanitation, or, finally, their opposition to *haole*, in the end they were just *naturally* doomed," Osorio explains.[43]

In the 1880s, as the American settler colonial elites steadily increased land holdings, they moved toward seizing direct political control of the Hawaiian Islands. As they successfully recruited new settlers to relocate in Hawai'i, the Americans continued to "remonstrate for the sale of government lands." US settler colonials secured government approval of land acts in 1884 and 1885 that "augmented the alienation of lands from Hawaiians."[44]

Even as they took possession of colonial space, the white elite experienced "chronic anxiety" over the uncertain political future of the islands. Any potential threat to the windfall profits of the sugar industry "struck terror" within the tight circle of *haole* elites. Strategic ambitions married economic self-interest. Mahan emphasized "over and over, in crucial moments the primary importance of Hawai'i to America's global strategy."[45]

The American elite led by Lorrin Thurston and Sanford Dole formed the Hawaiian League, a "shadow organization" that plotted "insurrection" at a meeting in Dole's home. Thurston and Dole were prominent men from well-established missionary families; both were attorneys and both had been elected to the Hawaiian legislature. They and their followers in the Hawaiian League secretly vowed "to persuade the dusky monarch into subjection." After overthrowing the monarchy, the *haole* elite would have complete control of the islands and could orchestrate their eventual annexation by the United States.[46]

In July 1887, the *haole* initiated the seizure of power by forcing King Kalakaua to sign the "Bayonet Constitution" in which the monarch turned over executive powers to the oligarchy of planters and businessmen, making them the de facto rulers of the islands. Mirroring the spread of Jim Crow segregation on the mainland, the new constitution disenfranchised the indigenes as well as Asian immigrants. It "was the very first time that democratic rights were determined by race in any Hawaiian constitution," Osorio notes. The United States at this time also claimed an "exclusive right" to build and maintain a coaling station at Pu'uloa (Pearl Harbor) in conjunction with a renewed reciprocity treaty. Hawaiians had vigorously opposed and successfully fought off previous American efforts to take control of the coveted harbor.[47]

The Kanaka Maoli bitterly protested and resisted the coup but the elite-controlled militia took to the streets with bayonets in place. Prepared to shed blood if necessary, the coup plotters had imported 900 rifles from San Francisco. A "white crowd that at times functioned as a vigilante mob" threatened to hang a small group of ambivalent American advisers to the King who stood in opposition to the gutting of the monarchy.[48]

The Hawaiians defied the colonial stereotypes of primitive, indolent islanders by holding mass meetings, signing petitions, attempting to work within the colonial legal system while at the same time plotting conspiracies against it. "One of the most persistent and pernicious myths of Hawaiian history is that the Kanaka Maoli passively accepted the erosion of their culture and the loss of their nation,"

Neone K. Silva points out. "The myth of nonresistance was created in part because mainstream historians have studiously avoided the wealth of material written in Hawaiian."[49]

The undermining of the language of the Kanaka Maoli was an important component of the settler colonial project. Beginning in the mid-nineteenth century, the *haole* disparaged the Hawaiian language "as inadequate to the task of 'progress.' " The Americans subsequently outlawed teaching of Hawaiian in the schools and established English as the official language. In the absence of Hawaiian sources, a "colonial historiography" subsequently evolved, rendering the indigenous people "nearly invisible in the historical narratives of their own places, while making the actions of the colonizers appear to be the only ones of any importance."[50]

As they strove to contain the indigenous Hawaiians, the *haole* elite moved to terminate the monarchy and to annex Hawai'i to the United States. In 1889 Blaine appointed John Stevens, a close associate from their native Maine and an avowed annexationist, as US minister to Hawai'i. In January 1893 Stevens launched a coup, reporting back to Washington, "The Hawaiian pear is now fully ripe, and this is the golden hour for the United States to pluck it." US marines landed, ostensibly to protect property, as Stevens declared Hawai'i a protectorate under the benevolent guidance of the United States.[51]

American settler colonialists in Hawai'i, joined by US officials and journalists on the mainland, demonized the reigning monarch Lili'uokalani on at least three levels: as a monarch, as a woman, and as the representative of a backward race. Editorial cartoons invariably depicted "Negroid features and black skin, signifiers to Americans that the queen was of a race unsuitable to rule." Lili'uokalani refused to give up the throne, however, and used the Yankee legal structures as a tool of resistance. The Queen attempted to work through the political system to promulgate a new constitution affirming the authority of the monarchy. She proved so nettlesome that the Americans finally seized the monarch's land, put her on trial, and placed her under house arrest in 1895.[52]

The indigenous *hui* (associations) anchored grassroots resistance, backed by the native language papers, but the Hawaiians "had no arms of consequence" whereas the *haole were* "armed to the teeth." An attempt at armed resistance in 1893 would have amounted to a "ritualized sacrifice." Arriving back in Maine, Stevens crowed that the "semi-barbaric monarchy" had been rendered "dead in everything but its vice."[53]

Stevens spoke too soon, however, as the US-led coup became a contentious issue as a result of ambivalent opposition within the United States. A large segment of American public opinion perceived that "the United States did wrong by Hawai'i in the 1893 revolution even when judged by 1890s standards and practices."[54] The takeover had been too blatant thus undermining the imperial project and delaying annexation to a more propitious moment.

In a reflection of the triangulated framework typical of settler colonialism, metropolitan authority attempted to rein in the settlers. President Grover Cleveland, a Democrat, condemned US imperialism in Hawai'i and rejected the treaty of annexation submitted by his Republican predecessor. "The provisional government owes its existence to an armed invasion by the United

States," Cleveland flatly declared, yet he made no effort to restore the Hawaiian monarchy.[55] Cleveland's anti-imperialism like that of the nation he represented proved ephemeral.

On July 4, 1894, with opposition fading and an economic depression setting in at home, the oligarchy proclaimed the existence of the new Republic of Hawai'i. The United States proffered immediate recognition, with Great Britain and most European countries following suit. Thousands of Kanaka Maoli protested the hoisting of the American flag outside the Iolani Palace and continued to sign petitions against the dissolution of the monarchy.[56]

Amid the manic energies unleashed by the Spanish-American War in 1898, the United States annexed Hawai'i by joint resolution of the Congress, which required only a simple majority rather than the two-thirds required in the Senate for approval of treaties. Annexation guaranteed continuing access to US and global markets thus assuring the continuation of high profits for the *haole* owned sugar industry. Annexation also mollified the "large policy" strategists—Roosevelt, Mahan, and Lodge—who convinced President William McKinley to annex the islands in the name of "manifest destiny." Roosevelt had long been demanding that the United States should seize control of Hawai'i "in the interests of the white race." In 1897 he declared, "If I had my way we would annex those islands tomorrow."[57]

Even as the United States went to war in April 1898 ostensibly to liberate Cuba and other Spanish possessions, the oligarchy worked assiduously to foreclose the possibility of any actual democracy in Hawai'i. The *haole* elite admitted to McKinley that in the event of a referendum on annexation in the islands that they would lose. "The files they so carefully left behind," Tom Coffman points out, "are littered with the theme of preventing a free and open vote."[58]

Unlike other colonies taken from Spain, which would require indirect strategies of colonial control, the United States annexed Hawai'i, making it, as one congressman put it, "the only true American colony." In the debate over annexation, proponents emphasized that Hawai'i was a US settler society colonized by an American Christian and economic elite, with an established constitutional government, and widespread use of the English language. In other words, unlike the other "primitive" and racially suspect possessions, annexationists averred, Hawai'i had already achieved a level of civilization and control that made it ripe for territorial status and eventual statehood.[59]

In a reflection of continuity over the *longue dureé* of American colonialism, imperialists outmaneuvered ambivalent opponents of annexation by using the history of Indian dispossession against them. The so-called anti-imperialists who argued that the United States was abandoning its tradition of advancing republicanism and self-determination were indulging in "a strange forgetfulness of the facts of American history," an Iowa congressman reminded them. After all, "Every American State was made by dispossessing the native Indians."[60]

Although indigenous Hawaiians were incapable of governing themselves, they were not "savages" but rather "barbarians of a milder and more progressive type," Lodge assured his colleagues. The Massachusetts senator pointed out that physically the Hawaiians had features "resembling the Europeans" and were "olive" in color rather than "yellow like the Malay nor red like the American Indian."

Hawaiian women, he added, were a "dazzling vision of sparkling eyes, pearly teeth, bright flowers, and bare legs . . . her voluptuous bust rounding in graceful curves." As Lodge's florid description attests, feminine representations could provide "an important justification for U.S. political and cultural hegemony."[61]

As occurred throughout the history of American and other settler colonialisms, the colonizers of Hawai'i rationalized their destruction of indigenous cultures by celebrating their own inherent goodness in advancing progress, under God. The manifestation of aggression under the guise of good works reflects pathologies identified by Sigmund Freud and later analyzed by Jacques Lacan (see Chapter 1). As the Americans were advancing Christian civilization and progress, the settler takeover was ultimately a good thing and enjoyed the blessings of Providence. Similarly, the application of American place names to streets, buildings, and sites, as well as the association of the takeover of a foreign government with the Declaration of Independence, offer examples of what Mary Louise Pratt described as "anti-conquest" rhetoric—"strategies of representation" in which imperialists "seek to secure their innocence in the same moment as they assert hegemony."[62]

Asian Settler Colonialism in Hawai'i

As the elite US minority seized the land and controlled the politics and economy of the islands, Hawai'i appeared to be a classic colonial state. Hawai'i, however, functioned not only as a colonial state but also as a distinctive *settler* colonial state comprised overwhelmingly of *Asian* settlers imported in large numbers to perform the labor on the sugar, coffee, and pineapple plantations. Following the arrival of the first major contract labor group of Chinese in 1852, the sugar planters imported thousands of Portuguese, Japanese, Filipino, and Korean laborers. As Asian contract laborers settled in Hawai'i in large numbers, the indigenous Kanaka Maoli became further marginalized.[63] The large influx of Asian settlers—"made possible by U.S. settler colonialism"— became the majority population on the islands. The early Asian settlers "were both active agents in the making of their own histories and unwitting recruits swept into the service of empire."[64]

In sum, US colonialism created an Asian settler colonial state in postcolonial Hawai'i. In an astonishingly rapid demographic transformation, US-sponsored Asian settler colonialism in Hawai'i quickly dwarfed the indigenous population. A census conducted in 1872 found the island comprised of 86 percent Hawaiians and another 4–5 percent of half-Hawaiians. By 1890, as a result of the rapid influx of Asian laborers and settlers, Kanaka Maoli comprised only 38 percent of the population, with part-Hawaiians comprising another 7 percent. The number of American settlers steadily increased yet they comprised a mere 2 percent of the population even as they dominated the islands politically and economically.[65]

Japan, a rising world power in the wake of industrialization and the Meiji restoration, sharply opposed the US takeover of Hawai'i. The Japanese protested and dispatched warships to Hawai'i. These actions aroused racially charged American concerns about rising Japanese power in the Pacific. Alarm over the "Japanese menace" in Hawai'i undercut anti-imperial discourse in the United

States while spurring congressional approval of the annexation of Hawai'i. As with the history of continental settler colonialism, racial formation married imperial ambitions and economic self-interest in the US takeover of Hawai'i.[66]

While Japan proved unable to impede US annexation, Japanese immigrants continued to flood into Hawai'i. By the beginning of the twentieth-century Japanese workers had become the largest foreign group in Hawai'i. Americans remained concerned that "the Japs" were "getting too numerous" in the Hawaiian Republic.[67] The oligarchy nonetheless sought to exploit the Japanese labor for the sugar industry even as they determined to fend off, as Dole put it, "the desire on the part of the Japs to control Hawai'i." Accordingly, the *haole* elite reinforced policies of "systematically granting extraordinary rights to immigrant whites while systematically denying those rights to Japanese and other Asian immigrants."[68]

From annexation of Hawai'i to 1946, a few score *haole* accumulated massive wealth and power over the Islands. During the Territorial period these men owned outright almost half of the land while the government that they controlled owned most of the rest. It was a more far-reaching concentration of wealth and power than anywhere else in the United States.[69]

The colonizing elite supported the maintenance of territorial status for Hawai'i for more than 60 years, as state and federal laws otherwise might preclude ongoing importation of cheap Asian labor. Two waves of Korean immigrants arrived in the first quarter of the twentieth century. As American Indians would do, Asian immigrants led by the Japanese began to employ the colonizer's own laws and institutions to press for rights and equality. By 1910, workers had begun to unionize and shed the contract labor system. Union leaders now argued that the plantation system was "undemocratic and un-American."[70]

As the Asian immigrant population proliferated, the ruling *haole* combined ambivalent gestures toward the Kanaka Maoli with continuing dispossession. In 1921, passage of the Native Hawaiian Homes Commission Act (HHCA) set aside land for indigenous people along with provisions to promote assimilation. However, much like the Dawes Act for Indians, the legislation enabled the taking of more land by the *haole*. The HHCA set aside prime agricultural land for the sugar industry and enabled pineapple corporations to sublease Hawaiian homelands.[71]

The HHCA thus ultimately constituted "a colonial project in the service of land alienation and dispossession." Even the some 200,000 acres set aside for the Kanaka Maoli required that individuals meet a 50 percent blood quantum rule in order to establish their status as "native Hawaiians." Blood quantum undermined efforts to build Kanaka Maoli political power by excluding rather than including people as Hawaiians.[72]

The Japanese attack in December 1941 on US-occupied Hawai'i followed by the Pacific War underscored the strategic importance of the Islands and paved the way for eventual statehood. The status of the Kanaka Maoli continued to decline in the 1940s and 1950s, as their percentage of the electorate and thus their political influence declined. In the postwar era both Asian settlers and indigenous Hawaiians faced growing "pressures to assimilate to the dominant white culture." Indigenous Hawaiian language fell increasingly out of favor and its use discouraged if not prohibited in schools.[73]

With the Kanaka Maoli marginalized and the white mainlanders dramatically outnumbered, the Asian settlers were ascendant. In the 1950s, as the children of the Asian immigrants gained citizenship status, they were primarily responsible for voting out the Republicans, long the party of the plantation elite. The Asian settlers joined with the *haole* in massive land development projects of mutual economic benefit. By exploiting the law, educational opportunity, unionization, and military service during the war, the Asian immigrants led by the Japanese had overcome segregation and exclusion to gain dominant influence in Hawai'i. In March 1959 Congress passed the Hawai'i Admission Act and President Dwight D. Eisenhower signed the fiftieth state into the Union. In subsequent years Japanese-American political influence, as symbolized by the political power accumulated by Senator Daniel Inouye, "left Native Hawaiian interests largely ignored."[74]

Emboldened by global decolonization and the reform spirit of the 1960s, indigenous Hawaiians, like American Indians, called attention to colonialism and injustice, and mounted various strategies of resistance and accommodation (see Chapter 9).

American Settler Colonialism in Alaska

When Europeans began to arrive in "Alaska" (derived from the Aleut word meaning "great land") indigenous people lived in myriad and complex social formations. To simplify the matter Aleuts lived in the island chain now named for them that trickles southeast from Alaska into the Bering Sea; the Inupiat and Yup'ik lived along the Arctic coast; Athabascans were scattered throughout the Alaskan interior; and the Tlingit and Haida occupied the southeast coast, which eventually comprised the population center of American settler colonialism. As with continental Indians, the best evidence suggests these peoples originally crossed from Asia on the once extant Siberian-Alaskan land bridge.

In the Arctic indigenes relied on seals for food and other fur-bearing animals for clothing and shelter. They hunted whales, walrus, and sea lion at sea and caribou, moose and polar bear on land. The interior Athabaskans hunted and built reliable birch canoes to facilitate fishing and riverine travel. Wherever it was possible the indigenes of Alaska worked the streams for migrating salmon. In southeastern Alaska indigenes benefited from a rich environment with plentiful food sources. Like Indians Alaskan spirituality was closely linked with the natural environment. Although some societies operated on the basis of matrilineal kinship, generally women were not much empowered in the indigenous cultures of Alaska.[75]

The colonial encounter began in the eighteenth century when the Dane Vitus Bering "discovered" Alaska for Europeans. Bering explored and mapped Alaska and the northern Pacific Coast along Puget Sound and down the coast of modern-day Oregon. Bering sailed for Tsar Peter the Great thus laying the foundation for the Russian claim to Alaska and the Aleutian islands. In 1741, Bering died on an island near the Kamchatka Peninsula that is now named for him, as are the Bering Strait and the Bering Sea between Russia and Alaska. Following in Bering's wake was the ubiquitous Captain Cook, first joined and then succeeded by fellow British explorer George Vancouver. These expeditions laid the foundation for competing British claims to the region.[76]

From 1799 to 1867, the Russian-American Company, a joint stock company authorized by the tsar, dominated the Alaskan fur trade. The Russians encountered and "subdued quickly and easily" the Aleuts and Kodiaks living in small coastal villages, but the Tlingit would be a different story. The Aleuts suffered extensively from disease, forced labor, rape, and murder at the hands of Russian fur hunters. The Russians expanded their forts and settlements as far south as Sonoma County, California. Competition from the British and then the Americans led to treaties in the mid-1820s. As with the Indians, the modernist nations negotiated their trade and occupation rights in the northwest Pacific without involvement or consideration of indigenous interests.[77]

Colonial ambivalence materialized from the start as the Russians, despite their episodic violence against the indigenes, became "dependent upon the Aleuts, Kodiaks, and Tlingit for such basics as furs, provisions, labor, and sex." Like the first Europeans on the Atlantic coast, the colonizers did not know how to fend for themselves in the new environment. They depended on the indigenes to provide meat, primarily from deer hunting, and fish to eat until the Russians learned better how to secure these on their own. As relatively few Russians proved willing to migrate to Alaska, the Russian-American Company depended on indigenous labor. Moreover, only the indigenes knew how to hunt the elusive sea otters from their kayaks on the open sea.

The Tlingit, a coalescence of competing clans, resisted colonization and proved to be tenacious fighters. Moreover, they had traded for arms from Americans passing through on "Yankee coasters" and they learned to "shoot very accurately." The Tlingit "hated the Russians for having seized their ancestral lands, occupied their best fishing and hunting grounds, desecrated their burial sites, and seduced their women." Like the American colonists in their "stations" on the borderlands, the Russians had to hole up in forts, as the "well-armed savages" were "always ready to take advantage of our negligence." No Russian "dared to go fifty paces from the fort."[78]

By the 1830s and 1840s, smallpox and other diseases had weakened the Tlingit but colonial ambivalence also ameliorated the relationship between the Russians and the indigenes. The Russians traded flour, rice, molasses, tobacco, and vodka and showed the indigenes how to grow potatoes. In a pattern familiar to the ambivalent Indian history on the mainland, the Aleuts allied with Russians in battles against their indigenous rivals the Tlingit.[79] With precious few Russian women willing to migrate to the "barbarous, desolate" realm, the Russian men established sexual relationships with indigenous women. As many of the hardened Russian colonizers were "depraved, drunk, violent, and corrupted," many of these relationships were coerced. Within the first generation, a substantial number of "creoles" began to appear.[80]

In the mid-1850s the Crimean War pitting Russia against the allied nations of Britain and France marked a turning point leading to the eventual sale of Alaska to the United States. Defeated in the Crimean War, the Russians feared further encroachments in the northern Pacific by the British and also cast a wary eye on the United States, which was attempting to reinvigorate Manifest Destiny now that the Civil War had come to an end. The Russians had gone to Alaska for the fur trade not to establish a settler colony. With only 658 Russians in residence, and the fur trade having peaked, the Russians were open to selling Alaska.

In 1867, as a result of late-night meetings and questionable financial arrangements involving the Russians and a handful of congressmen, Secretary of State Seward secured the Alaska Purchase at a cost of US$7.2 million. Despite scattered references to "Seward's folly" and "Walrussia," most Americans approved of the extension of the nation's power into the Arctic northwest. As noted, together with Hawai'i the Alaska Purchase anchored American power in the northern Pacific, enabling the eventual rise of the United States as a global power.[81]

As with settler colonialism on the mainland, the United States had once again expanded by virtue of signing a treaty in which a European power handed over vast lands inhabited by indigenous people. As the bearers of civilization, the Americans, consistent with the history of settler colonialism over the *longue durée*, had no intention of respecting indigenous land rights. In October 1867 when the US Army arrived in Sitka to set up administration, the United States had neither recognized the indigenous Alaskans as American citizens nor entered into any treaties with them. In fact the Americans knew virtually nothing about the local tribes.[82]

The 1867 Treaty of Cession had provided a path to US citizenship for any Russians or other Europeans who wished to remain in Alaska, but the provision pointedly excluded "uncivilized native tribes." Under this colonial discourse, the indigenous people would be "subject to such laws and regulations as the United States may, from time to time, adopt in regard to aboriginal tribes."[83] In 1869, after leaving office and visiting his prized possession, Seward applied the indigenous "vanishing race" discourse to Alaskans. He declared that the indigenes though "vigorous" would "steadily decline in numbers" as they "can neither be preserved as a distinct social community, nor incorporated into our society."[84]

Protected by the US Army, American settlers confiscated islands that the Tlingit and Haida had occupied for a millennium. "Vagabonds, adventurers, and not a few criminals" ascended on southeastern Alaska. Capitalists from Seattle and San Francisco built salmon canneries and fish traps that "made their absentee owners millions of dollars by overharvesting the Indians' most important subsistence resource." While the Army, the capitalists, and the adventurers took possession of colonial space, Congress provided enabling legislation "with slight regard for the impact of their decision making on the indigenous population."[85]

Like indigenous people everywhere, the southeastern indigenes resented the encroachment of the technologically advanced invaders. In 1869 the Army commander at Sitka reported that the Tlingit "frequently take the occasion to express their dislike at not having been consulted about the transfer of the territory. They do not like the idea of whites settling in their midst without being subjected to their jurisdiction."[86]

Much like Hawai'i and in contrast to the mainland, only scattered violent clashes rather than indiscriminate killing characterized American settler colonialism in Alaska. US soldiers generally coexisted peacefully with the indigenes, but as usual settlers proved more likely to get into direct conflict.

The army invariably defended the settlers and not the indigenous people in such clashes. On at least two occasions, the Army opted for collective punishment by burning down entire villages when the indigenes failed to turn over to the Americans those alleged to have killed individual white men. Consistent with most histories of settler colonialism, white men were immune from punishment for killing, raping, or injuring indigenous people. When the Army went so far as to jail a Sitka settler after he committed his second killing of indigenous men, "the settler community demanded his release," to which the Army promptly acquiesced.[87]

Playing their accustomed role as agents of colonial ambivalence, Protestant missionaries ventured north to civilize and save the souls of indigenous Alaskans. The Russian Orthodox Church had laid the groundwork, as it had some 50 missions in Alaska at the time of the sale to the United States. As the Russians departed, American Presbyterians, Quakers, and Catholics assumed the proselytizing mission.[88]

As in Hawai'i and on the mainland, the missionaries undermined indigenous culture by insisting on the primacy of their own spiritual beliefs. They prized individualism over group identity and demanded reshaping of gender roles. Most missionaries sympathized with the indigenes, however, and in 1884 their influence helped spur Congress to pass the Organic Act, which terminated US military rule, provided for the establishment of schools to educate the indigenous people, and included some tepid provisions intended to safeguard Alaska indigenes on their land. The Organic Act perceived Alaska as a "district" and not as a territory on the road to eventual statehood.[89]

Settler colonialism evolved slowly in Alaska before accelerating in the 1890s. Until that time settlers frequently expressed anxiety about being outnumbered by the indigenes that comprised some 90 percent of the population at the passage of the Organic Act. A federal land act in 1891 authorized homesteading and town sites to encourage settlement and capitalist development, especially in the salmon canning and sawmill industries. The act "facilitated the beginning of a permanent pioneer population in Alaska."[90]

In 1896, the discovery of gold in the Klondike region transformed Alaska much as the allure of gold had spurred settler colonial expansion onto Cherokee lands in the 1830s and especially to California in 1849. The familiar "gold fever" incited a stampede of some 100,000 men from the mainland to the Yukon Territory in northwestern Canada. The majority of Americans traveled through Alaska and had a dramatic impact on the land and people. Most of them failed, of course, to fulfill their dreams of unearthing overnight riches and many of the disappointed prospectors settled in Alaska.

At the outset of the Klondike gold rush, indigenous people got work as packers, stevedores, and woodcutters while others sold indigenous arts and crafts to the incomers. However, "Whites quickly and easily replaced the Indians in nearly all aspects of economic life." Thus most of the indigenes were soon unemployed and segregated with many turning to alcohol and prostitution. They became "increasingly dependent on white goods and the white economy" and were "regularly subject to segregation and discrimination." Prospectors and developers "ignored Native land use patterns, appropriating land and water and forcing the Natives to relocate." Missionaries helped to mitigate the impact of indigenous social problems but could not eliminate them.[91]

The influx of prospectors and developers spread diseases and impacted the environment through removal of vegetation; building of roads; construction of homes, stores, and taverns; and poisoning of streams. Indigenous Alaskans had suffered the effects of the new diseases in earlier years but the rapid six- to seven-fold increase in the settler population now made a devastating impact, as thousands of indigenes succumbed to influenza, measles, and other diseases. The Americans reduced the game populations, mainly caribou and moose, upon which the Alaskans depended for food. While indigenous population growth stagnated, the US population in Alaska grew to about 30,000 by 1910.[92]

In contrast to the approach to Indians on the mainland, until the twentieth century there were no treaties, no reservations, and no demand that the indigenous Alaskans renounce a tribe. "What really set Alaska's experience apart," Donald C. Mitchell explains, "was its very low population, enormously high percentage of federal lands, and lack of any provision made over the years—dictatorial or otherwise—for Alaska Native land ownership claims."[93]

In 1906, the situation began to change when the US Congress passed the Alaska Native Allotment Act. Based loosely on the Dawes Act, the legislation aimed to give indigenous Alaskans possession of individual plots of land. However, most indigenous Alaskans probably did not know about or understand the provisions of the allotment act yet many signed on the dotted line as instructed. In 1912 the Alaska Native Brotherhood was founded as a self-help organization to assist the indigenous people in responding to the settler influx. That same year Alaska officially became an American territory but one that lacked local autonomy, as major decisions still emanated from Washington, D.C. In 1924 the United States granted citizenship under the law to all indigenous peoples, including Alaskans.[94]

While American settler colonialism took hold mostly in southeastern Alaska, the northern reaches and the Bering Sea had long been the province of whale and seal hunters. European whalers depleted this vital indigenous resource and compounded the problem by trading whiskey at their ports, which had the predictable "malevolent effect on the northern Eskimos." The Americans sought with limited success to contain pelagic sealing—the killing on the open sea of fur-bearing seals, which had a severe impact on the population as the female seals did most of the open-water hunting. In 1911, the North Pacific Fur Seal Convention signed by the United States, Russia, Britain, and Japan, the first of its kind, ended pelagic sealing (at least *de jure*) and recognized US primacy in managing the on-shore slaughter of the animals.[95]

As with indigenes on the mainland, the Depression–New Deal and World War II era brought significant changes. In 1931, the Bureau of Indian Affairs began to extend services to the Alaska indigenes. In 1936, Congress applied the comprehensive Indian Reorganization Act (IRA) to Alaskan indigenes, "thereby equating the status of Alaska Natives to that of Native Americans in general." The IRA provided for the creation of local indigenous governments, though with only six indigenous reserves created these failed to extend throughout the vast reaches of the territory.[96]

US involvement in World War II brought another burst of settler colonial expansion to Alaska and attendant marginalization of indigenous people. Fearing a Japanese assault on the Aleutians, US authorities subjected the indigenous Alaskans to the same internment program that they enforced on Japanese-Americans and Japanese immigrants primarily in the Western states of the mainland—property seizures, prolonged confinement in makeshift camps, and wholesale violations of civil liberties. For reasons that defy rational explanation, the US military subjected 881 Aleuts to wartime internment. "Evacuations were marked by confusion and chaos, poor accommodations and meager rations, and an appalling degree of insensitivity," Mitchell points out. "From forced evacuation, to dubious confinement, to desolate homecoming, it is very difficult to imagine that American citizens of the white race would have been treated in a similar manner."[97]

As in Hawai'i, the ultimate impact of World War II was the militarization of Alaska and the closing of ties with the United States leading to eventual statehood. The Americans fortified the Aleutians, built military installations throughout the state, and constructed the Alaska Highway, all of which pumped billions of dollars into the territory. By 1943, some 154,000 American servicemen were stationed in Alaska. As the territory never became a major theater of the war, the men had plenty of time to hunt, fish, carouse, and alter the landscape.[98]

The discourse of global cold war increased the militarization and strategic significance of Alaska. It also unleashed competition for control of the Arctic involving the Soviet Union, the United States, Canada, Greenland, and Denmark. Caught in the middle were the indigenous Arctic residents, among them the Inuit. Over the years indigenous people of the Arctic, including more than 650,000 in Alaska, have been subjected to land loss and forced relocations, mining intrusions, and pollution. Not surprisingly, many now advocate a sovereign Arctic state.[99]

Anxious to disassociate itself from colonialism in the postwar era, the United States moved toward statehood for Alaska and Hawai'i. In 1946, the same year as Philippine independence, Alaskans voted 9,630 to 6,822 for statehood. Alaska became a political football, however, as congressional Republicans during the Eisenhower years feared that statehood would tilt political power in favor of the Democrats. Over the next few years Alaska politicians led by Ernest Gruening and Robert Bartlett persisted in lobbying and publicizing the territory's colonial status. Both the House and Senate eventually passed bills for statehood, which Eisenhower signed into law on January 3, 1959, making Alaska the 49th state in the Union.[100]

Statehood did not liberate the indigenous people of either Alaska or Hawai'i from the profound legacies of settler colonialism, as the postcolonial history of the two states (Chapter 9) would reveal.

8

"Things Too Scandalous to Write": The Philippine Intervention and the Continuities of Colonialism

Postcolonial analysis illuminates continuity in the history of US colonialism. The counterinsurgency war waged by the United States at the turn of the century in the Philippine archipelago, though not a settler project, was nonetheless a colonial project. The argument for viewing the "Spanish-American War" and the "Philippine Insurrection" as discontinuous rests on a disavowal of the prior history of settler colonialism. By relegating Indian removal to domestic history, thus keeping it quarantined from the broader history of US foreign relations, a colonialist historiography has obscured the fundamental continuities of US empire building.[1]

In the wake of the Spanish-American War, the United States established a new hegemony in the Caribbean and, with Hawai'i and Alaska as the pivot, emerged as a Pacific and global power. By seizing Puerto Rico, Guam, the Philippines, and Samoa, "the United States had become a formal overseas colonial empire just like its European counterparts," Julian Go observes.[2] After 1898, as Lanny Thompson explains, "The culture of imperialism in the United States drew upon and extended the continental colonial experience in the elaboration of the fundamental alterity of the subject peoples."[3]

Entering into new colonial spaces in Southeast Asia, the United States carried out an intensive counterinsurgency campaign that would ensconce the Philippine archipelago within an emerging American global security regime. As with the history of settler colonialism on the continent, the United States engaged in indiscriminate warfare to defeat the Philippine revolutionaries. In order to achieve "pacification" of the Philippine archipelago through a lethal application of asymmetrical warfare, the United States caused the deaths albeit mostly indirectly of at least 250,000, probably closer to 400,000, and perhaps as many as 800,000 Filipinos, while suffering a dramatically disproportionate 4,234 deaths of its own.[4]

As in the Indian wars, colonial ambivalence materialized alongside exterminatory violence in the Philippines. The United States ultimately succeeded in quelling the "insurrection"—in actuality an anticolonial revolution—through the ambivalent inducements of "nation building" in tandem with the willingness to kill and to destroy. The US Army capitalized on the disorganization and weaknesses of the resistance as it effectively combined lethal aggression with effective civic action programs and cooptation. While the US intervention ultimately proved effective, only by overlooking the high level of death and destruction and the essence of the intervention as a colonial project can it ultimately be viewed through a triumphal lens.[5]

Rather than simply "exporting" racial discourse and colonialism abroad, the United States had to adopt different approaches and strategies to fit "specific patterns of imperial rule." The new possessions in the Caribbean and the Pacific constituted an "internally differentiated imperial archipelago" requiring "multiple ruling strategies." Cuba, Puerto Rico, and the Panama Canal Zone facilitated regional economic linkages and reinforced the Monroe Doctrine, whereas Guam and Samoa served primarily as coaling stations and naval bases. In the Philippines removal of the indigenous people followed by direct US settlement was neither desirable nor remotely possible; the archipelago instead facilitated the emergence of the United States as a Pacific power. In all of these cases the Americans instituted colonial rule that precluded the pursuit of self-determination by the subject peoples.[6]

In 1898, at the outset of the conflict, the Spanish, not the Filipinos, constituted the enemy of the United States, thus enabling as in Cuba an alliance between the Americans and the indigenous people. Several US officials told Emilio Aguinaldo, a Filipino elite and leader of the anti-Spanish rebels, that the United States came as a liberator and had no intention of colonizing the islands. In June 1898, a few weeks after the US Navy crushed the decadent Spanish fleet in Manila Bay, Aguinaldo declared the Philippines independent. He called the United States an "honorable friend" and set about much the same way that many Indians and Hawaiians had done to try to impress the Americans with the potential of the Philippines to adapt and stand on its own as a "civilized" society.

As they attempted to bring to fruition the first successful nationalist revolution in Asia, the Philippine revolutionaries drafted a constitution, opened a newspaper, refrained from indiscriminate slaughter of the Spaniards, and discussed Philippine culture and their plans for its advancement. Apolinario Mabini, a close adviser to Aguinaldo and "one of the most determined and acute proponents of independence," suspected the United States of harboring imperial ambitions that would blunt Filipino nationalism. He called for preempting US colonization by convincing the Americans that they would confront "a strong and organized people who know how to defend the laws of justice and their honor."[7]

Much like the history of settler colonization in North America, nothing would deter the Americans once they had set their course of empire. The United States took Spain's surrender by treaty in December 1898, hoisting the American flag in Manila and pointedly excluding the Filipinos from the diplomatic stage. President William McKinley framed his decision to annex the islands as "benevolent assimilation" of the indigenes, a discourse that paralleled Indian assimilation under the Dawes Act. "Benevolent assimilation" also constituted a familiar discourse of disavowal of the colonizing act.[8]

The American colonialist fantasy as applied to the Philippines perceived the United States as undertaking a humanitarian project of replacing savagery with "uplift" to the ultimate benefit of the indigenous "tribes." Common application of the trope "tribes" to the Philippines reinforced continuity with the history of North American Indian removal. Americans began to "racialize Philippine society into a set of fragmented and warring 'tribes' that were incapable of nationality," Paul Kramer explains. Citing various groupings—Malays, Tagalogs, Moros—US "experts" depicted the Philippines as an inchoate colonial space inhabited by an "aggregate of tribes," Thompson notes. "The analogy of tribes, which originally suggested a rough equivalence of the North American Indian tribes and those of the Philippines, provided a powerful justification for U.S. hegemony."[9]

On February 4, 1899, as Americans undertook their new colonial project, a firefight broke out outside Manila and quickly escalated into a full-scale war. The American public blamed the savage and backward Filipinos, as typically had occurred in Indian "uprisings," for the outbreak of violence. The *New York Times* declared that the Filipinos' "insane attack . . . upon their liberators" was sufficient evidence of "their incapacity for self-government." The elite US newspaper, purveyor of all the news fit to print, thus equated anticolonialism with madness, which in turn justified the ensuing counterinsurgency campaign. As in previous and future wars, "The overriding sentiment of the American press was enthusiasm for war and empire," David Brody points out.[10]

The US soldiers who had crossed the Pacific to go to war with Spain had been left unfulfilled and languishing in "masculinist angst" as a result of the quick Spanish capitulation. Reminiscent of volunteers in the Mexican War, "The soldiers all want to fight, and would be terribly disappointed and chagrined if they didn't get what they came over here for." Branding the Filipinos as disrespectful and ungrateful for their liberation, many of the soldiers expressed "an earnest desire to be turned loose on them and kill them." Added a US volunteer, "If they would turn the boys loose, there wouldn't be a nigger left in Manila twelve hours after."[11]

Unleashed by the outbreak of the resistance, the Americans quickly established military supremacy over Philippine conventional forces, as they "inflicted terrible casualties on Aguinaldo's soldiers." On February 5 the United States prevailed after fighting in and around Manila in the largest and bloodiest battle of the entire Philippine War waged over a 16-mile front. The Americans went on to capture several cities, including the Revolutionary capital of Malolos to the north of Manila, which they subjected to a punishing naval bombardment with a high rate of civilian casualties. In a sign of things to come, dead bodies, human as well as horses and dogs, littered the streets of the town in which "every house was burned." Although the United States had shown its military superiority, the army lacked a sufficient force to hold the areas that it had "liberated." The Americans soon learned they were in for a much longer struggle than anticipated when in November 1899 Aguinaldo abandoned the conventional war effort and called for guerrilla resistance.[12]

While the regular troops and the thousands of volunteers showed a zeal for war, US commanders were not uniformly sanguine. The Americans had taken control of Manila and other urban enclaves, taking thousands of Filipino casualties, but a major effort would be required to quell guerrilla resistance throughout the countryside. General Samuel B. Young declared it was "doubtful whether in modern days any military force has ever found itself with a more difficult problem . . . the task of dealing with eight millions of primitive people of various races, tribes, customs, and languages, dispersed over many islands, embracing an area of fifty thousand square miles." In order to defeat and pacify "a despotism of the worst Asiatic type," the US forces would have to track down Aquinaldo, now branded "a fugitive and an outlaw" for waging a war for independence against foreign invaders.[13]

As the fighting unfolded, Americans justified the Philippine intervention with "racial stereotypes that were previously used to justify the enslavement of Africans, the removal of the Indians, and the expulsion of the Mexicans." "Imagine an Indian 'crossed' with a negro, the product of this union married to a Chinese" and one could grasp the inferior "mental and moral attitudes" of the Filipino, one soldier explained. Scores of American newspaper editorial cartoons depicted McKinley or Uncle Sam attempting to tame caricatured, recalcitrant natives replete with bones through their noses or engaged in chucking spears. Nearly always darkened in skin color, "the Negrito became the metaphor for the Filipinos." Some, as in an editorial cartoon in the magazine *Judge*, explicitly linked Filipinos to Indians. The cartoon depicted an Indian drawing on his direct experience with the United States to inform a Filipino native, "Be good or you will be dead!"[14]

As the American public, geographically challenged in any case, had focused attention overwhelmingly on Cuba, the eruption of major conflict in the Philippines came as a shock. It also provoked over time a vocal albeit minority opposition. The so-called anti-imperialists, having disavowed the long history of colonialism on the North American continent, viewed the Philippine war as discontinuous. They thus depicted the intervention as a deviation from republican virtue and what they believed to be an American history of anticolonialism. Between the signing of the Treaty of Paris in December 1898 and its narrow ratification February 6, 1899, Congress debated the issue of overseas empire. Despite disagreement virtually all of the speakers in these exchanges "believed that the United States was a nation of white Protestants under a special mandate from God to represent freedom."[15]

The leading imperialists were better historians than their opponents, as they directly linked Indian and Philippine resistance to colonialism, thus justifying the violence that ensued. Their arguments ultimately proved convincing, as most Americans understood that "wild" Indians had needed to be tamed on the "frontier." If the Filipinos like the Indians were backward peoples resisting civilization by means of dishonorable and "savage" guerrilla resistance, then it made sense to most Americans that they should be brought under the control of a superior and chosen race.

Imperialists argued convincingly that subduing and civilizing savages was both legitimate and continuous with national history. During congressional debate in

1900, Senator Henry Cabot Lodge, one of the main architects of Pacific expansion, declared that if subjugation of the Philippines was a crime, as anti-imperialists charged, "then our whole past record of expansion is a crime." Senator Orville Platt, architect of an amendment that enabled US hegemony over "liberated" Cuba, declared that anti-imperialists "would have turned back the Mayflower from our coast and would have prevented our expansion westward." The outspoken imperialist Senator Albert Beveridge explained that the United States had long "governed the Indian without his consent. And if you deny it to the Indian at home how are you to grant it to the Malay abroad?" Former Senator Henry Dawes drew on his reputation for expertise on assimilation to advise that the history of Indian relations should guide the nation's "experience with other alien races whose future has been put in our keeping" as a result of the Spanish-American War. "Our policy with the Indians becomes an object lesson." As guerrilla resistance unfolded in the Philippines, Secretary of War Elihu Root urged adoption of "methods that have proved successful in our Indian campaigns in the West."[16]

The most prominent and popular imperialist, however, was the Rough Rider hero of the battle of Cuba's San Juan Hill, Theodore Roosevelt. A man of boundless energy, a unique amalgam of patrician and rugged individualist, Roosevelt resonated authority not only because of his courage under fire but also as the author of the four-volume *The Winning of the West*, published from 1889 to 1896. The account emphasized atavistic Indian violence and atrocities in defiance of the march of civilization. The settlers "had justice on their side. This great continent could not have been kept as nothing but a game preserve for squalid savages," Roosevelt explained in the first volume. In a tidy summation of settler colonialism, Roosevelt declared, "The man who puts the soil to use must of right dispossess the man who does not, or the world will come to a standstill." Roosevelt famously played off Philip Sheridan's reference to genocidal violence against Indians as he quipped, "I don't go so far as to think that the only good Indians are dead Indians, but I believe nine out of ten are, and I shouldn't like to inquire too closely in the case of the tenth."[17]

Roosevelt accurately invoked the authority of history to counter the argument that the United States was "violating" a mythic anti-colonial tradition. The Seminoles, he explained, "rebelled and waged war exactly as some of the Tagals have rebelled and waged war in the Philippines . . . we are making no new departure." For the United States the conflicts were "precisely parallel between the Philippines and the Apaches and Sioux." Reports of atrocities upset many Americans, but Roosevelt reminded them that they "happened hundreds of times in our warfare against the Indians," as extreme violence was an inevitable component of the struggle between savagery and civilization.[18]

Some imperialists cited the colonization of Hawai'i as reason for optimism in taking civilization to the Philippines. "The example of Hawai'i gives great encouragement to the philanthropist and the Christian who may look hopefully to the future," as Senator John T. Morgan put it. While some based their opposition to the Philippine intervention on assumption of responsibility for inferior races, Morgan turned the argument on its head by suggesting that the Philippines might serve as a colonial space to alleviate the "Negro problem" at home. The Alabama senator argued that the South might purify itself by shipping to the Philippines the "alien race" of African-Americans.[19]

Guerrilla Resistance and Indiscriminate Warfare

Having been driven into the countryside by the occupiers, the Filipinos waged a guerrilla resistance encompassing tactics of sniping, stabbings with their *bolos* (long knives easily hidden in clothing), ambush and hit-and-run assaults, sabotage of roads and telegraph lines. The rebels could move seamlessly in and among the populace, which largely supported them but whose loyalty could otherwise be demanded at penalty of death. The United States responded by waging indiscriminate warfare while demanding unconditional surrender of the enemy.

Enraged by the Filipinos' resort to guerrilla resistance against the civilizing efforts of a superior race, the American occupiers embarked on a lethal campaign of counterinsurgency warfare. Alfred McCoy describes the conflict as "a dirty war marked by clandestine penetration, psychological warfare, disinformation, media manipulation, assassination, and torture." Citing the "barbarous savagery" of the Filipino rebels, the Americans rationalized an indiscriminate campaign of exterminatory warfare.[20] As savage tribes in the midst of an irrational revolt, the various Negritos, Tagalogs, Malays, and Moros would be met, as were the Mexicans, Indians, and Confederates, with uncompromising aggression. Once they had been pacified, like the Indian tribes, the Filipinos could then be shepherded to civilization.

Confronted with the age-old problem of identifying rebels within the populace, the army took the approach, as General Elwell S. Otis, military governor of the Philippines, acknowledged, that "every Filipino was really an insurgent." The lack of discrimination led to "the oppression of thousands of innocent natives," Otis admitted. Like the Union during the Civil War, the Americans invoked General Order 100, based on the Lieber Code in which irregular forces could be denied protection under the international laws of war. Torture, collective punishment, and indiscriminate killing followed. As US forces patrolled the cities and set out into the "boondocks" (*bunduk*, in Tagalog, for mountains), only those Filipinos who displayed "strict obedience" to US authority were safe. And even they often were not given a chance.[21]

US forces spoke openly of indiscriminate killing, employing the metaphors of "hiking" or "hunting" as did earlier generations on the US borderlands, as well as other colonials across the Australian outback, the South African veld, and myriad other settings. As Americans reinforced segregation at home through law, lynching, and terror, they went on "nigger hunts" abroad. The troops were "hiking all the time killing all we come across . . . killing niggers by the hundreds." It was merely "sport to hunt the black devils," soldiers acknowledged. The islands would not be pacified, a soldier from Kansas explained, "until the niggers are killed off like the Indians." "Just back from the fight," wrote a US infantryman. "Killed twenty-two niggers captured twenty-nine rifels [sic] . . . we just shot the niggers like a hunter would rabbits."[22]

Nearly 90 percent of generals and many other officers were veterans of the Indian wars and thus experienced in campaigns focused on "extirpation of guerrilla bands." Many officers had little interest in disciplining soldiers in a race war against "treacherous and cowardly" rebels who, like Indians, engaged in sniping and hit-and-run attacks. In addition to indiscriminate killing, Americans deported and tortured prisoners, notably by the water cure, carried out collective punishments and arbitrary arrests; conducted summary executions; raped Filipino women; destroyed food, crops and farm animals; and confined masses of people in disease-ridden camps contributing to the staggering death toll of the conflict. US forces generally occupied "the best houses in every town" which they frequently "ransacked in hope of booty of Eastern lands . . . They looted everything and destroyed for the fun of it." "In considering possible violations of the laws of war," Brian Linn notes, "most senior officers preferred a policy of 'don't ask, don't tell.' "[23]

As in previous wars, the United States depended on a large volunteer force that proved to be better trained and more organized and effective than in the earlier nineteenth-century conflicts. In contrast to the Mexican War, for example, army officers effectively led both the state and national volunteers and often praised their efforts. Taken as a whole, the US volunteers were "outstanding soldiers" and "far from being the bloody-handed butcher of fable," Linn avers. Linn is no doubt correct that most soldiers were not butchers yet many did kill indiscriminately and regular officers criticized as well as praised them.[24]

The Volunteers sometimes did "things too scandalous to write," as Major Matthew A. Batson put it. During the capture of San Fernando north of Manila in the spring of 1899, as Batson informed his wife, the volunteers

> ransacked churches, private houses, and wantonly destroyed furniture . . . they enter the cemeteries, break open the vaults and search the corpses for jewelry . . . They make no distinction, they simply loot everything they come to . . . We come as a Christian people to relieve them from the Spanish yoke and bear ourselves like barbarians . . . Why, if I was a Filipino I would fight as long as I had a breath left.

The volunteers were equally undisciplined in battle, Batson complained, as "they hear a shot, and then they turn loose and fire on everything they see—man, woman, or child. Then they report that they have been attacked by the Insurgents, and have driven them off with great loss to the Insurgents." Batson's ambivalence, much like George Crook's in Indian country, had its limits: he later ordered an entire town destroyed after rebels ambushed and killed a close friend.[25]

The army carried out a deadly assault and occupation of Cebu in which from 1898 to 1906 some 100,000 of the approximately 600,000 residents died from warfare and disease. In 1901, as guerrilla attacks continued on the mountainous island in the center of the archipelago, "American troops took to the field in earnest." Angered by the continuing guerrilla resistance, "many of the American sorties at this time were plain killing expeditions." Reports revealed "many cases of Filipinos killed or imprisoned on mere suspicion of being insurgents: carrying a bolo, refusing to act as a guide, transporting rice to the mountains, or 'acting like a spy.' "

The destruction of houses, farms, and food supplies forced the population into concentration camps, where disease especially cholera spread rapidly. "Death and famine stalked the land."[26]

As in the Indian Wars, atrocities against indigenes went unpunished whereas the US forces went on the rampage in response to "massacres" directed against them by the Filipinos. In September 1901, in the famous incident at Balangiga on the island of Samar, villagers orchestrated a surprise attack with their *bolos*, slaughtering 48 unsuspecting American soldiers at an early Sunday morning breakfast. In the weeks leading up to the attack the officer in charge of US forces in Balangiga, Capt. Thomas Connell, had tried to clean up the city and attempted to keep a tight rein on his rowdy soldiers who had arrived in Samar pumped up by "two months of drinking and whoring in Manila." The US infantrymen had little interest in winning over hearts and minds in "the heart of Googooland" and believed their "nigger lover" commander was too hard on them and too soft on the indigenes. Rapes and other assaults enraged the villagers, who began to plot their revenge.[27]

Similar to the response to Indian massacres, the traumatized Americans responded to Balangiga with an indiscriminate campaign not just in Samar but also throughout the Philippine archipelago. Reviving American cultural memory of the aftermath at Little Big Horn, the dead at Balangiga were reported to have been "mutilated and treated with indescribable indignities." The victims included Connell, who was found decapitated. The Americans claimed that other victims had their bodies cut open and filled with food from the mess hall, though the Filipino guerrilla leader strongly disputed such accounts, explaining that there had been no time for desecrating bodies and that such acts violated indigenous taboos. Newspapers avoided such subtleties as they filled in the nation, already in shock over the McKinley assassination, with detailed accounts of the "treacherous savagery" on the part of the "despicable" natives. The images of slaughter and the trope of the "treachery" at Balangiga became "the guiding principle of American actions on Samar," Louise Barnett explains. To most Americans Balangiga provided "indisputable evidence that force was the only proper policy."[28]

The recently appointed new commander of US forces in the Philippines, General Adna Chaffee, drawing on his experience in the Indian wars, had little patience with "false humanitarianism." He blamed the Balangiga assault on "soft mollycoddling of treacherous natives" by civilian officials. Chaffee relished the authorization received from the newly inaugurated President Roosevelt to apply "the most stern measures to pacify Samar . . . in no unmistakable terms." Primed for a campaign of "Injun warfare," Chaffee declared, "The situation calls for shot, shells and bayonets as the natives are not to be trusted."[29]

The enraged Americans thus responded to the trauma inflicted at Balangiga with a spurt of genocidal violence and military injustice. General Jacob H. Smith, a close associate of Chaffee in the Indian Wars and a veteran of Wounded Knee, issued his famous order to convert Samar into a Biblical "howling wilderness," as he authorized the killing of any Filipino aged ten or above. "I want no prisoners," Smith famously advised. "I wish you to kill and burn, the more you kill and burn the better you will please me." The troops followed their orders, as they razed the town and killed indiscriminately. "We did not take any prisoners," a volunteer acknowledged. "We shot everybody on sight." As a result of his blatant violations of the rules of war, Smith was brought before a court martial and convicted but merely admonished and retired. Another officer who summarily burned scores of villages and executed his Filipino auxiliaries in a fit of rage was found not guilty. The verdict in this case, which outraged even the hardliner Chaffee, came after "Every military witness ritualistically invoked treachery, this central principle of Filipino character and motivation."[30]

The boomerang of indiscriminate violence reverberated throughout the archipelago in the wake of Balangiga. In 1902, US forces, both volunteers and regulars, under General J. Franklin Bell conducted an undisciplined and brutalizing campaign to subdue the rebels in the province of Batangas on Luzon. Reminiscent of previous and future US wars, Americans meant to punish the Filipinos until they surrendered unconditionally to the superior US forces.

Angered by the continuing Filipino campaign of homeland defense, Bell asserted, "civilization demands that the defeated side, in the name of humanity, should surrender and accept the result." When the rebels refused to comply, Bell believed they deserved whatever consequence they might suffer, the same as Indians who had refused to report to the reservations, or Mexicans, Confederate rebels, and subsequently "Viet Cong" who persisted in guerrilla resistance. Bell's forces conducted summary executions and tortured other captives, as they liberally employed the water cure. "It got results," one veteran later recalled, sentiments echoed more than a century later by defenders of torture in the Iraq War.[31]

The US forces wantonly destroyed Filipino property to punish acts of resistance. "After an attack on one of their patrols, the US troops usually burned the houses in the nearest barrio" regardless of whether the residents were in any way connected with the resistance. In the course of search and destroy operations "women were molested by officers and soldiers alike without any kind of consideration; those who resisted such barbarity were threatened with imprisonment, deportation, or death."[32] As in the previous wars, the Americans conducted scorched-earth policies by killing cattle and other farm animals, destroying crops and gardens, and generally laying waste to the province. "Much of the devastation occurred for the simple reason that Bell's subordinates wanted to destroy and Bell chose not to upbraid them for doing so," Glenn May explains. "The predictable result of such behavior was ecological destruction on a massive scale."[33]

One of the officers unleashed by Bell, Col. William E. Birkhimer, increasingly frustrated over the pace of the pacification effort, proposed one of two genocidal approaches to end it: "first, to kill off all the males; second, capture and deport them ... Either plan properly put into execution would accomplish the object sought," he explained. Unsurprisingly, such attitudes produced an "astoundingly high level of civilian mortality in the zones of concentration and led to widespread abuses on the part of the U.S. military." Bell acknowledged that US confiscations of food stores "have made it difficult for the people to obtain rice," hence many were starving.[34]

While the US forces carried out torture, assassination, and indiscriminate killing, diseases took the greatest toll on the people of Batangas as a result of their close confinement in horrific conditions in the US re-concentration camps. Much like the destruction of Indian horses and food stores, the policy in the Philippines "aimed at the isolation and starvation of guerrillas through the deliberate annihilation of the rural economy," Kramer explains. The army conducted a "scorched-earth policy, burning residences and rice stores, destroying or capturing livestock, and killing every person they encountered" while driving the peasantry into the fortified encampments. Tens of thousands died of malaria, measles, dysentery, and cholera as "wartime health and sanitary conditions facilitated the spread of the disease." As May notes, it is "clear beyond a shadow of a doubt that death rates soared in the province during the period January–April 1902, when the civilians were confined."[35]

As a result of "rigorous censorship of foreign correspondents by the U.S. Army," news of atrocities filtered across the Pacific slowly, but Bell's egregious campaign eventually came under investigation. Lodge, however, closed to the public the hearings of his Committee on Insular Affairs while the army conducted a "charade" in which it claimed that war criminals had been brought to justice. In fact—consistent with virtually the entire history of American warfare—very few were actually punished, the overwhelming majority of those in the Philippines for minor offenses.[36] "By early 1903, the Philippine-American War was already becoming a dim memory to the U.S. public," notes May, hence Bell escaped unscathed and went on to become army chief of staff.[37]

Worn down and brutalized by US forces, the Philippine revolutionaries were also demoralized by the marginalization of the ambivalent anti-imperialists in the United States, who had been repudiated by McKinley's reelection in 1900. At the same time US counterinsurgency efforts prompted defections by Filipino elites including insurgent leaders. In March 1901, the revolutionary forces suffered a crippling blow with the capture of Aguinaldo. The rebel leader acknowledged US suzerainty, prompting the defections of additional insurgent leaders. Sporadic resistance continued, however, even after the last of the revolutionary leaders surrendered in June 1902.[38]

Indiscriminate violence infused with Orientalist religious discourse characterized the US occupation of Muslim Mindanao, the second largest island, located in the far south of the Philippine archipelago. The "Moro problem . . . was not only a question of governing uncivilized tribes but of controlling the dominant Mohammedan element," a US official explained.[39] In 1899 the United States in a strategic move signed an agreement recognizing the Muslim faith and allowing the sultan to rule "Moroland." At the time Mindanao was not a high priority in the US pacification campaign and the agreement pleased the sultan, as the Muslims had long been in conflict with Christian Filipinos to the north.

Despite the agreement with the sultan, the Americans viewed the "Moros," as the Spanish had dubbed the various ethnic groups who had converted to Islam, as religious fanatics. Following the defeat of the revolutionary forces in 1902, Muslims in Mindanao violently opposed the US-backed Filipino colonial government led by Catholic elites. Ultimately, "Force seems to be the only method of reaching them," Secretary of War William Howard Taft avowed. The Americans would impose control "through a series of merciless military campaigns," a "brutal pacification program" carried out through the establishment of army outposts and police forces placed in strategic locations throughout the province.[40]

As a vast and sparsely populated "frontier," Mindanao "inevitably drew comparisons with the Western frontier where 'unexplored' territory was populated with small groups of 'savage Indians.' Indeed, the most effective Americans in this tropical frontier were the veterans of the Apache war," Patricio Abinales points out. General Leonard Wood, a fellow Rough Rider hero and close confidant of Roosevelt, drew such comparisons, noting that a Muslim leader was of "the Geronimo type."[41]

Wood viewed the Muslims as "religious and moral degenerates" and proceeded to launch a genocidal campaign against them. Driven by a "toxic confluence of careerism, progressive ideology, and Muslim discourse," Wood set out to overthrow "the ridiculous little sultan of Sulu." In March 1906 Wood unleashed a three-day artillery assault against some 1,000 "Moro malcontents" who had taken refuge in Bud Dajo, an extinct volcano. "At least six hundred Muslims, including hundreds of unarmed women and children, perished" compared to 20 US personnel dead. Army Major Hugh Scott acknowledged that the people on Dajo "declared they had no intention of fighting—ran up there only in fright." The slaughter of these terrified refugees "would soon vanish from public consciousness" and like many Indian and colonial massacres remains widely unknown today.[42]

Wood and General John Pershing led other campaigns of slaughter in Mindanao, with Wood rationalizing, "Our Mohammedan friends . . . have to be thumped a little now and then." Pershing asserted, "The Mohammedan Malay" possessed "a fanatical disregard of the consequences of crime and an inborn desire to fight and plunder" and hence was among "the most aggressive and determined Orientals." This discourse justified another "asymmetric bloodbath" in June 1913 at Bud Bagsak in which US forces slaughtered "between three and four hundred hopeless fanatics and cattle thieves" compared to 14 US personnel dead. Like the other massacres, "Bud Bagsak barely registered on the metropolitan consciousness."

In both the Indian Wars and in Muslim Mindanao, Joshua Gedacht argues, "The anxieties that accompanied the initial work of colonial conquest—combined with the ambitions of military officers and religious fears—repeatedly proved conducive to excessive, indiscriminate use of force." Like General Nelson Miles in his justification of liquidating the Ghost Dancers at Wounded Knee, Wood and Pershing embraced "phantasmagorias of religious insurrection" that rationalized the subsequent slaughters of hundreds of innocent people. "Instead of stigmas, these massacres propelled the three officers to the highest echelons of the military establishment."[43]

Ambivalences in the Philippine War

As in previous US wars, colonial ambivalences, both on the part of the Americans as well as the Filipinos, played a critical part in the conflict and its resolution.

From the outset McKinley had framed the US intervention as a campaign of "benevolent assimilation" in which he glibly averred that the United States would "win the confidence, respect and affection of the inhabitants." Following the lead of the commander in chief, from the outset the army focused on establishing municipal government, schools, and police forces as the anchors of the American *mission civilisatrice.* "Visible advances in education and health, both hallmarks of colonial order, helped legitimate the occupation in the eyes of ordinary Filipinos."[44]

Much like President Grant's "peace policy," the United States would pursue a non-violent albeit ethnocentric reform program—but only so long as the indigenes accepted US colonial rule. "America's benevolence was thus predicated on violence," Julian Go points out.[45] As in the Indian wars, many US commanders had more enthusiasm for waging war than trying to implement a project of nation building. Nonetheless, beyond question the United States devoted substantial energies and resources to road building, sewer construction, food distribution, literacy programs, disease control, and municipal, legal, economic, educational, and judicial reform.

US reform efforts won over many Filipinos, especially as the guerrilla effort waned and the civilian population suffered from the conflict. While the Americans could involve Filipinos in a variety of civic action programs, "the guerrillas could offer little positive inducement to avoid cooperating with the occupiers . . . beyond the ever diminishing hope of independence." The Americans thus combined the allure of safety and, at least for some, opportunity with the visible threat of death and destruction. This ambivalent approach ultimately made the Philippine intervention, argues Linn, "the most successful counterinsurgency campaign in U.S. history."[46]

In the ambivalent colonial setting the Americans thus simultaneously carried out *both* reform and exterminatory violence. General Young reported that the army had supervised elections, instituted local governments, and built roads and bridges while at the same time waging counterinsurgency warfare by employing, as he wrote to Roosevelt, "measures that proved so effective with the Apaches."[47] The United States set up municipal governments as soon as an area could be pacified, a practice that began in the mountains around Luzon where hill tribes offered no resistance to American authority.

While colonial discourse depicted the Filipinos as "savage" and "treacherous," they were alternatively viewed as childlike and thus in need of nurture and education. Children, with their undeveloped minds, required scolding and punishment. With the outbreak of guerrilla resistance, Americans embraced a "widespread characterization of Filipinos as uncivilized and unruly 'children' who had dishonored the United States and now required discipline and order." Under ambivalent colonial policies, Americans built scores of schools enrolling thousands of children while at the same time destroying cities and towns and killing Filipinos young and old by the tens of thousands.[48]

Gender and racial discourses added to the complexity of the US occupation. Although thousands of American soldiers accessed the sexual services of Filipino women, and some courted women as girlfriends and as wives, Filipinas were also sometimes linked invidiously with Indian "squaws." Colonial discourse often represented Filipino women as less attractive and more dangerous than Hawaiian and other "exotic" women who had recently come under American colonial influence. Jose de Olivares introduced Americans to the new islanders in the book *Our Islands and Their People*, published in 1899, which included hundreds of sketches and photographs. Filipino women came in "many grades," some "highly cultivated," he allowed, yet "a majority of the women of this archipelago belong to a low grade of civilization, and some are but little above the condition of beast of field and forest."[49]

Racial ambivalences in the Philippines included the US deployment of two African-American units. The Filipino revolutionaries made a propaganda appeal for solidarity directed to "the Colored American Soldier," but to little effect. In either the high or the low point of colonial ambivalence, on one occasion during a firefight some Filipinos reportedly yelled to the American "Buffalo soldiers," "What are you coons doing here?" The American blacks responded, "We have come to take up the White Man's Burden!" Years later a journalist explained, "It was commonsensical from an American standpoint, 'niggers' being 'niggers,' to let 'niggers' fight Filipino 'niggers.' "[50]

Clearly, US racial discourse encompassed the readymade pejorative N-word along with "goo-goo" and other slurs, yet the soldiers and officials also conducted commercial interactions, went to local dances and concerts, and often professed admiration for the dark-skinned Filipinos. Admiral Dewey found the Filipinos "far superior in their intelligence" and "more capable of self-government" than were the Cubans.[51] "They are not savages," Major Batson wrote to his wife. "There is scarcely a boy that cannot read, write, and do a little arithmetic . . . I find them exceedingly interesting people." Although Batson thus seemed to suggest that the Filipinos were already civilized, nonetheless he orchestrated an indigenous counterinsurgency campaign against them.[52]

Batson's fondness for the Filipinos made him the ideal officer to organize the Macabebe "scouts," native auxiliaries employed in pacification. The Americans had used indigenous scouts in the Indian wars, just as the Australians had dispatched the Native Police to help subdue the outback, as the use of auxiliaries in pacification efforts was a common practice under colonialism. The Macabebes, an ethnic group from the province of Pampanga, had collaborated with the Spaniards and were historic enemies of the Tagalog and other Filipino ethnic groups. In June 1898, as the Spanish fled the town of Macabebe, Filipino rebels plundered and burned the town and beheaded scores of Macabebe soldiers. As the sworn enemy of other Filipino groups, the Macabebes were ripe for recruitment as part of the US counterinsurgency effort and proved highly effective in their campaigns. On October 29, 1899, Batson gleefully reported, "With my battalion of Macabebe Scouts I am spreading terror among the *Insurrectos*." The Americans recruited other indigenous forces as well. By 1901, 50 "Native Scout" companies of 50 men each had been organized. Thousands of other Filipinos served in paramilitary units, militia, police, and as guides and scouts.[53]

The Macabebes and other "scout" units underscore internal divisions and ambivalences of Philippine society, not only ethnic but also regional, social, and economic, all of which the Americans effectively exploited. The term "Filipino" had been applied broadly by among others José Rizal—the brilliant revolutionary leader executed by the Spanish in 1896—as part of an effort to promote an inchoate anticolonial nationalism in the archipelago. The term was both inclusive as well as exclusive, especially excluding the non-Christian "Moros." "Philippine" society was further divided by social banditry, local fiefdoms and geographic divisions, and especially by the economic and social gulf between elites and the peasantry. During the war Filipinos "fought not only against the Americans but also against each other."[54]

The tribalization of the Filipinos in colonial discourse hardened the categorizations and divisions of Filipino society—contrary to what Rizal had tried to achieve—and helped justify US intervention. Framing the archipelago as a colonial space in which a primitive amalgam of ethnic groups competed, from "uncivilized hill tribes" to "savage Muslims," the Americans promoted a discourse in which "only a paternalistic colonial state could discipline, contain, and transform this complexity into a civilized nation." Colonial discourse thus "re-inscribed internal categories of difference" because they functioned to justify external colonial authority.[55]

The McKinley administration created the Philippine Commission to effect the transition from military rule to civil government by exploiting the cleavages within Philippine society. In 1900, the second Philippine Commission under the well-connected Taft clashed with the army command under General Arthur MacArthur, who eventually was forced out for challenging "the administration's cherished dogma that the Filipino people wanted United States rule and opposed it only out of fear and ignorance." The Filipinos displayed remarkable adaptability, as they "cooperated enthusiastically with the civic action aspect of pacification—the roads, schools, sanitation projects, improved trade—but they resisted all efforts to use these municipal governments for the purposes of military pacification, and they continued to support the guerrillas with contributions, recruits, and shelter."[56]

As the United States pacified areas and cultivated defections of insurgent leaders, it evolved "complex structures of collaboration." The elite became "essential to 'pacification,' mediating between U.S. colonial authorities and the Filipino masses." US colonialism, as Kramer explains, established a "tutelary framework" that "accommodated elite demands for political participation while forestalling broader and deeper questions of independence."[57]

US authorities thus mobilized a largely oligarchic elite as part of the broader colonial project of reining in the insurgency and establishing postcolonial authority. By showing respect for and empowering a Christian Filipino elite, including priests and members of the Catholic hierarchy, the United States cultivated alliances in order to quell the revolution and establish a framework for colonial rule. In Batangas, as in Manila and on Luzon, American colonialism, as May points out, "forged an alliance of a sort with the elites, but made no effort to meet the needs of poor peasants." Likewise in Cebu, as Resil Majares has shown, the Americans "provided Filipino leaders with an expanding arena for political participation" yet "politics remained an elite preserve."[58]

US authorities encouraged Hispanicized Filipino elites centered in the cities to establish racial hierarchies and to project wartime discourses of savagery onto non-Christians and ethnic minorities. By separating out Muslims and other minority groups, the Americans and Filipino elites established a foundation for postwar collaboration within an emerging postcolonial framework. "The animists and Muslims of the archipelago, never defeated by the Spanish, would not for the most part be embraced within the emergent category of the Filipino," Kramer explains. US military colonialism left a legacy of "anti-center, specifically anti-Manila and anti-Christian sentiments among its people, the reverberations of which would continue well into the post-colonial period," Abinales points out.[59]

Within this "joint American-Filipino venture situated inside a broader, evolving colonial project," a bifurcated racial state emerged in which Muslims and mountain peoples were excluded. Within colonial discourse the oligarchic Philippine elite thus transitioned from "treacherous savages" to "little brown brothers" and partners against an internal opposition. US authorities set up the Philippine Constabulary, comprised mostly of younger male Filipinos, to establish order and help rein in the "Moros" through merciless military campaigns that flowed out of the new arrangement.[60]

The postcolonial framework enabled the occupation to move forward with modernist initiatives to develop commercial infrastructure, make sanitary improvements, and evolve a pervasive police state apparatus of surveillance and often-brutal suppression of revolution and reform efforts, as well as of freedom of speech and political activism. These characteristics outlived the US occupation and became thus far permanent features of an inveterately corrupt and often repressive Philippine society. "In the accommodation of American and Filipino conservatisms, much was preserved," Majares points out. "The basic problems of poverty and dependency remained and were heightened, the basic social configuration was preserved, and the character of the economy sustained." After "massive destruction wrought by the American invasion," what emerged was "a neo-colonial Philippines."[61]

The Postcolonial Philippines

Although some 300 years of Spanish colonization left an imprint on Philippine society, primarily in the form of Catholicism, the US occupation established the enduring framework of postcolonial history. As scholars point out, "The broad contours of recent Philippine history are best understood not against the backdrop of 'traditional' Filipino culture or Hispanicized society, but rather in the context of the state structures erected and imposed in the course of the American colonial era." Building upon the collaborative arrangements established during the counterinsurgency war, the United States and a privileged minority of Filipino elites established a security state backed by a "ubiquitous secret police."[62]

US military presence, covert operations, security assistance, political frameworks, and hundreds of millions of dollars outlasted the US pacification campaign normally framed from 1898 to 1902. Within the first decade of civil rule, as McCoy notes, "the colonial government covered the archipelago with a coercive apparatus that was invisible in its covert penetrations, omnivorous in its appetite for information, and enveloping in its omnipotence." In each postcolonial decade thereafter, the United States "intervened to revitalize the country's security forces with massive infusions of aid and advisory support, a process that continues today."[63]

The Americans and the Filipino elites collaborated on a postcolonial project centered on stifling reform, destroying the left, enriching the oligarchy, and securing the archipelago as a formidable US military asset. During the continuing occupation in the early twentieth century, the Americans oversaw transformation of the judicial and political systems including the establishment of a powerful executive branch limited by few checks and balances and thus open to myriad abuses of power. The postcolonial system empowered elite Filipino businessmen, local bosses, and politicians while the security state protected their interests and insulated them from accountability. Security forces policed the press, the church, political parties, labor unions, and fraternal organizations, keeping them compliant.[64]

The domination of the Philippines by an oligarchy of landowners, commercial magnates, and politicians from connected families reflects "enduring patterns of narrow class rule already discernible before independence."[65] The American colonial framework perpetuated elite rule and enabled widespread corruption. Philippine society became "essentially a multi-tiered racket" through the establishment of a "complex set of predatory mechanisms for private exploitation and accumulation of the archipelago's human, natural, and monetary resources."[66] As Eva-Lotta Hedman and John Sidel point out, "The features of Philippine politics most frequently derided and diagnosed as pathologically 'Filipino'—'bossism,' 'corruption,' 'personalism,' and 'rampant' criminality and political violence—are best understood as reflections of enduring American colonial legacies."[67]

While Filipino elites dominated politics and society, the United States solidified the Philippines as an imperial outpost within its burgeoning postwar global security regime. After the United States and the Philippines allied against the Japanese in World War II, the Philippines received independence in 1946. In the postwar period the United States built Clark Field Air Force base and Subic Bay naval base into the two largest overseas US military bases in the world. With the United States controlling external security, "internal security remained the primary concern of the coercive apparatuses of the Philippine state."[68]

As Americans conceptualized a global cold war, and conceived of Filipino space as vital to containment of communism across the "great crescent" of Asia, they collaborated with the internal security regime in a campaign against the left. The Hukbalahap—the People's Army Against the Japanese—had led the resistance during World War II, liberating most of Luzon, yet after the war the Americans arbitrarily arrested, disarmed, and incarcerated the Huks as alleged radicals and subversives.

The Huk resistance movement had "evolved out of earlier uprisings and acts of resistance against the unequal landowning system and repression of the U.S.-Philippine colonial government." Comprised "largely of rural peasants and farmers," the Huks pursued land reform and had sought to work within the political system for "social and economic justice."

In the midst of the global campaign against communism, including massive violence on the Korean peninsula, the United States in collaboration with the Filipino elite denied the Huks access to the political process and launched campaigns of annihilation. "The Filipino military police and civilian guards massacred Huk members and civilians believed to be supporters of the Huk movement," often as Kathleen Nadeau points out, "with the knowledge of American military officers."[69] Remaining members of the movement went underground and started a guerrilla war of resistance against the US-Filipino security regime. In the mid-1950s, the counterinsurgency campaign led by a shrewd and popular Filipino elite, Ramon Magsaysay, undermined the Huks through reorganization of the Philippine armed forces, economic incentive programs, and various psychological warfare operations devised by Magsaysay's close adviser, Edward Lansdale of the Central Intelligence Agency. "In a Cold War version of the 'Injun Warfare' of several decades earlier," Hedman and Sidel point out, "this anti-Huk 'psywar' campaign involved the mobilization of volunteers into 'hunter-killer' units called the Scout Rangers."[70]

After liquidating the Huks, the United States embraced the regime of President Ferdinand Marcos, who came to office in 1965. That same year the United States encouraged mass murder of communists, reformers, and intellectuals by the military dictatorship in Indonesia while unleashing its own bombers and "search and destroy" units in Vietnam.[71] Supported by the United States despite blatant corruption and human rights abuses, Marcos ruled under martial law from 1972 to 1986. In 1983 the regime assassinated exiled senator Benigno Aquino when he stepped off the plane in a return to Manila. Marcos tried to smooth over relations with the United States, where Aquino had lived in exile, by contributing US$10 million to President Ronald Reagan's reelection campaign in 1984.[72]

Reformers had gained strength in opposition to the Marcos regime but more ominously from the US and elite Filipino perspective, so had the Communist Party of the Philippines. The New People's Army, the armed wing of the Communist Party, had grown dramatically, establishing armed units and networks in the countryside as well as in urban barrios. The Filipino elite and US national security advisers viewed the NPA as a greater threat than the Huks had been three decades earlier. Another wave of violent repression against the left ensued.

The counter-subversion campaign unfolded following the ouster of the Marcos family (given asylum in Hawai'i by Reagan) and the ascension to the presidency of Aquino's widow, Corazon, in 1986. Aquino called for "not social and economic reform but police and military action" to combat the NPA. From 1986 to 1992, Aquino—advised, funded, and equipped by the United States—oversaw a counterinsurgency war against the NPA, social activists, labor organizers, and church and human rights groups. Behind the smiling façade of Aquino's much trumpeted "People Power" movement was a campaign to re-entrench the oligarchy while containing and destroying leftists and reformers.[73]

The Philippine government unleashed paramilitary units and irregular vigilantes to hunt down leftists and reformers in "campaigns of sustained intimidation and spectacular violence." International human rights monitors cited "a widespread pattern of extra-judicial execution, torture and illegal arrest throughout the Philippines." This latest cycle of political violence affirmed that the "decentralization and privatization of coercive state apparatuses encouraged under American auspices remained an enduring and powerful legacy under Philippine colonial democracy even several decades after Independence in 1946."[74]

Tension arose to some degree in the 1990s after breakdown in negotiations over re-authorization of the two massive US military bases, but the events that transpired after September 11, 2001, quickly reinvigorated the US-Filipino security relationship. In 1992 the United States closed Subic Bay and Clark Field but in the late 1990s the two countries signed the Visiting Forces Agreement, restoring military ties through joint training and exercises, as both nations cast a wary eye on China. After September 11, Philippine President Gloria Macapagal-Arroyo offered "unqualified support" in the "Global War on Terror," which eventually brought in hundreds of millions of dollars of security assistance to the Philippines. The United States sent hundreds of elite troops into the southern Philippines where they joined the Philippine security forces in tracking down the Muslim insurgent group Abu Sayyaf and assassinating its leaders. Arroyo exploited the climate of suppression amid the war on terror as she "unleashed military death squads for a lethal assault on the Philippine left."[75]

The US-Philippine postcolonial relationship remains close today more than a century after the original US intervention and establishment of the collaborative security framework. The Philippines served as an "ad hoc laboratory for counterinsurgency," a colonial space in which the "striking continuity in U.S. policy" spanned more than a century. Philippine society continues to be polarized between an increasingly wealthy minority, a shrinking middle class (many of which are forced to seek work overseas), and an impoverished mass, from the slums of Manila to the southern islands. "For the past half century," McCoy notes, "Washington has found it far easier to revitalize Philippine security forces than to reform the country's underlying social reality."[76]

9

"A Very Particular Kind of Inclusion": Indigenous People in the Postcolonial United States

In settler societies colonizing discourse invariably depicted the indigene as a premodern primitive and moreover as a member of a vanishing race. Death and destruction became normalized insofar as the indigene was after all part of a dying race. This rationalizing discourse helped justify dispossession, assuage guilt, and establish a framework for historical denial. To end the discussion with Wounded Knee, ignoring the twentieth century, would be to affirm the colonial mythology of the vanishing race.

The indigenes did not in fact "die off." In the 2010 US census, 5.2 million people identified as Indian or as indigenous Alaskan; 1.4 million identified as indigenous Hawaiian or Pacific islanders.[1] Some 560 indigenous bands exist in the United States though not all receive federal recognition. Nearly 20 percent of the indigenous population lives in Alaska, with Oklahoma and California having the next largest state populations.[2]

The postcolonial history of settler colonialism does not come to an end with the dispossession and demographic swamping of indigenous people. Indigenous people survived, many cultures remain intact, and they have continued to struggle variously for land, control of resources, compensation, civil rights, autonomy, and sovereignty. The structure and legacies of settler colonialism remain powerful, as does historical denial, and settler societies typically mobilize to contain indigenous challenges both to history and to the postcolonial condition. "The overall colonialist drive persists, even when expressed ambivalently," Kevin Bruyneel points out, "and to this day continues to place indigenous people and their sovereignty in a second-class status."[3]

Indians and Hawaiian and Alaskan indigenes variously participated in and resisted colonizing society throughout the twentieth century and into the twenty-first. By the 1960s, in the midst of a global movement trumpeting decolonization, anticolonial revolution, civil rights, and youth and women's movements, indigenous people gained unprecedented exposure and recognition. They staged protests and occupations but just as importantly they mounted significant challenges to historically exclusive claims to colonial space. Indigenes and their attorneys turned legal frameworks on their heads, as they took the colonizer to court and won several meaningful victories that brought increased visibility, respect, and empowerment. This activism emerged in the context of the global indigenous rights movement, which evolved in tandem with the broader international movement for human rights. The global indigenous rights movement achieved a milestone in September 2007 when the United Nations General Assembly adopted the Declaration on the Rights of Indigenous Peoples.[4] The Declaration was an important achievement, yet denial and reaction remained powerful forces within settler colonial societies.

Indians within the Postcolony

By 1890, disease and warfare had reduced the indigenous population from some 18 million living north of Mexico when the Europeans arrived to about one quarter of a million, yet Indians refused to play out the scripted role of a vanishing race. The settler state continued to express its sovereignty over Indians and over geographic space after the cessation of hostilities. Throughout the twentieth century and to the present, indigenous people have engaged in anticolonial resistance while simultaneously pursuing civil rights. "Indian people reworked a sense of distinctiveness and difference," Philip Deloria explains, "fighting off the colonizing ways the United States sought to include them, and demanding a very particular kind of inclusion, one based on unique political status."[5]

In the early twentieth century, the US Supreme Court in a series of decisions known as the Insular Cases upheld US sovereignty over the "unincorporated territories" seized in the context of the Spanish-American War. Around the same time—and underscoring the continuities of domestic and overseas colonialism—the high court ruled in *Lone Wolf v. Hitchcock* (1903) that Congress had complete authority over Indian affairs, including the power to abrogate treaty rights. This decision, sometimes called the Dred Scott decision for Indians, brought them into the new century, like Puerto Ricans and Hawaiians, as colonized subjects under the law.

Despite rigid racial lines and legal constraints, "Some Indian people—more than we've been led to believe—leapt quickly into modernity," Deloria notes, and became "acculturated into the educational, political, and economic order of twentieth century America."[6] As Americans began to cultivate the mythology of the frontier, Indians participated in the "Wild West" shows made famous by William "Buffalo Bill" Cody. However hackneyed, the shows were wildly popular and many of the "show Indians" enjoyed playing their roles as well as the travel and other opportunities.[7]

Indians achieved regional and national reputations in sports. Louis Sockalexis, a member of the Penobscot tribe from Maine, distinguished himself in baseball before succumbing to alcoholism. Sockalexis inspired the Cleveland franchise to adopt in 1915 the Indians moniker that it still sports today (along with the racially charged "Chief Wahoo" logo). Jim Thorpe, born in Oklahoma in 1887 to the Sauk and Fox tribe and a survivor of Carlisle, was an accomplished multisport athlete who won two gold medals for the United States in the 1912 Olympics in Stockholm.[8]

Indians, like African Americans, Hispanics, and Asian Americans, strove for political participation within the racial state. In 1911, a group of acculturated indigenes known as "Red progressives" founded the Society of American Indians. In 1917, US involvement in World War I created opportunity for thousands of Indian men to assume a role deeply ensconced in their traditions, that of warrior, though other indigenes resisted fighting on behalf of the colonial state. The Iroquois Confederation solved this dilemma by issuing its own declaration of war against Germany.[9]

The participation by some 16,000 Indians in the US armed forces during the Great War helped clear the path to voting rights and full citizenship, which came in 1924 by an act of Congress. Many of the 300,000 or so Indians living in the country at the time did not care to be US citizens and many states for their part did not care to enforce the law granting the indigenes legal equality. Ironically, the national crisis of the Great Depression created new opportunities for Indians through the New Deal reforms under President Franklin D. Roosevelt.

John Collier, a reformer with a longtime passion for indigenous affairs, spearheaded the Indian New Deal as commissioner of Indian affairs from 1933 to 1945. In 1934 the Indian Reorganization Act revoked the Dawes Act, bringing an end to the misguided effort at Indian assimilation and the cultural genocide that it entailed. Although paternalistic, and yet another top-down American "solution" to the "Indian problem," the Indian New Deal brought relief, expanded educational opportunities, and community building. Still, many Indians had no use for such federal initiatives. Influential tribes refusing to participate in the reforms included the Iroquois, the Crows, and the Navajo.[10]

Some 25,000 indigenous warriors fought in World War II and thousands more including Indian women took part in war related industries. Service in the armed forces helped develop a "hybrid American patriotism" in which Indians "imagined an American nationalism that drew upon rather than destroyed their values," Paul Rosier points out. Indigenous people thus "defended their right to be both American and Indian." As with other minorities, participation in US militarism abroad carved out cultural space to pursue rights and opportunities at home.[11]

Following World War II, the Indian Claims Commission, established in 1946, took up tribal grievances over treaty violations and other state actions affecting indigenous people. Over the next three decades the Commission settled scores of cases and paid out millions of dollars in settlements. While the Crows, for example, received a US$10 million payment, other tribes refused to settle for monetary compensation and demanded instead the return of colonized space.[12]

With the New Deal gone and conservatism on the rise in the 1950s, Congress terminated federal oversight of Indian affairs with scores of tribes deemed to have made the most "progress" toward assimilation. Once again, as with allotment, termination denied indigenous autonomy and subjected Indians to legal jurisdiction of the various states. The removal of government services hurt many tribes, forcing some to sell land to raise revenue. During this time hundreds of thousands of Indians moved into cities, a migration facilitated by federal relocation funding, though not enough of it to ward off poverty, inadequate housing, and disease. The Indian urban migration continued; by 2000 more than two-thirds of Indians lived in cities.[13]

The history of crimes and injustices against Indians, as well as activism on the part of indigenous people, received widespread visibility amid the reform and countercultural movement of the 1960s and 1970s. As the civil rights, youth, and antiwar movements gained strength, the Red Power movement also flourished, educating many Americans for the first time about indigenous cultures, the long history of racism, violent dispossession, violation of indigenous treaty rights, and resistance to colonial rule. The American Indian Movement (AIM), created in 1968, spurred indigenous activism, though many indigenes did not agree with AIM nor accept the group as their representative. Dee Brown's *Bury My Heart at Wounded Knee* (1970) and the popular book and film "Little Big Man" (1970) made vast audiences more aware of the colonial past. Vine Deloria's classic *Custer Died for Your Sins: An American Indian Manifesto* (1969) emphasized that Indians remained very much alive, as he illuminated indigenous worldviews with biting insight and some humor as well.

Indians remained heavily marginalized in the colonial state, hence the Red Power movement gained strength from the support and solidarity provided albeit unevenly and haltingly from other activists and organizations. As Sherry Smith points out, "The political and social movements of the 1960s and 1970s were very much intercultural and interracial."[14] The diverse array of supporters included Ken Kesey, Marlon Brando, Peter Coyote, Dick Gregory, Jane Fonda, the Black Panthers, Stokely Carmichael, Quakers and other church groups, the Whole Earth Catalog, Chicano activists, hippies, counterculturalists, Vietnam War protesters, and even the Nixon administration.

Like civil rights and antiwar activists, Indians mounted protests and occupations calling attention to the colonizing past while demanding reforms and autonomy in the present. In 1969, indigenes embarked on a 19-month occupation of Alcatraz Island calling attention to "broken treaties and broken promises" and calling for self-determination for the tribes. In 1972, AIM, the Native American Rights Fund, and other groups organized the "Trail of Broken Treaties," a march on Washington, D.C. patterned along the lines of the massive 1963 civil rights demonstration in the nation's capital. Indian activists occupied—and trashed—the Bureau of Indian Affairs headquarters before negotiations ended the occupation.[15]

Indian direct action peaked with an occupation of Wounded Knee, on the bitterly divided Pine Ridge Reservation. The tribal leader, Dick Wilson, opposed the activists, mounted "goon squads" to carry out violent attacks against them, and then collaborated with federal authorities in a massive display of militancy, as the US government dispatched riot control units, Phantom jets, and armored personnel carriers to the impoverished rural reservation in the South Dakota Badlands. The occupation lasted 71 days, featured hundreds of arrests, and commanded national attention. As Smith notes, "Many Americans—probably for the first time in the twentieth century—now knew this was a place where something had gone terribly wrong eighty years before."[16] The reservation remained the site of simmering resentments between the rival Sioux factions and on the part of the activists toward the federal government. In 1975, two FBI agents died in a shootout as they approached a farmhouse on the reservation.[17]

The Red Power movement succeeded in drawing unparalleled national attention to the North American indigenous past but also to the demands of the present. Indians pursued civil rights and treaty rights but also put forward an anticolonial agenda emphasizing self-determination. "The Red Power movement refused the false choice of either the assimilatory aims of the civil rights movement or the nationalist separatism of Third World anti-colonialism," Bruyneel explains. Instead Indians occupied an ambivalent "third space" in an effort to "work across spatial and temporal boundaries demanding rights and resources from the liberal democratic settler state while also challenging the imposition of colonial rule on their lives."[18]

"Multicultural" Hawai'i

Indigenous Hawaiians like American Indians derived inspiration from the reform spirit of the 1960s and from the global decolonization movement. The unique feature in postcolonial Hawai'i of a non-white, Asian majority gives the appearance of a "multicultural" immigrant success story. However, the "fantasy" of Hawaiian multiculturalism elides the dispossession and marginalization of the indigenous people.[19]

Like the "Vanishing American," indigenous Hawaiians had long been depicted as a dying race within a society dominated by the Americans and Asian Americans primarily of Japanese and Chinese extraction. Yet the Kanaka Maoli persisted and resisted. According to the 2010 census, Hawaiians and other Pacific Islanders comprised about 10 percent of the population of the islands; about one-quarter of Hawai'i's population was "white" and about 39 percent were Asian. Just under a quarter of the population reported two or more races of origin.[20]

In Hawai'i, as on the mainland, in Australia, and in other settler societies, historical denial is intrinsic to the legitimation of settler colonial society. Settler-centric historiography "attempts to redeem the settler state by casting it as a multicultural nation." In Hawai'i, the "scarcity of direct references to colonialism coupled with virtual absence of references to settler colonialism" in museums, exhibitions, and public discourse perpetuates historical denial.[21]

A movement for Hawaiian sovereignty began to gain momentum in the 1980s and 1990s in tandem with the rise of the global indigenous rights movement. Some Kanaka Maoli refused to recite the Pledge of Allegiance, file US or state tax returns, or get a driver's license, explaining that American laws were illegitimate and that Hawai'i was under colonial occupation. With the UN Human Rights Commission and other nongovernmental organizations providing a forum, the legacies of colonialism and postcolonial condition of indigenous peoples garnered unprecedented international attention. Pressured by the rise of the indigenous rights movement, settler states acknowledged the colonial past as a means of declaring closure to the issue.[22]

In 1993, on the centennial anniversary of the US-led coup, the US Congress passed an Apology Resolution, which President Bill Clinton duly signed. The resolution conferred no new rights, privileges, or compensation nor did it address the destruction of Kanaka Maoli culture.[23] Postcolonial Hawai'i remained firmly in US hands, a critical outpost in the global US military and security empire.[24]

Also marking the centennial of annexation in 1993 was the Peoples' International Tribunal, which conducted hearings and proceedings throughout the Hawaiian Islands. The Tribunal, based on the model established by Bertrand Russell during the Vietnam War, convened for 12 days, visited five islands, and involved hundreds of scholars and activists. In the end, the Tribunal leveled nine charges of human rights violations against the United States including illegal annexation, forced assimilation and imposition of statehood, environmental destruction, and genocide. The Tribunal based the latter charge on the appalling and still deteriorating health conditions and deliberate destruction of indigenous culture, including historically imposed restrictions on the use of the Hawaiian language. The Tribunal's records and findings became part of the international human rights regime. The Tribunal was the subject of a documentary film ("The Tribunal," 1994) and a book (*Islands of Captivity*, 2004). While it "received a significant amount of press coverage in Hawai'i" the Tribunal was "largely ignored by the U.S. media."[25]

Meanwhile, the legacies of settler colonialism remain palpable on the Islands. Ultimately, less than 5 percent of Hawaiian land was set aside as indigenous homelands, reflecting the near-total usurpation of colonial space. Colonialism thus created "the very structure of the settler state and its persistent, institutionalized policies of elimination."[26] In addition to being dispossessed, indigenous Hawaiians like Indians and other colonized peoples around the world face higher rates of homelessness, unemployment, poverty, declining health, substance abuse, crime, and incarceration, all legacies of American and Asian American settler colonialism.[27] Some analysts have characterized as a "hidden holocaust" the rates of infant mortality and the shorter lifespan of Hawaiians in comparison to virtually all other US ethnicities.[28]

The high level of homelessness of the Kanaka Maoli is a bitterly ironic albeit "frequently overlooked part of the ongoing legacy of settler colonialism." Homelessness underscores a "transformation of the indigenous into the indigent." Thousands of indigenous Hawaiians are unable to afford housing in one of the most expensive real estate markets in the United States and are simultaneously faced with "ever-dwindling state assistance." New laws clamped down on the homeless, making it illegal to sleep in public parks or beaches, casting these Hawaiians "as a blight on the landscape damaging the state's touristic image."[29]

The blood quantum provision defining Hawaiian identity remains contentious, as it minimizes rather than maximizes the number of people who can claim indigenous status. Blood quantum also perpetuates notions of the Kanaka Maoli as "a racial minority rather than indigenous people with national sovereignty claims" and frames indigenous policy as colonial welfare rather than entitlement to the land. Moreover, J. Kehaulani Kauanui explains, many indigenous Hawaiians oppose the blood quantum criterion today, because it "undercuts indigenous Hawaiian epistemologies that define identity on the basis of one's kinship and genealogy."[30]

Today a vocal contingent of Kanaka Maoli demands full sovereignty and separation from the United States while others seek a degree of autonomy. Some identify with Asian settlers generically as "locals," drawing a distinction with the *haole* and mainlanders, while others link the Asian settlers with whites as invaders of the islands. Many work within the American legal system in pursuit of civil rights and welfare reform while also advancing an agenda of indigenous rights. Collectively, they have called attention to indigenous issues and sparked a "resurgence of Hawaiian language and culture."[31]

Over a Barrel: The Politics of Alaskan Indigeneity

As in Hawai'i, statehood brought indigenous Alaskans *de jure* legal equality yet they remained second-class citizens in terms of income, housing, education, health care, and almost any other quality of life measure, a federal study concluded in 1968.[32] At the same time, the rise of rights consciousness in the 1960s—not only the African-American civil rights movement but the American Indian movement as well—galvanized indigenous protests and legal challenges in Alaska. American settler colonial migrants, meanwhile, anchored the state's economic development, which increasingly revolved around the drive to tap Alaska's massive oil reserves.

The legacies of settler colonialism remained strongly entrenched in Alaska, as many Americans opposed any settlement with the indigenes and continued to view them as primitives who had no legitimate claim to the land. "They wouldn't use it," explained Alaska's lone congressman, Ralph Rivers. "It would just lie there." The Alaska Miners Association declared, "Neither the U.S., the state of Alaska, nor any of us gathered here as individuals owes the Natives one acre of ground or one cent of taxpayers' money."[33]

Despite these hostile sentiments, the US economic and political elite could not dispense with the legacies of colonialism so easily, mainly because indigenous claims posed an obstacle to the proposed Alaska oil pipeline project as well as the broader development agenda. A negotiated settlement unique to Alaska emerged, yet included characteristics redolent of a long history of treaty making with indigenous people, who had given up land as whites pledged their commitment to benevolent assimilation. What made the Alaska settlement unique, however, was the extent to which the indigenes participated in forging the agreement.

In 1971, indigenous activists and US negotiators came to terms on the historic Alaska Native Claims Settlement Act (ANCSA). Under ANCSA, Congress paid US$962.5 million in compensation for extinguishing indigenous title to all but 44 million acres of Alaska land. Under the settlement, the indigenes relinquished claims to 330 million acres of land in return for stock in village corporations. "The chief objective of the complex landmark act," Stephen Haycox explains, "was to free Alaska's potential economic development from Native protest while simultaneously empowering Natives through economic capitalization and achieving justice in terms of Aboriginal land claims."[34]

As with the Dawes Act and other settler colonial initiatives, promoting indigenous assimilation was "a principal objective of the ANCSA settlement," though the agreement did not force indigenous Alaskans to leave their villages. The agreement provided economic incentives to indigenes albeit with attendant social values that were "antithetical to those embodied in traditional cultures." Although ANCSA did little to preserve indigenous culture, and its corporate structure clearly reflected a modernist framework, indigenous leaders participated meaningfully at every level in the drafting of the agreement. ANCSA provided unprecedented empowerment of indigenous Alaskans, as some of new corporations became large and prosperous. The settlement also provided for parks, wildlife refuges, and protection of wild and scenic rivers. In a subsequent out-of-court settlement, the state agreed to provide village schooling for indigenes at a substantial cost.[35]

The active role played by indigenous Alaskans was unprecedented in the history of American settler colonialism. "In Alaska the act was received by Natives and non-Natives alike as a great milestone in the history of the territory and its people." As Mary Clay Berry pointed out, despite its flaws the settlement "was an extraordinary agreement in view of the United States' traditional way of settling its Indian problems."[36]

Despite the high level of consultation afforded indigenes in the ANCSA, the results were ambiguous at best and did not relieve indigenous Alaskans from economic and social marginalization. While ANCSA removed obstacles in the path of development, enabling completion of the oil pipeline in 1977, the settlement "has done little to alleviate the economic and social problems that are pandemic in Native villages." Some of the village corporations made poor investments and then sold off their debts for cash payments. Swept into the modern world, indigenes bought snowmobiles, ATVs, vacations to the lower 48, and some managed college tuition for their children. As Donald Mitchell notes, "Alaska Natives have sought as much access as possible to modernity and the constantly expanding array of goods that modernity provides."[37]

Modernization and the changes wrought by the ANCSA had a traumatic impact on many indigenous people and their cultures. Most of the nearly 134,000 indigenes in Alaska (about 19 percent of the state's total population in the 2010 census) still lived in villages. "Poverty, though high, is much reduced since ANCSA's enactment, but many of ANCSA's benefits have not reached the villages," a recent study found. "Perhaps one half of natives alive today do not own ANCSA stock."[38] The regional corporations failed to create sufficient employment opportunities in the rural areas, forcing many to leave for the cities. "If you leave the village, you desert your family," an Alaska mental health counselor has pointed out. "If you stay in the village, you desert your future."[39] Faced with such a Hobson's choice, many indigenes turned to alcohol or substance abuse and crime, as their incarceration and suicide rates exceeded those of the colonizing population.

Though ANCSA made Alaska unique, the relationship between indigenous Alaskans, the federal government, and settler society remains similar to the mainland. In 1988, Congress restructured ANCSA to make indigenous Alaskans eligible for all federal Indian programs on the same basis as Indians on the mainland. In both cases human service programs expanded substantially following passage of the Indian Self-Determination and Education Assistance Act in 1975.[40]

The suggestion by indigenes and their supporters that more ought to be done to redress the continuing legacies of settler colonialism has received little traction in the politically conservative "red" state of Alaska. Suppressed feelings of guilt and rationalization are common, as some settlers aver that the indigenes have been "given" enough, a viewpoint that elides the colonial past. "I get tired of [hearing] they gave us forty four million acres and a billion dollars," an indigenous Alaskan shoots back. "They didn't give us shit. They stole it, and the only time they were interested in settling it was when they found a few barrels of oil."[41]

Indigenous Alaskans, increasing in numbers and assertiveness, still "own or control substantial lands and resources either as corporations or tribes." Indigenous people and their governments are well positioned to reinvigorate their cultures and traditions. Indigenous empowerment offers the possibility that, in the twenty-first century, Alaska "will eventually find a place where the relationships between immigrant and indigenous Americans may enrich each other."[42]

Taking Colonialism to Court

ANCSA underscores the role of law and reconceptualization of space in postcolonial society, and here some of the most significant reversals in the history of American settler colonialism have unfolded. Just as the colonizer used the law to deliver a number of nasty surprises over centuries of dispossession and treaty making, Indians turned the tables by marshaling legal precedent as a weapon of redress and even repossession of land. Thus the quest to disavow the colonizing act by using the law as the primary tool of dispossession boomeranged on the colonizer, as the indigenes and their lawyers resurrected old treaties, sued for legal enforcement, and variously demanded expanded jurisdiction, exclusive rights, compensation, and autonomy.

By the 1970s, the Red Power movement and indigenous activism produced change in public perceptions that carried over into the law. The Nixon administration backed Indian self-determination while the Supreme Court issued the landmark Boldt decision (1974), restoring exclusive indigenous rights to a portion of the Puget Sound salmon fishery on the basis of treaty rights dating to the mid-nineteenth century. Congress weighed in with a series of legislative reforms, including the Indian Self-Determination and Education Assistance Act (1975); the Native American Religious Freedom Act (1978); the Indian Child Welfare Act (1978); the Indian Gaming Regulatory Act (1988); the Native American Graves Protection and Repatriation Act (1990); the Native American Languages Act (1990); and the Indian Tribal Energy Development and Self Determination Act (2005).

Spurred by the Boldt decision, Indians and their supporters mounted an ongoing series of legal challenges based on historic treaty violations. After the Penobscot and Passamaquoddy Indians brought suit in Maine, the tribes in 1980 received US$81.5 million in compensation for lands illegally taken from them. Several Iroquois bands followed suit, literally, and won substantial land claims in the courts during the 1980s.[43]

These and other successful indigenous legal challenges ultimately produced a backlash within settler society. In an effort to reassert authority, the colonizer effects an inversion in which tribes are framed as the colonizers (if not as "socialists") demanding special privileges.[44] Under this frame, the ethnic minority becomes the aggressor and the majority population the victims deprived of their prerogative through, for example, the enforcement of treaties or restoration of exclusive rights. Anticolonial activism and legal challenges have thus spurred political conflict within a settler society that continues to feel threatened by indigenous people, no matter how marginalized.

By the time of the conservative Rehnquist Court (1986–2001), the Supreme Court as well as lesser courts began to shoot down indigenous claims. "The late twentieth century to the present has seen a consistent erosion of the federal common law rights of indigenous peoples," legal scholars pointed out in 2012. Supreme Court decisions turned against the trend toward broadened recognition of tribal jurisdiction and un-extinguished claims to colonized space. "As the progressive era of Indian law jurisprudence has receded, the new tendency in the Court's tests, rules, and rhetoric is to define tribal powers according to policies, values, and assumptions prevalent in non-Indian society."[45]

The struggle for legal rights included efforts to protect indigenous land from natural resource extraction industries, which placed "enormous pressure" on the tribes. As Colin Calloway has noted, "In the nineteenth century the United States wanted Indian land; in the twentieth century it wanted Indian resources such as coal, natural gas, uranium, timber and water."[46] Mining operations scarred Indian land and often had damaging health impacts such as excessive levels of radiation from uranium mining. Indians sued for damages in some of these cases yet the tribes faced difficult choices of their own between profiting from the use of their land balanced against the impact on the quality of life. Bands could be divided, for example, on whether to allow strip mining or to accept toxic wastes on reservations, which became a favored dumping ground for industry.

As they pursued both rights and anticolonial politics, Indians as well as Alaskans and Hawaiians thus had to consider the extent that they wished to join or maintain distance from capitalist development and mainstream lifestyles in order to preserve culture and community. Indian gaming is a case in point. In 1983 a Pequot band won federal recognition and tribal autonomy that enabled casino gambling. The tribe proceeded to open the massive Foxwoods Resort Casino in eastern Connecticut, which generated enormous profits in a state that otherwise outlawed casino gaming. Throughout the country various tribes have turned their land into gaming meccas, yet many Indians view gambling as a scourge that erodes indigenous culture and community while promoting addiction among tribal members. Thus while some bands generate wealth through gaming, others remain mired in abject poverty with few routes of escape.

Indigenous people in North America, as in other postcolonial settings, continue to suffer disproportionately from childhood mortality, sharply lower rates of life expectancy, disease and limited access to health care, lack of education and employment opportunities, alcoholism and drug abuse, crime and incarceration, and other social problems. In 2003, the US Commission on Civil Rights issued a report entitled "A Quiet Crisis" concluding that indigenous people continued to rank at or near the bottom of almost all social health and economic indicators. The report recommended increased funding for health care, infrastructure development, tribal courts, as well as allocations to "permit tribes to pursue their own priorities and allow tribal governments to respond to the needs of their citizens."[47] A conservative Congress and fiscal crises have not been conducive to addressing these needs.

It is not difficult to see the grinding poverty and dilapidated infrastructure on many Indian reservations, especially those, like the Sioux reservations, that remain isolated from large urban areas. The Sioux have the prospect of providing some redress for their people, including the possibility of sizable cash payments to individual tribal members, on the basis of a 1980 Supreme Court decision, which ruled that the Black Hills had been seized illegally and without compensation. The monetary award for the seizure of Sioux land, held in trust by the Interior Department, now exceeds US$1 billion. But the Great Sioux Nation has thus far rejected the award because it would require renunciation of ownership of the sacred Black Hills. Taking the money would entail acceptance of the colonizer's claims on colonial space. Various legislative and negotiated settlements remain in play but for now the postcolonial politics of the Sioux rest on principle rather than profit.[48]

As the ongoing struggle for the Black Hills underscores, the colonial past persists in the present. The postcolonial framework thus illuminates the past even as it offers a glimmer of hope for a brighter future.

Conclusion: The Boomerang of Savagery

American settler colonialism was a winner-takes-all proposition that demanded the removal of indigenous peoples and the destruction of their cultures. Even Americans who empathized with the indigenes urged them to abandon their cultures and vacate colonial space for white settlers. Indians participated at every level of the colonial encounter and, contrary to settler fantasies, the indigenes did not "vanish." Nonetheless, they overwhelmingly were dispossessed, their cultures and way of life assaulted, and the consequences of this postcolonial history remain apparent in indigenous communities today.

Americans including scholars shy away from the "c" and "g" words, as if they could not possibly apply to American history, yet colonialism and genocide inhered in the settler project. Dispossession, forced assimilation, compulsory religious conversions, forced reconfiguration of gender roles, child removal, and often-indiscriminate killing aimed to destroy the Indian way of life. Although contextualized by all manner of ambivalent relationships, in the final analysis the United States pursued a continuous "foreign policy" of colonial genocide targeting indigenous North Americans as well as Hawaiians. Americans also carried out indiscriminate campaigns against the Hispanic other, against masses of Filipinos, and even against one another in the American Civil War. Violence between and among Indians, Hispanics, and American settlers occurred more or less continuously across nearly four centuries of borderlands history, with profound consequences for national identity and subsequent foreign policy.

While the violence of borderlands history can be narrated and documented, its implications for national identity and foreign policy cannot be demonstrated empirically. The argument I construct in this regard ultimately rests on theorization. Postcolonial analysis, although eschewed by most historians, illuminates continuities and historical implications that otherwise elude the discipline.

I argue that the history of American settler colonialism, and the indiscriminate violence that it entailed, burrowed into US national identity and foreign relations. Colonized peoples invariably resist their colonizers and Indians with their own powerful warrior cultures put up a long and bloody resistance even as they also traded, accommodated, converted, and otherwise responded ambivalently. Indigenous resistance traumatized settlers, hardened the mythology of providential destiny, and fueled an often-indiscriminate response.

Americans thus internalized a propensity for traumatic, righteous violence, and a quest for total security, which came to characterize a series of future conflicts. Violence against Indians, replete with demonizing colonial discourse and indiscriminate killing, established a foundation for virulent national campaigns against external enemies across the sweep of American history. The long history of settler colonialism also adds depth of understanding to the persistent US affinity for "special relationships" with other "white" settler states such as Great Britain, Canada, Australia, South Africa, and Israel.

In recent years scholars have begun to call attention to continuities of American history rooted in settler colonization. "Settler exclusion," Aziz Rana argues, "was more than just a distant period of conquest and subordination; it provided the basic governing framework for American life for over three centuries." Paul Rosier takes as a "basic premise" that "the United States has practiced imperialism since its founding" and that the colonial encounter with Indians shaped the nation's subsequent "engagement with new peoples on new global frontiers—'Indian country' migrating west to the Philippines and beyond." In settler colonial societies, "aggressive instincts turned towards the outside world remain active" even after indigenous resistance has been overcome, Lorenzo Veracini points out. "Even demographic takeover cannot dissipate settler aggressiveness."[1]

Born of settler colonialism, indiscriminate violence against savage foes forged an American way of war and a pathway first to continental and then to global empire. "When warfare occurs with considerable frequency as it did in early America," John Ferling points out, "war shapes the character and identity of a people." As Colin Calloway notes, "The Indian wars, some would say, left a more sinister mark on American culture: a nation built on conquest could not escape the legacy of its violent past." "If imperial rule had such a profound influence on the colonized we might well ask whether it had an equally significant impact on the colonizer," Alfred McCoy observes in articulating the evolution of an "imperial mimesis" that grew out of the US-Filipino construction of a postcolonial security state.[2]

The American way of war carried beyond the wars narrated in this study, through the twentieth century, and to the present day. Although obscured by the trope of the "good war," indiscriminate violence characterized the United States' role in World War II, particularly in the relentless bombing of civilian targets in Germany and Japan. The indiscriminate killing in the Pacific War, culminating in the atomic bombings of Hiroshima and Nagasaki, came naturally to the traumatized Americans, as "the treacherous Japs" like the skulking Indian savages had attacked without warning in the US-occupied colonial space of Hawai'i. Few Americans know the extent of "collateral damage" that occurred during the supposedly "limited war" in Korea, a war characterized by saturation bombing and indiscriminate killing of civilians. Little more than a decade later the United States invaded Indochina, conducting lethal search and destroy operations into the "Indian country" of Vietnam, defoliating the countryside, and subjecting the region to the most intensive bombing in human history, causing the deaths of at least a million people and perhaps twice that number. American *Apache* and *Black Hawk* helicopters along with *Tomahawk* missiles have conveyed US militarism to Iraq where hundreds of thousands of people have died as a result of the US interventions.[3]

Americans have a remarkable capacity, as John Tirman points out, to elide "the deaths of others" in warfare. "One salient effect of indifference or callousness toward large-scale human suffering in U.S. wars," Tirman notes, "is to permit *more* such wars." As other scholars have pointed out, despite the ubiquity of violence in popular culture, regular occurrence of public mass killings, as well as a comparatively high homicide rate, "the history of American violence as a whole has attracted relatively little attention."[4]

American history is not a simple story of brutal and relentless violence against other peoples but brutal and relentless violence is undeniably a critically important *part* of American history. When we deny it, or decline to study it, or marginalize it, we are complicit in its recurrence. American drives and ambitions have made possible many great things, countless historic achievements, but they have also made possible the destruction of other peoples who got in the way of those drives, who resisted the imposition of American imperial will, who challenged the nation's towering hubris.

Americans, like other peoples throughout history, have rationalized warfare and glossed over extreme violence by emphasizing the ultimate justification of the cause, whether the wars were for civilization or against communism or terrorism. As Americans ultimately were performing good works, almost any level of violence could be rationalized and justified. Such rationalizations and exceptionalist mythologies must be unpacked and violence over the *longue dureé* systematically chronicled and analyzed. As the Lacanian scholar Jennifer Rutherford notes, by "speaking against the grain of the good and its incumbent fantasies" we can better recognize "the propinquity of our most moral ideals and sordid deeds."[5]

A long overdue genuine reckoning with the nation's propensity for indiscriminate violence against other peoples must begin with early American history and work its way forward, but this is something that settler colonial societies resist with a vengeance. It is important to remember that the United States is not exceptional but rather part of a broader settler colonial and global history. Historical denial is intrinsic to settler colonial societies no matter how "free" that they think they might be, as cultural campaigns against "revisionist history" and "black armband" versions of the past attest.

American willingness to take responsibility for destruction of indigenous cultures has been limited, belated, muted in comparison to other countries, and designed to deflect meaningful restitution. Most Americans are not even aware of official US apologies for the colonial past. Tellingly, in December 2010 the official US apology to Indians was squirreled away deep inside *a defense appropriations bill* wherein the United States expressed "official apologies for the past ill-conceived policies by the U.S. government toward native peoples of this land and reaffirm our commitment toward healing our nation's wounds and working toward establishing better relationships rooted in reconciliation." Like the apology in 1993 to indigenous Hawaiians, the United States took no legal responsibility and offered no relief or compensation.

The "quiet" of the US apology stands out, as Audra Simpson notes, in comparison with the "apologies of the Australian and Canadian states to indigenous peoples in February 2008 and June 2008, respectively." These apologies were directed toward survivors and descendants and "performed in Parliament and received extensive national and international coverage." Critics wonder, "Is an apology that is not said out loud really an apology?"[6]

On September 13, 2007, the United States, joined by Australia, Canada, and New Zealand, settler colonial states all, cast the four negative votes—compared with 143 in favor—against the UN General Assembly's historic Declaration on the Rights of Indigenous Peoples.[7] The United States has since offered a tepid, carefully qualified endorsement with a "finalizing disclaimer" reasserting its ultimate sovereignty over indigenous people.[8] The legacies of settler colonialism including the hoary legal Doctrine of Discovery continue to impede reform and judicial adjustments.[9]

Unlike "conventional" colonialism, which at least since World War II has evolved a narrative of decolonization and self-determination, a definitive narrative of settler colonial decolonization has yet to take hold. This absence leaves "a narrative gap that contributes crucially to the invisibility of anti-colonial struggles." Settler colonialism first must be broadly acknowledged and its significance grasped before narratives of settler decolonization and rectification can take hold..[10] "It is not about shaming or 'guilting' or blaming," Larissa Behrendt points out. "It is about acknowledging the truth, and with that acknowledgement will come reconciliation, healing, empowerment and pride . . . It is a mistake to think of Indigenous rights and well-being as merely an 'Indigenous issue' or 'Indigenous problem.' "[11]

As other scholars note, by identifying the United States as a settler state "we can more effectively work toward justice for Native people and, by extension, for settlers as well."[12] Especially for the United States—with its driving sense of mission, its incomparable military power and global influence, but also its propensity for destruction—a more honest reckoning with the past is an indispensable prelude to the construction of a more peaceful future.

Notes

Preface

1. For the sake of clarity, I employ the English names of indigenous tribes, hence the Lenni Lenape will be referred to as the Delaware, the Ani–yun Wiya as the Cherokee, the Haudensaunee as the Iroquois, and so on. Likewise, individual Indians will be referenced through their English names; hence Thayendanegea will be referred to as Joseph Brant, Mishikinakwa as Little Turtle, and so on. As all names and designations ultimately are problematic, in this study I apply commonly used terms such as "Indians," "indigenous people," or "indigenes." I try to avoid the term "Native," which seems to me to connote primitivism. Though terms such as "tribes" and "bands" also are problematic, so are most alternatives; hence I use such references for the sake of clarity and convenience.
2. Stephen Warren, "The Ohio Shawnees' Struggle against Removal, 1814–30," R. David Edmunds., ed., *Enduring Nations: Native Americans in the Midwest* (Urbana and Chicago, IL: University of Illinois Press, 2008), 73–88.
3. See the evidence and literature cited throughout this book.
4. Leonard Sadosky, "Rethinking the Gnadenhutten Massacre: The Contest for Power in the Public World of the Revolutionary Pennsylvania Frontier," in David C. Skaggs and Larry Nelson, eds., *The Sixty Years' War for the Great Lakes, 1754–1814* (East Lansing, MI: Michigan State University Press, 2001), 187–214; Rob Harper, "Looking the Other Way: The Gnadenhutten Massacre and the Contextual Interpretation of Violence," in Philip G. Dwyer and Lyndall Ryan, "Introduction: The Massacre in History," in Dwyer and Ryan, eds., *Theatres of Violence: Massacre, Mass Killing and Atrocity Throughout History* (New York: Berghahn Books, 2012), 81–93; R. Douglas Hurt, *The Ohio Frontier: Crucible of the Old Northwest, 1720–1830* (Bloomington, IN: Indiana University Press, 1996), 91; Earl P. Olmstead, *David Zeisberger: A Life Among the Indians* (Kent, OH: Kent State University Press, 1997), 325–337.
5. Hurt, *Ohio Frontier*, 92; Colin Calloway, *The American Revolution in Indian Country: Crisis and Diversity in Native American Communities* (New York: Cambridge University Press, 1995), 294.
6. Sadosky, "Rethinking the Gnadenhutten Massacre," 201.
7. Karl Jacoby, *Shadows at Dawn: An Apache Massacre and the Violence of History* (New York: Penguin Books, 2008), 2.
8. Helen Hunt Jackson, *A Century of Dishonor: A Sketch of the United States Government's Dealings With Some of the Indian Tribes* (Norman, OK: University of Oklahoma Press, 1995; 1881); Dee Brown, *Bury My Heart at Wounded Knee: An Indian History of the American West* (New York: Bantam, 1970).
9. Amié Césaire, *Discourse on Colonialism* (New York: Monthly Review Press, 1972; 1950), 41.

Chapter 1

1. The term *ethnic cleansing*, which arose in the context of the former Yugoslavia, can be defined as a systematic effort to remove a defined group of people from a given territory based on ethnic or religious grounds. Ethnic cleansing invariably entails violence including massacres, rape, collective punishment, and other violations of human rights. The term is gaining credence among scholars, as demonstrated by the citations throughout this and other works. See also the forthcoming book by Gary C. Anderson tentatively entitled *The Ethnic Cleansing of the Indian* (University of Oklahoma Press).
2. The American way of war is an important interpretive concept for understanding American history, but at this point it has been undertheorizied and poorly developed. American military history was long disdained by the vast majority of social and cultural historians, hence the historical profession bears some responsibility for the failure to develop an adequate intellectual foundation for assessing the most powerful and consequential military state—the United States—in human history. The phrase "American way of war" originated with Russell F. Weigley's classic though now outdated military history. See Weigley, *The American Way of War: A History of United States Military Strategy and Policy* (Bloomington, IN: Indiana University Press, 1973). More recent studies that emphasize unconventional and indiscriminate warfare while arguing for an "American way of war" rooted in the colonial era and carrying to the present include Eliot A. Cohen, *Conquered into Liberty: Two Centuries of Battles along the Great Warpath That Made the American Way of War* (New York: Free Press, 2011); John Grenier, *The First Way of War: American War Making on the Frontier, 1607–1814* (New York: Cambridge, 2005); and Fred Anderson and Andrew Cayton, *The Dominion of War: Empire and Liberty in North America, 1500–2000* (New York: Viking, 2005).
3. Aziz Rana, *The Two Faces of American Freedom* (Cambridge,MA: Harvard University Press, 2010), 8–14; Anders Stephanson argues that dispossession "reached its purest and most lethal expression" in colonial America and the United States. See "An American Story? Second Thoughts on Manifest Destiny," in David Maybury-Lewis, Theodore Macdonald, and Biorn Maybury-Lewis, eds., *Manifest Destinies and Indigenous Peoples* (Cambridge, MA: Harvard University Press, 2009), 33.
4. See Ania Loomba, Suvir Kaul, Matti Bunzl, Antoinette Burton, and Jed Esty, eds., *Postcolonial Studies and Beyond* (Durham, NC: Duke University Press, 2005); Joanne P. Sharpe, *Geographies of Postcolonialism: Spaces of Power and Representation* (Thousand Oaks, CA: Sage Publications, 2009); Sankaran Krishna, *Globalization and Postcolonialism: Hegemony and Resistance in the Twenty-first Century* (Lanham, MD: Rowan and Littlefield, 2009); Henry Schwarz, "Mission Impossible: Introducing Postcolonial Studies in the U.S. Aacdemy," in Henry Schwarz and Sangeeta Roy, eds., *A Companion to Postcolonial Studies* (Malden, MA: Blackwell Publishers, 2000); and the citations below.
5. Associated with the French Annales School, the *longue dureé* emphasized long-term economic and social analysis rather than viewing history conventionally through a series of reigns of kings and queens. In the pre–World War II era, Marc Bloch and Lucien Febvre launched a journal centered on the "longue dureé linking mentalities with economic forces." In the postwar era, Fernand Braudel added prominence to the Annales School with two major works focusing on the *longue dureé* of the Mediterranean world and on civilization and capitalism. Fernand Braudel, *The Mediterranean and the Mediterranean World in the Age of Phillip II* (London: Harper-Collins, 1972).

6. John McLeod, ed., *The Routledge Companion to Postcolonial Studies* (London and New York: Routledge, 2007), 8–9.
7. With a vocabulary drawn from myriad disciplines as well as theoretical realms, including Marxism, poststructuralism, postmodernism, and psychoanalysis, postcolonial studies can be daunting. Research methodology is highly interdisciplinary and can center on archives and/or literary texts; sources can be both fictional and nonfiction. Postcolonial studies take up "issues of hybridity, creoloization, and mestizaje—with the in-betweenness, diaspora, mobility and cross-overs of ideas and identities generated by colonialism." As Robert Young notes, "Those encountering postcolonial theory for the first time can be intimidated or baffled by the terminology, concepts and apparently cryptic language being used." However, "It is also the case," Ania Loomba points out, "that the newer critical vocabularies are not always merely 'jargon.' " See Robert J. C. Young, *Postcolonialism: An Historical Introduction* (Oxford, UK, Walden, MA: Blackwell Publishers, 2001), 67; and Ania Loomba, *Colonialism/Postcolonialism* (New York: Routledge, 1998; 2005), 145, 2. For criticisms of postcolonial analysis, see Arif Dirlik, Vinay Bahl, and Peter Gran, *History After the Three Worlds: Post-Eurocentric Historiographies* (Lanham, MD: Rowan and Littlefield, 2000), 10; Neil Lazarus, *Nationalism and Cultural Practice in the Postcolonial World* (New York: Cambridge University Press, 1999).
8. Anthony C. Alessandrini, ed., *Frantz Fanon: Critical Perspectives* (New York: Routledge, 1999), 91; Frantz Fanon, *Black Skin, White Masks* (New York: Grove Press, 1967; 1952), 10–14.
9. Frantz Fanon, *The Wretched of the Earth* (New York: Random House, 1961), quotations on 313, 311; see also Nigel C. Gibson, ed., *Rethinking Fanon: The Continuing Dialogue* (Amherst, NY: Humanity Books, 1999).
10. Aimé Césaire, *Discourse on Colonialism* (New York: Monthly Review Press, 1972; 1950), 35–43, 71, 85; Albert Memmi, *The Colonizer and the Colonized* (Boston, MA: The Beacon Press, 1970; 1965), 88–89, 61.
11. Edward W. Said, *Orientalism* (New York: Pantheon, 1978); Said, *Culture and Imperialism* (New York: Vintage Books, 1993).
12. "Combining a Fanonian model of resistance with Lacanian psychoanalytic theory," Jenny Sharpe explains, "Bhabha identified in colonial discourse an inherent 'ambivalence' that allowed for slippages and native appropriations." Jenny Sharpe, "Postcolonial Studies in the House of U.S. Multiculturalism," Schwarz and Roy, eds., *Companion to Postcolonial Studies*, 112.
13. Homi Bhaba, *The Location of Culture* (New York: Routledge, 1994), 112 and passim.
14. Lorenzo Veracini, *Settler Colonialism: A Theoretical Overview* (New York: Palgrave Macmillan, 2010), 15.
15. Ibid., 14.
16. Caroline Elkins and Susan Pedersen, eds., *Settler Colonialism in the Twentieth Century* (New York: Routledge, 2005), 2; Veracini, *Settler Colonialism*, 35; See also "Settler Colonialism," *South Atlantic Quarterly*, 107, 4 (special edition, Fall 2008).
17. Patrick Wolfe, *Settler Colonialism and the Transformation of Anthropology: The Politics and Poetics of an Ethnographic Event* (London: Cassell, 1999), 2; James Belich, *Replenishing the Earth: The Settler Revolution and the Rise of the Anglo World, 1783–1939* (New York: Oxford University Press, 2009), 21–23.
18. John C. Weaver, *The Great Land Rush and the Making of the Modern World, 1650–1900* (Montreal: McGill-Queen's University Press, 2003), 12, 104.
19. Veracini, *Settler Colonialism*, 16, 18.
20. Belich, *Replenishing the Earth*, 558.

21. Ibid., 81, 554.
22. Annie E. Coombes, ed., *Rethinking Settler Colonialism: History and Memory in Australia, Canada, Aotearoa New Zealand and South Africa* (Manchester: Manchester University Press, 2006), 2; Belich, *Replenishing the Earth*, 554–558.
23. Nicholas Blomley, David Delaney and Richard T. Ford, *The Legal Geographies Reader: Law, Power and Space* (Oxford, UK: Blackwell Publishers, 2001), xvi; David Delaney, *The Spatial, The Legal and the Pragmatics of World Making: Nomospheric Investigations* (New York: Routledge, 2010); see also David Featerstone and Joe Painter, *Spatial Politics: Essays for Doreen Massey* (Malden, MA: Wiley Blackwell, 2013).
24. See Chapter 2.
25. Ibid., 90.
26. Lynette Russell, ed., *Colonial Frontiers: Indigenous-European Encounters in Settler Societies* (Manchester, UK: Manchester University Press, 2001), 3.
27. Ibid., 3; Weaver, *Great Land Rush*, 5.
28. British settler societies can be distinguished from exploitative British colonies such as India.

    > In settler societies, extensive settlement, natural population increase, the consolidation of power by self-confident native-born elites and the more or less successful transformation of these societies into highly Anglicized colonial variance of British Metropolitan culture had by the mid 18th-century not only differentiated these colonies from newer and more marginal American colonies, but also differentiated them from every other area in the world where Britain had a presence.

    Trevor Burnard, "Placing British Settlement in the Americas in Comparative Perspective," in H. V. Bowen, Elizabeth Mancke, and John G. Reid, eds., *Britain's Oceanoic Empire: Atlantic and Indian Ocean worlds c. 1550–1850* (New York: Cambridge University Press, 2012), 411.
29. Weaver, *Great Land Rush*, 18–19.
30. See Jill St. Germain, *Indian Treaty-Making in the United States and Canada, 1867–1877* (Lincoln, NE: University of Nebraska Press, 2001).
31. Roger L. Nichols, "National Expansion and Native Peoples of the United States and Canada," in Maybury-Lewis, MacDonald and Maybury-Lewis, eds., *Manifest Destinies and Indigenous Peoples*, 162; see also Nichols, *Indians in the United States and Canada: A Comparative History* (Lincoln, NE: University of Nebraska Press, 1998); and Bruce Vandervort, *Indian Wars of Mexico, Canada, and the United States, 1812–1900* (New York: Routledge, 2006).
32. Nigel Penn, "The Northern Cape Frontier Zone in South African Frontier Historiography," in Russell, ed., *Colonial Frontiers*, 19–21; Martin Meredith, *Diamonds, Gold, and War: The British, the Boers, and the Making of South Africa* (New York: Public Affairs, 2007), 7.
33. Weaver, *Great Land Rush*, 148; 160–167; see also Robert Ross, *A Concise History of South Africa* (New York: Cambridge University Press, 1999), 21–53.
34. Grant Morris, " 'The Final Legal Frontier': The Treaty of Waitangi and the Creation of Legal Boundaries between Maori and Pakeha in New Zealand Society," in Russell, ed., *Colonial Frontiers*, 119–133.
35. Michael King, *The Penguin History of New Zealand* (New York: Penguin Books, 2003), 211.
36. Weaver, *Great Land Rush*, 145–147.
37. Philippa Mein Smith, *A Concise History of New Zealand* (New York: Cambridge University Press, 2012), 72–81.

38. A. Dirk Moses, "Genocide and Settler Society in Australian History," in Moses, ed., *Genocide and Settler Society: Frontier Violence and Stolen Indigenous Children in Australian History* (New York: Berghahn Books, 2004), 3–48; Margaret D. Jacobs, *White Mother to a Dark Race: Settler Colonialism, Maternalism, and the Removal of Indigenous Children in the American West and Australia, 1880–1940* (Lincoln, NE: University of Nebraska Press, 2009); Stuart McIntyre and Anna Clark, *The History Wars* (Melbourne: Melbourne University Press, 2003).
39. Stuart Macintyre, *A Concise History of Australia* (London: Cambridge University Press, 2004), 4.
40. Macintyre, *Concise History of Australia*, 28; see also Stuart Banner, *Possessing the Pacific: Land, Settlers, and Indigenous People from Australia to Alaska* (Cambridge, MA: Harvard University Press, 2007), 13–46.
41. Henry Reynolds, *The Other Side of the Frontier: Aboriginal Resistance to the European Invasion of Australia* (Sydney: University of New South Wales Press, 2006; 1981), 31.
42. Benjamin Madley, "Tactics of Nineteenth-Century Colonial Massacre: Tasmania, California and Beyond," in Philip G. Dwyer and Lyndall Ryan, eds., *Theatres of Violence: Massacre, Mass Killing and Atrocity Throughout History* (New York: Berhahn Books, 2012), 112–113.
43. Raymond Evans, Kay Saunders, and Kathryn Cronin, *Race Relations in Colonial Queensland: A History of Exclusion, Exploitation and Extermination* (St. Lucia, Queensland: University of Queensland Press, 1988; 1975); Henry Reynolds and Dawn May, "Queensland," in Ann McGrath, ed., *Contested Ground: Australian Aborigines Under the British Crown* (Crows Nest, New South Wales: Allen and Unwin, 1995); Moses, "Genocide and Settler Society in Australian History"; Colin Tatz, "Genocide in Australia," in Samuel Totten and William S. Parsons, eds., *Centuries of Genocide: Essays and Eyewitness Accounts* (New York: Routledge, 2013).
44. Robert J. Miller, Jacinta Ruru, Larissa Behrendt, and Tracey Lindberg, *Discovering Indigenous Lands: The Doctrine of Discovery in the English Colonies* (New York: Oxford University Press, 2010), 186–206; Lisa Ford, *Settler Sovereignty: Jurisdiction and Indigenous People in America and Australia, 1788–1836* (Cambridge, MA: Harvard University Press, 2010).
45. Jennifer Rutherford, *The Gauche Intruder: Freud, Lacan and the White Australian Fantasy* (Melbourne: Melbourne University Press, 2000), 9; Russell, ed., *Colonial Frontiers*, 91; Miller, Ruru, Behrendt, and Lindberg, *Discovering Indigenous Lands*, 186–206; Rod Macneil, "Time After Time: Temporal Frontiers and Boundaries in Colonial Images of the Australian Landscape," in Russell, ed., *Colonial Frontiers*, 47–48; See also McGrath, ed., *Contested Ground*, 1.
46. Stuart Hall and Paul du Gay, eds., *Questions of Cultural Identity* (Thousand Oaks, CA: Sage Publications, 1996); I have dealt with the role of the other in US foreign policy in *The Myth of American Diplomacy: National Identity and U.S. Foreign Policy* (New Haven, CT: Yale University Press, 2008).
47. Fanon, *Wretched of the Earth*, 102; Kevin Bruyneel, *The Third Space of Sovereignty: The Post-Colonial Politics of U.S.-Indigenous Relations* (Minneapolis, MN: University of Minnesota Press, 2007), 8.
48. Veracini, *Settler Colonialism*, 61; Etienne Balibar and Immanuel Wallerstein, eds., *Race, Nation, Class: Ambiguous Identities* (London: Verso, 2010), 96.
49. Loomba, *Colonialism/Postcolonialism*, 99; Norbert Finzsch, "Discourses of Genocide in Eighteenth- and Nineteenth-Century America and Australia," A. Dirk Moses, ed., *Empire, Colony, Genocide: Conquest, Occupation, and Subaltern Resistance in World History* (London: Berghahn Books, 2008), 3–4. See also David Theo Goldberg, *The Racial*

State (Malden, MA: Blackwell, 2002) and the classic work by Winthrop Jordan, *White over Black: American Attitudes toward the Negro, 1550–1812* (New York: Norton, 1968).

50. Anne McClintock, *Imperial Leather: Race, Gender, and Sexuality in the Colonial Contest* (New York: Routledge, 1995), 24; Joan Scott, *Gender and the Politics of History* (New York: Columbia University Press, 1999); Jacobs, *White Mother to a Dark Race.*
51. Colin Calloway, *The American Revolution in Indian Country: Crisis and Diversity in Native American Communities* (New York: Cambridge University Press, 1995), 294; Andrea Smith, *Conquest: Sexual Violence and American Indian Genocide* (Cambridge, MA: South End Press, 2005); Kathryn Zabelle Derounian-Stodola, ed., *Women's Indian Captivity Narratives* (New York: Penguin Books, 1998); Robert F. Berkhofer, Jr., *The White Man's Indian* (New York: Alfred A. Knopf, 1978), 84.
52. Loomba, *Colonialism/Postcolonialism*, 141.
53. Anna Johnston and Alan Lawson, "Settler Colonies," in Schwarz and Roy, eds., *Companion to Postcolonial Studies*, 364–366.
54. Ibid., 364; Philip J. DeLoria, *Playing Indian* (New Haven, CT: Yale University Press, 1998), 184; Renato Rosaldo, *Culture and Truth: The Remaking of Social Analysis* (Boston, MA: Beacon Press, 1993), 68–87.
55. Edward T. Linenthal and Tom Engelhardt, eds., *The History Wars: The Enola Gay and Other Battles for the American Past* (New York: Henry Holt, 1996); McIntyre and Clark, *History Wars*; Ross, *Concise History of South Africa*, 198–201; Laurence J. Silberstein, ed., *Postzionism: A Reader* (New Brunswick, NJ: Rutgers University Press, 2008).
56. Johnson and Lawson, "Settler Colonies," 362; Sharpe, "Postcolonial Studies in House of U.S. Multiculturalism," 122.
57. Quoted in Amy Kaplan and Donald Pease, *Culture of United States Imperialism* (Durham, NC: Duke University Press, 1993), 3; Julius W, Pratt, *America's Colonial Experiment: How the United States Gained, Governed, and in Part Gave Away a Colonial Empire* (New York: Prentice-Hall, 1950), 2–3.
58. Schwarz, "Mission Impossible," 10; Donald E. Pease, *The New American Exceptionalism* (Minneapolis, MN: University of Minnesota Press, 2009), 205.
59. Pease, "U.S. Imperialism: Global Dominance with Colonies," in Schwarz and Roy, eds., *Companion to Postcolonial Studies*, 205.
60. Malani Johar Schueller and Edward Watts, eds., *Messy Beginnings: Postcoloniality and Early American Studies* (New Brunswick, NJ: Rutgers University Press, 2003), 2; see also, Carroll Smith-Rosenberg, *This Violent Empire: The Birth of an American National Identity* (Chapel Hill, NC: University of North Carolina Press, 2010).
61. For overview see R. David Edmunds, "Blazing New Trails or Burning Bridges: Native American History Comes of Age," *Western Historical Quarterly* 39 (Spring 2008), 4–15. John R. Wunder, "Native American History, Ethnohistory, and Context," *Ethnohistory* 54 (Fall 2007), 591–604; see also the studies cited below and in Chapters 2–6.
62. The "metaphysics of Indian hating" is a reference drawn from Herman Melville's novel, *The Confidence Man* (1857) and was applied by scholars such as Roy Harvey Pearce and later Richard Drinnon. See Pearce, *Historicism Once More: Problems and Occasions for the American Scholar* (Princeton, NJ: Princeton University Press, 1969) and Drinnon, *Facing West, The Meta-Physics of Indian hating and Empire-Building* (Minneapolis, MN: University of Minnesota Press, 1980); Drinnon's classic study enjoyed a long shelf life precisely because it did effectively draw connections between Indian removal and subsequent US imperial history, but scholars have since allowed that connection to wane. See also Dee Brown, *Bury My Heart at Wounded Knee: An Indian History of the American West* (New York: Bantam, 1970).

63. Daniel Richter, *Facing East from Indian Country: A Native History of Early America* (Cambridge, MA: Harvard University Press, 2001); see also the studies cited below and in Chapters 2–6.
64. Samuel Truett and Eliott Young, *Continental Crossing: Remapping U.S.-Mexico Borderlands History* (Durham, NC: Duke University Press, 2004); the classic work is Herbert E. Bolton, *The Spanish Borderlands: A Chronicle of Old Florida and the Southwest* (New York: United States Publishers Association, 1977; 1921) see also David Weber, *The Mexican Frontier, 1821–1846: The American Southwest Under Mexico* (Albuquerque, NM: University of New Mexico Press, 1982); for some qualifications see Jeremy Adelman and Stephen Aron, "From Borderlands to Borders: Empires, Nation-States, and the Peoples in Between North American History," *American Historical Review* 104 (June 1999), 814–841; the reference to "middle ground" is from Richard White's now classic, *The Middle Ground: Indians, Empires, and Republics in the Great Lakes Region, 1650–1815* (New York: Cambridge University Press, 2011; 1991).
65. Lance R. Blyth, *Chiricahua and Janos: Communities of Violence in the Southwestern Borderlands, 1680–1880* (Lincoln, NE: University of Nebraska Press, 2012), 211; Andrew R. L. Cayton, "Writing Native American History," *Journal of the Early Republic* 22 (Spring 2002), 105–111; Colin G. Calloway, "2008 Presidential Address: Indian History from the End of the Alphabet; And What Now?" *Ethnohistory* 58 (Spring 2011), 197–211. For the dialogue on global, world, and transnational histories, see "AHR Conversation: On Transnational History," *American Historical Review* 111 (December 2006), 1440–1464; Ian Tyrrell, *Transnational Nation: United States History in Global Perspective Since 1789* (New York: Palgrave Macmillan, 2007); Thomas Bender, *A Nation among Nations: America's Place in World History* (New York: Hill and Wang, 2006); Michael Adas, "From Settler Colony to Global Hegemon: Integrating the Exceptionalist Narrative of the American Experience into World History," *American Historical Review* 106 (December 2001), 1692–1720; David Thelen, "The Nation and Beyond: Transnational Perspectives on United States History: A Special Issue," *Journal of American History* 86 (December 1999).
66. Nicole M. Guidotti-Hernandez, *Unspeakable Violence: Remapping the U.S. and Mexican National Imaginaries* (Durham, NC Duke University Press, 2011), 30.
67. James F. Brooks, *Captives and Cousins: Slavery, Kinship, and Community in the Southwest Borderlands* (Chapel Hill, NC: University of North Carolina Press, 2002), 3; and passim.
68. See Chapter 2.
69. R. Brian Ferguson and Neil L. Whitehead, *War in the Tribal Zone: Expanding States and Indigenous Warfare* (Santa Fe, NM: School of American Research Press, 1992), 3; see also Chapter 2.
70. Frederick E. Hoxie, "Retrieving the Red Continent: Settler Colonialism and the History of American Indians in the U.S.," *Ethnic and Racial Studies* 31 (2008), 1153–1167; Calloway, "2008 Presidential Address"; Joseph Genetin-Pilawa, *Crooked Paths to Allotment: The Fight Over Federal Indian Policy after the Civil War* (Chapel Hill, NC: University of North Carolina Press, 2012), 9. See also Nancy Shoemaker, "Categories," in Shoemaker, ed., *Clearing a Path: Theorizing the Past in Native American Studies* (New York: Routledge, 2002), 51–74.
71. Berkhofer, Jr., *White Man's Indian*, 176; Peka Håmålåinen *The Comanche Empire* (New Haven, CT: Yale University Press, 2008), 369n.
72. Richter, *Facing East*; Bernard DeVoto Introduction to Joseph K. Howard, *Strange Empire: A Narrative of the Northwest* (Westport, CT: Greenwood Press, 1974; 1952), 8–9.

73. Kerwin Lee Klein, *Frontiers of Historical Imagination: Narrating the European Conquest of Native America, 1890–1990* (Berkeley, CA: University of California Press, 1997), 211.
74. Hoxie, "Red Continent;" Ian Tyrrell, "Beyond the View from Euro-America: Environment, Settler Societies, and the Internationalization of American History," in Bender, ed., *Rethinking American History in Global Age,* 168–191; Michael Adas, "From Settler Colony to Global Hegemon: Integrating the Exceptionalist Narrative of the American Experience into World History," *American Historical Review* 106 (December 2001), 1692–1720; Patricia Nelson Limerick, "Going West and Ending Up Global," *Western Historical Quarterly* 32 (2001), 5–23; Elizabeth A. Fenn, "Whither the Rest of the Continent?" *Journal of the Early Republic* 24 (2004), 167–175; for a survey of relevant literature, see Paul A. Kramer, "Power and Connection: Imperial Histories of the United States in the World," *American Historical Review* 116 (December 2011), 1348–1391.
75. Karl Jacoby, *Shadows at Dawn: An Apache Massacre and the Violence of History* (New York: Penguin Books, 2008), 2; Ned Blackhawk, *Violence over the Land: Indians and Empires in the Early American West* (Cambridge, MA: Harvard University Press, 2008), 3; Richard White, "The American West and American Empire," in Maybury-Lewis and Macdonald, eds., *Manifest Destinies and Indigenous Peoples,* 204.
76. Carroll P. Kakel, III, *The American West and the Nazi East: A Comparative and Interpretive Perspective* (New York: Palgrave Macmillan, 2011), 179; Gray H. Whaley, *Oregon and the Collapse of Illahee: U.S. Empire and the Transformation of an Indigenous World, 1792–1859* (Chapel Hill, NC: University of North Carolina Press, 2010), 226.
77. In addition to the works cited below see the broad range of essays in Dan Stone, ed., *The Historiography of Genocide* (New York: Palgrave Macmillan, 2008). Other comprehensive studies include Michael Mann, *The Dark Side of Democracy: Explaining Ethnic Cleansing* (Cambridge, UK: Cambridge University Press, 2005); Ben Kiernan, *Blood and Soil: A World History of Genocide and Extermination from Sparta to Darfur* (New Haven, CT: Yale University Press, 2007); and Daniel Jonah Goldhagen, *Worse Than War: Genocide, Eliminationism, and the Ongoing Assault on Humanity* (New York: Public Affairs, 2009).
78. John Docker, *The Origins of Violence: Religion, History and Genocide* (London: Pluto Press, 2008), 2. "The hour hand, which historians largely ignore, is the evolution of human beings as a species," David Courtwright reminds us. See David T. Courtwright *Violent Land: Single Men and Social Disorder from the Frontier to the Inner City* (Cambridge, MA: Harvard University Press, 1996), 7. The apes that are our human forbears engage in indiscriminate violence, aggressive raids, even search and destroy operations. With human evolution thousands of years ago, as expanding agricultural-commercial societies encountered hunter-gatherer societies, settler colonial type violent conflicts erupted over possession of the land. See Jane Goodall, *50 Years at Gombe* (New York: Stewart, Tobaori and Chang, 2010); Jared Diamond, *The Third Chimpanzee: Evolution and Future of the Human Animal* (New York: Harper-Collins, 1992); and Hugh Brody, *The Other Side of Eden: Hunters, Farmers, and the Shaping of the World* (New York: North Point Press, 2000).
79. Docker, *Origins of Violence,* 130, 115, 122.
80. United Nations, "Convention on the Prevention and Punishment of the Crime of Genocide," 1948, http://www.un.org/millennium/law/iv-1.htm
81. On Argentina, see Claudio N. Briones and Walter Delrio, "The 'Conquest of the Desert' as a Trope and Enactment of Argentina's Manifest Destiny," in Maybury-Lewis, Macdonald, and Maybury-Lewis, eds., *Manifest Destinies and Indigenous Peoples,* 51–83 and Ricardo D. Salvatore, "The Unsettling Location of a Settler Nation: Argentina

from Settler Economy to Failed Developing Nation." *South Atlantic Quarterly* 107, 755–789. In the late nineteenth century, Argentinians drove indigenes out of Pampa and Patagonia through settlement and direct military aggression memorialized in Argentine history as the "Conquest of the Desert" (eliding the conquest of *people*). When Argentines did acknowledge indigenous people, they depicted them, as in other settler colonial settings, as savages doomed to extinction. Argentines conducted murders and massacres, massive deportations and confinement as well as separation of families and other de-tribalization measures, all of which have been obscured in Argentine history.

82. Moses, ed., *Empire, Colony, Genocide*; Norman Finkelstein, *The Holocaust Industry: Reflections on the Exploitation of Jewish Suffering* (London: Verso, 2000); Gudrun Kramer, *A History of Palestine: From the Ottoman Conquest to the Founding of the State of Israel* (Princeton, NJ: Princeton University Press, 2011); Schlomo Sand, *The Invention of the Jewish People* (London: Verso, 2010); Lorenzo Veracini, *Israel and Settler Society* (London: Pluto Press, 2006); and Avi Shlaim, *Israel and Palestine: Reappraisals, Revisions, Refutations* (London: Verso, 2009).
83. Jürgen Zimmerer, "The Birth of Ostland out of the Spirit of Colonialism: a Postcolonial Perspective on the Nazi Policy of Conquest and Extermination," in Moses, ed., *Empire, Colony, Genocide*, 115; Kakel, *American West and Nazi East*, 218.
84. Kakel, *American West and Nazi East*, 7, 216–218; see also Jens-Uwe Guettel, "From the Frontier to German South-West Africa: German Colonialism, Indians, and American Westward Expansion," *Modern Intellectual History*, 7 (2010), 523–552.
85. Shelley Baranowski argues that the Nazi "Final Solution" evolved from a "confluence of roadblocks" to the colonial project in the quest for *Lebensraum*. See *Nazi Empire: German Colonialism and Imperialism from Bismarck to Hitler* (New York: Cambridge University Press, 2011), 297. See also Kakel, *American West and Nazi East*, 212–228; Zimmerer, "Birth of Ostland: Postcolonial Perspective on Nazi Policy of Conquest and Extermination"; and Arno Mayer, *Why Did the Heavens Not Darken? The Final Solution in History* (New York: Pantheon, 1988).
86. Philip G. Dwyer and Lyndall Ryan, "Introduction: The Massacre in History," in Dwyer and Ryan, eds., *Theatres of Violence: Massacre*, xi–xxv; Tatz, "Genocide in Australia," 60.
87. Weaver, *Great Land Rush*, 148.
88. McClintock, *Imperial Leather*, 8; Geoff Eley, *A Crooked Line: From Cultural History to the History of Society* (Ann Arbor,MI: University of Michigan Press, 2005), 155; See also Dominick LaCapra, *Writing History, Writing Trauma* (Baltimore, MD: Johns Hopkins University Press, 2001).
89. Ashis Nandy, *The Intimate Enemy: Loss and Recovery of Self under Colonialism* (Delhi, New York: Oxford University Press, 1983), xi, xxi; Veracini, *Settler Colonialism*, 76–81; see also Maria Teresa Savio Hooke and Salman Akhtar, *The Geography of Meanings: Psychoanalytic Perspectives on Place, Space, Land, and Dislocation* (London: International Psychoanalytic Association, 2007).
90. Nandy, *Intimate Enemy*, 30.
91. Pease, *New American Exceptionalism*; Anders Stephanson, *Manifest Destiny: American Expansion and the Empire of Right* (New York: Harper Collins, 1995); Rutherford, *The Gauche Intruder*, 26; on Zionism see footnote 83 above.
92. Rutherford, *The Gauche Intruder*, 10; see also Richard Feldstein, Maire Jaanus, and Bruce Fink, eds., *Reading Seminars I and II: Lacan's Return to Freud* (Albany, NY: State University of New York Press, 1996); Sean Homer, *Jacques Lacan* (New York: Routledge, 2005); Slavoj Zizek, *How to Read Lacan* (New York: Norton, 2006); Zizek, "Superego by

Default," in *The Metastases of Enjoyment: Six Essays on Women and Causality* (London and New York: Verso, 2005; 1994); Zizek, *Looking Awry: An Introduction to Jacques Lacan through Popular Culture* (Boston, MA: MIT Press, 1991); Zizek, *The Sublime Object of Ideology* (New York: Verso, 1989).

93. Loomba, *Colonialism/Postcolonialism*, 119; Mary-Jo DelVecchio Good, Sandra Teresa Hyde, Sarah Pinto, and Byron J. Good, eds., *Postcolonial Disorders* (Berkeley, CA: University of California Press, 2008), 106; Octave Mannoni, *Prospero and Caliban: The Psychology of Colonization* (Ann Arbor, MI: University of Michigan Press, 1990; 1950), vi, 98, 106; see also Philip Chassler, "Reading Mannoni's Prospero and Caliban Before Reading Black Skin, White Masks," *Human Architecture: Journal of the Sociology of Self-Knowledge* 5 (June 2007), 71–81.
94. Zizek, *How to Read Lacan*, 105.
95. DeLoria, *Playing Indian*, 37.
96. Johnson and Lawson, "Settler Colonies," 374; DelVecchio Good, Hyde, Pinto, and Good, eds., *Postcolonial Disorders*, 6.
97. Abigail Ward, "Psychological Fomulations," in McLeod, ed., *Routledge Companion to Postcolonial Studies*, 201.
98. Tzvetan Todorov, *The Conquest of America: The Question of the Other* (New York: Harper and Row, 1984), 4.

Chapter 2

1. No one knows precisely when human habitation began in North America. The most common estimates are 12,000–14,000 years ago, very likely as a result of migration across the Bering Strait land bridge.
2. Charles C. Mann, *1491: New Revelations of the Americas* (New York: Vintage Books, 2006).
3. The above generalizations are based on readings cited through the chapter.
4. Timothy Pauketat, *Cahokia: Ancient America's Great City on the Mississippi* (New York: Penguin, 2009), 13; Pauketat and Thomas R. Emerson, *Cahokia: Domination and Ideology in the Mississippian World* (Lincoln, NE: University of Nebraska Press, 1997), 267, 269, 278.
5. John F. Scarry, ed., *Political Structure and Change in the Prehistoric Southeastern United States* (Gainesville, FL: University Press of Florida, 1996), 245.
6. Matthew Jennings, "Violence in a Shattered World," in Robbie Ethridge, "Introduction," in Robbie Ethridge and Sheri M. Shuck-Hall, eds., *Mapping the Mississippian Shatter Zone: The Colonial Indian Slave Trade and Regional Instability in the American South* (Lincoln, NE: University of Nebraska Press, 2009), 272.
7. Ibid., 274; Robbie Ethridge, "The Making of a Militaristic Slaving Society," in Alan Gallay, ed., *Indian Slavery in Colonial America* (Lincoln, NE: University of Nebraska Press, 2009), 245; Scarry, *Political Structure and Change in Prehistoric Southeastern United States*, 181.
8. Robbie Ethridge, "Afterword," in Ethridge and Shuck-Hall, eds., *Mapping Mississippian Shatter Zone*, 421.
9. These generalizations are drawn from the scores of works cited throughout this and subsequent chapters. See especially Armstrong Starkey, *European and Native American Warfare* (Norman, OK: University of Oklahoma Press, 1998); and Alan Taylor, *American Colonies: The Settling of North America* (New York: Penguin, 2001), 3–66.

10. Alan Gallay, *The Indian Slave Trade: The Rise of the English Empire in the American South, 1670–1717* (New Haven, CT: Yale University Press, 2002), 308.
11. David H. Dye, "Warfare in the Protohistoric Southeast, 1500–1700," in Cameron B. Wesson and Mark A. Rees, eds., *Between Contacts and Colonies: Archaeological Perspectives in the Protohistoric Southeast* (Tuscaloosa, AL: University of Alabama Press, 2002), 141.
12. See Stuart Hall and Paul du Gay, eds., *Questions of Cultural Identity* (Thousand Oaks, CA: Sage Publications, 1996) and Nancy Shoemaker, "Categories," in Shoemaker, ed., *Clearing a Path: Theorizing the Past in Native American Studies* (New York: Routledge, 2002), 51–74;); for a classic account of the colonial binary see Roy Harvey Pearce, *The Savages of America: A Study of the Indian and the Idea of Civilization* (Baltimore, MD: The Johns Hopkins University Press, 1953).
13. Jerald T. Milanich, *Florida Indians and the Invasion from Europe* (Gainesville, FL: University Press of Florida, 1995).
14. Jennings, "Violence in Shattered World," 278, 279; Patricia Galloway, ed., *The Hernando de Soto Expedition: History, Historiography, and "Discovery" in the Southeast* (Lincoln, NE: University of Nebraska Press, 1997); for a first-hand account of the Soto expedition see Rodrigo Rangel, "Account of the Northern Conquest and Discovery of Hernando de Soto (c. 1546)," in Colin G. Calloway, ed., *First Peoples: A Documentary Survey of American Indian History* (New York: Bedford-St. Martin's, 3d ed., 2008), 108–112.
15. J. H. Elliott, *Empires of the Atlantic World: Britain and Spain in America, 1492–1830* (New Haven, CT: Yale University Press, 2006), 38–44; Taylor, *American Colonies*, 50–90; David J. Weber, *The Spanish Frontier in North America* (New Haven, CT: Yale University Press, 1992).
16. David J. Weber, *Barbaros: Spaniards and the Savages in the Age of Enlightenment* (New Haven, CT: Yale University Press, 2005).
17. Gary Clayton Anderson, *The Indian Southwest, 1580–1830: Ethnogenesis and Reinvention* (Norman, OK: University of Oklahoma Press, 1999), 82, 91; Weber, *Barbaros*, 84.
18. Calloway, *First Peoples*, 88–92; Edward Countryman, "The Pueblo Revolt," http://www.gilderlehrman.org/history-by-era/early-settlements/essays/pueblo-revolt.
19. Weber, *Barbaros*, 5–6.
20. Galloway, "Introduction," in Patricia Galloway, ed., *LaSalle and His Legacy: Frenchmen and Indians in the Lower Mississippi Valley* (Jackson, MS: University Press of Mississippi, 1982), xii, xiii.
21. Cornelius J. Jaenen, "Amerindians View of French Culture in the Seventeenth Century," in Peter C. Mancall and James H. Merrell, eds., *American Encounters: Natives and Newcomers from European Contact to Indian Removal, 1500–1850* (New York: Routledge, 2000), 91; see Taylor, *American Colonies*, 363–395; Richard White, *The Middle Ground: Indians, Empires, and Republics in the Great Lakes Region, 1650–1815* (London: Cambridge University Press, 1991).
22. Timothy J. Shannon, *Iroquois Diplomacy on the Early American Frontier* (New York: Viking, 2008), 30–38; Calloway, *First Peoples*, 98.
23. Thomas S. Abler, "Beavers and Muskets: Iroquois Military Fortunes in the Face of European Colonization," 151–174; R. Brian Ferguson and Neil L. Whitehead, *War in the Tribal Zone: Expanding States and Indigenous Warfare* (Santa Fe, NM: School of American Research Press, 1992), 159.
24. Shannon, *Iroquois Diplomacy*, 32–33.
25. Elliott, *Empires of the Atlantic World*, 38–44; Taylor, *American Colonies*, 50–90; Weber, *Spanish Frontier in North America*.

26. Elliott, *Empires of the Atlantic World*, 47; James Mahoney, *Colonialism and Postcolonial Development: Spanish America in Comparative Perspective* (Cambridge, UK: Cambridge University Press, 2010), 235.
27. Karen Ordahl Kupperman, "International at the Creation: Early Modern American History" in Thomas Bender, ed., *Rethinking American History in a Global Age* (Berkeley, CA: University of California Press, 2002), 103–122; Helen C. Rountree and E. Randolph Turner, III, "On the Fringe of the Southeast: The Powhatan Paramount Chiefdom in Virginia," in Charles Hudson and Carmen Chaves Tesser, eds., *The Forgotten Centuries: Indians and Europeans in the American South, 1521–1704* (Athens, GA: University of Georgia Press, 1994), 355–372.
28. Karen Ordahl Kupperman, *The Jamestown Project* (Cambridge, MA: Harvard University Press, 2007), 210–240.
29. Daniel Richter, *Facing East from Indian Country: A Native History of Early America* (Cambridge, MA: Harvard University Press, 2001), 69–78.
30. Kupperman, *Jamestown Project*, 253–254; see also Kathleen M. Brown, *Good Wives, Nasty Wenches, and Anxious Patriarchs: Gender, Race, and Power in Colonial Virginia* (Chapel Hill, NC: University of North Carolina Press, 1996).
31. Ibid., 287, 295.
32. Jon Reyhner and Jeanne Eder, *American Indian Education: A History* (Norman, OK: University of Oklahoma Press, 2004), 25–26; Kupperman, *Jamestown Project*, 295–299.
33. John Smith, "Of the Natural Inhabitants of Virginia," in Brett Rushforth and Paul W. Map, eds., *Colonial North America and the Atlantic World: A History in Documents* (Upper Saddle River, NJ: Pearson, 2009), 91; John Ferling, *Struggle for a Continent: The Wars of Early America* (Arlington Heights, IL: Harlan Davidson, 1993), 19–21.
34. Richter, *Facing East from Indian Country*, 75; Taylor, *American Colonies*, 135.
35. Ferling, *Struggle for a Continent*, 21–27; Kupperman, *Jamestown Project*, 304–324.
36. "Nathaniel Bacon Justifies Rebellion," in Rushforth and Map, eds., *Colonial North America and the Atlantic World*, 104–105.
37. Taylor, *American Colonies*, 138–157.
38. William Bradford, *Of Plymouth Plantation*, Samuel E. Morison, ed., (New York: Knopf, 1952).
39. Alfred Cave, *The Pequot War* (Amherst, MA: University of Massachusetts Press, 1996), 11; Ferling, *Struggle for a Continent*, 28.
40. Cave, *Pequot War*, 1–12.
41. Bradford, *Of Plymouth Plantation*, 296; Ferling, *Struggle for a Continent*, 36–38; Calloway, *First Peoples*, 102.
42. Cave, *Pequot War*, 3, 168.
43. Reyhner and Eder, *American Indian Education*, 26–34.
44. Richter, *Facing East from Indian Country*, 90–105.
45. Jenny Hale Pulsipher, *Subjects unto the Same King: Indians, English, and the Contest for Authority in Colonial New England* (Philadelphia, PA: University of Pennsylvania Press, 2005), 118.
46. Pulsipher, *Subjects unto the Same King*, 134, 190; King Philip's speech quoted in Calloway, *First Peoples*, 134.
47. John Grenier, *The First Way of War: American War Making on the Frontier, 1670–1840* (New York: Cambridge University Press, 2005), 43.
48. Ann M. Little, *Abraham in Arms: War and Gender in Colonial New England* (Philadelphia, PA: University of Pennsylvania Press, 2007), 7–8; Gina Martino-Trutor, "'Her Extraordinary Sufferings and Services': Women and War in New England and New France," PhD diss., University of Minnesota, 2013.

49. Ferling, *Struggle for a Continent*, 52.
50. Jill Lepore, *In the Name of War: King Philip's War and the Origins of American Identity* (New York: Vintage, 1999), ix–xvi; 173–178; Ferling, *Struggle for a Continent*, 57; Pulsipher, *Subjects unto the Same King*, 236.
51. Pulsipher, *Subjects unto the Same King*, 158; Grenier, *First Way of War*, 43; "Minister Daniel Gookin Discusses the Dilemmas Confronting Christian Indians," in Rushforth and Map, eds., *Colonial North America and the Atlantic World*, 152.
52. Pulsipher, *Subjects unto the Same King*, 112; Daniel R. Mandell, *King Philip's War: Colonial Expansion, Native Resistance, and the End of Indian Sovereignty* (Baltimore, MD: The Johns Hopkins University Press, 2010), 144; Lepore, *In the Name of War*, xiv.
53. Margaret Newell, "Indian Slavery in Colonial New England," in Gallay, ed., *Indian Slavery in Colonial America*, 47; Lepore, *In the Name of War*, 182.
54. Jean M. O'Brien, *Dispossession by Degrees: Indian Land and Identity in Natick, Massachusetts, 1650–1790* (Lincoln, NE: University of Nebraska Press, 1997), 6.
55. Taylor, *American Colonies*, 252.
56. Donna Merwick, *The Shame and the Sorrow: Dutch-Amerindian Encounters in New Netherland* (Philadelphia, PA: University of Pennsylvania Press, 2006); Taylor, *American Colonies*, 255.
57. Gunlog Fur, *Colonialism in the Margins: Cultural Encounters in New Sweden and Lapland* (Leiden, The Netherlands: Brill, 2006), 247–277; Lorraine E. Williams, "Indians and Europeans in the Delaware Valley, 1620–1655," in Carol E. Hoffecker, et al., ed., *New Sweden in America* (Newark, NJ: University of Delaware Press, 1995), 112–120.
58. Gallay, ed., *Indian Slavery in Colonial America*, 2–3.
59. Ethridge and Shuck-Hall, eds., *Mapping the Mississippian Shatter Zone*, 1–2.
60. Ferguson and Whitehead, *War in the Tribal Zone*, 159; Ethridge, *Mapping the Mississippi Shatter Zone*, 20.
61. Christina Snyder, *Slavery in Indian Country: The Changing Face of Captivity in Early America* (Cambridge, MA: Harvard University Press, 2010), 13–45; Jennings, "Violence in Shattered World," 289.
62. Gallay, "South Carolina's Entrance into the Indian Slave Trade," in Gallay, ed., *Indian Slavery in Colonial America*, 109.
63. Shannon, *Iroquois Diplomacy*, 14; Ethridge, "Introduction," in Ethridge and Shuck-Hall, eds., *Mapping the Mississippi Shatter Zone*, 1–62; William A. Fox, "Events as Seen from the North: The Iroquois and Colonial Slavery," in Ethridge and Shuck-Hall, eds., *Mapping the Mississippi Shatter Zone*, 63–80.
64. Margaret Newell, "Indian Slavery in Colonial New England," in Gallay, ed., *Indian Slavery in Colonial America*, 33–66.
65. C. S. Everett, "Indian Slaves in Colonial Virginia," in Gallay, ed., *Indian Slavery in Colonial America*, 67–108.
66. Gallay, "South Carolina's Entrance into the Indian Slave Trade"; Jennings, "Violence in Shattered World," 287.
67. Ibid., 125.
68. Ethridge, "Introduction," 24.
69. Denise I. Bossy, "Indian Slavery in Southeastern Indian and British Societies, 1670–1730," in Gallay, ed., *Indian Slavery in Colonial America*, 207–250.
70. Jennings, "Violence in Shattered World," 287.
71. Gallay, "South Carolina's Entrance into the Indian Slave Trade."
72. Milanich, *Florida Indians and Invasion from Europe*, 173, 204.

73. John E. Worth, "Razing Florida: The Indian Slave Trade and the Devastation of Spanish Florida, 1659–1715," in Ethridge and Shuck-Hall, eds., *Mapping Mississippi Shatter Zone*, 295; Milanich, *Florida Indians and Invasion from Europe*, 230.
74. Scarry, "Stability and Change in the Appalachee Chiefdom," in Scarry, ed., *Political Structure and Change in the PreHistoric Southeastern United States* (Gainesville, FL: University Press of Florida, 1996), 192–228; John H. Hahn, "The Apalachee of the Historic Era," in Charles Hudson and Carmen Chaves Tesser, eds., *The Forgotten Centuries: Indians and Europeans in the American South, 1521–1704* (Athens, GA: University of Georgia Pres, 1994), 327–354.
75. Ethridge, "Introduction"; Gallay, "Introduction: Indian Slavery in Historical Context," in Gallay, ed., *Indian Slavery in Colonial America*, 1–32; Vernon James Knight, Jr., "The Formation of the Creeks," in Hudson and Tesser, eds., *Forgotten Centuries*, 373–392; Ned J. Jenkins, "Tracing the Origins of the Early Creeks, 1050–1700 CE," in Ethridge and Shuck-Hall, eds., *Mapping Mississippi Shatter Zone*, 188–249; Tom Hatley, *The Dividing Paths: Cherokees and South Carolinians through the Era of Revolution* (New York: Oxford University Press, 1993), 3–41; Patricia Galloway, "Confederacy as a Solution to Chiefdom Dissolution: Historical Evidence in the Choctaw Case," in Hudson and Tesser, eds., *Forgotten Centuries*, 393–420; Ethridge, "The Making of a Militaristic Slave Society: The Chickasaws and the Colonial Indian Slave Trade," 252–276; Greg O'Brien, ed., *Pre-Removal Choctaw History: Exploring New Paths* (Norman, OK: University of Oklahoma Press, 2008); Maureen Myers, "From Refugees to Slave Traders: The Transformation of the Westo Indians," in Ethridge and Shuck-Hall, eds., *Mapping Mississippi Shatter Zone*, 81–103; Stephen Warren and Randolph Noe, " 'The Greatest Travelers in America': Shawnee Survival in the Shatter Zone," in Ethridge and Shuck-Hall, eds., *Mapping Mississippi Shatter Zone*, 163–187.
76. Shannon, *Iroquois Diplomacy*, 68–73.
77. Bossy, "Indian Slavery in Southeastern Indian and British Societies," 207–250; William L. Ramsey, *The Yamassee War: A Study in Culture, Economy, and Conflict in the Colonial South* (Lincoln, NE: University of Nebraska Press, 2008).
78. Ramsey, *The Yamassee War*; Gallay, *Indian Slave Trade*, 338; Peter H. Wood, *Black Majority: Negroes in Colonial South Carolina from 1670 Through the Stono Rebellion* (New York: Norton, 1996; 1974).
79. Brett Rushforth, "The Origins of Indian Slavery in New France," 353; E. A. S. Demers, "John Askin and Indian Slavery at Michilimackinac," 391; both in Gallay, ed., *Indian Slavery in Colonial America*.
80. Carl J. Ekbert, *Stealing Indian Women: Native Slavery in the Illinois Country* (Urbana and Chicago, IL: University of Illinois Press, 2007), 25–30.
81. Ian Brown, "An Archeological Study of Culture Contact and Change in the Natchez Bluffs Region," in Galloway, ed., *LaSalle and His Legacy*, 176–193; George E. Milne, "Picking Up the Pieces: Natchez Coalescence in the Shatter Zone," in Ethridge and Shuck-Hall, eds., *Mapping Mississippi Shatter Zone*, 388–417; Ethridge, "Introduction," 16.
82. Colin G. Calloway, *New Worlds for All: Indians, Europeans, and the Remaking of Early America* (Baltimore, MD: The Johns Hopkins University Press, 1997), 102, 98.
83. Juliana Barr, "A Spectrum of Indian Bondage in Spanish Texas," in Gallay, ed., *Indian Slavery in Colonial America*, 277–318.
84. Ned Blackhawk, *Violence Over the Land: Indians and Empires in the Early American West* (Cambridge, MA: Harvard University Press, 2008), 70–78, 148.
85. Leland Donald, *Aboriginal Slavery on the Northwest Coast of North America* (Berkeley, CA: University of California Press, 1997), 310–312.
86. Ethridge, "Introduction," 421.

Chapter 3

1. Robert J. Miller, Jacinta Ruru, Larissa Behrendt, and Tracey Lindberg, *Discovering Indigenous Lands: The Doctrine of Discovery in the English Colonies* (New York: Oxford University Press, 2010).
2. Stuart Banner, *How the Indians Lost Their Land: Law and Power on the Frontier* (Cambridge, MA.: Harvard University Press, 2007), 82; see also the path-breaking work by Dorothy Jones, *License for Empire: Colonialism by Treaty in Early America* (Chicago: University of Chicago Press, 1982).
3. I base these generalizations about diplomacy and those that follow on a range of readings, but see especially James H. Merrell, *Into the American Woods* (New York: Norton, 1999); Eric Hinderaker, "Diplomacy Between Britons and Native Americans, c. 1600–1800," in H. V. Bowen, Elizabeth Mancke, and John G. Reid, eds., *Oceanic Empire: Britain's Atlantic and Indian Ocean Worlds* (Cambridge, UK: Cambridge University Press, 2012), 218–248; and Greg O'Brien, "The Conqueror Meets the Unconquered: Negotiating Cultural Boundaries on the Post-Revolutionary Southern Frontier," in O'Brien, ed., *Choctaws in a Revolutionary Age*, 148–182; and Juliana Barr, *Peace Came in the form of a Woman: Indians and Spaniards in the Texas Borderlands* (Chapel Hill, NC: University of North Carolina Press, 2007).
4. O'Brien, "Conqueror Meets the Unconquered," 156–157.
5. See Armstrong Starkey, *European and Native American Warfare, 1675–1815* (Norman, OK: University of Oklahoma Press, 1998); Eliot A. Cohen, *Conquered Into Liberty: Two Centuries of Battles along the Great Warpath That Made the American Way of War* (New York: Free Press, 2011); John E. Ferling, *Struggle for a Continent: The Wars of Early America* (Arlington Heights, IL.: Harlan Davidson, 1993); John Grenier, *The First Way of War: American War Making on the Frontier, 1607–1814* (New York: Cambridge, 2005); Patrick M. Malone, *The Skulking Way of War: Technology and Tactics Among the New England Indians* (Lanham, MD: Madison Books, 1991).
6. Daniel Richter points out that the Anglo-Iroquois covenant was not monolithic but rather ebbed and flowed over time and in different spaces in conjunction with the actions of "individual cultural brokers" and "intercultural politics." Richter, "Cultural Brokers and Intercultural Politics: New York-Iroquois Relations, 1644–1701," *Journal of American History* 75 (June 1988), 40–67; see also Timothy J. Shannon, *Iroquois Diplomacy on the Early American Frontier* (New York: Viking, 2008).
7. Spain declined to ally with France in the French and Indian War mainly out of concern that France would dominate the northwest and thereby access to the Pacific. See Paul W. Mapp, *The Elusive West And the Contest for Empire, 1713–1763* (Chapel Hill, NC: University of North Carolina Press, 2011).
8. Neal Salisbury, "The Indians' Old World: Native Americans and the Coming of Europeans," in Peter C. Mancall and James H. Merrell, eds., *American Encounters: Natives and Newcomers from European Contact to Indian Removal, 1500–1850* (New York: Routledge, 2000), 21.
9. Merrell, *Into the American Woods*, 295, 37–38.
10. Daniel H. Usner, Jr., "The Frontier Exchange Economy in the Lower Mississippi Valley in the Eighteenth Century," in Mancall and Merrill, eds., *American Encounters*, 216–239.
11. Peter Silver, *Our Savage Neighbors: How Indian War Transformed Early America* (New York: W.W. Norton, 2008), 35; Eric Hinderaker, *Elusive Empires: Constructing Colonialism in the Ohio Valley, 1673–1800* (London: Cambridge University Press, 1997), 102, 128.

12. Daniel P. Barr, "'The Land is Ours and Not Yours': The Western Delawares and the Seven Years' War in the Upper Ohio Valley, 1755–1758," in Daniel P. Barr, ed., *The Boundaries Between Us: Natives and Newcomers along the Frontiers of the Old Northwest Territory, 1750–1850* (Kent, OH.: Kent State University Press, 2006), 29; "Disaster in the Forest," in Rushforth and Map, eds., *Colonial North America and the Atlantic World*, 315.
13. As Peter Silver points out, "Almost no one in eighteenth-century America or England seems to have realized that Indian war was designed by its practitioners to be precisely as terrifying as they found it." See Silver, *Our Savage Neighbors*, 57.
14. Silver, *Our Savage Neighbors*, 80–83, 284; Richard White, *The Middle Ground: Indians, Empires, and Republics in the Great Lakes Region, 1650–1815* (London: Cambridge University Press, 1991), 366; Starkey, *European and Native American Warfare*, 112.
15. Silver, *Our Savage Neighbors*, xix–xx.
16. Robert F. Berkhofer, Jr., *The White Man's Indian: Images of the American Indian from Columbus to the Present* (New York: Alfred A. Knopf, 1978), 84–85; Silver, *Our Savage Neighbors*, 80–83; Christina Snyder, *Slavery in Indian Country: The Changing Face of Captivity in Early America* (Cambridge, MA: Harvard University Press, 2010), 4.
17. Fred Anderson, *The Crucible of War: The Seven Years War and the Fate of Empire in British North America, 1754–1766* (New York: Vintage Books, 2000), 185–201; Ian K. Steele, *Betrayals: Fort William Henry and the "Massacre"* (New York: Oxford University Press, 1990).
18. Gregory E. Dowd "'Insidious Friends': Gift Giving and the Cherokee-British Alliance," in Andrew R. L. Clayton and Fredrika J. Teute, eds., *Contact Points: American Frontiers from the Mohawk Valley to the Mississippi, 1750–1830* (Chapel Hill, NC: University of North Carolina Press, 1998), 125.
19. David L. Preston, *The Texture of Contact: European and Indian Settler Communities on the Frontiers of Iroquoia, 1667–1783* (Lincoln, NE: University of Nebraska Press, 2009), 226; Merrell, *Into the Woods*, 247.
20. Grenier, *First Way of War*, 145; Stephen Brumwell, *White Devil: A True Story of War, Savagery, and Vengeance in Colonial America* (Cambridge, MA: Da Capo Press, 2004): 17, 166–167.
21. Brumwell, *White Devil*, 197, 262.
22. W. J. Eccles, "French Imperial Policy for the Great Lakes Basin," 21–41; Keith R. Widder, "The French Connection: The Interior French in the Western Great Lakes Region, 1760–1775," 125–143; and Susan Sleeper-Smith, "'Ignorant Bigots and Busy Rebels': The American Revolution in the Western Great Lakes," 145–165; quotation p. 160, all in David C. Skaggs and Larry L. Nelson, *Sixty Years' War for Great Lakes* (East Lansing, MI: Michigan State University Press, 2001).
23. White, *Middle Ground*; Dowd "Insidious Friends," 150.
24. On this point see Greg O'Brien, "Protecting Trade through War: Choctaw Elites and British Occupation of the Floridas," 103–122, in Greg O'Brien, ed., *Pre-Removal Choctaw History: Exploring New Paths* (Norman, OK: University of Oklahoma Press, 2008).
25. John Oliphant, *Peace and War on the Anglo-Cherokee Frontier, 1756–1763* (London: Palgrave, 2001), 20, 104.
26. Tom Hatley, *The Dividing Paths: Cherokees and South Carolinians through the Era of Revolution* (New York: Oxford University Press, 1993), 101–102.
27. Dowd "Insidious Friends," 114–150; M. Thomas Hatley, "The Three Lives of Keowee: Loss and Recovery in the Eighteenth-Century Cherokee Villages," in Rushforth and Map, eds., *Colonial North America and the Atlantic World*, 240–260.

28. Anderson, *Crucible of War*, 466; Hatley, *Dividing Paths*, 139; Oliphant, *Peace and War on the Anglo-Cherokee Frontier*, 206.
29. James H. Merrell, *The Indians' New World: Catawbas and Their Neighbors from European Contact through the Era of Removal* (Chapel Hill, NC: University of North Carolina Press, 1998), 170, 225.
30. Dixon, "We Speak as One People," 56; Gregory Evans Dowd, *Pontiac, the Indian Nations, and the British Empire* (Baltimore, MD: Johns Hopkins University Press, 2002).
31. Grenier, *First Way of War*, 144–145; Silver, *Our Savage Neighbors*, 132; Anderson, *Crucible of War*, 541–546; E. A. Fenn, "Biological Warfare in Eighteenth-Century North America," *Journal of American History* 86 (June 1999), 552–558; Elizabeth Fenn, *Pox Americana: The Great Smallpox Epidemic of 1775–82* (New York: Hill and Wang, 2001).
32. Gregory Evans Dowd, *War under Heaven: Pontiac, the Indian Nations, and the British Empire* (Baltimore, MD: Johns Hopkins University Press, 2002), 233; John C. Weaver, *The Great Land Rush and the Making of the Modern World, 1650–1900* (Montreal: McGill-Queen's University Press, 2003), 154–156.
33. David Dixon, " 'We Speak as One People': Native Unity and the Pontiac Indian Uprising," in Barr, ed., *Boundaries between Us*, 59; see also Nancy Shoemaker, "How Indians Became Red," *American Historical Review* 102 (June 1997), 625–644; and Shoemaker, *A Strange Likeness: Becoming Red and White in Eighteenth-Century North America* (New York: Oxford University Press, 2004), 141.
34. Colin Calloway, *The Scratch of a Pen: 1763 and the Transformation of North America* (New York: Oxford University Press, 2006), 98.
35. Patrick Griffin, *American Leviathan: Empire, Nation, and Revolutionary Frontier* (New York: Hill and Wang, 2007), 16.
36. White, *Middle Ground*, 317; Calloway, *Scratch of a Pen*, 100.
37. Starkey, *European and Native American Warfare*, 115.
38. R. Douglas Hurt, *The Ohio Frontier: Crucible of the Old Northwest, 1720–1830* (Bloomington, IN: Indiana University Press, 1996), 56.
39. Preston, *Texture of Contact*, 165; Richter, *Facing East*, 201–208; Silver, *Our Savage Neighbors*,172.
40. James Axtell, "The White Indians of Colonial America," in Mancall and Merrell, eds., *American Encounters*, 324–350.
41. White, *Middle Ground*, 351; Shannon, *Iroquois Diplomacy on Early American Frontier*, 168.
42. White, *Middle Ground*, 362, 364.
43. Starkey, *European and Native American Warfare*, 128.
44. Hinderaker, *Elusive Empires*, 186–187.
45. Andrew R. L. Cayton, "The Meanings of the Wars for the Great Lakes," in Skaggs and Nelson, eds., *Sixty Years' War for the Great Lakes*, 388.
46. Alan Taylor, *The Divided Ground: Indians, Settlers, and the Northern Borderland of the American Revolution* (New York: Vintage Books, 2006), 80–88.
47. Glenn F. Williams, *Year of the Hangman: George Washington's Campaign against the Iroquois* (Yardley, PA: Westholme Publishing, 2006), 131.
48. Eric Hinderaker, *The Two Hendricks: Unraveling a Mohawk Mystery* (Cambridge, MA: Harvard University Press, 2010), 10, 16; Preston, *Texture of Contact*; see also Shannon, *Iroquois Diplomacy on Early American Frontier*.
49. Williams, *Year of the Hangman*, 284–294, x.
50. Hinderaker, *Elusive Empires*, 193.

51. Ibid., 208, 211; John Mack Faragher, *Daniel Boone: The Life and Legend of an American Pioneer* (New York: Owl Books, 1992), 156.
52. White, *Middle Ground*, 368–377; on Clark see also the essays in Kenneth C. Carstens and Nancy S. Carstens, eds., *The Life of George Rogers Clark, 1752–1818: Triumphs and Tragedies* (Westport, CT: Praeger, 2004); and Lowell H. Harrison, *George Rogers Clark and the War in the West* (Lexington, KY: University Press of Kentucky, 1976).
53. Silver, *Our Savage Neighbors*, 276.
54. Colin Calloway, *The American Revolution in Indian Country: Crisis and Diversity in Native American Communities* (New York: Cambridge University Press, 1995), 48.
55. See next chapter.
56. Hatley, *Dividing Paths*, 197, 136, 185.
57. Ibid., 192–234; Calloway, *American Revolution in Indian Country*, 290.
58. Hatley, *Dividing Paths*, 192–234; Hatley, "Three Lives of Keowee," 240–260; William G. McGloughlin, "Cherokee Anomie, 1794–1810: New Roles for Red Men, Red Women, and Black Slaves," in Rushforth and Map, eds., *Colonial North America and the Atlantic World*, 453–476.
59. White, *Middle Ground*, 276.
60. Hurt, *Ohio Frontier*, 98–99; Faragher, *Daniel Boone*, 254.
61. Faragher, *Daniel Boone*, 121, 170–174, 251–254.
62. Cayton, "Meanings of Wars for Great Lakes," 382.

Chapter 4

1. Kevin Bruyneel, *The Third Space of Sovereignty: The Post-Colonial Politics of U.S.-Indigenous Relations* (Minneapolis, MN: University of Minnesota Press, 2007), 8.
2. Alan Taylor, *Divided Ground: Indians, Settlers, and the Northern Borderland of the American Revolution* (New York: Vintage Books, 2006), 107; J. Edward Chamberlin, "Homeland and Frontier," in David Maybury-Lewis, Theodore Macdonald, and Biorn Maybury-Lewis, eds., *Manifest Destinies and Indigenous Peoples* (Cambridge, MA: Harvard University Press, 2009), 194.
3. John C. Weaver, *The Great Land Rush and the Making of the Modern World, 1650–1900* (Montreal: McGill-Queen's University Press, 2003), 159–160; Colin Calloway, *The American Revolution in Indian Country: Crisis and Diversity in Native American Communities* (New York: Cambridge University Press, 1995), 293.
4. http://www.law.cornell.edu/wex/commerce_clause; Frank Pommersheim, *Broken Landscape: Indians, Indian Tribes, and the Constitution* (New York: Oxford University Press, 2009), 33–86; Cynthia Cumfer, "Local Origins of National Indian Policy: Cherokee and Tennessean Ideas about Sovereignty and Nationhood, 1790–1811," *Journal of the Early Republic* 23 (Spring 2003), 21–46.
5. Stuart Banner, *How the Indians Lost Their Land: Law and Power on the Frontier* (Cambridge, MA: Harvard University Press, 2005), 113; Dorothy V. Jones, *License for Empire: Colonialism by Treaty in Early America* (Chicago: University of Chicago Press, 1982), 186.
6. Banner, *How Indians Lost Their Land*, 112; Taylor, *Divided Ground*, 10.
7. Elizabeth Fenn, *Pox Americana: The Great Smallpox Epidemic of 1775–1782* (New York: Hill and Wang, 2001), 260–261; Paul Grant-Costa and Elizabeth Mancke, "Anglo-Amerindian Commercial Relations," in H. V. Bowen, Elizabeth Mancke, and John G. Reid, eds., *Oceanic Empire: Britain's Atlantic and Indian Ocean Worlds* (Cambridge, UK: Cambridge University Press, 2012), 372.

8. Text of the Northwest Ordinance online at: http://www.historyplace.com/unitedstates/revolution/nwest-ord.htm
9. Frazier D. McGlinchey, "'A Superior Civilization': Appropriation, Negotiation, and Interaction in the Northwest Territory, 1787–1795," in Daniel P. Barr, ed., *The Boundaries Between Us: Natives and Newcomers along the Frontiers of the Old Northwest Territory, 1750–1850* (Kent, OH: Kent State University Press, 2006), 126–127.
10. Robert J. Miller, Jacinta Ruru, Larissa Behrendt, and Tracey Lindberg, *Discovering Indigenous Lands: The Doctrine of Discovery in the English Colonies* (New York: Oxford University Press, 2010), 26.
11. Anders Stephanson, *Manifest Destiny: American Expansionism and the Empire of Right* (New York: Hill and Wang, 1995), 33.
12. Robert M. Owens, "Jeffersonian Benevolence on the Ground: The Indian Land Cession Treaties of William Henry Harrison," *Journal of the Early Republic* 22 (Autumn 2002), 405–435.
13. Anthony F.C. Wallace, *Jefferson and the Indians: The Tragic Fate of the First Americans* (Cambridge, MA: Harvard University Press, 1999), 1–20, viii.
14. Taylor, *Divided Ground*, 245.
15. Richard White, *The Middle Ground: Indians, Empires, and Republics in the Great Lakes Region, 1650–1815* (London: Cambridge University Press, 1991), 416.
16. Ibid., 418; R. Douglas Hurt, *The Ohio Frontier: Crucible of the Old Northwest, 1720–1830* (Bloomington, IN: Indiana University Press, 1996), 104.
17. Stephen Aron, *How the West Was Lost: The Transformation of Kentucky from Daniel Boone to Henry Clay* (Baltimore, MD: The Johns Hopkins University Press, 1996), 49–50.
18. Lisa Brooks, "Two Paths to Peace: Competing Visions of Native Space in the Old Northwest," in Barr, ed., *Boundaries Between Us*, 92; Taylor, *Divided Ground*, 281–282.
19. Armstrong Starkey, *European and Native American Warfare, 1675–1815* (Norman, OK: University of Oklahoma Press, 1998), 137–149; Hurt, *Ohio Frontier*, 111–118.
20. Hurt, *Ohio Frontier*, 133.
21. Andrew R. L. Cayton, "The Meaning of the Wars for the Great Lakes," in David C. Skaggs and Larry L. Nelson, eds., *Sixty Years' War for Great Lakes* (East Lansing, MI: Michigan State University Press, 2001), 386.
22. White, *Middle Ground*, 458; Colin G. Calloway, *The Shawnees and the War for America* (New York: Penguin, 2007), 85–108.
23. "'Mad Anthony' Wayne's Campaign against the Indians in Ohio, 1792–1794," by H.L. Robb, Captain, Corps of Engineers, November 1921, Box 8, Order of Indian Wars (OWI) Collection, United States Army Military History Institute, Carlisle Barracks, Pa. Hereafter cited as Carlisle Barracks; Calloway, *Shawnees and War for America*, 95–105.
24. Calloway, *Shawnees and War for America*, 87, 105; see also John Sugden, *Blue Jacket: Warrior of the Shawnees* (Lincoln, NE: University of Nebraska Press, 2000).
25. Andrew R. L. Cayton, *Frontier Indiana* (Bloomington, IN: Indiana University Press, 1996), 157.
26. Stephen Warren, "The Ohio Shawnees' Struggle against Removal, 1814–1830," in R. David Edmunds, ed., *Enduring Nations: Native Americans in the Midwest* (Champaign, IL: University of Illinois Press, 2008), 72–93; Andrew R. L. Cayton, "'Noble Actors' upon 'The Theatre of Honor': Power and Civility in the Treaty of Greenville," in Cayton and Fredrika Teute, eds., *Contact Points: American Frontiers from the Mohawk Valley to the Mississippi, 1750–1830* (Chapel Hill, NC: University of North Carolina Press, 1998), 235–269.
27. Cayton, *Frontier Indiana*, 199–200; White, *Middle Ground*, 489.

28. Alan Taylor, *The Civil War of 1812: American Citizens, British Subjects, Irish Rebels, and Indian Allies* (New York: Alfred A. Knopf, 2010), 126; Cayton, *Frontier Indiana*, 202.
29. R. David Edmunds, *The Shawnee Prophet* (Lincoln, NE: University of Nebraska Press, 1983); R. David Edmunds, *Tecumseh and the Quest for Indian Leadership* (New York: Pearson-Longman, 2007); Gregory Evans Dowd, *A Spirited Resistance: The North American Indian Struggle for Unity, 1745–1815* (Baltimore, MD: The Johns Hopkins University Press, 1992), xv, 33.
30. On Tecumseh see Edmunds, *The Shawnee Prophet* and John Sugden, *Tecumseh: A Life* (New York: Henry Holt, 1997); Cayton, *Frontier Indiana*, 218–219.
31. William Henry Harrison, "Official Report of the Campaign and Battle of Tippecanoe," November 8, 1811, Box 11, OWI, Carlisle Barracks; Taylor, *Civil War of 1812*, 127; Calloway, *Shawnees and War for America*, 140.
32. Taylor, *Civil War of 1812*, 126–128.
33. Ibid., 126; 203–233; Ben Kiernan, *Blood and Soil: A World History of Genocide and Extermination from Sparta to Darfur* (New Haven, CT: Yale University Press, 2007), 375.
34. Taylor, *Civil War of 1812*, 210–217; Starkey, *European and Native American Warfare*, 161.
35. Starkey, *European and Native American Warfare*, 162.
36. Taylor, *Civil War of 1812*, 409–440.
37. Steven Watt, *The Republic Reborn: War and the Making of Liberal America, 1790–1820* (Baltimore, MD: Johns Hopkins University Press, 1987), 283.
38. David C. Skaggs, "The Sixty Years' War for the Great Lakes, 1754–1814: An Overview," in Skaggs and Nelson, eds., *Sixty Years' War for the Great Lakes*, 17.
39. Taylor, *Civil War of 1812*, 409–440.
40. The Treaty of Ghent can be accessed online at: http://avalon.law.yale.edu/19th_century/ghent.asp
41. Brian L. Dunnigan, "Fortress Detroit, 1701–1826," in Skaggs and Nelson, eds., *Sixty Years War for Great Lakes*, 167–185.
42. Taylor, *Civil War of 1812*, 10; Warren, "Ohio Shawnees' Struggle against Removal."
43. R. David Edmunds, "Forgotten Allies: The Loyal Shawnees and the War of 1812," in Skaggs and Nelson, eds., *Sixty Years War for Great Lakes*, 337–351.
44. Warren, "Ohio Shawnees' Struggle against Removal."
45. Edmunds, "Forgotten Allies: Loyal Shawnees and the War of 1812," 347; Warren, "Ohio Shawnees' Struggle against Removal"; Dowd, *Spirited Resistance*, 194.
46. Dana D. Nelson, *National Manhood: Capitalist Citizenship and the Imagined Fraternity of White Men* (Durham, NC: Duke University Press, 1998) and Michael A. Morrison and James B. Stewart, eds., *Race and the Early Republic: Racial Consciousness and Nation-Building in the Early Republic* (Lanham, MD: Rowan and Littlefield, 2002); David R. Roediger, *The Wages of Whiteness: Race and the Making of the American Working Class* (London: Verso, 2007); Noel Ignatiev, *How the Irish Became White* (New York: Routledge, 1995).
47. See Chapter II.
48. Susan Sleeper-Smith, "Resistance to Removal: The 'White Indian,' Frances Slocum," in Edmunds, ed., *Enduring Nations*, 109–123.
49. Warren, "The Ohio Shawnees' Struggle against Removal"; James Belich, *Replenishing the Earth: The Settler Revolution and the Rise of the Anglo World, 1783–1939* (New York: Oxford University Press, 2009), 226.
50. John W. Hall, *Uncommon Defense: Indian Allies in the Black Hawk War* (Cambridge, MA: Harvard University Press, 2009), 244–245.

51. Patrick J. Jung, *The Black Hawk War of 1832* (Norman, NE: University of Oklahoma Press, 2007), 172–174; Thomas B. Colbert, "The Hinge on Which All the Affairs of the Sauk and Fox Indians Turn: Keokuk and the United States Government," in Edmunds, ed., *Enduring Nations*, 67.
52. R. David Edmunds, *The Potawatomis, Keepers of the Fire* (Norman, OK: University of Oklahoma Press, 1978); Hall, *Uncommon Defense*, 236; Jung, *The Black Hawk War*, 185.
53. Calloway, *American Revolution in Indian Country*, 197, 290.
54. John Grenier, *The First Way of War: American War Making on the Frontier, 1607–1814* (New York: Cambridge University Press, 2005), 182.
55. Theda Perdue and Michael D. Green, *The Cherokee Nation and the Trail of Tears* (New York: Penguin Books, 2007), 48.
56. Claudio Saunt, *A New Order of Things: Property, Power, and the Transformation of the Creek Nations, 1733–1816* (Cambridge, UK: Cambridge University Press, 1999), 69, 205–206, 272.
57. Andrew Burstein, *The Passions of Andrew Jackson* (New York: Vintage Books, 2003), 106.
58. Ibid., 16, 90.
59. David J. Weber, *Barbaros: Spaniards and the Savages in the Age of Enlightenment* (New Haven, CT: Yale University Press, 2005), 215–217.
60. James G. Cusick, *The Other War of 1812: The Patriot War and the American Invasion of Spanish East Florida* (Gainesville, FL: University Press of Florida, 2003), 8, 219, 278; see also J. C. A. Stagg, *Borderlines in Borderlands: James Madison and the Spanish-American Frontier, 1776–1821* (New Haven, CT: Yale University Press, 2009), 52–133; John Missall and Mary Lou Missall, *The Seminole Wars: America's Longest Indian Conflict* (Gainesville, FL: University Press of Florida, 2004), 245; see also Andrew F. McMichael, *Americans in Spanish West Florida, 1785–1810* (Athens, GA: University of Georgia Press, 2008).
61. Saunt, *New Order of Things*, 288.
62. Scholars disagree on the body count. Claudio Saunt cites the figure of 40 deaths whereas John and Mary Lou Missall put the figure at more than 250. See Saunt, *New Order of Things*, 288; and, Missall and Missall, *Seminole Wars*, 30. Historical markers at the Negro Fort site use the figure of 300.
63. Missall and Missall, *Seminole Wars*, 30; David S. and Jeanne T. Heidler, *Old Hickory's War: Andrew Jackson and the Quest for Empire* (Baton Rouge, LA: Louisiana State University Press, 1996), 154, 203.
64. An abundant literature exists on Jackson and the Indians. Two standard accounts are Robert V. Remini, *Andrew Jackson and His Indian Wars* (New York: Viking, 2001) and Anthony F. C. Wallace, *The Long, Bitter Trail: Andrew Jackson and the Indians* (New York: Hill and Wang, 1993).
65. William E. Unrau, *The Rise and Fall of Indian Country, 1825–1855* (Lawrence, KS: University Press of Kansas, 2007), 61–62; Alfred A. Cave, "Abuse of Power: Andrew Jackson and the Indian Removal Act of 1830," *The Historian* 65 (Winter 2003), 1330–1353; Removal Act (1830) online: https://www.mtholyoke.edu/acad/intrel/removal.htm
66. Brian W. Dippie, *The Vanishing American: White Attitudes and U.S. Indian Policy* (Lawrence, KS: University Press of Kansas, 1982), 61–70.
67. Mary Hershberger, "Mobilizing Women, Anticipating Abolition: The Struggle against Indian Removal in the 1830s," *Journal of American History* 86 (June 1999), 15–40; Natalie Joy, "Cherokee Slaveholders and Radical Abolitionists," http://www.commonplace.org/vol-10/no-04/joy/.

68. Clara Sue Kidwell, "Choctaws and Missionaries in Mississippi Before 1830," in Greg Obrien, ed., *Pre-Removal Choctaw History: Exploring New Paths* (Norman, OK: University of Oklahoma Press, 2008), 200–220.
69. Mary Elizabeth Young, *Redskins, Ruffleshirts and Rednecks: Indian Allotments in Alabama and Mississippi, 1830–1860* (Norman, OK: University of Oklahoma Press, 1961), 191; Perdue and Green, *Cherokee Nation and Trail of Tears*, 63.
70. Dippie, *The Vanishing American*, 61–70.
71. Donna L. Akers, *Living in the Land of Death: The Choctaw Nation, 1830–1860* (East Lansing, MI: Michigan State University Press, 2004), 20, James T. Caron, "Native Americans, the Market Revolution, and Cultural Change: The Choctaw Cattle Economy, 1690–1830," in O'Brien, ed., *Pre-Removal Choctaw History*, 183–199.
72. Akers, *Living in the Land of Death*, 88–89.
73. Remini, *Jackson and his Indian Wars*, 243–253.
74. Michael D. Green, *The Politics of Indian Removal: Creek Government and Society in Crisis* (Lincoln, NE: University of Nebraska Press, 1982), 141–186.
75. Dowd, *Spirited Resistance*, 194.
76. The two Supreme Court decisions can be read online at http://supreme.justia.com/us/30/1/case.html; and http://supreme.justia.com/us/31/515/case.html; see also Pommersheim, *Broken Landscape: Indians and the Constitution*, 87–124; and "Settler Colonialism," *South Atlantic Quarterly* 107 4 (special edition, Fall 2008), 839–854.
77. Banner, *How Indians Lost Their Land*, 221.
78. "Movement of the Cherokee Indians, 1838," Box 2, Smith-Kirby-Webster-Black-Danner Family Papers, Box 2, Carlisle Barracks; Green and Perdue, *Cherokee Nation and Trail of Tears*; Remini, *Jackson and Indian Wars*, 268–270.
79. William Loren Katz, *Black Indians: A Hidden Heritage* (New York: Atheneum, 1986), 50–69; Missall and Missall, *Seminole Wars*, 103.
80. Missall and Missall, *Seminole Wars*, 178; Remini, *Jackson and Indian Wars*, 276.
81. Missall and Missall, *The Seminole Wars*, 196, 203.
82. Dippie, *Vanishing American*, xii, 12.
83. Susan Schekel, *The Insistence of the Indian: Race and Nationalism in Nineteenth-Century American Culture* (Princeton, NJ: Princeton University Press, 1998), 99–126.
84. John Hausdoerffer, *Catlin's Lament: Indians, Manifest Destiny, and the Ethics of Nature* (Lawrence, KS: University Press of Kansas, 2009); Dippie, *Vanishing American*, 26.

Chapter 5

1. The reference is to President Abraham Lincoln's annual message to the Congress delivered on December 1, 1862. http://showcase.netins.net/web/creative/lincoln/speeches/congress.htm.
2. David J. Weber, *Barbaros: Spaniards and the Savages in the Age of Enlightenment* (New Haven, CT: Yale University Press, 2005), 94–95; 148, 77–78.
3. Brian DeLay, *War of a Thousand Deserts: Indian Raids and the U.S.-Mexican War* (New Haven, CT: Yale University Press, 2008), 12–14; Richard V. Francaviglia and Douglas W. Richmond, *Dueling Eagles: Reinterpreting the U.S.-Mexican War, 1846–1848* (Fort Worth, TX: Texas Christian University Press, 2000), 146.
4. Weber, *Barbaros*, 269; DeLay, *War of a Thousand Deserts*; Ned Blackhawk, *Violence over the Land: Indians and Empires in the Early American West* (Cambridge, MA: Harvard University Press, 2008), 148.

5. DeLay, *War of Thousand Deserts*, 118, xv; Pekka Håmålåinen, *The Comanche Empire* (New Haven, CT: Yale University Press, 2008).
6. Gary Clayton Anderson, *The Indian Southwest, 1580–1830: Ethnogenesis and Reinvention* (Norman, OK: University of Oklahoma Press, 1999), 204–250; on women, gender, and diplomacy, see Juliana Barr, *Peace Came in the Form of a Woman: Indians and Spaniards in the Texas Borderlands* (Chapel Hill, NC: University of North Carolina Press, 2007).
7. Håmålåinen, *Comanche Empire.*
8. Anderson, *The Indian Southwest*, 204–250; Håmålåinen, *Comanche Empire.*
9. Anderson, *The Indian Southwest*, 258–259; Jacki Thompson Rand, *Kiowa Humanity and the Invasion of the State* (Lincoln, NE: University of Nebraska Press, 2008), 26–27.
10. DeLay, *War of a Thousand Deserts*, xiii, 114–138.
11. Håmålåinen, *Comanche Empire*, 2, 142; see also Brian DeLay, "The Wider World of the Handsome Man: Southern Plains Indians Invade Mexico, 1830–1848," *Journal of the Early Republic* 27 (Spring 2007), 83–113.
12. Jesus f. de la Teja, "Discovering the *Tejano* Community in 'Early' Texas," *Journal of the Early Republic* 18 (Spring 1998), 73–98.
13. Daniel Walker Howe, *What Hath God Wrought: The Transformation of America, 1815–1848* (New York: Oxford University Press, 2007), 658–671.
14. Gary C. Anderson, *The Conquest of Texas: Ethnic Cleansing in the Promised Land, 1820–1875* (Norman, OK: University of Oklahoma Press, 2005), 7–8.
15. Ibid., 41, 57, 80; on the failure of Houston's efforts to negotiate, 153–171.
16. Ibid., 360.
17. See, for example, S. C. Gwynne's bestseller *Empire of the Summer Moon: Quanah Parker and the Rise and Fall of the Comanches* (New York: Scribner, 2010); which was nominated for a Pulitzer Prize yet leans heavily on hoary and unverified accounts of Indian atrocity while failing to consult authoritative, peer-reviewed scholarship, award-winning in its own right, such as Anderson's *Conquest of Texas* or Peka Håmålåinen, *The Comanche Empire.*
18. Anderson, *Conquest of Texas*, 128–129.
19. Ibid., 160, 57, 80, 174, 319.
20. Ibid., 182–183.
21. David Clary, *Eagles and Empire: The United States, Mexico, and the Struggle for a Continent* (New York: Bantam Dell, 2009), 53.
22. DeLay, *War of a Thousand Deserts*, 248.
23. William Earl Weeks, *The New Cambridge History of American Foreign Relations (Vol. I): Dimensions of the Early American Empire, 1754–1865* (Cambridge, UK: Cambridge University Press, 2013), 122; see also Anders Stephanson, *Manifest Destiny and the Empire of Right* (New York: Hill and Wang, 1995).
24. David Pletcher, *The Diplomacy of Annexation: Texas, Oregon, and the Mexican War* (Columbia, MO: University of Missouri Press, 1973); Clary, *Eagles and Empire*, 74.
25. DeLay, *War of a Thousand Deserts*, 248.
26. Clary, *Eagles and Empire*, 74, 85, 99.
27. http://www.dmwv.org/mexwar/documents/polk.htm
28. Francaviglia and Richmond, *Dueling Eagles*, 16; for Mexican perspectives, see Cecil Robinson, ed., *The View from Chapultepec: Mexican Writers on the Mexican-American War* (Tucson, AZ: University of Arizona Press, 1989).
29. David Clary and David Pletcher, both authors of surveys of the Mexican War (though written 36 years apart), agree that Polk's aggressiveness to the point of recklessness brought on a war that could have been avoided while US expansionist goals still

achieved through ongoing settler colonialism and dedicated diplomacy. Clary judged Polk as "impatient . . . ignorant and pig-headed" whereas Pletcher argued that Polk, like his mentor Jackson, "epitomized aggressive self-centered nationalism." Along those same lines, Thomas Hietala suggests that the "anxious aggrandizement" that brought on the war stemmed from a conviction that rapid westward expansion would ward off federalism and thus preserve the sovereignty (and the right to own slaves) of the individual states. See Clary, *Eagles and Empire*, 452–453; Pletcher, *The Diplomacy of Annexation*, 605; and Thomas R. Hietala, *Manifest Design: Anxious Aggrandizement in Late Jacksonian America* (Ithaca, NY: Cornell University Press, 1985). See also Amy S. Greenberg, *A Wicked War: Polk, Clay, Lincoln, and the U.S. Invasion of Mexico* (New York: Knopf, 2012).

30. Francaviglia and Richmond, *Dueling Eagles*, 132.
31. Andrés Reséndez, "National Identity on a Shifting Border: Texas and New Mexico in the Age of Transition, 1821–1848," *Journal of American History* 86 (September 1999), 668–688.
32. Richard B. Winders, *Mr. Polk's Army: The American Military Experience in the Mexican War* (College Station, TX: Texas A&M University Press, 1997), 195; see also James M. McCaffrey, *Army of Manifest Destiny: The American Soldier in the Mexican War, 1846–1848* (New York: New York University Press, 1992).
33. Paul Foos, *A Short, Offhand, Killing Affair: Soldiers and Social Conflict during the Mexican-American War* (Chapel Hill, NC: University of North Carolina Press, 2002), 31; Robert W. Johannsen, *To the Halls of the Montezumas: The Mexican War in the American Imagination* (New York: Oxford University Press, 1985), 5–10, 29.
34. Johannsen, *To the Halls of Montezumas*, 11; Foos, *Short, Offhand Killing Affair*, 58–59.
35. Pletcher, *Diplomacy of Annexation*, 463; Joseph E. Chance, ed., *Mexico under Fire: The Diary of Samuel Ryan Curtis* (Fort Worth, TX: Texas Christian University Press, 1994), 19.
36. Isaac Bowen to Katie Bowen, December 23–24, 1846, Box 2, Isaac Bowen Papers, United States Army Military History Institute, Carlisle Barracks, PA. Hereafter cited as Carlisle Barracks.
37. Clary, *Eagles and Empire*, 120.
38. Chance, ed., *Mexico under Fire*, 20–24, 30.
39. Clary, *Eagles and Empire*, 141; Foos, *Short, Offhand, Killing Affair*, 131.
40. Chance, ed., *Mexico under Fire*, 174.
41. Isaac Bowen to Katie Bowen, July 27, 1846, Box 2, Bowen Papers, Carlisle Barracks.
42. Winders, *Mr. Polk's Army*, 197.
43. Foos, *Short, Offhand, Killing Affair*, 113; Clary, *Eagles and Empire*, 145.
44. Chance, ed., *Mexico under Fire*, 171–172; Clary, *Eagles and Empire*, 168.
45. Francaviglia and Richmond, *Dueling Eagles*, 171–172.
46. Isaac Bowen to Katie Bowen, September 27, 1846, Box 2, Bowen Papers, Carlisle Barracks.
47. Clary, *Eagles and Empire*, 201–202; Nathaniel C. Hughes, Jr., and Timothy D. Johnson, *A Fighter from Way Back: The Mexican War Diary of Lieutenant Daniel Harvey Hill* (Kent, OH: The Kent State University Press, 2002), 44.
48. Clary, *Eagles and Empire*, 279–280, 221.
49. Luther Giddings, *Sketches of the Campaign in Northern Mexico in Eighteen Hundred Forty-Six and Forty-Seven* (electronic resource; G. P. Putnam and Co., 1853), 324; Foos, *Short, Offhand Killing Affair*, 121.
50. Chance, ed., *Mexico under Fire*, 174.

51. Foos, *Short, Offhand Killing Affair*, 120–121; Clary, *Eagles and Empire*, 143; Hughes and Johnson, *Fighter from Way Back*, 28; Johannsen, *To the Halls of Montezumas*, 37–38.
52. Foos, *Short, Offhand Killing Affair*, 121.
53. Samuel E. Chamberlain, *My Confession: The Recollections of a Rogue* (Lincoln, NE: University of Nebraska Press, 1987; 1956), 86–88; Clary, *Eagles and Empire*, 268–269.
54. Foos, *Short, Offhand Killing Affair*, 123–124.
55. Clary, *Eagles and Empire*, 284; Chance, ed., *Mexico under Fire*, 176.
56. Chance, ed., *Mexico under Fire*, 173.
57. Clary, *Eagles and Empire*, 206, 248–249.
58. James F. Brooks, *Captives and Cousins: Slavery, Kinship, and Community in the Southwest Borderlands* (Chapel Hill, NC: University of North Carolina Press, 2002), 284.
59. Francaviglia and Richmond, *Dueling Eagles*, 127–154; Clary, *Eagles and Empire*, 176–177.
60. Clary, *Eagles and Empire*, 168.
61. "Part IX, The Abridged Diaries of William Gibbs McAdoo, 1846–," Carlisle Barracks.
62. Clary, *Eagles and Empire*, 299–304.
63. Krystyna M. Libura, et al., eds., *Echoes of the Mexican-American War* (Toronto: Groundwood Books, 2004), 149.
64. Foos, *Short, Offhand Killing Affair*, 126; Clary, *Eagles and Empire*, 380.
65. Foos, *Short, Offhand Killing Affair*, 126; Clary, *Eagles and Empire*, 383.
66. John H. Schroeder, *Mr. Polk's War: American Opposition and Dissent, 1846–1848* (Madison, WI: University of Wisconsin Press, 1973), 162–163; on this point, see also Greenberg, *A Wicked War*.
67. Amy S. Greenberg, *Manifest Manhood and the Antebellum American Empire* (Cambridge, UK: Cambridge University Press, 2005), 106; Clary, *Eagles and Empire*, 386.
68. Foos, *Short, Offhand Killing Affair*, 134; Francaviglia and Richmond, *Dueling Eagles*, 60; "End of Mexican War," Box 2, Smith-Kirby-Webster-Black-Danner Family Papers, Carlisle Barracks; Transcript of Treaty of Guadalupe Hidalgo online: http://www.ourdocuments.gov/doc.php?flash=true&doc=26&page=transcript.
69. Johannsen, *To the Halls of Montezumas*, 204, 297.
70. Anderson, *Conquest of Texas*, 213, 35, 14; Philip Weeks, *Farewell, My Nation: The American Indian and the United States in the Nineteenth Century* (Wheeling, IL: Harland Davidson, 1990), 85.
71. Weeks, *Farewell, My Nation*, 84–85.
72. De la Teja, "Discovering the *Tejano* Community in 'Early' Texas," 87.
73. Håmålåinen, *Comanche Empire*, 309; Anderson, *Conquest of Texas*, 190, 222, 285.
74. Anderson, *Conquest of Texas*, 229, 325–326.
75. Robert E. May, *Manifest Destiny's Underworld: Filibustering in Antebellum America* (Chapel Hill, NC: University of North Carolina Press, 2002), 9.
76. Ibid., 14.
77. Tom Chaffin, *Fatal Glory: Narciso Lopez and the First Clandestine U.S. War against Cuba* (Charlottesville, VA: University of Virginia Press, 1996).
78. May, *Manifest Destiny's Underworld*, 69; Joseph Allen Stout, *The Liberators: Filibustering Expeditions into Mexico, 1848–1862* (Los Angeles, CA: Westernlore Press, 1973), 47.
79. Stout, *The Liberators*, 1, 43–68.

80. On Walker and his legacy, see Brady Harrison, *Agent of Empire: William Walker and the Imperial Self in American Literature* (Athens, GA: University of Georgia Press, 2004); see also Amy S. Greenberg, "Grey-Eyed Man: Character, appearance, and Filibustering," *Journal of the Early Republic* 20 (Winter 2000), 673–699.
81. Harrison, *Agent of Empire*, 81–101.
82. Myriad accounts assess Walker's invasion; for Nicaraguan perspectives, see Michael Gobat, *Confronting the American Dream: Nicaragua under U.S. Imperial Rule* (Durham, NC: Duke University Press, 2005).
83. Ibid., 3, 38, 41.
84. "In the history of filibusterism," Charles H. Brown has pointed out, "it seems that nothing succeeded like failure." Brown, *Agents of Manifest Destiny: The Life and Times of the Filibusters* (Chapel Hill, NC: University of North Carolina Press, 1980), 68.
85. Gobat, *Confronting the American Dream*, 22.
86. The violent contradictions of the settler colonial project played out over a generation rather than merely four years of the traditional periodization from Fort Sumter (April 1861) to Appomattox (April 1865). As other scholars have suggested, the Civil War might more fruitfully be conceptualized as an era beginning with "Bleeding Kansas" in the mid-1850s if not even earlier and ending with the Compromise of 1877. See Stanley Harrold, *Border War: Fighting over Slavery before the Civil War* (Chapel Hill, NC: University of North Carolina Press, 2010), 15; Nicole Etcheson, *Bleeding Kansas: Contested Liberty in the Civil War Era* (Lawrence, KS: University Press of Kansas, 2004); see also David S. Reynolds, *John Brown, Abolitionist: The Man Who Killed Slavery, Sparked the Civil War, and Seeded Civil Rights* (New York: Vintage Books, 2005), 138–178.
87. Something resembling a culture of death materialized during the Civil War, as shared assumptions about the righteousness of the cause on both sides enabled and sustained an unprecedented level of violence. See Mark S. Schantz, *Awaiting the Heavenly Country: The Civil War and America's Culture of Death* (Ithaca, NY: Cornell University Press, 2008), 2, 67, 125; see also Drew Gilpin Faust, *This Republic of Suffering: Death and the American Civil War* (New York: Knopf, 2008).
88. J. David Hacker, "A Census-Based Count of the Civil War Dead," *Civil War History* 57 (December 2011), 307–348.
89. Jonathan D. Sarris, "'Shot for Being Bushwhackers': Guerrilla War and Extralegal Violence in a North Georgia Community, 1862–1865," in Daniel Sutherland, ed., *Guerrillas, Unionists, and Violence on the Confederate Home Front* (Little Rock, AR: University of Arkansas Press, 1999), 43–44.
90. Robert R. Mackey, *The Uncivil War: Irregular Warfare in the Upper South, 1861–1865* (Norman, OK: University of Oklahoma Press, 2004); Clay Mountcastle, *Punitive War: Confederate Guerrillas and Union Reprisals* (Lawrence, KS: University Press of Kansas, 2009); Daniel E. Sutherland, *Savage Conflict: The Decisive Role of Guerrillas in the American Civil War* (Chapel Hill, NC: University of North Carolina Press, 2009); Sutherland, ed., *Guerrillas, Unionists, and Violence on Confederate Home Front*. See also Philip S. Paludan, *Victims: A True Story of the Civil War* (Knoxville, TN: University of Tennessee Press, 1981).
91. Sutherland, ed., *Guerrillas, Unionists, and Violence on Confederate Home Front*, 28; Harrold, *Border War*, 1.
92. James A. Ramage, *Grey Ghost: The Life of Colonel John Singleton Mosby* (Lexington, KY: University Press of Kentucky, 2007); Ramage, *Rebel Raider: The Life of General John Hunt Morgan* (Lexington, KY: University Press of Kentucky, 1986); Jack Hurst, *Nathan Bedford Forrest: A Biography* (New York: Knopf, 1993).

93. Michael Fellman, *Inside War: The Guerrilla Conflict in Missouri during the American Civil War* (New York: Oxford University Press, 1989), 18, 19, 35, 41.
94. Mountcastle, *Punitive War*, 53; Fellman, *Inside War*, 25.
95. T. J. Stiles, *Jesse James: Last Rebel of the Civil War* (New York: Vintage Books, 2003), 93; Fellman, *Inside War*, 151.
96. Michael Fellman, "Inside Wars: The Cultural Crisis of Warfare and the Values of Ordinary People," in Sutherland, ed., *Guerrillas, Unionists, and Violence on Confederate Home Front*, 190–191, 203; see also Stiles, *Jesse James*.
97. Mackey, *The Uncivil War*, 30, 36.
98. Ibid., 39–41.
99. Sutherland, *Savage Conflict*, 228–239.
100. Ibid., 224–226.
101. Ibid., 50; David Paul Smith, "The Limits of Dissent and Loyalty in Texas," in Sutherland, ed., *Guerrillas, Unionists, and Violence*, 134.
102. Smith, "Limits of Dissent and Loyalty in Texas," 135, 141.
103. Ibid., 152–170.
104. Mountcastle, *Punitive War*, 32.
105. Sutherland, *Savage Conflict*, 240; Mountcastle, *Punitive War*, 82, 1, 40.
106. Sutherland, *Savage Conflict*, 253.
107. Ibid., 271–272.
108. Mackey, *Uncivil War*, 117; Sutherland, *Savage Conflict*, 240.
109. Sarris, "Shot for Being Bushwhackers," 32; Lesley J. Gordon, " 'In Time of War:' Unionists Hanged in Kinston, North Carolina, February 1864," 47, both in Sutherland, ed., *Guerrillas, Unionists, and Violence.*
110. B. Frank Cooling, "A People's War: Partisan Conflict in Tennessee and Kentucky," in Sutherland, ed., *Guerrillas, Unionists, and Violence.*, 122, 124.
111. George C. Rable, *But There Was No Peace: The Role of Violence in the Politics of Reconstruction* (Athens, GA: University of Georgia Press, 1984), 13, 1.
112. Smith, "The Limits of Loyalty in Texas," 148–149.
113. Rable, *But There Was No Peace*, 29–52.
114. Ibid., 143.
115. Laurence M. Hauptman, *Between Two Fires: American Indians in the Civil War* (New York: The Free Press, 1995), 186.
116. Ibid., passim.
117. Clarissa W. Confer, *The Cherokee Nation in the Civil War* (Norman, OK: University of Oklahoma Press, 2007), 145.
118. David La Vere, *Contrary Neighbors: Southern Plains and Removed Indians in Indian Territory* (Norman, OK: University of Oklahoma Press, 2000), 169.

Chapter 6

1. As Pablo Mitchell observes, "The American railroad was none other than the ultimate agent of modernity and imperialism." Pablo Mitchell, *Coyote Nation: Sexuality, Race, and Conquest in Modernizing Mexico, 1880–1920* (University of Chicago Press, 2005), 3; see also William G. Robbins, *Colony and Empire: The Capitalist Transformation of the American West* (Lawrence, KS: University Press of Kansas, 1994).
2. "No other nation has taken a time and place from its past and produced a construct of the imagination equal to America's creation of the West," David H. Murdoch declares. The West also served as "Hollywood's most popular single genre." David H. Murdoch,

The American West: The Invention of a Myth (Reno, NV: University of Nevada Press, 2001), vii; See also Robert G. Athearn, *The Mythic West in Twentieth-Century America* (Lawrence, KS: University Press of Kansas, 1986); Albert Hurtado, "Romancing the West in the Twentieth Century: The Politics of History in a Contested Region," *Western Historical Quarterly* 32 (Winter 2001), 417–435; and Helen McLure, "The Wild, Wild Web: The Mythic American West and the Electronic Frontier," *Western Historical Quarterly* 31 (Winter 2000), 457–476.

3. William Cronon, George Miles, and Jay Gitlin, *Under an Open Sky: Rethinking America's Western Past* (New York: W.W. Norton, 1992), 9.
4. Jacki Thompson Rand, *Kiowa Humanity and the Invasion of the State* (Lincoln, NE: University of Nebraska Press, 2008), 56.
5. Lorenzo Veracini, *Settler Colonialism: A Theoretical Overview* (New York: Palgrave Macmillan, 2010), 44.
6. As Frank Van Nuys points out the West "helped consolidate the widely held assumption of American identity as fundamentally white and Anglo-Saxon." Frank Van Nuys, *Americanizing the West: Race, Immigrants, and Citizenship, 1890–1930* (University Press of Kansas, 2002), xii.
7. John Mack Faragher, "'More Motley than Mackinaw': From Ethnic Mixing to Ethnic Cleansing on the Frontier of the Lower Missouri, 1783–1833," in Andrew R. L. Clayton and Fredrika J. Teute, eds., *Contact Points: American Frontiers from the Mohawk Valley to the Mississippi, 1750–1830* (Chapel Hill, NC: University of North Carolina Press, 1998), 304–326.
8. Stephen Aron, *American Confluence: The Missouri Frontier from Borderland to Border States* (Bloomington, IN: Indiana University Press, 2006), 151, 162–163.
9. Aron, *American Confluence*, 226.
10. Ibid., 183, 209, 207.
11. Kathleen DuVal, *The Native Ground: Indians and Colonists in the Heart of the Continent* (Philadelphia, PA: University of Pennsylvania Press, 2006).
12. William E. Unrau, *The Rise and Fall of Indian Country, 1825–1855* (Lawrence: University Press of Kansas, 2007), 61; James P. Ronda, "'We Have a Country': Race, Geography and the Invention of Indian Territory," *Journal of the Early Republic* 19 (Winter 1999), 740.
13. Frank McLynn. *Wagons West: The Epic Story of America's Overland Trails* (New York: Grove Press, 2002); Unrau, *Rise and Fall of Indian Country*, 148, 125.
14. Unrau, *Rise and Fall of Indian Country*, 142.
15. David J. Wishart, *An Unspeakable Sadness: The Dispossession of the Nebraska Indians* (Lincoln, NE: University of Nebraska Press, 1994), viii; see also William E. Unrau, *The Kansa Indians: A History of the Wind People, 1673–1873* (Norman, OK: University of Oklahoma Press, 1971).
16. Unrau, *Rise and Fall of Indian Country*, 11.
17. Wishart, *Unspeakable Sadness*, 69, 111, 104, 107.
18. Ibid., 110, 132, 143, 187, 201.
19. James F. Brooks, *Captives and Cousins: Slavery, Kinship, and Community in the Southwest Borderlands* (Chapel Hill, NC: University of North Carolina Press, 2002), 265.
20. David La Vere, *Contrary Neighbors: Southern Plains and Removed Indians in Indian Territory* (Norman, OK: University of Oklahoma Press, 2000), 91.
21. Ronda, "We Have a Country."
22. La Vere, *Contrary Neighbors*, 139.
23. Elliott West, *The Contested Plains: Indians, Goldseekers, and the Rush to Colorado* (Lawrence, KS: University Press of Kansas, 1998), 95.

24. Ned Blackhawk, *Violence over the Land: Indians and Empires in the Early American West* (Cambridge, MA: Harvard University Press, 2008), 262; Sherry L. Smith, *The View from Officers' Row: Army Perceptions of Western Indians* (Tucson, AZ: University of Arizona Press, 1990); see also Smith, "Lost Soldiers: Re-searching the Army in the American West," *Western Historical Quarterly* 29 (Summer 1998), 149–163 and Robert Wooster, *The Military and the Indian Wars, 1865–1903* (New Haven, CT: Yale University Press, 1988).
25. Michael Fellman, *Citizen Sherman: A Life of William Tecumseh Sherman* (New York: Random House, 1995), 260.
26. Wooster, *The Military and the Indian Wars*, 41–110.
27. Jon Reyhner and Jeanne Eder, *American Indian Education: A History* (Norman, OK: University of Oklahoma Press, 2004), 70.
28. Philip Weeks, *Farewell, My Nation: The American Indian and the United States in the Nineteenth Century* (Wheeling, IL: Harland Davidson, 2001), 171; Reyhner and Eder, *American Indian Education*, 71–72.; Karl Jacoby, *Shadows at Dawn: An Apache Massacre and the Violence of History* (New York: Penguin Books, 2008), 127.
29. William T. Sherman, "We Do Our Duty According to Our Means," in Cozzens, ed., *Eyewitnesses to Indian Wars, V*, 2–4; Sherman, "The Indian Question," Ibid., 109–113; Weeks, *Farewell, My Nation*, 125–126; Fellman, *Citizen Sherman*, 260–271.
30. James Donovan, *A Terrible Glory: Custer and the Little Big Horn—The Last Great Battle of the American West* (New York: Back Bay Books, 2008) 17–18; Peka Håmålåinen, *The Comanche Empire* (New Haven, CT: Yale University Press, 2008), 328; Weeks, *Farewell, My Nation*, 159.
31. West, *Contested Plains*, 174, 201.
32. David F. Halaas and Andrew E. Masich, *Halfbreed: The Remarkable True Story of George Bent Caught between the Worlds of the Indian and the White Man* (New York: Da Capo Press, 2004), 127, 138.
33. West, *Contested Plains*, 299–319.
34. Halaas and Masich, *Halfbreed*, 113–153; See also Jerome A. Greene and Douglas D. Scott, *Finding Sand Creek: History, Archeology, and the 1864 Massacre Site* (Norman, OK: University of Oklahoma Press, 2004); http://www.kclonewolf.com/History/SandCreek/sc-documents/sc-01hearing.html.
35. West, *Contested Plains*, 299–319; Halaas and Masich, *Halfbreed*, 113–153; Cozzens, ed., *Eyewitnesses to Indian Wars, III*, xxii; The Secretary of War's report on the Sand Creek massacre can be accessed online at: http://www.kclonewolf.com/History/SandCreek/sc-documents/sc-01hearing.html.
36. Håmålåinen, *Comanche Empire*, 324.
37. Blackhawk, *Violence over the Land*, 215; Henry E. Stamm, IV, *People of the Wind River: The Eastern Shoshones, 1825–1900* (Norman, OK: University of Oklahoma Press, 1999), 236; On the buffalo see Andrew C. Isenberg, *The Destruction of the Bison: An Environmental History, 1750–1920* (Cambridge: Cambridge University Press, 2000).
38. Brig. Gen. Edward S. Godfrey, "Some Reminiscences, Including the Washita Battle," November 27, 1868, Box 3, Godfrey Papers, United States Army Military History Institute, Carlisle Barracks, Pa. (hereinafter cited as Carlisle Barracks); Jerome A. Greene, *Washita: The U.S. Army and the Southern Cheyenne, 1867–1869* (Norman, OK: University of Oklahoma Press, 2004); Cozzens, ed., *Eyewitnesses to Indian Wars, III*, 339–403.
39. Benjamin Madley, "Tactics of Nineteenth Century Colonial Massacre: Tasmania, California and Beyond," in Philip G. Dwyer and Lyndall Ryan, eds., *Theatres of*

Violence: Massacre, Mass Killing and Atrocity Throughout History (New York: Berghan Books, 2012), 110–125; see also James Wilson, *The Earth Shall Weep: A History of Native America* (New York: Atlantic Monthly Press, 1998), 228.

40. Stuart Banner, *Possessing the Pacific: Land, Settlers, and Indigenous People from Australia to Alaska* (Cambridge, MA: Harvard University Press, 2007), 184–188.
41. Albert L. Hurtado, *Indian Survival on the California Frontier* (New Haven, CT.: Yale University Press, 1988); Wilson, *The Earth Shall Weep*, 244.
42. Hurtado, *Indian Survival on the California Frontier*, 213; Steven W. Hackel, *Children of Coyote, Missionaries of Saint Francis: Indian-Spanish Relations in Colonial California, 1769–1850* (Chapel Hill, NC: University of North Carolina Press, 2005), 8, 39; Clifford E. Trafzer and Joel R. Hyer, eds., *"Exterminate Them!": Written Accounts of Murder, Rape, and Slavery of Native Americans During the California Gold Rush, 1848–1868* (East Lansing: Michigan State University Press, 1999), 9.
43. Trafzer and Hyer, eds., *"Exterminate Them!"*, 12.
44. George Harwood Phillips, *Indians and Intruders in Central California, 1769–1849* (Norman, OK: University of Oklahoma Press, 1993); Trafzer and Hyer, eds., *"Exterminate Them!"*, 13.
45. Hurtado, *Indian Survival on the California Frontier*, 213; Trafzer and Hyer, eds., *"Exterminate Them!"*, 30; Benjamin Madley, "The Genocide of California's Yana Indians," in Samuel Totten and William S. Parsons, eds., *Centuries of Genocide: Essays and Eyewitness Accounts* (New York: Routledge, 2013), 174; Banner, *Possessing the Pacific*, 165.
46. Russell Thornton, *American Indian Holocaust and Survival: A Population History Since 1492* (Norman, OK: University of Oklahoma Press, 1987), 109–112; Madley, "Genocide of California's Yana Indians," 17–53.
47. Wilson, *Earth Shall Weep*, 229–230; Trafzer and Hyer, eds., *"Exterminate Them!"*, 14, 21.
48. Benjamin Madley, "When 'The World Was Turned Upside Down': California and Oregon's Tolowa Indian Genocide, 1851–1856," in Adams Jones, ed., *New Directions in Genocide Research* (New York: Routledge, 2012), 171–196.
49. Trafzer and Hyer, eds., *"Exterminate Them!"*, 27; James J. Rawls, *Indians of California: The Changing Image* (Norman, OK: University of Oklahoma Press, 1984), 152–164; Ben Kiernan, *Blood and Soil: A World History of Genocide and Extermination from Sparta to Darfur* (New Haven, CT: Yale University Press, 2007), 352–354.
50. Phillips, *Indians and Intruders*, 161; on Garra, see George Harwood Phillips, *Chiefs and Challengers: Indian Resistance and Cooperation in Southern California* (Berkeley, CA: University of California Press, 1975).
51. Trafzer and Hyer, eds., *"Exterminate Them!"* contains reprints of accounts over several years from the *Daily Alta California* and other newspapers; Kiernan, *Blood and Soil*, 350–352.
52. Wilson, *Earth Shall Weep*, 238; Kiernan, *Blood and Soil*, 352.
53. On this point, see Smith, *View from Officers' Row*, 184.
54. Azor H. Nickerson, "Major General George Crook and the Indians: A Sketch," Crook-Kennon Papers, Box 1, Carlisle Barracks; John G. Bourke, "General Crook in Indian Country," in Cozzens, ed., *Eyewitnesses to Indian Wars, V*, 149–202.
55. Jean Pfaelzer, *Driven Out: The Forgotten War Against Chinese Americans* (Berkeley, CA: University of California Press, 2007), xxv–xxvii; David T. Courtwright, *Violent Land: Single Men and Social Disorder from the Frontier to the Inner City* (Harvard University Press, 1996), 158.
56. Blackhawk, *Violence over the Land*, 20, 148.

57. Julianna Barr, "From Captives to Slaves: Commodifying Indian Women in the Borderlands," *Journal of American History* 92 (June 2005), 21–46; see also Michael Lansing, "Plains Indian Women and Native and Interracial Marriage in the Upper Missouri Trade, 1804–1868," *Western Historical Quarterly* 31 (Winter 2000), 413–433.
58. Blackhawk, *Violence over the Land*, 162, 172.
59. Ibid., 249, 263–267.
60. Jane Lahti, "Colonized Labor: Apaches and Pawnees as Army Workers," *Western Historical Quarterly* 39 (Autumn 2008), 283–302.
61. Blackhawk, *Violence over the Land*, 240.
62. Virginia McConnell Simmons, *The Ute Indians of Utah, Colorado, and New Mexico* (Boulder; CO: University Press of Colorado, 2000), 90.
63. Blackhawk, *Violence over the Land*, 231–244.
64. Simmons, *Ute Indians of Utah*, 78.
65. Blackhawk, *Violence over the Land*, 225.
66. Simmons, *Ute Indians of Utah*, 120–125; "Ute War," in Peter Cozzens, ed., *Eyewitnesses to the Indian Wars, III Conquering the Southern Plains* (Mechanicsburg, PA: Stackpole Books, 2003), 598–641.
67. Brooks, *Captives and Cousins*, 363.
68. Peter Iverson, *Diné: A History of the Navahos* (Albuquerque, NM: University of New Mexico Press, 2002), 36–51; Brooks, *Captives and Cousins*, 331–334.
69. Frederick W. Rathjen, *The Texas Panhandle Frontier* (Lubbock, TX: Texas Tech University Press, 1998), 144.
70. Hamelein, 303–313; Anderson, 302–317.
71. Cozzens, ed., *Eyewitnesses, III*, xxxix; Hâmålåinen, *Comanche Empire*, 297.
72. Rathjen, *Texas Panhandle Frontier*, 173–174; Cozzens, ed., *Eyewitnesses to Indian Wars, III*, 448–565.
73. Jacoby, *Shadows at Dawn*, 60–61.
74. Frederik G. Hughes, "The Military and Cochise," in Cozzens, ed., *Eyewitnesses to Indian Wars*, I, 132–137; Jacoby, *Shadows at Dawn*, 60–61.
75. Edward Palmer, "A Great Slaughter of Apaches," in Cozzens, ed., *Eyewitnesses to Indian Wars*, I, 5–6; Charles B. Genung, "Indians and Indigo," Ibid., 84; Jacoby, *Shadows at Dawn*, 114, 122.
76. James Deine, "An Incident of the Hualapais War," in Cozzens, ed., *Eyewitnesses to Indian Wars*, I, 5–6; William S. Oury, "Historical Truth: The So-Called 'Camp Grant Massacre' of 1871," Ibid., 57–58; Jacoby, *Shadows at Dawn*, 122; see also Peter Aleshire, *Reaping the Whirlwind: The Apache Wars* (New York: Facts on File, 1998).
77. Oury, "Historical Truth," 61; Brig, Gen. T. H. Slavens, "San Carlos, Arizona in the Eighties: The Land of the Apache," Box 11, OIW, Carlisle Barracks; Jacoby, *Shadows at Dawn*, 139; Nicole M. Guidotti-Hernandez, *Unspeakable Violence: Remapping U.S. and Mexican National Imaginaries* (Durham, NC: Duke University Press, 2011), 81–132.
78. Guidotti-Hernandez, *Unspeakable Violence*, 132.
79. Jacoby, *Shadows at Dawn*, 92, 222–225.
80. Ibid., 139, 229; Aleshire, *Reaping the Whirlwind*, 100–143.
81. Charles P. Elliott, "Campaign against Chiricahua Apache Indians, Geronimo, and Others, 1885, 1886," Box 2, OIW, Carlisle Barracks; see also Section V, "Chasing Geronimo, 1885–1886," in Cozzens, ed., *Eyewitnesses to Indian Wars*, I, 425–589.
82. "Apache Campaign, 1886," Box 2, Nelson A. Miles Papers; "Extracts from the Personal Memoirs of Brigadier General James Parker, U.S. Army," Box 11, Order of the Indian Wars; Secretary of War R.C. Drum to Miles, August 25, 1886, Box 2, Miles Papers, all

at Carlisle Barracks; Elliott, "Campaign against Apache Indians, Geronimo"; In 2009 Geronimo's great-grandson sued Skull and Bones over the alleged desecration. The grave at Fort Sill is open to the public.

83. Gray H. Whaley, *Oregon and the Collapse of Illahee: U.S. Empire and the Transformation of an Indigenous World, 1792–1859* (Chapel Hill, NC: University of North Carolina Press, 2010), 161.
84. Hampton Sides, *Blood and Thunder: An Epic of the American West* (New York: Doubleday, 2006): 85–88.
85. Cameron Addis, "The Whitman massacre: Religion and Manifest Destiny on the Columbia Plateau, 1809–1858," *Journal of the Early Republic* 25 (Summer 2005), 221–258; Elliott West, *The Last Indian War: The Nez Perce Story* (New York: Oxford University Press, 2009).
86. Banner, *Possessing the Pacific*, 238; Whaley, *Oregon and the Collapse of Illahee*, 216–225.
87. Whaley, *Oregon and the Collapse of Illahee*, 216–225.
88. Ibid., 203, 231.
89. Banner, *Possessing the Pacific*, 253; Robert R. McCoy, *Chief Joseph, Yellow Wolf, and the Creation of Nez Perce History in the Pacific Northwest* (New York: Routledge, 2004), 84; Whaley, *Oregon and the Collapse of Illahee*, 218.
90. West, *The Last Indian War*, 23.
91. Ibid., 20–136.
92. "Nez Perce Campaign: Official Reports and Letters," Box 2, Miles Papers; Charles N. Loynes, "From Fort Fizzle to the Big Hole," 432–440; John B. Caitlyn, "The Battle of Big Hole," 441–446; Duncan McDonald, "The Nez Perce War of 1877—The Inside Story from Indian Sources"; Henry Buck, "The Story of the Nez Perce Campaign During the Summer of 1877," 496–538, 451–493; Chuslum Moxmox (Yellow Bull), "Yellow Bull's Story," 494–495, all in Peter Cozzens, ed., *Eyewitnesses to the Indian Wars, 1865–1890, II, The Wars for the Pacific Northwest* (Mechanicsburg, PA: Stackpole Books, 2002); West, *The Last Indian War*, 186–266.
93. West, *The Last Indian War*, 291; McCoy, *Chief Joseph, Yellow Wolf, and Creation of Nez Perce History*, 128; Miles to President Hayes, January 19, 1881, Box 2, Miles Papers; "Chief Joseph: An Indian's View of Indian Affairs (1879)," in Colin Calloway, ed., *First Peoples: A Documentary Survey of American Indian Peoples* (New York: Bedford St. Martin's, 2008), 349–355.
94. West, *Last Indian War*, 301–321.
95. James Jackson, "The Modoc War: Its Origin, Incidents, and Peculiarities," 98–109; George W. Kingsbury, "The Twelfth U.S. Infantry in the Lava Beds," 274–275, both in Cozzens, ed., *Eyewitnesses to Indian Wars, II*; Charles B. Hardin, 1st U.S. Cavalry, "The Modoc War, 1872–1873", January 12, 1926, Box 10, OIW, Carlisle Barracks.
96. J. O. Skinner, "Correspondence with the Army War College Concerning the Modoc War and the Murder of General Canby," undated, Box 11, Carlisle Barracks; "Veritas," "The Capture of Captain Jack," in Cozzens, ed., *Eyewitnesses to Indian Wars, II*, 284–286; Bruce Vandervort, *Indian Wars of Mexico, Canada, and the United States, 1812–1900* (New York: Routledge, 2006), 189; Ian Hernon, *Massacre and Retribution: Forgotten Wars of the Nineteenth Century* (London: Sutton Publishing, 1998), 131–154.
97. Whaley, *Oregon and the Collapse of Illahee*, 220, 238.
98. Oliver O. Howard, "The Bannock War," 604–664; William C. Brown and Charles B. Hardin, "The Sheepeater Campaign," 676–706, in Cozzens, ed., *Eyewitnesses to Indian Wars, II*; Wooster, *Military and U.S. Indian Policy*, 174–178.

99. Ted Binnema and William A. Dobak, "'Like the Greedy Wolf': The Blackfeet, the St. Louis Fur Trade, and War Fever, 1807–1831," *Journal of the Early Republic* 29 (Fall 2009), 413.
100. Theodore Binnema, "Allegiances and Interests: Niitsitapi (Blackfoot) Trade, Diplomacy, and Warfare, 1801–1836," *Western Historical Quarterly* 37 (Autumn 2006), 327–349; John C. Ewers, *The Blackfeet: Raiders on the Northwestern Plains* (Norman, OK: University of Oklahoma Press, 1958), 251–252; Blanca Tovias, "A Blueprint for Massacre: The United States Army and the 1870 Blackfeet Massacre," in Dwyer and Ryan, eds., *Theatres of Violence*.
101. Jerry Kennan, *The Great Sioux Uprising: Rebellion on the Plains August-September 1862* (Cambridge, MA: Da Capo Press, 2003); Sylvia D. Hoffert, "Gender and Vigilantism on the Minnesota Frontier: Jane Gregy Suisshelm and the U.S.-Dakota Conflict of 1862," *Western Historical Quarterly* 29 (Autumn, 1998), 342–362.
102. Hoxie, *Parading Through History*, 88.
103. Richard White, "The Winning of the West: The Expansion of the Western Sioux in the Eighteenth and Nineteenth Centuries," in Peter C. Mancall and James H. Merrell, eds., *American Encounters: Natives and Newcomers from European Contact to Indian removal, 1500–1850* (New York: Routledge, 2000), 542–561.
104. Jeffrey Ostler, *The Lakotas and the Black Hills: The Struggle for Sacred Ground* (New York: Viking, 2010), 42–45.
105. Jeffrey Ostler, *The Plains Sioux and U.S. Colonialism From Lewis and Clark to Wounded Knee* (New York: Cambridge University Press, 2004), 20–21, 46; Hoxie, *Parading through History*, 113.
106. Ostler, *The Lakotas and the Black Hills*, 58–79.
107. Hoxie, *Parading through History*, 48–124.
108. Anson Mills, "Remarks—Battle of the Rosebud," 1917, Box 6, OIW, Carlisle Barracks; Donovan, *A Terrible Glory*, 143.
109. Donovan, *A Terrible Glory*, 261–278.
110. William H. C. Brown, "Remembrances of General Nelson A. Miles," Box 2, William Carey Brown Papers, Carlisle Barracks.
111. Nickerson, "Crook and the Indians"; Ostler, *Plains Sioux and U.S. Colonialism*, 78.
112. Ostler, *Plains Sioux and U.S. Colonialism*, 200.
113. C. Joseph Genetin-Pilawa, *Crooked Paths to Allotment: The Fight Over Federal Indian Policy after the Civil War* (Chapel Hill, NC: University of North Carolina Press, 2012), 156; Banner, *How the Indians Lost Their Land*, 257.
114. Helen Hunt Jackson, *A Century of Dishonor: A Sketch of the United States Government's Dealings with some of the Indian Tribes* (Norman, OK: University of Oklahoma Press, 1995; 1881); Miles to Senator A. Saunders, December 17, 1878, Box 2, Miles Papers, Carlisle Barracks.
115. Genetin-Pilawa, *Crooked Paths to Allotment*.
116. Rand, *Kiowa Humanity and the Invasion of the State*, 45; Genetin-Pilawa, *Crooked Paths to Allotment*, 155–56.
117. Reyhner and Eder, *American Indian Education*, 113, 42–43.
118. Margaret D. Jacobs, *White Mother to a Dark Race: Settler Colonialism, Maternalism, and the Removal of Indigenous Children in the American West and Australia, 1880–1940* (Lincoln: University of Nebraska Press, 2009), 4. As Jacobs points out in her Bancroft Prize-winning book, the child removal program proved paradoxical for American women. "In their own quest for independence public authority, and equality, many white women undermined Indian women through their support for the removal of indigenous children."(p. 433)

119. Reyhner and Eder, *American Indian Education*, 50, 73–74; Colin Calloway, *First Peoples: A Documentary Survey of American Indian History*, 3rd ed. (New York: St. Martin's Press, 2008), 386.
120. Ibid., 7, 143.
121. "In the White Man's Image: The Tragic Attempt to Civilize Native Americans in the 1870s," *The American Experience* video (PBS), 2007; 1992. Reyhner and Jeanne Eder, *American Indian Education*, 139–149.
122. Jacobs, *White Mother to a Dark Race*, 25.
123. Text of Dawes Act: http://www.nebraskastudies.org/0600/stories/0601_0200_01.html; Andrew Denson, *Demanding the Cherokee Nation: Indian Autonomy and American Culture, 1830–1900* (Lincoln: University of Nebraska Press, 2004), 202.
124. J. Edward Chamberlin, "Homeland and Frontier," in David Maybury-Lewis, Theodore Macdonald, and Biorn Maybury-Lewis, eds., *Manifest Destinies and Indigenous Peoples* (Cambridge, MA: Harvard University Press, 2009), 197.
125. Reyhner and Eder, *American Indian Education*, 85; Stuart Banner, *How the Indians Lost Their Land: Law and Power on the Frontier* (Cambridge, MA: Harvard University Press., 2005), 228.
126. Reyhner and Eder, *American Indian Education*, 82; A. M. Gibson, *The Kickapoos: Lords of the Middle Border* (Norman, OK: University of Oklahoma Press, 1963), 253; Weeks, *Farewell, My Nation*, 230.
127. Dippie, *Vanishing American*, 193.
128. Heather Cox Richardson, *Wounded Knee: Party Politics and the Road to an American Massacre* (New York: Basic Books, 2010).
129. Ostler, *Plains Sioux and U.S. Colonialism*, 168, 262; Blackhawk, Violence over the Land, 270.
130. Ibid., 61; Brig. Gen. G. W. McIver, "Account of the Participation of the Seventh U.S. Infantry in the Sioux Campaign of 1890–1891," Box 8, OIW, Carlisle Barracks.
131. "Sioux War, 1890–1891—Correspondence Relating to Wounded Knee"; "Sioux War, 1890–1891-Investigation of Wounded Knee," both Box 2, Miles Papers, Carlisle Barracks; McIver, Participation in Sioux Campaign.
132. Lt. Col. W. F. Drum, "Report on the Sitting Bull Affair" [order for arrest and killing], December 17, 1890; Capt. E. G. Fecht, "Report on the Sitting Bull Affair" [order for arrest and killing], December 17, 1890, both in Box 6, OIW, Carlisle Barracks.
133. Lieut. Alexander R. Paper, 8th Infantry to Marie Cozzens Piper, December 29, 1890, Box 6, OIW, Carlisle Barracks; "James Mooney Documents the Ghost Dance Religion and its Consequence, 1890," in Christopher Waldrep and Michael Bellesiles, eds., *Documenting American Violence: A Sourcebook* (New York: Oxford University Press, 2006), 238–243.
134. Ostler, *Plains Sioux and U.S. Colonialism*, 303, 360; "Scattered confrontations" between the US Army and Indians continued throughout the 1890s and irregular violence continued sporadically as well. Wooster, *Military and U.S. Indian Policy*, 174.

Chapter 7

1. Sally Engle Merry, *Colonizing Hawai'i: The Cultural Power of Law* (Princeton, NJ: Princeton University Press, 2000), 24.
2. Steven Haycox, *Alaska: An American Colony* (Seattle, WA: University of Washington Press, 2002), 175.

3. The "Pacific World" framework has been extensively and engagingly developed by Bruce Cumings in *Dominion from Sea to Sea: Pacific Ascendancy and American Power* (New Haven, CT: Yale University Press, 2009). Gary Y. Okihiro places Hawaiian history within a larger frame of Oceania in *Island World: A History of Hawai'i and the United States* (Berkeley, CA: University of California Press), 2008.
4. This brief portrait of indigenous Hawai'i draws on the works cited hereafter.
5. Houston Wood, *Displacing Natives: The Rhetorical Production of Hawai'i* (Lanham, MD.: Rowan and Littlefield, 1999), 32.
6. Marshall Sahlins, *Island of History* (Chicago: University of Chicago Press, 1985), 136.
7. Wood, *Displacing Natives*, 23.
8. Sahlins, *Island of History*, 104–135.
9. Noenoe K. Silva, *Aloha Betrayed: Native Hawai'ian Resistance to American Colonialism* (Durham, NC.: Duke University Press, 2004), 23.
10. Silva, *Aloha Betrayed*, 24; Candace Fujikane and Jonathan Y. Okamura, eds., *Asian Settler Colonialism: From Local Governance to Habits of Everyday Life in Hawai'i* (Honolulu, HI: University of Hawai'i Press, 2008), 5; see also Eleanor C. Nordyke, *The Peopling of Hawai'i* (Honolulu, HI: University of Hawai'i Press, 1989; 1977).
11. Tom Coffman, *Nation Within: The History of the American Occupation of Hawai'i* (2d ed., Kihei, HI: Koa Books, 2009; 1998), 54.
12. Linda S. Parker, *Native American Estate: The Struggle over Indian and Hawaiian Lands* (Honolulu, HI: University of Hawai'i Press, 1989), 6.
13. Okihiro, *Island World*, 96, 114; Jonathan K. Osorio, *Dismembering Lahui: A History of the Hawai'i an Nation to 1887* (Honolulu, HI: University of Hawai'i Press, 2002), 60–65.
14. Parker, *Native American Estate*, 89, 93; Ronald Takaki, *Pau Hana: Plantation Life and Labor in Hawaii, 1835–1920* (Honolulu, HI: University of Hawai'i Press, 1983), 4–6.
15. Merry, *Colonizing Hawai'i*, 20, 260.
16. Jennifer Fish Kashay, "From *Kapus* to Christianity: The Disestablishment of the Hawaiian Religion and Chiefly Appropriation of Calvinist Christianity," *Western Historical Quarterly* 39 (Spring 2008), 17–39.
17. Ibid., 13.
18. Osorio, *Dismembering Lahui*, 3.
19. Marshall Sahlins, "Hawai'i in the Early Nineteenth Century: The Kingdom and the Kingship," in Robert Borofsky, ed., *Remembrance of Pacific Pasts: An Invitation to Remake History* (Honolulu, HI: University of Hawai'i Press, 2000), 189.
20. Parker, *Native American Estate*, 97, 100.
21. Takaki, *Pau Hana*, 6–7.
22. Osorio, *Dismembering Lahui*, 13.
23. Parker, *Native American Estate*, 125.
24. Osorio, *Dismembering Lahui*, 251, 73.
25. Osorio, *Dismembering Lahui*, 65.
26. Stuart Banner, *Possessing the Pacific: Land, Settlers, and Indigenous People from Australia to Alaska* (Cambridge, MA: Harvard University Press, 2007), 128–162.
27. Parker, *Native American Estate*, 115.
28. Merry, *Colonizing Hawai'i*, 26.
29. Parker, *Native American Estate*, 21.
30. Takaki, *Pau Hana*, 8.
31. Patrica Grimshaw, *Paths of Duty: American Missionary Wives in Nineteenth-Century Hawai'i* (Honolulu, HI: University of Hawai'i Press, 1989), 154–178.

32. Ibid., 38; Likikala Kame'eleihiwa, "U.S. Merchants, Missionaries, and the Overthrow of the Hawaiian Government," in Ward Churchill and Sharon H. Venne, eds., *Islands in Captivity: The Record of the International Tribunal on the Rights of Indigenous Hawaiians* (Cambridge, MA: South End Press, 2004), 81.
33. Okihiro, *Island World*, 99.
34. Wood, *Displacing Natives*, 37–39.
35. Grimshaw, *Paths of Duty*, 172; Wood, *Displacing Natives*, 166; Merry, *Colonizing Hawai'i*, 25.
36. Merry, *Colonizing Hawai'i*, 22.
37. Takaki, *Pau Hana*, 19; Coffman, *Nation Within*, 62.
38. Cumings, *Dominion from Sea to Sea*, 176–177; Takaki, *Pau Hana*, 20.
39. Coffman, *Nation Within*, 63–64.
40. Blaine to Comly, December 1, 1881, Department of State, *Papers Relating to Foreign Relations of the United States for 1881* (Washington, D.C, 1882), 635–636.
41. Coffman, *Nation Within*, 69–90; Cumings, *Dominion from Sea to Sea*, 136–141.
42. Banner, *Possessing the Pacific*, 158.
43. Osorio, *Dismembering Lahui*, 224.
44. Parker, *Native American Estate*, 120–211.
45. Coffman, *Nation Within*, 91–92, 108.
46. Ibid., 79; Osorio, *Dismembering Lahui*, 240.
47. Osorio, *Dismembering Lahui*, 156.
48. Coffman, *Nation Within*, 79–83.
49. Silva, *Aloha Betrayed*, 1–2.
50. Ibid., 5, 163.
51. Parker, *Native American Estate*, 130.
52. Wood, *Displacing Natives*, 87; Cumings, *Dominion from Sea to Sea*, 185.
53. Coffman, *Nation Within*, 52, 177, 182.
54. William Michael Morgan, *Pacific Gibraltar: U.S.-Japanese Rivalry over the Annexation of Hawai'i, 1885–1898* (New York: Naval Institute Press, 2012), 241.
55. Parker, *Native American Estate*, 130; Cumings, *Dominion from Sea to Sea*, 185.
56. Silva, *Aloha Betrayed*, 123–163.
57. Coffman, *Nation Within*, 261, 217; Cumings, *Dominion from Sea to Sea*, 184–188.
58. Coffman, *Nation Within*, 208, 243.
59. Lanny Thompson, *Imperial Archipelago: Representation and Rule in the Insular Territories Under U.S. Dominion after 1898* (Honolulu, HI: University of Hawaii Press, 2010), 185, 9.
60. Ibid., 185.
61. Ibid., 113, 66, 79.
62. Mary Louise Pratt, *Imperial Eyes: Travel Writing and Transculturation* (New York: Routledge, 1992), 7.
63. Fujikane, "Introduction: Asian Settler Colonialism in the U.S. Colony of Hawai'i," 1–42.
64. Ibid., 7.
65. Coffman, *Nation Within*, 64.
66. Morgan, *Pacific Gibraltar*; see also Eric Love, *Race over Empire: Racism and U.S. Imperialism, 1865–1900* (Chapel Hill, NC: University of North Carolina Press, 2004).
67. Takaki, *Pau Hana*, 25.
68. Coffman, *Nation Within*, 234, 198, 202.

69. Sally Engle Merry, "Law and Identity in an American Colony," in Merry and Donald Brenneis, eds., *Law and Empire in the Pacific: Fiji and Hawai'i* (Santa Fe, NM: School of American Research Press, 2003), 135.
70. Ibid., 138.
71. Parker, *Native American Estate*, 191.
72. J. Kehaulani Kauanui, *Hawaiian Blood: Colonialism and the Politics of Sovereignty and Indigeneity* (Durham, NC: Duke University Press, 2008), 10.
73. Merry, "Law and Identity in an American Colony," 139.
74. Mililani B. Trask, "Hawaiian Sovereignty," in Fujikane and Okamura, eds., *Asian Settler Colonialism*, 73; see also, George Cooper and Gavan Davis, *Land and Power in Hawai'i: The Democratic Years* (Honolulu, HI: University of Hawai'i Press, 1985); Merry, "Law and Identity in an American Colony," 142–143.
75. Haycox, *Alaska: An American Colony*, 3–33.
76. Walter R. Borneman, *Alaska: Saga of a Bold Land* (New York: Harper Collins, 2003), 33–89.
77. James R. Gibson, "Russian Dependence on the Natives of Alaska," in Stephen W. Haycox and Mary Childers Mangusso, eds., *An Alaska Anthology: Interpreting the Past* (Seattle, WA: University of Washington Press, 1996), 27; Haycox, *Alaska: An American Colony*, 115–146; Borneman, *Alaska: Saga of a Bold Land*, 60–73.
78. Gibson, "Russian Dependence on the Natives of Alaska," 21–42.
79. Borneman, *Alaska: Saga of a Bold Land*, 60–66.
80. Gibson, "Russian Dependence on the Natives of Alaska," 35–37.
81. Cumings, *Dominion from Sea to Sea*, 191–196; Borneman, *Alaska: Saga of a Bold Land*, 106–112; Haycox, *Alaska: An American Colony*, 170–175; See also Paul S. Holbo, *Tarnished Expansion: The Alaska Scandal, The Press, and Congress, 1867–1871* (Knoxville, TN: University of Tennessee Press, 1983).
82. Haycox, *Alaska: An American Colony*, 175.
83. The Treaty of Cession can be accessed online at http://www.usgennet.org/usa/ak/state/1867cession_treaty.htm. See Article 3 on the citizenship provision.
84. Banner, *Possessing the Pacific*, 295.
85. Donald Craig Mitchell, *Sold American: The Story of Alaska Natives and their Land, 1867–1959* (Hanover, NH: University Press of New England, 1997), 6–7.
86. Haycox, *Alaska: An American Colony*, 175.
87. Ibid., 179–180.
88. Jon Reyhner and Jeanne Eder, *American Indian Education: A History* (Norman, OK: University of Oklahoma Press, 2004), 34–35.
89. Borneman, *Alaska: Saga of a Bold Land*, 128–232.
90. Haycox, *Alaska: An American Colony*, 200.
91. Ibid., 209.
92. Ibid., 201–235.
93. Mitchell, *Sold American*, 395.
94. Donald Craig Mitchell, *Take my Land, Take my Life: The Story of Congress's Historic Settlement of Alaska Native Land Claims, 1960–1971* (Fairbanks, AK: University of Alaska Press, 2001).
95. Mitchell, *Sold American*, 7; Borneman, *Alaska: Saga of a Bold Land*, 116–118.
96. David S. Case and David A. Voluck, *Alaska Natives and American Laws* (Anchorage, AK: University of Alaska Press 2012), 26–33.
97. Mitchell, *Sold American*, 345–346.
98. Ibid., 7.

99. See Barry Scott Zellen, *On Thin Ice: The Inuit, the State, and the Challenge of Arctic Sovereignty* (Lanham, MD: Lexington Books, 2009).
100. Haycox, *Alaska: An American Colony*, 257–272; Borneman, *Alaska: Saga of a Bold Land*, 395–403.

Chapter 8

1. Myriad histories continue to frame the Spanish-American War as discontinuous, as if it were the nation's first foray into imperialism. See, for example, Chapter 9, "The Birth of an American Empire, 1898–1902," in the recent military history by Allan Millett, *For the Common Defense: A Military History of the United States from 1607–2012* (New York: Free Press, 2012). It remains a common practice to begin surveys of diplomatic history with the Spanish-American War as the fulcrum of empire. See, for example, Jerald A. Combs, *The History of American Foreign Policy from 1895* (New York: M.E. Sharpe, 4th ed., 2012).
2. Julian Go, "Imperial Power and Its Limits: America's Colonial Empire in the Early Twentieth Century," in Craig Calhoun, Frederick Cooper, and Kevin Moore, eds., *Lessons of Empire: Imperial Histories and American Power* (New York: The New Press, 2006), 204.
3. Lanny Thompson, *Imperial Archipelago: Representation and Rule in the Insular Territories Under U.S. Dominion after 1898* (Honolulu, HI: University of Hawaii Press, 2010), 4.
4. Paul Kramer concludes, "The estimate of 250,000 Filipino war deaths appears conservative" whereas Julian Go declares "no less than 400,000 Filipino lives" were lost in the war. Paul A. Kramer, *The Blood of Government: Race, Empire, the United States, and the Philippines* (Chapel Hill, NC: University of North Carolina Press, 2006), 157; Go, "Imperial Power and Its Limits," 212. In *Arc of Empire: America's Wars in Asia from the Philippines to Vietnam* (Chapel Hill, NC: University of North Carolina Press, 2012), Michael H. Hunt and Stephen I. Levine aver, The best guess is that between 1899 and 1903 the death rate exceeded normal mortality by 750,000. This figure reflects war-related hardships such as severe food shortages and outbreaks of diseases such as malaria, dysentery, typhoid, smallpox, and cholera that shortened the lives of adults, raised infant mortality, disrupted pregnancies, and reduced fertility. These effects persisted well into peacetime.(58)
5. Both Brian M. Linn and John M. Gates offer well-researched studies published more than a generation apart that emphasize the success of US Army pacification and civic action programs in ultimately winning the Philippine War. These authors trumpet the success of the army's counterinsurgency campaign while marginalizing the indiscriminate violence of the war as aberrant rather than intrinsic to the colonial project. In a more recent work, Linn condemns "non-specialists" for perpetuating "clichés," "dogma," and the "myth" that violence, torture, and devastation lay behind the US war effort. Linn frames his own interpretation as objective scholarship whereas he finds it "distressing" that "many Americans, particularly in academia, interpret the Philippine War through an ideological perspective developed during the 1960s," which we are left to infer renders them automatically discredited. See Brian McAllister, *The Philippine War, 1899–1902* (Lawrence, KS: University Press of Kansas, 2000), 324–328; and John M. Gates, *Schoolbooks and Krags: The United States Army in the Philippines, 1899–1902* (Westport, CT: Greenwood Press, 1973).
6. Kramer, *Blood of Government*, 5; Go, "Imperial Power and Its Limits," 212.

7. Kramer, *Blood of Government*, 94–99; Hunt and Levine, *Arc of Empire*, 23, 28.
8. The text of McKinley's "benevolent assimilation" proclamation of December 21, 1898 can be accessed online at: http://www.historywiz.com/primarysources/benevolentassimilation.htm
9. Ibid., 91; Thompson, *Imperial Archipelago*, 252.
10. David Brody, *Visualizing Empire: Orientalism and Imperialism in the Philippines* (University of Chicago Press, 2010), 61.
11. Kramer, *Blood of Government*, 103–104; David J. Silbey, *A War of Frontier and Empire: The Philippine-American War*, 1899–1902 (New York: Hill and Wang, 2007), 68.
12. Linn, *Philippine War*, 42–52; Linn, *The U.S. Army and Counterinsurgency in the Philippine War, 1899–1902* (Chapel Hill, NC: University of North Carolina Press, 1989), 12–16; Kramer, *Blood of Government*, 111–112.
13. Samuel B. Young, "Philippine Insurrection, Letters Sent Letters Received," Box 4; "Remarks Delivered before the Middlesex Club," Boston, Box 6; Young to Major General Elwell S. Otis, November 17, 1899, all in Samuel B. M. Young Papers, U.S. Army Military History Institute, Carlisle, PA, hereinafter cited as Carlisle Barracks.
14. Servando D. Halili, Jr., *Iconography of the New Empire: Race and Gender Images and the American Colonization of the Philippines* (Quezon City: The University of the Philippines Press, 2006), xi, 61, 67.
15. Susan K. Harris *God's Arbiters: Americans in the Philippines, 1898 to1902* (New York: Oxford University Press, 2011), 180.
16. Walter L. Williams, "United States Indian Policy and the Debate over Philippine Annexation: Implications for the Origins of American Imperialism," *Journal of American History* 66 (March 1980), 810–831; Linn, *U.S. Army and Counterinsurgency in Philippine War*, 23.
17. Theodore Roosevelt, *The Winning of the West: (Vol. I) From the Alleghenies to the Mississippi, 1769–1776* (Lincoln, NE: University of Nebraska Press, 1995; 1889), 90, 92; Roosevelt quoted in Ben Kiernan, *Blood and Soil: A World History of Genocide and Extermination from Sparta to Darfur* (New Haven, CT: Yale University Press, 2007), 363.
18. Williams, "U.S. Indian Policy and Debate over Philippine Annexation," 825–827.
19. Harris, *God's Arbiters*, 64–65.
20. Alfred W. McCoy, *Policing America's Empire: The United States, the Philippines, and the Rise of the Surveillance State* (Madison, WI: University of Wisconsin Press, 2009), 5; Kramer, *Blood of Government*, 139, 122.
21. Linn, *Philippine War, 1899–1902*, 185–224.
22. Russell Roth, *Muddy Glory: America's 'Indian Wars' in the Philippines, 1899–1935* (Hanover, MA: Christina Publishing House, 1981), 54–55; Stanley Karnow, *In Our Image: America's Empire in the Philippines* (New York: Random House, 1989), 154; Kramer, *Blood of Government*, 144–145.
23. Roth, *Muddy Glory*, 21, 74; Angel Velasco Shaw and Luis H. Francia, eds., *Vestiges of War: The Philippine-American War and the Aftermath of and Imperial Dream, 1899–1999* (New York: New York University Press, 2002), 5–6; Linn, *Philippine War*, 224.
24. Linn, *Philippine War*, 326.
25. Major Matthew A. Batson to his wife, April 21, 1899, "Letters of Major Matthew A. Batson, Cuban and Philippine Campaigns, 1898–1901," Box 3, Carlisle Barracks; Karnow, *In our Image*, 154.
26. Resil B. Majares, *The War against the Americans: Resistance and Collaboration in Cebu, 1899–1906* (Manila: Ateneo de Manila University Press, 1999), 133–157.

27. Stuart Creighton Miller, *"Benevolent Assimilation": The American Conquest of the Philippines, 1899–1903* (New Haven, CT: Yale University Press, 1982), 199–201; Linn, *Philippine War*, 306–321.
28. Miller, *"Benevolent Assimilation,"* 204; Louise Barnett, *Atrocity and American Military Justice in Southeast Asia* (New York and London: Routledge, 2010), 65; Linn, *Philippine War*, 310–312.
29. Miller, *"Benevolent Assimilation,"* 196–218.
30. Silbey, *War of Frontier and Empire*, 195–196; Barnett, *Atrocity and American Military Justice in Southeast Asia*, 77.
31. Kramer, *Blood of Government*, 135; Glenn Anthony May, *Battle for Batangas: A Philippine Province at War* (New Haven, CT: Yale University Press, 1991), 147.
32. May, *Battle for Batangas*, 149; Angel Velasco Shaw and Luis H. Francia, eds., *Vestiges of War: The Philippine-American War and the Aftermath of and Imperial Dream, 1899–1999* (New York: New York University Press, 2002), 15.
33. May, *Battle for Batangas*, 256; Bell Telegraphic Circular No 37 from Batangas, April 7, 1902, Box 1, James Franklin Bell Papers, Carlisle Barracks.
34. May, *Battle for Batangas*, 161, 243.
35. Kramer, *Blood of Government*, 152–153; May, *Battle for Batangas*, 274, 264.
36. "Cover-up, if at all possible, would always appear to be the best policy of the military." Barnett, *Atrocity and American Military Justice in Southeast Asia*, 26.
37. Kramer, *Blood of Government*, 145; May, *Battle for Batangas*, 284.
38. Linn, *U.S. Army and Counterinsurgency in Philippine War*, 26–27.
39. "A Synopsis of the Progressive Development of the Moro Province, 1903–12," Box 1, John P. Finley Papers, Carlisle Barracks.
40. Patricio N. Abinales, "The U.S. Army as an Occupying Force in Muslim Mindanao, 1899–1913," in Alfred W. McCoy and Francisco Scarano, eds., *Colonial Crucible: Empire in the Making of the Modern American State* (Madison, WI: University of Wisconsin Press, 2009), 416; Kramer, *Blood of Government*, 217.
41. Abinales, "U.S. Army as Occupying Force in Muslim Mindanao," 412.
42. Ibid., 411; Joshua Gedacht, "Mohammedism Religion Made it Necessary to Fire: Massacres on the American Imperial Frontier from South Dakota to the Southern Philippines," in McCoy and Scarano, eds., *Colonial Crucible*, 397–409.
43. Gedacht, "Mohammedism Religion Made It Necessary to Fire."
44. McCoy, *Policing America's Empire*, 62.
45. Go, "Imperial Power and Its Limits," 212.
46. Linn, *Philippine War*, 324, 328.
47. Samuel B. Young to Theodore Roosevelt, May 26, 1900, Box 12, Young Papers, Carlisle Barracks.
48. Thompson, *Imperial Archipelago*, 166; Young to Roosevelt, May 26, 1900, Box 12, Young Papers, Carlisle Barracks.
49. Thompson, *Imperial Archipelago*, 73.
50. Kramer, *Blood of Government*, 116–130; Roth, *Muddy Glory*, 60.
51. Kramer, *Blood of Government*, 102–103.
52. Batson to his wife, May 21, 1899, Box 3, Batson Papers, Carlisle Barracks.
53. "Letters of Major Matthew A. Batson, Cuban and Philippine Campaigns, 1898–1901," Box 3, Batson Papers, Carlisle Barracks; Linn, *Philippine War*, 216; McCoy, *Policing America's Empire*, 83.
54. Kramer, 73–82; Majares, *War against the Americans*, 209.
55. Thompson, *Imperial Archipelago*, 174; Kramer, *Blood of Government*, 85.
56. Linn, *Philippine War*, 218, 213.

57. Kramer, *Blood of Government*, 29, 434–435.
58. May, *Battle for Batangas*, 200; Majares, *War against the Americans*, 280.
59. Kramer, *Blood of Government*, 67; Patricio Abinales, "An American Colonial State: Authority and Structure in Southern Mindanao," in Shaw and Francia, eds., *Vestiges of War*, 109.
60. Kramer, *Blood of Government*, 435, 217.
61. Majares, *War against the Americans*, 209–210.
62. Eva-Lotta E. Hedman and John T. Sidel, *Philippine Politics and Society in the Twentieth Century: Colonial Legacies, Post-colonial Trajectories* (New York: Routledge, 2000), 7; McCoy, *Policing America's Empire*, 125.
63. McCoy, *Policing America's Empire*, 29, 10.
64. Ibid., 59–205.
65. Hedman and Sidel, *Philippine Politics and Society in Twentieth Century*, 15.
66. John T. Sidel, *Capital, Coercion, and Crime: Bossism in the Philippines* (Stanford, CA: Stanford University Press, 1999), 146.
67. Hedman and Sidel, *Philippine Politics and Society in Twentieth Century*, 8.
68. Ibid., 41.
69. Kathleen M. Nadeau, *The History of the Philippines* (Westport, CT: Greenwood Press, 2008), 60, 69–71.
70. Robert Nashel, *Edward Lansdale's Cold War* (Amherst, MA: University of Massachusetts Press, 2005); Hedman and Sidel, *Philippine Politics and Society in Twentieth Century*, 42.
71. On Indonesia see Bradley R. Simpson, *Economists with Guns: Authoritarian Development in U.S.-Indonesian Relations, 1960–1968* (Stanford, CA: Stanford University Press, 2008); the literature on the Vietnam War is massive; for an excellent recent overview see Scott Laderman and Edwin Martini, eds., *Four Decades On: Vietnam, the United States, and the Second Indochina War* (Durham, NC: Duke University Press, 2013.
72. Nadeau, *History of the Philippines*, 94.
73. Hedman and Sidel, *Philippine Politics and Society in Twentieth Century*, 36; McCoy, *Policing America's Empire*, 433–451.
74. Hedman and Sidel, *Philippine Politics and Society in Twentieth Century*, 51–58.
75. McCoy, *Policing America's Empire*, 511–515, 519.
76. Ibid., 1, 20; Patricio N. Abinales, "Notes on the Disappearing 'middle' in Post-authoritarian Philippine Politics," in Shiraishi Takashi and Pusuk Phongpaichit, eds., *The Rise of Middle Classes in Southeast Asia* (Kyoto: Kyoto University Press, 2008), 176–193.

Chapter 9

1. "The American Indian and Alaska Native Population: 2010 Census Briefs." http://www.census.gov/prod/cen2010/briefs/c2010br-10.pdf
2. Colin Calloway, *First Peoples: A Documentary Survey of American Indian History* (New York: St. Martin's, 2008), 525.
3. Kevin Bruyneel, *The Third Space of Sovereignty: The Post-Colonial Politics of U.S.-Indigenous Relations* (Minneapolis, MN: University of Minnesota Press, 2007), 12.
4. United Nations Declaration on the Rights of Indigenous People. http://www.un.org/esa/socdev/unpfii/documents/DRIPS_en.pdf; see also Elvira Pulitano, ed., *Indigenous Rights in the Age of the UN Declaration* (New York: Cambridge University Press, 2012); the literature on the global human rights movement is rapidly emerging. For overviews see Jack Donnelly, *Universal Human Rights in Theory and Practice* (Ithaca, NY: Cornell

University Press, 2013) and Aryeh Neier, *The International Human Rights Movement: A History* (Princeton, NJ: Princeton University Press, 2012).

5. Philip J. Deloria, *Indians in Unexpected Places* (Lawrence, KS: University of Kansas Press, 2004), 237.
6. Deloria, *Indians in Unexpected Places*, 231.
7. Ibid., 52–80; Louis S. Warren, *Buffalo Bill's America: William Cody and the Wild West Show* (New York: Vintage Books, 2005).
8. Deloria, *Indians in Unexpected Places*, 109–135; Calloway, *First Peoples*, 400–401; see also David L. Fleitz, *Louis Sockalexis: The First Cleveland Indian* (Jefferson, NC: McFarland, 2002).
9. Calloway, *First Peoples*, 399–402.
10. Paul C. Rosier, *Serving Their Country: American Indian Politics and Patriotism in the Twentieth Century* (Cambridge, MA: Harvard University Press, 2009), 42–70; Calloway, *First Peoples*, 438–445.
11. Rosier, *Serving Their Country*, 9–11.
12. Calloway, *First Peoples*, 448.
13. Rosier, *Serving Their Country*, 109–160.
14. Sherry L. Smith, *Hippies, Indians, and the Fight for Red Power* (New York: Oxford University Press 2012), 13.
15. Ibid., 78–11; 170–184.
16. Ibid., 183–212; quotation, 186.
17. For an in-depth account see Peter Matthiessen, *In the Spirit of Crazy Horse* (New York: Viking, 1991).
18. Bruyneel, *The Third Space of Sovereignty*, 220, xvii.
19. Candace Fujikane, "Introduction: Asian Settler Colonialism in U.S. Colony of Hawai'i,"in Candace Fujikane and Jonathan Y. Okamura, eds., *Asian Settler Colonialism: From Local Governance to Habits of Everyday Life in Hawai'i* (Honolulu, HI: University of Hawai'i Press, 2008), 11.
20. http://quickfacts.census.gov/qfd/states/15000.html; David Stannard, "The Hawaiians: Health, Justice and Sovereignty," in Fujikane and Okamura, eds., *Asian Settler Colonialism*, 161–169.
21. Fujikane, "Introduction," 26; Karen K. Kosasa, "Searching for the 'C' Word: Museums, Art Galleries, and Settler Colonialism in Hawai'i," in Fiona Bateman and Lionel Pilkington, eds., *Studies in Settler Colonialism: Politics, Identity and Culture* (New York: Palgrave Macmillan, 2011), 153–168.
22. Sally Engle Merry, "Law and Identity in an American Colony," 144–145; and Mililani B. Trask, "Hawaiian Sovereignty," 71–75, both in Merry and Donald Brenneis, eds., *Law and Empire in the Pacific: Fiji and Hawai'i* (Santa Fe, NM: School of American Research Press, 2003); see also Pulitano, ed., *Indigenous Rights in Age of UN Declaration*.
23. The Apology can be accessed online at http://www.hawaii-nation.org/publawall.html; Fujikane, "Introduction," 14.
24. Kyle Kajihiro, "The Militarizing of Hawai'i: Occupation, Accommodation, and Resistance," in Fujikane and Okamura, eds., *Asian Settler Colonialism*, 170–194.
25. Elivira Pulitano, "Kanawai, International Law, and the Discourse of Indigenous Justice: Some Reflections on the Peoples' International Tribunal in Hawai'i," in Pulitano, ed., *Indigenous Rights in Age of UN Declaration*.
26. Linda S. Parker, *Native American Estate: The Struggle over Indian and Hawaiian Lands* (Honolulu, HI: University of Hawai'i Press, 1989), 122; Fujikane, "Introduction," 10.
27. Ibid., 1–5; Helani Sonoda, "A Nation Incarcerated," in Fujikane and Okamura, eds., *Asian Settler Colonialism*, 99–115.

28. Jo Ann Umilani Tsark, "Native Hawaiian Health Data: Contours of a Hidden Holocaust," in Ward Churchill and Sharon Venne, eds., *Islands in Captivity: The International Tribunal on the Rights of Indigenous Hawaiians* (Boston, MA: South End Press, 1997), 273–276.
29. Laura E. Lyon, "From the Indigenous to the Indigent: Homelessness and Settler Colonialism in Hawai'i," in Bateman and Pilkington, eds., *Studies in Settler Colonialism*, 140–152.
30. J. Kehaulani Kauanui, *Hawaiian Blood: Colonialism and the Politics of Sovereignty and Indigeneity* (Durham, NC: Duke University Press, 2008), 3.
31. Gary Okihiro, *Island World: A History of Hawai'i and the United States* (Berkeley, CA: University of California Press, 4); Trask, "Hawaiian Sovereignty," 71–75; Merry, "Law and Identity," 144–145.
32. Donald Craig Mitchell, *Take my Land, Take my Life: The Story of Congress's Historic Settlement of Alaska Native Land Claims, 1960–1971* (Fairbanks, AK: University of Alaska Press, 2001), 278.
33. Walter R. Borneman, *Alaska: Saga of a Bold Land* (New York: Harper Collins, 2003), 465–467.
34. Haycox, *Alaska: An American Colony*, 283; the ANCSA can be accessed online at: http://www.alaskool.org/projects/ancsa/reports/rsjones1981/ANCSA_History71.htm
35. Mitchell, *Take my Land, Take my Life*, 11; Haycox, *Alaska: An American Colony*, 285–286.
36. Stephen Haycox, *Alaska: An American Colony* (Seattle: University of Washington Press, 2002), 283; Borneman, *Alaska: Saga of a Bold Land*, 471.
37. Mitchell, *Take my Land, Take my Life*, 10, 504.
38. David S. Case and David A. Voluck, *Alaska Natives and American Laws* (Anchorage, AK: University of Alaska Press, 2012), 198.
39. Mitchell, *Take my Land, Take my Life*, 495.
40. Case and Voluck, *Alaska Natives and American Laws*, 264.
41. Borneman, *Alaska: Saga of a Bold Land*, 471.
42. Case and Voluck, *Alaska Natives and American Laws*, 443.
43. Calloway, *First Peoples*, 467–468; 525.
44. Rosier, *Serving Their Country*, 277.
45. Case and Voluck, *Alaska Natives and American Laws*, 4–5.
46. Ibid., 160; Calloway, *First Peoples*, 470.
47. US Commission on Civil Rights, "A Quiet Crisis: Federal Funding and Unmet Needs in Indian Country." http://www.usccr.gov/pubs/na0703/na0204.pdf
48. Jeffrey Ostler, *The Lakotas and the Black Hills: The Struggle for Sacred Ground* (New York: Viking, 2010), 139–191; Tim Giago, "Black Hills Settlement Funds Top $1 Billion." http://www.huffingtonpost.com/tim-giago/black-hills-claims-settle_b_533267.html

Conclusion: The Boomerang of Savagery

1. Aziz Rana, *The Two Faces of American Freedom* (Cambridge, MA: Harvard University Press, 2010), 13; Paul C. Rosier, *Serving Their Country: American Indian Politics and Patriotism in the Twentieth Century* (Cambridge, MA: Harvard University Press, 2009), 3; Lorenzo Veracini, *Settler Colonialism: A Theoretical Overview* (New York: Palgrave Macmillan, 2010), 94.

2. John E. Ferling, *Struggle for a Continent: The Wars of Early America* (Arlington Heights, IL: Harlan Davidson, 1993), 6; Colin G. Calloway, *New Worlds for All: Indians, Europeans, and the Remaking of Early America* (Baltimore, MD: Johns Hopkins University Press, 1997), 114; Alfred W. McCoy, *Policing America's Empire: The United States, the Philippines, and the Rise of the Surveillance State* (Madison, WI: University of Wisconsin Press, 2009), 37, 540; see also the classic work by Richard Drinnon, *Facing West: The Meta-physics of Indian Hating and Empire Building* (Minneapolis, MN: University of Minnesota Press, 1980).
3. On World War II see William Hitchcock, *The Bitter Road to Freedom: The Human Cost of Allied Victory in World War II Europe* (New York: The Free Press, 2009); John Dower, *War Without Mercy: Race and Power in the Pacific War* (New York: Pantheon, 1986); and Michael S. Sherry, *The Rise of American Air Power: The Creation of Armageddon* (New Haven, CT: Yale University Press, 1987); on the legacies of World War II and Korea, see Sahr Conway-Lanz, *Collateral Damage: Americans, Noncombatant Immunity, and Atrocity after World War II* (New York: Routledge, 2006); on the Korean War see *The Korean War: A History* (New York: Modern Library, 2010) by Bruce Cumings, who estimates that the US Air Force killed one ninth of the Korean population; on Vietnam, see Bernd Greiner, *War Without Fronts: The USA in Vietnam* (New Haven, CT: Yale University Press, 2009). John Tirman (see footnote 4) has chapters on all these conflicts and more. See also Michael S. Sherry, *In the Shadow of War: The United States Since the 1930s* (New Haven, CT: Yale University Press, 1995); Yuki Tanaka and Marilyn B. Young, *Bombing Civilians: A Twentieth Century History* (New York: The New Press, 2009); and Dower, *Cultures of War: Pearl Harbor/ Hiroshima/ 9–11/ Iraq* (New York: W.W. Norton, 2010).
4. John Tirman, *The Deaths of Others: The Fate of Civilians in America's Wars* (New York: Oxford University Press, 2011), 5, 15; Christopher Waldrep and Michael Bellesiles, eds., *Documenting American Violence: A Sourcebook* (New York: Oxford University Press, 2006), 6.
5. Jennifer Rutherford, *The Gauche Intruder: Freud, Lacan and the White Australian Fantasy* (Melbourne: Melbourne University Press, 2000), 207–208.
6. Rob Capriccioso, "A Sorry Saga: Obama Signs Native American Apology Resolution; Fails to Draw Attention to It," January 13, 2010: http://www.indianlaw.org/node/529; Audra Simpson, "Settlement's Secret," *Cultural Anthropology* 26 (May 2011), 205–217; see also Roy L. Brooks, ed., *When Sorry Isn't Enough: The Controversy over Apologies and Reparations for Human Injustice* (New York: New York University Press, 1999).
7. As Elvira Pulitano has pointed out the UN Declaration is an ambiguous and in some respects contradictory document, yet "UNDRIP constitutes, with all its imperfections and among all the controversy, a significant achievement for peoples worldwide." Clint Carroll adds, "In highlighting on a global stage the persistence of colonial relations between indigenous peoples and settler states, it seems that the Declaration has already served an important purpose." Elvira Pulitano, ed., *Indigenous Rights in the Age of the UN Declaration* (New York: Cambridge University Press, 2012), 25, 143.
8. On the disclaimer, see the explanation by US Advisor Robert Hagen, "On the Declaration on the Rights of Indigenous Peoples, to the UN General Assembly," September 13, 2007, http://usun-ny.us/press_releases/20070913_204.html.
9. Robert J. Miller, Jacinta Ruru, Larissa Behrendt, and Tracey Lindberg, *Discovering Indigenous Lands: The Doctrine of Discovery in the English Colonies* (New York: Oxford University Press, 2010), 266.

10. Lorenzo Veracini, "Telling the End of the Settler Colonial Story," in Fiona Bateman and Lionel Pilkington, eds., *Studies in Settler Colonialism: Politics, Identity and Culture* (New York: Palgrave Macmillan, 2011), 209.
11. Larissa Behrendt, *Achieving Social Justice: Indigenous Rights and Australia's Future* (New South Wales: The Federation Press, 2003), 5, 176; see also Manfred Berg and Bernd Schaefer, eds., *Historical Justice in International Perspective: How Societies are Trying to Right the Wrongs of the Past* (Washington, DC: German Historical Institute and Cambridge University Press, 2009).
12. Candace Fujikane and Jonathan Y. Okamura, eds., *Asian Settler Colonialism: From Local Governance to Habits of Everyday Life in Hawai'i* (Honolulu, HI: University of Hawai'i Press, 2008), 13.

Index

Note: Locators followed by 'fn' refer to foot notes.

Printed and bound in Great Britain by
CPI Group (UK) Ltd, Croydon, CR0 4YY